ISBN 978-1-330-51599-0
PIBN 10072441

1 MONTH OF
FREE
READING

at

www.ForgottenBooks.com

By purchasing this book you are eligible for one month membership to ForgottenBooks.com, giving you unlimited access to our entire collection of over 700,000 titles via our web site and mobile apps.

To claim your free month visit:

www.forgottenbooks.com/free72441

English
Français
Deutsche
Italiano
Español
Português

www.forgottenbooks.com

Mythology Photography **Fiction**
Fishing Christianity **Art** Cooking
Essays Buddhism Freemasonry
Medicine **Biology** Music **Ancient**
Egypt Evolution Carpentry Physics
Dance Geology **Mathematics** Fitness
Shakespeare **Folklore** Yoga Marketing
Confidence Immortality Biographies
Poetry **Psychology** Witchcraft
Electronics Chemistry History **Law**
Accounting **Philosophy** Anthropology
Alchemy Drama Quantum Mechanics
Atheism Sexual Health **Ancient History**
Entrepreneurship Languages Sport
Paleontology Needlework Islam
Metaphysics Investment Archaeology
Parenting Statistics Criminology
Motivational

PUBLIC UTILITY RATES

A DISCUSSION OF THE PRINCIPLES AND PRACTICE
UNDERLYING CHARGES FOR WATER, GAS,
ELECTRICITY, COMMUNICATION AND
TRANSPORTATION SERVICES

BY

HARRY BARKER, B.S.

*Mechanical and Electrical Engineer, Associate Editor of Engineering
News, Member American Institute of Electrical Engineers.*

FIRST EDITION

McGRAW-HILL BOOK COMPANY, INC.

239 WEST 39TH STREET. NEW YORK '

LONDON: HILL PUBLISHING CO., LTD.

6 & 8 BOUVERIE ST., E. C.

1917

Stanhope Press
F. H. GILSON COMPANY
BOSTON, U.S.A.

PREFACE

THE collection and formulation of these notes have been under way about eight years. Before utility questions had attained their present popularity, the author felt (in following the discussion of public-service questions at engineering conventions and from the varied acquaintance of an engineering editor) that a comprehensive discussion of (1) such corporation and municipal activities as affect service and rates, (2) the trend of public opinion and court and commission decisions, and (3) the most important engineering and economic problems involved, would be useful to many who have to deal first-hand with one phase or another of public service. Very many men who have seemed to be interested in all phases of these problems have not had the time or opportunity to study the conflicting and reiterative ideas of the scattered documents, pamphlets, and papers which very largely form the literature of the subject. There has seemed to be a desire among public utility officials to throw off the blinders of daily duties, and to study what some are pleased to call "the academic questions" of their business. The writer hopes to make that possible here.

It has seemed, as the notes have grown in these years, that if the main lines of some broad survey of the rate problem could be given, free from the mass of obscuring detail which necessarily marks individual cases, then the contemplated review would be of some service to lawyers and legislators, to editorial writers of the daily press, to students of municipal affairs and even to some part of the general public. For this varied service, although the inherent nature of these studies demands essentially an engineering and economic analysis, an attempt has been made to keep the pages understandable to men not technically trained. Partly for such readers are the brief reviews of history and technology of railroads, electric railways, water-works, and gas, electricity and telephone utilities, given in the chapters on special problems. But even the technical reader of these pages must give heed to the history and technology of any utility whose rates he studies.

This is particularly true in comparing the fixed charges in different fields.

A presentation of rate problems cannot be evolved out of inner consciousness as can a novel or poem. It must be based on an accumulation of separate contributions to the thought on the subject — with perhaps new explanations here, a realinement there, and a different deduction elsewhere. It is hoped, however, that the mere presentation, in one volume, of the diverse phases of rate making may be of service in provoking thought — in spite of the inherent shortcomings of the text..

The author has felt that such a review of essential facts and principles can best be arranged by some third impartial party, such as an editor of an engineering journal — being affiliated neither with a public-service corporation nor a regulating commission, but in touch with both and not confining all his attention to the field of one utility class. It seems reasonable that such a third party can most easily attempt to approach the several and conflicting viewpoints and can best endeavor to pick out the essential elements of the problems in the most nearly unbiased manner because free from the pursuit of petty details and the irritating distractions of daily administration.

With the foregoing ideas in mind, the author has carefully studied the wealth of discussion that has come to him and he has very gradually formulated this presentation. It is admittedly incomplete and possibly defective, but it is hoped that continued open-minded study and discussion may enable the reader to bridge gaps and eliminate fallacies. It is only fair to all approaching the subject with open mind, to warn them that some of the author's opinions, while supported by the views of many eminent engineers and economists, are not yet accepted by some others equally prominent. An attempt has been made where such divergence exists, to present the diverging ideas. Acknowledgment is here made to many prominent specialists in the several utility branches for their ready coöperation and frank criticism of the author's notes at various stages of growth. Their number and modesty prevent more complete and specific credit.

It probably will seem to the public commissioner, to the company official, or the consulting engineer, that innumerable important details have been omitted. The author feels, however, that, in spite of the importance of interpretations of principles in each concrete case, the inclusion of more detail here would obscure the fundamental points that need to be emphasized — besides giving a book that would rival an unabridged dictionary in size and require a lifetime to prepare.

It might be well to remark, perhaps, that the author does not believe in any inherent iniquity of corporations, in spite of the occasional mismanagement of officers of quasi-public enterprises and the laxity of directors. He trusts that these notes accordingly will be found temperate in tone and fair toward such organizations. On the other hand, he recognizes, in the magnitude and complexity of modern organization schemes, opportunities for hiding grave abuses; and he does not feel that any man who has the requisite ability and energy to cultivate or exploit public service should be allowed to do so solely for private profit, without some effective oversight and chance for restraint. It is to be hoped that the author will not be classed as an apologist for the cartoon type of public-service magnate if such exists to-day; he agrees that with the absolute disappearance of the men who organize corporations solely for the sake of large and speculative promotion profits, and not for the more moderate and certain returns of daily service, there will come a better day, for both the public and the corporations.

H. B.

New York City,
January, 1917

CONTENTS

CHAPTER V

CHAPTER VI

CHAPTER XIII

CHAPTER XIV

CHAPTER XV

CHAPTER XVI

PUBLIC UTILITY RATES

CHAPTER I

DEVELOPMENT OF UTILITY REGULATION; UTILITY PRIVILEGES AND OBLIGATIONS; RIGHTS OF THE PUBLIC

Political Place of Utility Regulation. — It is obvious that a second great American experiment in civil government is under way. The primary experiment, of course, is our particular arrangement of a democracy under a legislative-executive-judicial division of function; the second is the control of quasi-public industry by powerful combined-function agents (railroad and utility commissions) of the legislatures, both state and national.

The best forms of regulative legislation evidently were framed by men who saw possibilities of curing grave corporate abuses, though the passage of regulating acts probably was helped by those who saw new prospects of political capital.

Good state-commission regulation and the appointment of capable and conscientious commissioners, on the whole, continues steadily to increase. The evidences of superior value in state regulation over local legislative control must be appreciated by the mass of thinking and influential voters of the country or this could not be true.

These commissions are given powers, more or less broad in the several cases, over financial arrangements, general operating results desired, and over rates. At first only operation and rates were put under scrutiny; but it was found in very many cases that full control of service and rates was impractical without a considerable power over capitalization and the issue of securities, so that the tendency is to add this last.

There are many who decry this supervision over corporations, forgetting perhaps that the corporation is a creation of the state, an artificial personal entity brought into being primarily for the

1

promotion of public welfare — directly or indirectly. If it be a child of the people's creation, surely it ought to answer to the public for its acts and be willing to give all information about its activities that may not adversely affect its business, perhaps eventually confidentially reporting to the state or national government what is reserved from general publication.

A common avenue for commission control is in the matter of charges. This directly affects the people and makes a greater impression on the body politic than any equal attention to safety and adequacy of service or to the issue of securities. It is therefore of immediate use to have widely disseminated sound knowledge of how rates may be fairly governed. Fortunately, general principles are more crystallized here than in many other matters of regulation, for the latter depend much more on local necessities and often involve the application of a mere sense of common justice rather than any economic principles or elements of law and engineering. It must not be supposed, however, that local conditions may not profoundly affect rates. In any rate case, as complete a study of the local situation as is possible must be made — and some situations will arise when adequate precedents cannot be found and a logical analysis cannot be perfected. Throughout this work, therefore, emphasis will be placed on the latitude to be allowed rate makers from formal statements of principles and precedent which at times may be but convenient points of departure.

These studies into testing the reasonableness of charges for public service are made with a few basic propositions in view which it is well to state at the outset.

Definition of Public Utility. — A concern having special rights to use public property (like highways) and serving the general public conducts a true "public utility" when its service has passed the state of being a mere luxury or convenience for the few and has become a necessity in the conduct of business and ordinary life of the many. (Before that condition is reached, the concern does merely a "quasi-public" business, more or less of public interest and in which the government has specific limited rights to interfere.)

This definition does not exclude all concerns whose business does not immediately involve every citizen (as does that of a water company); it includes enterprises, like electricity-supply works, which serve many citizens, but by no means all, and whose service is a growing public convenience though seldom a complete necessity.

Privileges. — A concern furnishing a public service enjoys a privilege not to be unduly exploited by the company, not to be the excuse for abuse by the citizens and not to be the cause of harassment by the government.

A concern that has eliminated competition within some field of activity, or has come into a control of a trade without the approval of the customers and the public generally must always be prepared to justify every action or else permit and expect public scrutiny of every act. This applies to business in necessary commodities perhaps even more than to service concerns. There is reason to expect an extension of present utility-regulation ideas more and more into general business.

Obligations. — The conduct of a true public-utility business involves several definite obligations. There is first that of giving the most satisfactory and complete service which the needs of the people, the state of the art involved, and the local physical limitations and finances permit. Secondly, there is need of securing from the customers the common local rates of interest on property involved, plus a just compensation for all the risks of the business as a venture and perhaps some small extra return for giving especially good and careful service, or for the continued reduction of costs and rates through careful attention to improved processes, or for the pursuit of an especially broad and beneficent public policy.

Rights of the Public. — The public may properly take all precautions to protect itself, as a civic unit, as customers or as stockholders, against vicious franchise obligations and privileges, and against pernicious activity either by or against the public-utility concern. In the conflict of interests, however, the principle of "the greatest good to the greatest number" is to be applied.

No distinction has been made in these discussions between personal or corporate ownership of a public utility, and little for municipal operation. For convenience, reference has been made throughout to public-utility "companies." But the remarks apply equally whether one man holds the property or a thousand own the stock of a service corporation; they should apply also

to the public-utility departments of a municipality like the water-
or electric-supply works. There is possibly no greater field
(geographically and in aggregate injustice) of discrimination and
unfair rates than among the municipally owned utilities. For
instance, in a water-works department the charges for fire-hydrant
service, which are assessed on each taxpayer, may be heavy to
permit of low rates for general supply or may be so light as to
throw an undue burden on the consumer — distinguished from
the taxpayer. In gas or electric service a deficit from supplying
ordinary consumers at too low rates may be prevented by high
charges for street lights. The municipalities should be amen-
able to the same demands for reasonable rates and adequate services as private plants. This sort of control has been exercised in
Massachusetts and Wisconsin for many years but is not yet
broadly exercised beyond these states.

CHAPTER II

PRODUCT AND SERVICE COMPANIES; SOME DEFINITIONS OF RATES AND SERVICES

Two Classes of Companies. — Public utilities may well be separated into two classes in inquiring into rates; (1) those which store and *handle a product* and (2) those which *perform a service*. Into the first class, naturally fall most domestic water and gas companies, and perhaps sometimes sewerage and other wastes-disposal undertakings, or eventually, furnishers of domestic supplies like ice, coal and milk. In the second class are electricity-supply concerns, telephone and telegraph companies, steam- and electric-transportation lines generally, express companies, and the postal service.

Product Storage. — Perhaps the most distinguishing characteristic of the two classes of public utilities above made is in the ability of the first to produce (or acquire) and store a tangible substance, as compared with the inability of the second class to store a service in advance of demand. For instance, a water company often can continuously impound its supply at a uniform rate for a whole day, month, or season, drawing upon some reservoir in larger or smaller amounts as the demand may dictate. A gas company, similarly, may be producing gas at a comparatively small but uniform rate constantly, feeding most of it into its holders from whence the supply flows at times of larger demand.

Service Capacity. — An electricity-supply company must have ready for more or less quick service generators of a total capacity equal to the maximum demand its customers as a whole are apt to make at any time of the day or year. Necessarily this apparatus must be idle much of the time. Storage batteries, to serve the function of the water reservoir or gas holder, are not practicable or economical, except in small installations and for some special services. Street and suburban railways must have a reserve of employees and equipment, sufficient to handle the crowds which may travel to business in the morning and homeward at night. Railway companies must have spare equipment

5

to carry with minimum discomfort the crowds which travel at certain seasons or on certain holidays, and to move with minimum delay the crops which mature at certain seasons. The telephone companies must have central-office equipment enough to serve the greatest number of subscribers apt to call at one time.

Class Costs. — Thus it may be seen that the manufacturing plants of the first class of utility companies may work under conditions of maximum efficiency — that is, close to designed capacity and continuously. The investment per unit of product then may be small so far as generating plant goes, but it may be large for storage facilities. These conditions are reversed for the second class. The apparatus must work at reduced efficiency during light and discontinuous operation; there are apt to be considerable standby losses (as in keeping boilers hot and engines warm) and certainly there are heavy fixed charges on idle investment.

Two Classes of Rates. — Two broad schemes of charging for public service or supply may be discerned; (1) the *unit charge* and (2) the *flat rate*. These two have been dubbed also the "European" and the "American" plans, respectively.

The unit charge, or "European plan," involves measuring the amount of product handled or service rendered and making the payment bear some definite relation to such quantities. The flat-rate scheme, or "American plan," consists in charging a customer an agreed sum, more or less logically determined, irrespective of actual utilization of proffered product or service, or not based on varying factors which are measured. The first is the more logical and fair in principle but the expense of measuring product or service sometimes makes flat rates more economical all around — especially with small customers.

Split Rates. — A third scheme of stating rates is by a two- or three-part charge — under various names and disguises. This is more seen in service-type utilities than in product-type. By many this scheme is classed as a unit-charge plan, and truly such it is — but carried to a logical extreme. One part of the charge is based on the customer's maximum demand at any time (for this is related to the investment for that customer in the service-type of company). There is a second part, proportional to the amount of service shown by meter (for this is related to the actual operating cost of serving a particular customer). There may be sometimes a third part — a fixed sum to cover the cost per customer of expenses peculiarly proportional only to the number of customers. Sometimes the first and third parts are combined; where demand cuts no figure the split rate reduces to a simple unit charge.*

While the multi-part tariff may be wholly logical, it may be so complex and unintelligible to the customer that he cannot check up his bill by any instruments on his premises and this may create a fundamental prejudice against the utility. Then the disadvantages outweigh the benefits of the schedule in most cases.

Twilight Zones. — Many rates are not wholly flat nor yet quite like logical unit charges; for instance, take the postal letter rates. For all domestic and many foreign letters, the charge is flat with respect to distance, collection and delivery, but in units so far as weight and number go. For newspapers, the only unit basis is that of weight; in this case distance, collection, delivery and number of separate pieces are not separately considered and to that extent the charge is a flat rate. In the American parcel-post system, recently inaugurated, a much more definite proportionment is made, based on pieces, weight and distance, so as to be practically a unit-tariff plan. Some telephone rates at first seem like flat charges — being frequently so many dollars per installation per year; but closer inspection shows that there is a differentiation into classes, such as residence, commercial, etc., and further into single-party, two-party, etc., with different charges to each and with or without count of connections actually completed for a customer.

Sliding scales — so much for the first thousand cubic feet of gas or water (for example) and proportionately less for succeeding thousands — are unit charges with a device attempting to bring the price automatically close to the cost of serving large and small consumers.

In general, it may be stated that it is easier to test the adequacy of service and the reasonableness of rates in a company making a storable product than one performing a service.

* Credit for these schemes should go first to Dr. John Hopkinson who formulated in 1892 the demand and output division in a presidential address to the Junior Engineering Society (British). Shortly after Mr. Arthur Wright produced his well-known maximum-demand indicator and further developed the demand-output basis. In 1900 Mr. Henry Doherty, in the paper "Equitable, Uniform and Competitive Rates," before the National Electric Light Association split fixed charges into demand and customer factors.

ILLUSTRATIONS OF AMERICAN UTILITY RATE CLASSIFICATIONS

	FLAT	UNIT-CHARGE
Gas	$0.25 per lamp per month.	$0.70 to $1.25 per thousand cubic feet.
Electricity	$0.75 per lamp or motor per month or year.	$0.05 to $0.15 per kilowatt hour.
Water	$1 per fixture or person per quarter.	$2.25 to $5 per thousand cubic feet.
Street Railway	5c. per passenger trip.	5c. per passenger in first zone plus 2c. per added zone.
Steam Railway	Long excursion fares. Monthly commutation tickets.	2½c. per passenger mile (mileage books, trip tickets).
Sewerage	Various sums per outlet or per person or per inch of outlet.	Per thousand gallons or cubic feet discharged.
Telephone	$15 to $200 per year.	2 to 5c. per local call. Various toll charges for long distances.*
Telegraph	Various sums for leased lines.	Tolls based on number of words, distance and time of day.†
Postal Service	2c. per oz. for letters, to 1c. per lb. for newspapers.	Parcel-post zone-weight rates.

Relative Importance of Low Rates. — The expressions of public-utility officials seem to indicate that, after fair convenience and more or less attractive prices have been established for the proffered service, complete ability and readiness to serve all who apply is first to be secured; then a service is to be sought that will not cause complaint as to regularity, uniformity or reliability, and finally a lower rate established.

* For messages between New York and Chicago, a distance of 900 miles, the message charge is $5, or 0.19c. per mile per minute. An average of the New England Telephone & Telegraph Co. tolls, as found by D. C. Jackson in the Massachusetts Highway Commission studies, was 1.6 to 0.65c. per message mile.

† The telegraph charge for ten words from New York to Chicago in 1916 was 50c., or 0.0066c. per word mile. The similar charge from New York to San Francisco is $1, or 0.0031c. per word per mile. The New York-New Orleans charge is 60c. or 0.0045c. per word mile. For transmission during off-peak hours, 50 words are transmitted for the same price, which correspondingly reduces the word-mile charges to ⅕ those quoted.

What constitutes superior service beyond the essential qualities of adequacy outlined? Due regard for the preservation and enhancement of a community's external attractiveness, search for especially courteous and skillful employees, general wide use of safety precautions and devices for the protection of the public and employees — such are about all that can be named without study of specific cases. A closer study of adequacy is not attempted here, as such discussions turn on regulation rather than on rates.

CHAPTER III

VARIOUS BASES FOR RATES

Cost of Service a Necessary Approach. — To complete any survey of the justice and equity in a scheme of rates, the prices charged should be studied in their relations to the cost of the service and the income to be received. The deeper the probe, the more will this need appear — in spite of other matters that exert a profound influence (like the maximum price which small telephone users can afford to pay). When quality of service regulates some rates to certain classes of customers, as in telephone, telegraph, express and postal utilities, cost of service at least is a base of departure. It is obvious that a corporation will not long do business if cost of service is not met by income; the reasonableness of an aggregation of tariffs cannot be judged until the relations between income, expense, profits, dividends, surplus, etc., are known.

" Cost " is Replacing " Worth." — Time was when innumerable able men held that such a proposition was not tenable because it was strange and because it seemed to be an attempt to substitute an easy plan for the difficult scheme of determining "what a service was worth." It seems reasonable, however, to assert that such arguers deny the possibility of growth in legal and economic thought, even if the proposition were strange. This is not today a stranger doctrine than history shows was the one of 1875 that a state legislature could fix maximum utility rates so long as they allowed a fair return on the value of the utility. Yet, since the celebrated corner-stone case of *Munn v. Illinois* (94 U. S., 113; 1876) this principle has been unquestioned.

Use of Cost is Not New. — While in ordinary private transactions the worth of a service has depended on various external influences, yet, when a large part of the public has been affected, cost has been a large measure of worth. When industrial life was more simple than now and competition more free, the selling price of a manufactured product and the production cost were nearly parallel year after year. When virtual monopoly developed,

10

the manifest desire of the people nevertheless was *to continue the results* with which they had been so long familiar, i.e., they desired some assurance that production cost and selling price would continue to be parallel and separated at all times by profits no larger than obtained in other lines of manufacturing effort.

Thus the reason for the important rôle of cost of service in public-utility rates far antedates the utilities as now organized and is but one expression of a general treatment to be expected for monopolistic business. It is apparent then that even when it is attempted to apply "value-of-service" as the fundamental process of judgment (taking a well-known definition* of "value of service" as the "amount which a user would have to pay for the same or equivalent service under fair but not destructive competition"), it is not possible to cut loose from "cost-of-service."

An Unsound **Basis.** — A basis of rates, which once existed more broadly than now and one which is probably the oldest and possibly the simplest to follow, is often stated as "charging all the traffic will stand." Most rates which result from this plan are perhaps to be regarded as the outcome of a bargain, and in these cases they have probably been fixed blindly without considering what profits, or losses, might properly be assumed. Such a course, taken as the fundamental procedure of a true public utility, is not now regarded as generally fair to the consumer or to the utility concern; and sometimes it is in opposition to a wise public policy. It belonged, indeed, to the pioneer days when a given service was not a public necessity or even a convenience, and hence not subject to more public regulation than that afforded by common barter or by refusal to trade. (As a subordinate idea, however, it has still a certain important but restricted application as noted later.)

A Fair **Basis.** — A basis of rates for real public service now acknowledged to be generally equitable is one by which the legitimate expenses, and reasonable profits, are fairly distributed upon the total service or product given. This idea of a proper basis of rates is gaining wider recognition constantly. How this basis is to be secured may be seen in the trend of judicial and commission opinions, based on the constitutional principle that property cannot be taken without due process of law and on the

* Rate Research Committee, National Electric Light Association, 1914 Report.

concept (given in 1885 by *R. R. Commission Cases*, 116 U. S. 307, 331; and in 1888 by *Reagan v. Farmers Loan and Trust Co.*, 154 U. S., 362, 399) that a rate imposed on a concern by public mandate must permit a common profit in order not to be confiscatory. The oft quoted decision of the U. S. Supreme Court in *Smyth v. Ames* (169 U. S., 466) early outlined the idea applied to a railroad case. It is stated there:

We hold, however, that the basis of all calculations as to the reasonableness of rates to be charged by a corporation maintaining a highway under legislative sanction must be the fair value of the property being used by it for the convenience of the public. And, in order to ascertain that value, the original cost of construction, the amount expended in permanent improvements, the amount and market value of its bonds and stocks, the present as compared with the original cost of construction, the probable earning capacity of the property under particular rates prescribed by statute, and the sum required to meet operating expenses are all matters for consideration, and are to be given such weight as may be just and right in each case. We do not say that there may not be other matters to be regarded in estimating the value of the property.

Courts do not Fix Reasonableness. — It must be remembered, however, that neither legislation nor judicial opinion have yet made much closer determination of the relative importance or fixed the application of the elements which the Supreme Court, in the above case, held should be more or less influential. One cannot expect that courts will become very explicit as to what might be reasonable. It is the court's function to determine only if rate systems in specific cases are unreasonable and confiscatory, or perhaps on the other hand extortionate. It is the function of the legislatures and their agents, the commissions and municipalities, to find and prescribe the reasonable figures.

Moreover, such remarks as above quoted, found in typical court decisions, are only statements of an end to be sought. Such broad ideas, applied without qualifications, might be fair to the company in final result, especially as to protection of property rights, but still work injustice to a large percentage of the consumers through not charging individuals even roughly in accordance with the cost of serving them. How may the same result be secured to the company with substantial justice and approximate fairness in apportioning each consumer's burden? That is not to be answered easily or quickly in an offhand way, and the complete answer must remain as the object of all the studies which follow.

Need of Classifying Customers. — Ideas must differ as to what (speaking only of rates) constitutes "substantial justice" and "approximate fairness." It seems reasonable to consider those secured if a customer receives a rate that would be fair to the average customer of a class having wants similar to his. It may be assumed here as axiomatic that the unit cost of serving each customer will vary somewhat from that for all others, depending somewhat on the size of his demand for service, on his distance from service centers, on the times of service relative to the demand of other customers, etc., etc. The bearing of these affecting conditions will appear again later. It is generally manifestly unfair to compel a public-utility concern to compute a different basic rate for each small individual, or every time a bill has to be rendered. But that is what is sometimes seen, in effect, where a company adopts a multi-part tariff scheme where the change to any customer has different demand, service quantity and customer factors which vary from month to month. Concerns adopting such complicated schedules would perhaps complain if forced to adopt them by public service commissions. Moreover, with the difficulty of a customer's checking the charges, opportunity might here be seized by employees for petty harassment and discrimination. Common public knowledge of the basis for prices would become difficult and unreliable. Confidence in the existence of an equitable basis of computing charges would diminish.

It is general experience that the business of most utilities may be gathered into a few classes wherein the maximum and minimum costs of unit service (cubic feet of gas or water, kilowatt-hours, local telephone calls, etc.) vary but little from the average.

Classes Promote Simplicity. — This is fortunate, for simplicity in the rate system is usually a greater public benefit than perfect adherence to wholly logical or completely accurate individual rates. Moreover the ideal individual rates need not seriously differ from the practical class rates if the classifications are well drawn. In very many cases, the natural commercial separations are sufficient. For instance, it has been shown that cost of electricity supply often changes greatly with the size of a customer's load. Here individual rates become possible for very heavy consumers and perhaps segregation of the various smaller users between certain load limits, as 0 to 50 kw.-hr. per month,

51 to 500 kw.-hr., 501 to 1000 kw.-hr., 1001 to 3000 kw.-hr., etc.,
sufficient to secure the "approximate fairness" and "substantial
justice" mentioned.

Such class separation may exist but be indirect and even unrecognized, as by the use of discounts which increase in proportion
to the size of the customer's bill, or sliding scales of diminishing
prices.

Each classification needs to be closely scrutinized by managers
and regulators alike to avoid if possible large groups of customers
in each size class falling close to the limits with few between for
then some may be unduly favored or unjustly burdened. The
most desirable adjustment of size-class limits results when customers are generally scattered between, bunching, if at all, not
far from the mid-point.

Off-peak Classes. — A customer classification which greatly
affects cost is according to the time of service, or supply, relative
to the maximum daily or seasonal demand on the utility company.
This affecting condition is most pronounced in the cases of service
rendered rather than storable product supplied. For instance, the
capacity of generating machinery to be installed in a central
electric station is fixed generally by the maximum demand which
exists for a short time only once in one day. Investment charges
may then be apportioned more or less according to the demand
which the various customers exhibit at the time of maximum plant
load. Customers whose maximum demand comes at the time of
smallest station output may come into special classes or sub-
classes and may justly receive rates which include little or no
charge for investment in generating equipment.

This evidently has long been recognized by the Massachusetts
Board of Gas and Electric Light Commissioners, one of the earliest
and most far sighted utility commissions, though its opinions
discussing this point do not directly take up investment. Thus
in the 1908 petition case of the Public Franchise League relative
to the Boston Edison Electric Illuminating Co. (24th Ann. Rep.,
Jan., 1909) the Board stated:

In distinction from the large body of customers just mentioned [de-
pendent and non-contract] there is a considerable number, both actual
and possible, who may readily supply themselves . . . from some other
source. To such customers the value of the service furnished by the
company will probably depend to a considerable extent on the probable

cost of supplying themselves. If the company is to supply them, it is subject to the ordinary rules of business competition — it must meet prices established by conditions which it did not create and cannot control, or not do the business. . . .

In reaching out for additional business by making concessions from the average rate, it is plain that the only justification for the continuance of such a policy is that this additional business will be for the benefit of the large body of customers who must pay the regular rate. . . . In fact, the only means by which the average lighting customer can hope to see the price to him materially reduced is through a greater increase in the volume of business relative to the company's investment. Long use of a customer's installation, especially during parts of the day or year when otherwise a considerable proportion of the company's plant is standing idle, even at very low rates, provided they reasonably exceed proper "running costs" may yield a revenue otherwise not available, which will materially help to dilute the company's general expenses.

This has been re-affirmed in various more recent cases.

The history of a given utility, the industrial situation and various other local factors necessarily enter any opinion as to the extent to which special classes of customers may participate in investment-charge burdens.

Individual Diversity Factors. — Participation in investment charges may sometimes be made after a study of the individual diversity factors of various customers or subdivisions of an utility system. This idea has been developed for electric central-station conditions* and can be extended to other fields. The cost of gas and water-supply is much less affected by the time of a customer's demand (for the stored product) than is electricity.

"Group Diversity Factor" for such a study has been defined as "the ratio of the sum of the maximum power demands of any system or part of a system to the maximum demand of the whole system or a part under consideration." "Individual Diversity Factor" then becomes "the ratio of the maximum power demand made by any subdivision of a system to the coincident demand made by such subdivision at the hour of the maximum load upon the source of supply."

Strict Equity versus General Welfare. — It will not do to be dogmatic in saying on what fundamental basis new rates always are or are not to be built up or old ones scrutinized. For instance,

* "Application of Diversity Factor," H. B. Gear, National Electric Light Assoc., June, 1915.

it will not do even always to deny that the traffic is to be "charged all that it will stand" — if we dissociate from that phrase its sinister intimation of gentle highway robbery. A certain service or product may be very desirable for a given community and very few persons therein may be able to meet the cost that should fall on them. For the sake of having the convenience, some few may be willing and economically able to stand for more than their proper charge based on proportionate cost of service. Then, an "overcharge" to some, and as great as they would consent to, in connection with an "undercharge" (below the proportionate cost of service) to others, might be made to yield an income which would cover expenses and profit and justify the undertaking. The whole community would then be a gainer. Extortion may be guarded against for, with public supervision, it can be seen whether total operating income covers reasonable investment charges and still yields the concern enough for a proper reward or more than enough to attract needed capital.

For a specific example illustrating the point fairly well, we may take a telephone exchange in a small community. To a few it is evidently a real necessity; to the multitude it could be a great economizer of effort and time, but a luxury and even an extravagance if the charge equaled the cost. By charging those who most needed and most valued the telephone service, all they would stand, the service might be brought within reach of all and the business raised to a size worth the attention of men skilled in the industry.

Such a course in this one case perhaps also might be justified as following closely the real value and cost. The worth of telephone service increases in proportion to the total number of persons which a subscriber may call or be called by. This advantage of a very large list of subscribers is of greatest value to the already heavy user of a limited list like the merchant and of much less value to the average householder, who normally reaches the same few tradesmen and friends. In such a case the real individual cost of some subscribers might be considered to include a part of the book cost of others — the cost of having some one to call.

A similar condition exists in the postal service today. It is known that the expenses of collecting, assorting, transporting and delivering the several classes of mail matter are not at all evenly distributed. A logical basis of comparing class costs is not in use and some shifting of the burden from letter-rate matter probably would be seen dictated if such a logical basis were operative. At the same time, it is possible that were the newspapers and magazines to bear their full proportion of cost, then their distribution would be so restricted that there would be a consequent marked decrease in first-class matter — fewer letters being drawn out by advertisements, etc. Moreover, the transmission of intelligence and the spread of intellectual enjoyment might be so appreciably impaired in rural districts that the best development of the country would be hindered. If that result is expected, the country at large can fairly contribute to prevent it through slightly excessive first-class rates.

CHAPTER IV

DETAILS OF THE COST-OF-SERVICE STUDY OF RATES; TEST FOR FIXED AND OPERATING CHARGES

Test Schedules. — A good approach to the study of a concern's existing rates or the logical formulation of new ones is to build up independent or tentative schedules based on cost of service for various classes.

General Cost of Service. — It is necessary first to arrive at some knowledge of all the true annual expenses in giving the service as a whole (exclusive of return on capitalization, investment or value of property used). This true operating cost, of course, subtracted from the earnings of the service in question should establish the lump sum of net earnings and leads to the computation of the percentage return on value of plant, etc., for the particular service. (Discrepancies in true net earnings from the figures of official reports will often arise even if the proposed schedule of true annual costs is very carefully built up since some items of true cost are often neglected. They may not always be "expense," — in that they never have been paid out of cash, but they then represent value lost from the property investment and not compensated for by funds laid aside from earnings.)

Preliminary Survey of Profits. — If the computed rate of net earnings on value, investment or capitalization, as the case may warrant, is judged to be too low (the basis of opinion as to what constitutes a "fair return" is discussed later), then the conclusion may frequently be drawn that the existing rate schedule is unfair to the utility company at some point. However, before the opinion is further crystallized, close detailed scrutiny of the entire organization, equipment and daily activity of the concern may be necessary to see if the deficiency can arise from corporate or personal inefficiency, from plant troubles like excessive leaks or losses, from too many bad accounts, insufficient or undistributed load, poor detail management, etc., etc.

18

If the possibility is not disclosed of sufficient improvement to seem apt to raise the reduced profits, then it may be well carefully to look over the existing rate schedules. If at some point they are manifestly far below the rates seen in a number of plants under an approach to similar conditions, then the impression of rates unfair to the company is much strengthened Existence of compensating lower figures of expenses, due to local causes, are to be sought out. If the deficiency really comes from an unfair rate schedule, the conclusion is unescapable that the rates somewhere must be advanced. If the trouble is internal rather than external, the plant load must be improved or new economies found.

If the overall rate of net earnings is larger than those which are just necessary to attract fresh capital, and in the absence of cause for certain special rewards, discussed later, the common presumption is that the rate schedule somewhere is unreasonably heavy. Sometimes the presumption cannot be sustained, but the circumstance warrants study. The gross earnings of a company, for instance, may include income not at all from the public service, or income from traffic developed by the unusual activity of the officials in fields where a demand for services of the utility concern did not previously exist and where good earnings may be secured with prices not based at all on cost of service. The same close scrutiny of organization, equipment and activity, as noted already, still may well be made, for possibly no condition is more conducive to perpetuation of bad accounts, loose engineering and general inefficiency than the rarity, "easy money." Such a scrutiny may disclose definite sums which can be saved and in justice to the public, these are to be taken from the actual annual costs to arrive at proper figures.

True-cost Schedule. — The following schedule of a concern's annual service costs (not necessarily annual "expenses" under some managers' understanding of that term) is perhaps useful for examination at this point. These figures are easily found if the utility is keeping its accounts according to prescribed standards of most regulating commissions.

1 — Return on value of physical plant and allowed intangible elements.*

* This item is grouped here though when it is desired to test the percentage of net earnings on valuation or capitalization, it is to be excluded from the sum of expenses. Moreover, this item is capable of division into bond inter-

2 — Rentals on leased properties.*

3 — Annual allowances to recover for "depreciation" and "obsolescence."

4 — Annual appropriation for amortization of investment in intangible property.

5 — Taxes or equivalent, fire-, accident- and liability-insurance premiums.

6 — Annual appropriations for surplus funds to secure bond interest and dividends in lean years or for extreme contingencies.

7 — Salaries of administrative officers and clerks.

8 — Expenses of general offices, etc.

9 — Engineering department expense.

10 — Annual appropriations for hospital subsidies, welfare work, charities, etc.

11 — Advertising; new-business getting.

12 — Interest on working capital required.

13 — Bad accounts, etc.

14 — Meter reading, accounting, billing and collecting costs.

15 — Labor in service or upon plant.

16 — Supplies for service or plant.

18 — Repairs — distinct from depreciation.

19 — Losses between plant and customer.

Nothing is allowed for extensions to plant, for this item, in the great majority of cases, means fresh capital. The conditions which warrant reporting some part of the first cost of extensions as annual service costs, are so peculiar and are seen so rarely that their insertion is a special matter to be justified by special evidence to that end. This schedule is not the only arrangement that could be made and re-assignment of items is permissible. Further than already noted, these items are self-explanatory to a considerable extent, although various questions rise as to their determination and bearing; discussions of these points appear later.

If there is subtracted from the lumped gross earnings, the cost of service aggregated without Item 1 (and perhaps Item 6), then the remainder may be considered the lump net return. This, divided by the allowed valuation of the property, gives us the percentage return. It should be here particularly noted that Item 1, "return on value of plant," ought to work out to be such a percentage on combined bonds and stocks as will attract capital, or

est and dividends. Presumably, the bonds will not exceed bare physical property value, but the stock capitalization may bear no relation to the physical value less bonded and net floating debt.

* Rentals need to be studied to see that undue parts of any earnings are not being by-passed as rentals. The rented property ought not to be expected ordinarily to return more than say 10 to 20% net of actual value — as local conditions may disclose to be a proper rental change.

include all additions, above ordinary interest, for the risk of the business, special rewards, etc.

The Problem of Apportioning Costs on Customers. — Supposing, that we have reached the actual figures for true cost of service and income, and know the segregation of expenses according to such items as in the foregoing schedule, and have ample information about customers' load characteristics, then in the majority of cases we can go a long step beyond the lump-sum and percentage returns, and study the rates which should place on the ultimate consumers, the approximate costs of their respective services.

In apportioning expenses among the customers, it is almost obvious that a mere equal division of all expense and profit according to their number or to their maximum load, or to aggregate of service alone may not be fair.

At first glance, it may seem almost hopeless to attempt a logical apportionment of the items given. Indeed, the whole task of studying fairness of rates seems stupendous and hopeless in its entirety; but, like most other intricate problems when attacked step by step with engineering methods, it unfolds itself and loses its air of complexity and impenetrability.

It has been seen that the expenses fall into two classes (1) "fixed" — generally those continuing whether the plant is running or not, and (2) "operating" — mostly those which stop when service stops. For a complete analysis, it is well to further split up the first group into (a) fixed charges which actually do not vary with any fluctuations of business, and (b) customer costs which vary directly with the number of customers and which would disappear entirely with the complete loss of business.

A Test for Fixed Charges. — For the logical segregation of expense items, a simple test is available and that is to ask such questions as these: "Is this item most concerned with providing physical property?" (If so, it is a true fixed charge.) "Is this closest related to mere maintenance of corporate functions?" (If so, it usually is an operating expense, unless there are peculiar circumstances.) "Is this item dependent on actual daily amount of service furnished or accepted?" (If so, it is clearly a true operating expense.) "Is this expense caused by dealings with customers as individuals?" (Then it is a customer or "semi-fixed" charge.)

The common and generally acceptable sequel of such tests, as noted later, is to apportion rental, appropriation for obsolescence reserves, taxes and fire insurance, a small part of appropriations for amortization, parts of salaries of administration officers and part of general office expenses, upon the customers according to their proportion of peak-load demands. (On account of the diversity of the individual demands, which usually do not quite coincide with each other, each customer's share or peak load ordinarily is less than his own small peak.)

This apportionment is secured more typically in service utilities than in concerns which distribute a product like gas or water from cheap and easy storage. The argument for this test and distribution of fixed-cost items is that the actual equipment needed is fixed by the reserve necessary to meet the experienced coincident demands for service of those customers who cause the peak loads. Taxes, rentals, and allied outlays clearly are fixed by the amount of property needed for the business (the "load"). It perhaps is not so obvious, but it is seen on second thought, that part of the appropriations to surplus and for amortization of intangible purchases, parts of the salaries of administrative officers, and of the general office expense, etc., can be considered necessary to protect the integrity of such physical property (aside from wear), and so are to be borne by those who require equipment held in reserve. Peculiarities of electric-railway service need special application of this apportionment — as noted in Chapter XI.

In the case of those utilities handling a product out of storage, the manufacturing or generating equipment may be of small size but working very steadily; then the annual cost of such equipment may be assessed in proportion to total product irrespective of peaks, etc. But the storage plant, at first, might seem to be partly fixed by the peak loads or demands. Yet careful thought shows two things; (1) approximately, the total product enters the storage plant for a greater or lesser length of time, (2) the size of storage facilities is more or less proportioned to the total product to be delivered over the period of a short operating cycle and is very little affected by the rate of delivery (a high rate means a peak demand). So then this class of utilities may often properly assess all items except No. 13 and parts of Nos. 6 and 7, on the basis of total product supplied. Gas and water mains have to be designed to carry peak flow, and so may have a certain part of investment considered as reserve property and apportioned according to peak demand.

The result of a peak-load apportionment of fixed charges is that one or a few classes of customers may carry nearly all the investment charges since they cause practically all the maximum demand. Local conditions may fix the most desirable solutions in specific cases — remembering only that the peak customers get an indirect benefit from the development of off-peak business. Such benefits arise from the purchase of supplies in larger quantities, shorter life of equipment with less liability of heavy obsolescence, quicker installation of improved equipment by a broader distribution of depreciation charges, greater chance of reduced rates by reduction of operating expense through apportioning some items, like labor, over more units of service or product, benefits of higher-grade officials, employees and consultants attracted by the concern with the larger business.

Apportionment of Taxes. — Taxes and the various insurance premiums appear at first to be wholly concerned with the integrity of the property and hence fixed charges to be apportioned to the use of peak load capacity. However, further study shows that taxes (being contributions to the support of organized government with its fire and police protection, monetary system, etc.) may be considered a cost of maintenance of business as well — and hence to be sometimes in greater or less part distributed over all service rendered or product supplied. Local conditions may exert a profound influence on the proper apportionment of taxes.

Apportionment of Depreciation Expense. — Questions of " depreciation" are perhaps the greatest stumbling blocks in all rate discussions. Moreover, so involved is this subject in a maze of differing definitions that the terms employed, even when attempted to be used quite technically, convey different ideas to different persons. Therefore a later section has been devoted to a discussion of these difficult matters, and passing mention is made here only of the apportionment of current expense burdens commonly called "depreciation."

Modern practice is to pay for the annual deterioration or provide retirement-liability insurance by definite contributions from the rates intended to repay the actual cost of each item of property by the time it has to be retired.

Theoretically, it would be expected that the annual deterioration due alone to the year's unrepairable wear and tear (independent of any impairment of value due to antiquation through industrial advance) should have its repayment apportioned like fuel and operating labor — since it increases with the hours of use.

Theoretically, compensation for obsoletion and antiquation, when there is any, should be apportioned like interest — for obsoletion is a liability of change which is independent of the hours of service, heavy loads, etc., being only an expected impairment of the value of physical property.

Where wear-deterioration is the controlling phenomenon in limiting the life of apparatus, theory justifies apportioning the annual repayment burden entirely along with the operating expenses. Where, on the other hand, obsoletion and antiquation control the length of useful life, the entire annual insurance payment against these contingencies may enter the fixed charges.

In many practical situations, as in the case of product-storing utilities, it makes little or no difference which way the apportionment is regarded — since both operating and fixed charges are levied alike on quantity units. As a matter of commercial expediency in some cases of service-type utilities where either wear-deterioration or obsoletion may predominate, it may be advisable to distribute the annual burdens on the various customers according to their respective responsibility for the deterioration and the obsoletion. This division can be made fairly logical; but so far it has been more often arbitrary — perhaps through disregard of the principles underlying payment for depreciation.

Depreciation Expense as an Operating Cost. — In the actual practice of rate making, the assumptions as to expectation of equipment life (considering either deterioration or obsoletion) and the various approximations necessary (all of which crudities affect the annual "depreciation" burden) have given rise to the practice of treating all such expense burdens wholly as an operating expense — so far as apportionment goes. The lumping of all sorts of retirement contributions under the single heading of "depreciation expense" seems to have arisen through (1) railroad and similar utility management (street railways and telephone systems) with rates fixed more by external circumstances than the actual cost of the individual service or through (2) the accounting of product-selling utilities where peak loads have been so negligible that distinctions between fixed and operating expenses did not affect the unit cost of the single class of product supplied. To illustrate: the Interstate Commerce Commission states in its accounting rules ("Classification of Operating Revenues and Operating Expenses of Steam Roads," July 1, 1914, p. 31):

2. *Maintenance Expenses.* — The accounts provided for maintenance of fixed improvements and of equipment are designed to show the cost of repairs and also the loss through depreciation of the property used in operations, including all such expenses resulting from ordinary wear and tear of service, exposure to the elements, inadequacy, obsolescence or other depreciation, or from accident, fire, flood or other casualty.

Elsewhere the Commission has stated ("Uniform System of Accounts for Telephone Companies," Jan. 1, 1913, p. 67):

By expense of depreciation is meant (a) the losses suffered through the current lessening in value of tangible property from wear and tear (not covered by current repairs); (b) obsolescence or inadequacy resulting from age, physical change, or supercession by reason of new inventions and discoveries, changes in popular demand, or public requirements; and (c) losses suffered through destruction of property by extraordinary casualties.

Depreciation Expense as a Fixed Charge. — While it is seen to be common practice to regard depreciation levies on rates as an operating charge, yet there are numerous instances where utility officials regard it as a fixed or overhead charge. There is no reason why, in the formulation of adequate rates, this or the other course should not be followed if circumstances point to that plan as logical. Nor has there been any good reason set forth why a ratemaker may not divide his depreciation expense into some wear-deterioration and obsoletion payments which he thinks approximates the risks, and apportion them accordingly among his customers. When such a refinement is desirable, an official of course expects that his course will have to stand the future scrutiny of any regulating commission in authority as to the general fairness and reasonableness of the results.

Apportionment of Amortization. — Frequently sums for "amortization" are mentioned as a burden on rates distinct from depreciation allowances. Usually these are intended for the retirement of capital invested in franchises, development expenditures, engineering work not directly chargeable to specific equipment, early deficits which may have been capitalized, etc. Amortization charges are most necessary in the case of an utility with a limited-term franchise, where there is no certainty of selling out and receiving back the entire investment made. There are many who hold that all utilities should try thus to reduce their investment irrespective of their franchise term — so that all the present-day customers may pay all the possible cost of the present service, and pass along for another generation a burden of liabilities only equal to the ready-sale value of the property units. This is an ideal not often easily attainable though worth striving. for; the concern which can follow such a course will be on a more secure basis — for instance, free from undermining competition.

Not every utility can burden its rates to this extent; not every official believes it is a worthy ideal. The best argument against it is based on the fact that the overhead costs of today are a continually decreasing percentage of the total value of a growing and developing utility. That is true, of course, but each grand expansion brings in its additional overhead items and these pile up a possible weakness for the time when the utility must reach equilibrium. Something of this sort, it is commonly believed, has brought about the burdensome capitalization of British railways, on which no appreciable amortization of abandoned investment and development expenses has been made.

It might seem at first, applying the test for apportionment of annual amortization sums, that they were simple charges on investment and properly laid on demand or capacity units. Further consideration shows that it is desirable that all the customers should carry some share of this burden (except perhaps some desirable competitive business which cannot be held if so burdened) and this points to the inclusion of annual amortization in with operating expenses — apportioned among the customers according to quantity of service or product supplied.

If the annual amortization sums which can be secured are not too trifling they may be subdivided between quantity-unit and demand-unit charges. The subdivision ratio then would follow the relative proportions of the general organization and development investment to the incidental costs of physical plant — unassigned engineering, legal work for rights of way, etc.

Apportionment of **General Expense.** — The time and thought of administrative officers and general clerks by study will be found to be given largely to the business as a whole at times or in certain cases — but also partly to providing capital and equipment, and to such an extent in cost resembles taxes and insurance. The numerical division is not difficult to approximate. Then it is logical to apportion the same proportion of the salaries of these officers and clerks (1) as a per unit charge on all service rendered or product delivered and (2) on peak-load demand as a capacity-unit charge.

Distribution of rent, lighting, water, heat, and other such office services, of general office supplies and miscellaneous expenses may be similarly made, if it is worth while to have such refinement.

The expenses for maintenance of an engineering department are evidently partly connected with providing physical property and partly with actual operation. The head of the department should be able to make a fair estimate of the proportion applicable to each for division as noted.

Annual appropriations for hospitals, welfare work, charities, etc., are seen to be intimately associated with operating labor and virtually amount to an increase in labor cost. Therefore, they logically may be charged like labor, fuel, etc. However, if considerable benefits come to the employees in the administrative, engineering, and public-bureau departments, then a certain part of the welfare-work cost (generally according to numbers rather than salaries) may be allocated as per-capacity-unit charges according to peak-load demands and another part according to actual number of customers.

Advertising, bad accounts, and interest on working capital are seen to be associated with service rendered or product supplied more than anything else, and hence are like operating costs.

Distribution of Metering Cost. — Meter reading and accounting, billing, and collecting costs obviously are about as heavy for a small customer as a larger one and for an off-peak customer as a peak-load one. These then are expenses to be distributed on customers according to number.

Labor. — There can be usually little question about the distribution of labor (as part of service or upon plant repairs), operating supplies like fuel, etc., repair and maintenance materials, etc., — all as unit charges on quantity of service or product.

Service Losses. — There seems to be no better way, without undue complication, to apportion the losses between plant and customer than according to quantity of service given or product delivered. This item covers the energy loss of electrical transmission lines, the water and gas leakage from mains, etc. Some utilities have no such losses. Among such are telephone and telegraph services; in transportation utilities there may be a loss through uncollected fares but there is no way of accurately ascertaining the amounts so lost and service data is based on fares collected.

In gas, water and electricity distribution, the output of a station is metered and the difference between this figure and the sum of the customers' meters gives easily and fairly accurately the losses. Even though existing, the losses may not enter the analysis of costs and rates. For instance, if the total costs are figured for distribution on service actually rendered, or product actually supplied to the customers, and not on units of main-plant output, then these figures cover the cost of losses. However, there are many cases arising when it is desirable to know production costs and cost of losses separately, even if only as a measure of proper operation of the utility. In that case internally used service may require separation.

Limitations of Test for Apportionment. — Such a varied apportionment of expenses is, of course, to be carried out more or less completely as needed information can be secured. The number of customers and the total number of units of service rendered or product supplied should be known.. But the aggregate of maximum demands is very seldom known with any approach to exactitude; where no approximate idea can be had, or no reasonable assumptions are possible, of the individual contributions to the peak load, then the charges laid against demand or capacity must be apportioned like an operating charge on service units delivered. Such contingencies however will be rare.

Indeed, the maximum-demand apportionment of part of the expenses is of great effect on rates only in the case of service works. In the case of gas works as already outlined, much of the investment costs can be equitably borne directly by the total product supplied. Usually this is true also of waterworks — unless there is practically no long-storage capacity so that the size of the pumping installation is fixed by the maximum demand rather than daily consumption, and unless much larger pipes are required for maximum than average flow.

Where some of the expense items can be readily apportioned

but others cannot, it is common and reasonable practice to divide the sum of unapportioned items according to the aggregate assignments already made. Details of this scheme are shown in the chapters on problems of the specific utilities.

The general rules laid down for distribution of cost items have been so stated after debates in which arguments for or against the rules and sub-rules or exceptions have been weighed. However, the mere fact that most of these questions have two sides is enough to show that specific cases may arise which may decidedly alter the arguments for the methods given. In these exceptional cases the local necessities may prevent application of generalized ideas. But it is felt that such strange cases will be rare and that the effect of peculiar items on rates so minor that sufficient accuracy will be secured by any intelligent management which consistently and conscientiously strives to be fair and open minded and seeks competent advice.

Revised Cost Schedule. — Summarizing the results of such a scrutiny of expense apportionment, the following rearrangement of the former list of utility costs may be built up.

I. FIXED CHARGES. — (To be allocated according to participation in peak-load demands, wholly or largely, except in special circumstances or as noted in chapters on problems of specific utilities.)

1 — Return on value of plant and intangibles.

2 — Rentals on leased property.

3a — Annual allowance for retirements or replacements. (In part only, and in proportion to obsolescence factor or deterioration from. weather. See pages 24 and 111.)

4 — Taxes.

5 — Fire insurance premiums.

6a — Salaries of administration officers and clerks. (In small part only.)

7a — General office expenses. (In small part only.)

8a — Engineering department expense. (In part only.)

9a — Cost of repairs due to weathering.

10 — Appropriations to surplus reserve to secure bond interest and dividends in lean years or for contingencies.

II. OPERATING CHARGES. — (To be allocated according to quantity of service rendered or product manufactured or delivered.)

3a — Annual allowance for retirements or replacements. (In

part only, and in proportion to wear-deterioration factor.
See pages 24 and 111.)

6b — Salaries of administration officers and clerks (in part).

7b — General office expenses. (In part.)

8b — Engineering-department expense. (In part.)

11 — Operating labor.

12 — Operating supplies.

9b — Cost of repairs and maintenance. (Apart from replacements and recovery from weathering.)

13 — Appropriation for amortization of intangible values. (In large part.)

14 — Interest on working capital. (Funds on hand.)

15 — Cost of leaks, losses, etc.

16 — Bad accounts.

17 — Accident liability insurance costs or equivalent.

18 — Appropriations for hospital subsidies, welfare work, charities, etc.

19 — Advertising.

III. CUSTOMER CHARGES. — (To be equally allocated on individual customers.)

20 — Cost of meter reading or equivalent.

21 — Accounting, billing and collecting.

6c — Salaries of administrative officers and clerks (in small part only).

7c — General office expenses (in small part only).

Simplicity in Rates. — It is seen that the simplicity of a given rate schedule primarily depends on the simplicity of the business in question. If the customers' characteristics are all much alike then there is but one form necessary for the charge and this very frequently allows a flat rate. As the customers' demands become dissimilar we can see that a two-factor basis becomes more logical, while for all sorts of complications the full three-factor base seems to place on each class the burdens of its peculiar service.

It has been argued that this two- or three-part basis, directly visible in the published schedule of an utility, is the most equitable that can be devised. In theory surely this is so, but practically the complexity of such a schedule, the uncertainty in the approximations of each person's real participation in peak loads, the impossibility of the ordinary customer's checking his bills, etc., do not promote public confidence and pleasant relations.   Therefore the two and three-factor basis will often better form the foundation of rates to be expressed in more direct terms.

Customer Groups. — Simple tariffs are easily constructed if the customers can be arranged in groups wherein the individual requirements are not far from the average.   Then the fixed charges on the peak-load capacity required for all the members of a group, plus the operating costs of furnishing the aggregate of service or product to the class, plus the costs of dealing with the several individuals of the group, gives the total annual cost of furnishing the group.   If then this figure be divided by the total quantity of service or product for the group during a year, we have a unit price which it is generally fair to impose on all the members of the group.

This scheme is largely followed, and with widespread satisfaction.   The customers understand what they have to pay and their check on bills is obvious.   Of course, if the peculiarities of the classes change materially, then the old rates may be unfair either to the utility company or to the customer — to which depends on circumstances.

Distribution of Fixed Charges. — It has been noted that fixed charges were located "largely in accordance with participation in peak-load demands."   Usually for a group of small customers this participation may be found by a simple approximation for each class, being based on group maximum demand, actual maximum peak delivery of the utility, and the aggregate of the group demands, thus:

$$\text{Group Max.} \times \frac{\text{Actual Peak}}{\text{Aggreg. Group Max's.}}.$$

This averages the diversity of demand among the individuals inside a class but for small services it is simple, practical and reasonable.

Where there are large customers each one may be handled like a class in the computation, basing the approximate participation in fixed charges then on group maximum demands, large individual maximum demands, and actual peaks of delivery, thus:

$$\text{Group or Indiv. Max.} \times \frac{\text{Actual Peak}}{\text{Aggreg. Group and Indiv. Max's.}}.$$

A still further refinement in the approximation is possible by

assessing directly on each class and each large individual the whole
fixed charges on equipment allotted to each of them solely and
dividing charges on further equipment, used commonly by two
or more of the groups or individuals, according to:

$$\frac{\text{Indiv. or Group Max.} \times \text{Actual Peak on Joint Equipment}}{\text{Sum of Related Indiv. or Group Max's.}},$$

and apportioning charges on remaining plant serving all the customers (usually manufacturing or storage equipment) as before
by:

$$\frac{\text{Indiv. or Group Max.} \times \text{Actual Peak}}{\text{Aggreg. Indiv. and Group Max's.}}.$$

Importance of Studying Individual Diversity. — Individual
diversity of demands becomes of great importance in reducing
to a minimum the investment in plant required between an utility's manufacturing plant, or its equivalent, and a customer. It
is obvious that if the maximum of measured coincident demands
of the members of a group is only ⅓ the sum of the individual
maximum demands then the investment in joint-service distribution apparatus need have only ⅓ the maximum output capacity
which would have been required had not the individual diversity
existed. This effect has been studied most with central-station
electric service.

Ends, Not Means, Sought. — If study of annual costs shows
an increasing figure for each successive year, then the fairest adjustment for practical conditions may be above unit figures applying at the moment, and vice versa. Frequent scrutiny of
costs, rates, and profits is desirable. But most utility managers
will argue that the benefit of trifling changes is less than the expense and trouble involved, so that frequent and inconsequential
revisions are not worth while usually.

No one of various ways of expressing the resulting tariffs is to
be broadly recommended for all sorts of utilities. One town water-
works department may charge $5 per capita per year; another
similarly situated may charge $0.35 per 1000 gallons metered; a
third may assess a user $1.50 per outlet per year. All these may
amount to the same thing in the end. Some will prefer to give a
unit price for all comers with changing discounts for different
amounts of service or time of demands. The chances are that
all flat rates have been empirically established and tinkered up

from time to time to yield sufficient gross income without the responsible officials knowing what is the relation between rates and actual cost of the various customers. Very often diverse statements of rates will yield substantially the same results under similar conditions, and in such cases we may regard the rates as equivalent and cease striving for mere methods of expression — so long as intent to deal justly with all is seen.

Minimum Charges to Cover Readiness. — Practically all utilities have some form of minimum charge below which a customer's bill never descends, whatever the quantity of service rendered or product supplied. This enables them with certainty to secure the annual fixed and customer charges which have been computed as fair. In the greater number of utility companies the practice seems to be to use a straight monthly charge; water companies, however, very often adjust their minimums to an annual figure. An occasional electric company does the same — witness the Boston Edison Electric Illuminating Co. At least one company (Public Service Electric Co., Newark, N. J.) gives a concession in that it waives the minimum charge on application and renders no bill for periods of one month' or more when premises are closed or current cut off. Where no annual adjustment is made it is evident that an inequitable overcharge may easily be made since the rates are based on annual figures and since the maximum demand is an annual peak. A customer often may fairly be allowed to ease up the heavy consumption in one period of the year by the light consumption of another — provided always that the proper annual demand, customer and quantity costs are secured by the utility. The New Jersey Commission, however, has ruled * that simple monthly charges are logical as well as convenient, basing its contention on the fact that salaries are paid weekly or monthly, depreciation written up monthly, and interest met semi-annually — apparently overlooking the more fundamental facts that revenue to meet obligations is collected monthly or quarterly; that working capital is a part of rate-basis worth, and that the annual readjustment of minimum charges is a correction of overcharges beyond the actual proper ánnual figure based on the cost-of-service idea.

* Re *Minimum Monthly Charges for Lighting Service by Electric Companies;* Informal Proceedings, January, 1912.

Study of Hypothetical Case. — For a general illustration of
the development of simple unit rates based on cost of service we
may arrange a hypothetical case of the most difficult sort — that
of a service-furnishing utility as distinguished from the product-
supplying type. Assume that it has five classes of customers;
(1) large users (10,000 to 20,000 quantity units) whose maximum
demand falls in hours of peak load, (2) small users (500 to 1700
units) whose maximum demand falls in the same hours of peak
load, (3) large users (above 10,000 units) none of whose demand
comes at hours of peak load, (4) small users with similar off-
peak load, (5) miscellaneous users with maximum demands in
hours of heavy load but taking service only in summer. Assume
further that the utility has a peak-load output capacity of 35,000
units (gallons per hour, cubic feet per minute, kilowatts, etc.);
that the total of all services is expressed as 30,000,000 quantity
units per year (gallons, cubic feet, kilowatt-hours, etc.); that the
fixed charge, including 8% on the fair value of plant, etc., is
$340,000, while the general operating and individual customer
charges reach respectively $295,000 and $67,000. Assume that the
peak load comes in winter with Group 1 causing 60% of the peak
and Group 2, 40%. Let the annual aggregate quantity output
be taken up 55% by Group 1, 33% by Group 2, 7% by Group 3,
3% by Group 4, and 2% by Group 5. The number of customers
is: Group 1, 1500; Group 2, 13,000; Group 3, 205; Group 4,
120; Group 5, 55.

Then we can charge each and every consumer per annum
$9.70 $\left(= \frac{\$340,000}{35,000}\right)$ per peak-load capacity unit (maximum demand divided by individual diversity factor) plus $0.0098
$\left(= \frac{\$295,000}{30,000,000}\right)$ per unit of service, plus $4.50 per customer per
year. But the preparation of bills might be rather too burden-
some and the whole arrangement of rates too blind to most customers. Easy, fair and understandable class rates can be worked
out as follows:

Group 1 carries $204,000 (= $340,000 × 0.60) of the annual
fixed charges, plus $162,300 (= $295,000 × 0.55) of the operat-
ing costs, plus $6750 $\left(= \$67,000 \times \frac{1500}{14,880}\right)$ of the special customer

costs; the total is $373,050 and, divided by the total quantity of service furnished the group, gives a unit rate of $0.0230.

Group 2 similarly carries $136,000 in fixed charges, $97,350 in operating costs, and $58,500 in customer costs, making a total of $291,850 and a unit figure of $0.0295. Group 3 carries no part of fixed charges, not causing any of the peak load, — but it has a burden of $20,650 operating costs and $922 customer charges, a total of $21,572 and a unit price of $0.0103. Group 4 has no fixed charges to bear either, but carries $8850 of the operating burden and $540 of the customer costs, making $9390 total and $0.0104 unit price. Group 5 also carries no fixed charges, but has $5900 plus $248 and a unit price figure of $0.0102.

The hypothetical utility company might then fairly draw up the following preliminary rate schedule and claim it to be substantially just and reasonable; or new classifications might be sought and the process completed again.

(1) For long-hour peak-load customers whose annual consumption equals or exceeds 10,000 quantity units, 2.30c. per unit.

(2) For short-hour peak-load customers whose annual consumption is under 10,000 units, 3.00c. per unit.

(3) For off-peak customers, 1.10c. per unit.

To avoid the abrupt change in rate to peak-load customers some sliding scale scheme may be substituted for sections 1 and 2. For instance: For peak-load customers 3.00c. per unit for the first 1000 units, plus 2.20c. per unit for the next 9000 units, plus 1.50c. per unit for all additional above 10,000 units — or some equivalent advisable figure.

A minimum charge would probably be made also to cover the customer costs, the average fixed costs, and the average quantity found to be supplied to the minimum-charge customers; this would be, for instance, for the short-hour peak-load customer $4.50 per annum plus say $0.50 — the operating cost of 50 odd quantity units assumed to be taken here by the average minimum-charge customer — plus $7 fixed charge, amounting to $12.

It should be borne in mind that the foregoing case merely illustrates a method [of studying rates and does not show an example of a single utility to which the quoted dollars and cents apply. It does not even pretend to show a widely applicable form of schedule, or give the only approach to the problem.

CHAPTER V

FAIR VALUE OF UTILITY PROPERTY

What is Fair Value. — It has become common in dealing with public-service rates to say that they should yield a "reasonable return" on a "fair value." Such words sound innocent enough and indeed they are widely accepted as defining a condition desirable to secure. But arguments continue over the ways to attain this end — largely because one person has one idea of what is meant by "fair value" and "reasonable return" while to another the words do not convey the same ideas. If limitations of language could be obviated, each would better comprehend what the other was striving for and many of the apparent differences might disappear through harmonizing and adjustment.

Here, unless made obviously otherwise, "fair value" will be taken to mean a property worth, expressed in dollars and cents, on which the utility company, for justice and equity to the company and to the public, may earn a greater or less net percentage return free and clear of all further deductions. Sentimental value is discarded. This is a description of the results of an evaluation — not a statement of how a desirable end may be reached. Ideas of the proper road to travel are many, as a few paragraphs will show.

Market Value as a Basis. — In considering the many valuations of utility property for establishing rate-making bases that are now on record, it is seen that there are three general theories upon which they are founded. The first, and to many the most obvious, scheme (for years used in work prior to purchase and refinancing of a concern and therefore naturally transferred), seems to be to set up a "*market value*," a price which a willing purchaser would give a willing seller. In many cases of purchase, market value has been no more than "earning value" — capitalized net earnings; the weakness of this as a basis for rates is its circular reasoning, for this value depends on rates and rates in turn on value. Utility properties are not commodities that are traded so frequently as to establish a true market value and

36

appraisers, therefore, in trying to set up what they call such a basis, build up a hypothetical figure based on cost to reproduce, on notable appreciation of parts and estimated or revealed depreciation, effect of mistakes, and the expense of building up the organization and business.

Investment as a Basis. — A second plan upon which rate-making valuation has been based is the *investment* or *sacrifice theory*. This would give compensation for all that the investor has given up, first and last, legitimately and in good faith, less anything equivalent to a return of investment. The investor is penalized for any obvious lack of common prudence, ordinary foresight and good judgment of his agents, the utility officials, but not for unavoidable mistakes or unforeseen contingencies.

Equivalent Substitute Basis. — The third plan is the *equivalent-plant* theory which would give the old utility a value equal to what it would cost to produce a new going concern with the most economical plant equipment available, and an organization and business cheaply built up by having available the latest business experience and practice.

What Basis To Use. — The various decisions which can be generalized as noted in the immediately preceding paragraphs, it must be noted, do not often completely or exclusively embody a single theory, — or is it essential that they should when slavish adherence to a single theory is very apt to result in absurdity and inequity.

It appears as though some persons of pro-corporation affiliations employ whichever theory seems bound to result in the highest value, while others of anti-corporation leanings act as though the aim should be to produce the minimum value. Needless to say, the men of greatest influence exhibit no bias in either direction but apparently seek to employ such means as in the specific cases farthest push the attainment of fair treatment for all.

Frequently, in utility-rate controversies a "market value" is pitted against a "substitute-plant value" as being respectively what a willing seller would take and what a willing purchaser would give. The result in such cases is usually a compromise, in effect if not in aim, and this compromise figure is very apt to lie close to that determined by actual or probable investment.

Present tendency seems to be to give more and more weight to figures of investment and investors' sacrifice in determining

rate-basis worth.   With the general imposition of proper accounting systems figures of investments and sacrifice can be more completely secured than in the past so that a better basis for value
by investment can be established.   Where regulation has been
longest established, there investment has greatest weight; it is
not unreasonable to expect that in the course of time the entire
country may accept the theory.   To cite a specific instance of
the acceptance of the investment basis, the Massachusetts Public
Service Commission recently declared in the Middlesex & Boston
Street Railway case (No. 553; Oct. 1914):

It is argued by some of the counsel that the present value of the property used by the petitioner is the only amount upon which it can claim
to earn a return. . . . It is sufficient here to observe that few words
having a fundamental importance in dealing with questions of law and
finance have been found more difficult of accurate and generally accepted
definition. . . .

In this fairly consistent adherence to sound principle our Massachusetts public utility code is in striking contrast with the loose and hap-
hazard legislation as to capitalization in many other states, which has
recently resulted in compelling their regulating commissions to resort to
reproduction cost as perhaps the least unsafe basis for determining a fair
rate.   Accordingly, we rule that under Massachusetts law capital honestly
and prudently invested must, under normal conditions, be taken as the
controlling factor in fixing the bàsis for computing fair and reasonable
rates;   that if there is mismanagement causing loss, such loss must be
charged against the stockholders legally responsible for the mismanagement; that reproduction cost either with or without depreciation, while
it may be considered, is not, under our law, to be taken as the determining basis for reckoning rates.   .

It should be noted that the Massachusetts Commissions have
existed, under one title or another, many years and that this
policy may give equitable results under continuous and long-
standing regulation when it might not apply fairly to previously
unregulated properties.

Investment as a Datum. — In the absence of all the historical
facts to establish investment figures, it may well be the object of
an evaluation of the utility property to establish some figure as
what the actual legitimate investment of the moment reasonably
might be.   Legitimate investment may often be a datum below
which for common justice the actual agreed worth ought not to
drop unless there is some way of showing that original capital

probably has been returned to the investor or sacrificed by a lax management through neglect to provide for depreciation and in making renewals of worn-out plant out of new capital. What the agreed worth may be, above such a general minimum, may involve the effect of appreciation in market value of property like land (an increment to deprive a concern of which without compensation the courts have held, but may not always hold for quasi-public concerns, is confiscatory and unconstitutional). . This valuation figure must be carefully determined and based on good evidence to carry weight — especially in court. The highest courts repeatedly have thrown out parts of appraisals that were mere conjecture. For instance, all these several points are illustrated by the decision of the U. S. Supreme Court in the Minnesota Rate Cases (230 U. S. 352; June 1913). Two paragraphs are as follows:

It is clear that in ascertaining the present value we are not limited to the consideration of the amount of the actual investment. If that has been reckless or improvident, losses may be sustained which the community does not underwrite. As the company may not be protected in its actual investment, if the value of its property be plainly less, so the making of a just return for the use of the property involves the recognition of its fair value if it be more than its cost. The property is held in private ownership and it is that property, and not the original cost of it, of which the owner may not be deprived without due process of law.

Assuming that the company is entitled to a reasonable share in the general prosperity of the communities which it serves, and thus to attribute to its property an increase in value, still the increase so allowed, apart from any improvements it may make, cannot properly extend beyond the fair average of the normal market of land in the vicinity having a similar character. Otherwise we enter the realm of mere conjecture.

Court Decisions on Fair Value. — The courts have laid down some general requirements for determining "fair value." The most quoted is the opinion of the U. S. Supreme Court in the now famous case of *Smyth v. Ames* (169 U. S. 466).

The original cost of construction, the amount expended in permanent improvements, the amount and market value of its bonds and stock, the present as compared with original cost of construction, the probable earning capacity of the property under the particular rates prescribed by statute and the sum required to meet operating expenses, are all matters for consideration and are to be given such weight as may be just and right in each case.

It must be remembered that this was a broad outline made before many people had carefully considered these problems and an evident effort was made to warn appraisers of what they must examine in general to use or to discard, depending on purpose, etc.

Court Decisions not Yokes and Fetters. — So far in the history of this country, the highest court benches have been filled by the best men of learning, ideals and judgment which the country has developed and, while no one man can be infallible, yet in the aggregate their opinions command respect. Decisions of the highest federal courts then are usually to be taken not as yokes and fetters under which we must necessarily labor but as rules of conduct by which justice is to be promoted, by which political (economic) and industrial pitfalls are to be avoided and by which the will of the people is made clear. If the decisions seem wrong to the engineering view of economics, they are to be persistently studied to see if the conflicting ideas are not reconcilable. Engineers, however, have a duty in seeking recognition for their ideas.

There is perhaps a widespread impression that high-court civil-action decisions are necessarily based only on hard and fast statutes and difficultly appreciated pyramids of blind precedent. But that is not the actual case — they are in general rather the official interpretations not only of legislative will and common law but of inexorable economic principles, and they aim to apply common ideas of simple justice and equity.

Court Errors. — However, in spite of the ability and intent of the learned judges, there are cases where engineering knowledge and experience show fallacies; for instance, the point in the decision of the U. S. Supreme Court in the N. Y. Consolidated Gas Case where the court held that cast-iron gas mains in New York City would not withstand the equivalent of $2\frac{1}{2}$ in. water-head pressure without strengthening; again in the Minnesota Rate Case where Justice Hughes writes that railroad land must be valued at market value since the roads have the power of eminent domain to take land at market value — which is contrary to common experience in condemnation results. But such decisions probably come about through some inadequacy in each case in preparation or presentation of matters in which the judges are not as versed as in law and economics, and it is unsafe to generalize on one or a few selected decisions, which are apt to be suspended or reversed in apparent principle as soon as the subjects are presented in a better way in another case.

False Respect for Precedent. — There are people who hold as sacred and infallible principle any finding frequently affirmed in any court — like those, for instance, bearing on the idea which holds that all "unearned increments" of property must fully redound to the benefit of the owner, or on one which affirms that annual appreciation of property must not enter the accounts in the same way as obsolescence and amortization items, or one which maintains that public-utility franchises, having the attributes of property, must necessarily enter fair value.

The view that courts are tied to precedent and cannot strike out into fresh thought is not supported by law reports, and it seems to deny the possibility of advance in economic ideas, political principles and legal processes along open paths toward industrial and social democracy.

Other Values than " Rate-basis Worth." — Other phases of "value" in public-utility cases, besides basis of earnings, will not be dealt with at length here. It is necessary to note, however, that the restricted meaning given to "fair value" before makes it quite different from mere "earning value" (or capitalized net returns) which profoundly affects "market value" of stocks. It is also distinct from, because usually more inclusive than, "physical value" — i.e., the "cost to replace new" or the "reproduction cost less depreciation." Nor should the restricted meaning of "fair value" here employed be held synonymous with such unaccepted concepts as "service value" which has frequently denoted original total cost decreased in proportion to decreased ability to give the original service or original efficiency of operation.

Further, while fair value, as defined, is parallel to "going-concern value" in many respects, it is not necessarily the same thing. Fair value will usually contain a "going-concern" element since there has been considerable expense in welding equipment and organization together for effective, satisfactory and profitable activity. But "going-concern value," as generally meant, is a price which may be secured for an adjusted physical plant run in connection with a smooth-working organization, internal good will and external business satisfaction; it arose in sale and condemnation cases and it belongs there.

Some of these factors should be left out of account in rate making for some of the momentary sale value of a producing concern, even of a regulated monopoly, is due to a constant expense in keeping the internal organization "oiled," the product or service advertised, the customers satisfied, etc. Such costs are met from earnings and arise year after year. If the concern is to sell out they contribute to the price which a willing purchaser would pay; if rate making is under consideration any such sale value should not be considered when it arose first from regularly allowed development expense and has been maintained as a burden on earnings. Such value is like centrifugal force, — continued action is required for its perpetuation and the transferable value of past action is due to momentum; the impropriety of entering it in rate basis depends on its arising out of the service and rates.

Valuation for Various Purposes. — The determination of a worth on which the company may earn some reasonable net return is valuation for rate-fixing purposes. But this is not the only valuation that may be made of the same property. Even though the several valuations follow parallel paths, include some identical factors and are under equally wise and experienced legal and engineering advice, yet they may be distinct. There can be one valuation preliminary to a sale and transfer, one as an aid in fixing proper capitalization for reorganization, another to find a basis for the taxes which it is proper for the concern to pay, yet another to give some new accounting plan a more secure foundation based on the actual condition of an utility. Unless specifically stated or otherwise obvious, *"valuation" used hereafter will mean "valuation for rate making"* — the finding of rate-basis worth.

There are economists who hold that there can be no difference in the results of valuation for different ends. They maintain that for taxation, for sale or condemnation, and for fixing financial return there can be but one " value " — that of a sort of " constitutional property " which will stand in court. While true in some cases perhaps, this does not always seem equitable and just to either corporation or public, as will appear as the principles and practice of valuation are discussed. What many undoubtedly mean is that there can be but one result of a general inventory and appraisal.

Take, for instance, one phase of the very large and involved question of whether full original investment or some diminished figure is to be the basis of rates. In cases of sale it is obvious that most purchasers of a physical property will pay only a depreciated value (plus appreciation) for they assume the responsibility for approaching renewals; in rate making this burden on the owner may sometimes represent an investment on which a return may be required to be earned if it has continued unreturned or unsquandered while depreciation has been going on.

As a further instance: in valuation for taxation the several states' requirements vary greatly. There is supposedly some attempt to make a corporation contribute its just proportion of the expenses of organized government with its police and fire protection, stability of business conditions, etc. So far as the protection of mere physical property goes, the corporation of course should pay according to the same scheme as the individual citizens, and that is usually a certain annual percentage on "quick-sale value" which may vary in different localities say from 40 to 80% of actual legitimate investment. All the concerns "property" and business is protected by government and hence subject to taxation. But not all the "property" is "used and useful in service" — some valuable franchises for instance — and some may not enter the rate basis. Other tax burdens may be reasonable under special circumstances — as where presence of the utility on the highways brings added burdens to the municipality, but those are not pertinent to this discussion. This is sufficient to show, however, that a valuation (a "basis" it might be better to say) for taxation is for radically different ends from that of rate making and may be fairly attained through radically different theories of procedure.

Value of Favorable Contracts. — Contracts to supply special service at an attractive figure have been capitalized for transfer of property, since a bidder for the property would raise the sum of his bid as far as he could and still reap a little return on such favored business. But to include this in the basis of rates is obviously unfair through multiplication of profits. Such contracts are property but not "used and useful" in the public service. The question is thus disposed of by the New York Public Service Commission, First District, in the Kings County Lighting Case (No. 1273, Oct. 20, 1911):

When computing the capitalized value [of a favorable street-lighting contract] from the annual amount, he [company's expert witness] used a basis of $4\frac{1}{2}\%$. But when considering the fair rate of return on such capital value he used 10%. The fallacy of such a method is evident. Assume an annual profit of $90,000 to be a fair return. Capitalized upon a $4\frac{1}{2}\%$ basis the value of such a perpetual annuity would be $2,000,000. But 10% of this would be $200,000. The more the city pays the more the consumer must pay. If there is any relationship between these two factors, it is that the more the city pays, the less the consumer should pay. The argument of the company proves too much for if it is correct, it could be argued that every contract should be similarly treated. All are property and presumably all are profitable. Those that are could be capitalized if this one may and the more profitable they are, the higher must the rates to others be placed. Conversely if any one should not be profitable, the capitalized loss should be subtracted from the fair value of the other property and the rates lowered accordingly.

Worth as Disclosed by Accounts. — For aid in determining continuing investment in physical equipment, the accounts of a company should be thrown open. They will be invaluable if they have been properly kept in ways now approved and if there are sufficient memoranda on the conduct of replacement work, repairs, etc. However, the pioneer officials necessarily had a poorer understanding of present-day requirements, so that their accounts, even when preserved, are open to various interpretations with consequently limited reliability and value.

Worth as Disclosed by Appraisal. — In cases of inadequate records, it is necessary to work back from an inventory of the plant as it exists today, in fixing fair value. There are two associated ideas in the reason for this: First, it is a logical step in studying property "at present used and useful" which the U. S. Supreme Court has reminded us must be considered; secondly, it looks toward finding probable legitimate investment which is an important factor in fair value. Efforts to work up, from incomplete and vague accounts, a probable figure for actual legitimate investments in force are usually too speculative to carry weight. Sometimes the early affairs of a concern are so involved and the transactions so questionable that it is necessary to let the past lie dead and to find, instead, the investment required in such a property today.

Actual or Substitute Plant? — There may be special cases where the utility plant has been established by such incompetent hands that it is necessary in the public interest to fix the reasonable investment in such a plant as the probable total cost with a more modern equipment substituted for that in use. But in most cases appraisers are attempting to find the most probable investment in the actual plant as it was obliged to develop, and not in an ideal plant as it might be developed under later conditions.

This is usually necessary since there is too much difference of opinion as to the design of the substitute plant and too many ways of giving the desired service to allow close agreement among different appraisers or to approach a comparable basis in different cases; too much speculation is introduced. Further, justice to the investors indicates the need of taking equipment procurable at the time of installation and not the best the art affords today.

Bearing of Original Conditions. — The foregoing reasoning also logically advises us to take into account the environment of the works and local conditions existing during the development period. For example, if extensive city buildings have been erected, the razing of known or very probable old structures should be included in the cost of the new ones. If a reservoir has been created, the cost of buildings destroyed, the expense upon highways and railways that have been moved and for any special cleaning up of the site that was needed — these, logically and in fairness, all should be included in the cost of the reservoir. There should be some acceptable evidence, however, showing the extent of all such work. Mere conjecture is ruled out.

For establishing the most probable investment, as originally made, the unit prices of property items used would be those prevailing at the time of original construction. But where any considerable period has passed, the desired figure is a continuing investment — which is affected by changed prices of materials and labor, renewals of older equipment, etc., so that present prices are commonly combined with historical conditions. This gives a short cut over finding an original-investment figure and adjusting it to date.

There are vexatious problems, however, in considering the bearing of original conditions; take, for instance, the "paving over mains" cases. It is obvious that, if water or gas mains or electric conduits have been put down under expensive pavement which had to be torn up and replaced, then the cost of the installation is considerably greater than for streets with inexpensive surfacing. Therefore some companies claim, as the present value of their mains and conduits under improved streets, some figure approaching the present cost of putting down the pipes and ducts — irrespective of whether the new paving was laid before the mains or after. Justice to the public would seem to indicate that the increased value be admitted only in the case of subsequent mains, etc., otherwise for each such municipal improvement the city is to be penalized by higher utility rates. While the U. S. Supreme Court has held that a present worth is to be the fair value sought in general, yet it has specifically ruled (Des Moines Gas Case, June 1915) that new paving over old lines is to be excluded.

Some experts hold that strict adherence to a plan of estimating the cost of reproducing the actual existing property as though built today, is the only consistent attitude which will satisfy the courts. This has an apparent benefit at first of dispensing the same degree of justice to all — not discriminating between those properties whose history is obscure and those wherein the effect of historical conditions is apparent. To many others perfect consistency is not more apparent with the neglect of such historical facts so far as they are satisfactorily secured — it merely means establishing the cost of the property and its continuing value to date *so far as facts disclose it.* There seems to be no inconsistency between the use of current prices of materials and the consideration of past actions — it is using all the available data to full extent and neglecting none. However, valuation work is in a formative stage and the last word has not been said; all these points in specific cases are indeed often questions with two sides.

Depreciated Value as a Basis of Rates. — Many commissions sanction the use of actual (or reproduction) cost less accrued depreciation as the actual (or probable) investment of the moment. Many of the most eminent corporation officials condemn such a practice in strongest terms. Both parties are evidently striving for just treatment of either utility or customer. Since justice to corporation and public can usually be secured simultaneously, the contradictions of this question should be more apparent than real. The trouble is that these generalizations are put forth without some statement of underlying premises. *The proposition to subtract "depreciation" from actual or reproduction cost must not* *be separated from an explanation of the treatment of annual depreciation allowances.*

It is reasonable to expect that a concern should not earn on its original investment if there is evidence that extra large dividends have been passed back to the stockholders instead of providing for the inevitable depreciation in service value of plant or amortizing some of the early development costs, especially promoters' profits. There might then be good ground for holding that the investors had had returned to them that part of their investment represented by drop in value. But where very modest returns have been made, where management has been careful and where there is no suggestion of improper demands of the promoters, justice to the investors would indicate that they should not lose part of their funds just because the utility had not been able to lay up funds enough to pay for all replacements expected soon. The loss of this much capital can hardly be called one of the "risks of the business" covered by the expected dividends — especially since the importance of burdening rates with depreciation allowances was hardly appreciated fifteen or twenty years ago. But such deficits generally are counted in with cost of business development rather than with value of physical property.

Some argue that when depreciation allowances are being accumulated from earnings, a company ought not to earn on the present depreciation in physical worth. Really, equity depends on how one handles these annual contributions of the customers taken to offset depreciation. One popular scheme is to put in the rates such annual allowances as would, on being put out at compound interest, equal the unredeemed cost of the several items of property at the end of the useful life of each. In that scheme the annuity does not fully equal the depreciation; it is obvious that the sums derived from these allowances have to be invested somewhere in order to be ample. Therefore whether they are invested inside the business or outside, they are not free capital and are bringing in returns only for their own proper upbuilding. In such cases justice to the investor indicates that something equivalent to the full undepreciated investment should be in the earning basis. Conflicting views in this case are harmonized by noting that the sinking-fund reserve is analogous to reserve equipment, and fills the gap between depreciated value of plant and continuing investment.   (See further discussion of depreciation in Chapter VIII.)

Another scheme of providing funds to meet depreciation burdens the gross earnings with an equal sum each year, the sum being figured by dividing the total cost of each property item by its probable life.   Modifications of this plan make the payments unequal each year of probable life, being smaller at first and larger toward the last.   Such methods, it is plain, provide direct and immediate compensation for depreciation in worth and the allowances do not have to be put out at interest to assist in their own accumulation.   They are in the nature of a repayment of destroyed investment — sums which the company may re-invest as it sees fit.   As depreciation in value has thus been currently compensated for, then, and only then, is it just that a correspondingly diminished investment be used in the basis of earnings, instead of full investment as before.   (See also later discussions of depreciation.)

Use of Appreciation in Value. — There have been cases where it was attempted to have the appreciation of an utility's property (usually land) enter the income accounts, since the trend of court decisions is to denote such "increments in market value" as property and hence as an earning investment.   Any general doctrine that public utilities must expect to forego "unearned increments" in land has not been yet widely accepted — although there is some superficial plausibility in the oft-repeated claim that "unearned increments" should not enter fair value (for rates) in view of the increasing protection against "unearned decrements" in property.   It is necessary to inquire into the "increments" and "decrements" in specific cases really to understand when and why they should affect the valuation and the accounts.

The inclusion or exclusion of unearned increments in utility valuation is not a simple case like a boom or slump in real estate where no one knows with complete certainty whether a development will succeed or fail.   In general it is equitable to deny an increment only when protecting against a decrement.   The private real-estate promoter stands the chance of either loss or gain, but in an utility a certain loss in the value of original property is certain while any increase is doubtful.   Unless the protection against loss is complete there can be no equitable denial of increments.

What the utility is protected against is the financial loss due to a reduction in value of plant resulting from service. A certain deterioration is inevitable — the irreparable attrition due to service rendered. Even obsolescence and inadequacy, elements in depreciation which are expected to be problematical, in experience are found generally inevitable. None of the utility arts and sciences stand still long enough but what inadequacy and antiquation are manifested in service plants; one has only to think of telephone equipment, street-lighting apparatus, steam engines and turbines, street cars, railway locomotives and track, gas retorts and holders, reciprocating and centrifugal pumping engines, etc., to see the process. The public benefit of this protection is reflected in lower rates of return in capital, not in elimination of increments.

What the utility is not protected against, as yet, is a slump in market value of property (mostly land) due to outside influences not connected with the service. This is the antithesis of the unearned increment which some would deny. If the protection has not been given, denial of the effect of a boom does not seem equitable.

In some cases such protection is tacitly assumed. Take, for instance, the much debated case of new paving over old mains, a case of possible unearned increment generally denied the utility. If the pavement perchance became so peculiarly bad that it was cheaper than ever before for a concern to dig to its mains, or that it had to replace no street surfacing, then the earning power of the main would not decrease and there would be no demand that the value of mains be diminished. Here the company is protected against an unearned decrement and prevented from benefiting from a possible increment.

The arguments for balancing both appreciation and depreciation in valuation and operation accounts were best stated by M. R. Maltbie when on the New York Public Service Commission for the First District. His arguments in the first place seem to be based on a decision of Judge Hough in the earlier N. Y. Consolidated Gas case (157 Fed. Rep., 855), quoted thus:

Upon reason it seems clear that in solving this equation, the plus and minus quantities should be equally considered, and appreciation and depreciation treated alike.

In the opinion for the Queens Borough Gas & Electric Co. case (Informal Proceedings, June 1911), the Commissioner stated:

Thus land has been taken at its fair value and not at its original cost, and the annual appreciation of land has been treated as a profit. By this method all property is treated absolutely alike as Judge Hough suggests. No difference is made, except that as depreciation represents a decrease in assets, it is placed as a debit against operation, while appreciation is placed as credit because it is an increase in assets. If property is to be taken at its depreciated value where it has depreciated, an entry must regularly be made in estimated operating expenses equal to the average annual depreciation. Conversely if land or any other property which genuinely appreciates in value is to be taken at its appreciated value, then an entry must be made in the estimated receipts, equal to the average annual appreciation.

It is suggested that the annual increase in the value of land which is treated as income is not actually received. Increase in the value of unoccupied land is not realized until sold or put into use, but it is real, nevertheless, although payment may be deferred. Likewise, payments to the depreciation fund are not actually expended; yet they have been considered legitimate charges in practically every case. Furthermore, the annual increment is no more indefinite than the total increment — the present value. There is a further similarity, the exact amount of depreciation and the annual rate are not definitely known until the piece of property is actually replaced or has become useless. Total appreciation and the average annual rate are not known until the land is sold. The depreciation of the buildings is a charge against operation; why should not the appreciation of land be a credit?

In the later case of *Merihew v. Kings County Lighting Co.* (No. 1273, Nov. 1911), one reads:

The company apparently desires that the Commission shall increase the value of the land and then eliminate all reference to such increase in the profit and loss amounts, thereby the company would be enabled to collect from gas consumers 7 or 8% upon the value of the land and also retain the unearned increment from the land itself, thus obtaining double return. The profit obtained from increasing land values is just as real as any profit. The person who rents property that costs him $10,000 several years ago at a rental which yields him a return on $50,000 has just as certainly realized a profit from the increased value of the land as if he had sold it and invested the $50,000 elsewhere. The Commission has throughout, from 1909 to 1913, allowed $7\frac{1}{2}\%$ return upon the increasing value of the land, and it must, in order to be consistent, consider the annual increase as a profit for the purposes of this case."

But the highest court of the state threw out this annual appreciation allowance, confirming the court below which held that it was not income and an asset available for paying debts and so was not permissible in the annual accounts.

There still remains one unsettled problem connected with the Maltbie plan of entering the annual increment of land among the earnings. The treatment is not quite analogous to that of depreciation; the latter is paid for and a certain deduction made in the rate-basis worth and in the fixed charges. Where the increment is entered among earnings a certain addition is made to the rate-basis worth and the fixed charges are increased thereafter. In the case of depreciation the present customers pay the bill of loss and the deal ends there. In the case of appreciation the company pays the bill of gain and only the present consumers get the benefit; all the consumers of future years have to pay interest on what the present ones gain. That creates a tendency of fixed charges which is in the wrong direction — for effort should be made toward the reduction of fixed charges rather than their increase. It may be that this tendency is necessary in this case, but the last word has not been said.

CHAPTER VI

VALUATION AS AN ENGINEERING TASK; APPRAISAL OF LAND AND WATER RIGHTS

The General Problem. — Determination of reproduction cost or reproduction less depreciation is essentially an engineering problem. Theoretically, there is one true figure to be found in each case, but practically there are as many different sums as there are attempts to appraise — owing, in addition to the honest differences of opinion already noted, and even under the most favorable conditions, to error, unconscious prejudice, unrecognized influence, variable prices of materials and work, and the varied experiences of the engineers in charge.

It is almost trite to say that the appraisal should be under the guidance of the best engineer the available funds permit, for heretofore valuation has been made largely when subject to review by courts and commissions.

Selecting the Engineers. — To carry weight, the work must be consistently detailed and reasonably accurate; the engineer must have a reputation for conservatism, carefulness, and lack of prejudice either for or against corporations.

It is well to recognize that there are many able appraisers in this country whose experience has been all on one side or the other of these questions. While they believe themselves to be eminently fair, their figures have almost always been discounted by court or commission until experience warns that their employment will be regarded as special pleading and their results will weaken rather than strengthen the merits of their client's case. Indeed, some engineers seemingly will not accept appraisal tasks in actions against an utility corporation and others probably would not be employed by such concerns. On the other hand, there are many prominent men who seem to enjoy the confidence of public officials, corporations, courts and commissions alike; naturally their experience becomes more varied and valuable each year.

Helping or Hindering the Engineer. — In much of the work that valuation runs into, so many interpretations of fact can be made under any peculiarities of a particular case, that the employers must take their engineer into full confidence about every phase of their problem. Few would employ legal counsel without treating them so — if they expected good results; it is equally important on the engineering and economic sides. The engineer's experience always can bring out valuable suggestions of procedure, leading to greater public confidence in the client and fairer dealing all around. Yet many concerns secure an engineer to find the value of their property without advising him fully about every possible use of the results, which, if foreseen, might demand special consideration of fact.

Cost of Appraisal. — When an engineer of reputation is retained to organize and direct valuation, the whole work may be expected to cost from $0.25 to $1.25 per $1000 in property studied. The lower limit applies to large and uniform property arrangements, the higher limit covers smaller collections of diversified and scattered property. Some railroads have been appraised at $2 per mile (Texas Commission), but with much expense borne by the roads. Others have cost $6.50 per mile (Michigan) where everything was done by the appraisers. These sums amounted to about $0.137 and $0.424 per $1000 worth of property. The 1915 appraisal of the $84,000,000 property of the New York Telephone Co. cost $500,000 — $6 per $1000. This was intricate work.

Where men of broad experience and accepted standing can be employed to direct an appraisal it is frequently possible to cut down the cost by various approximations. But it has more often been considered that most cases might come before the courts and that, to stand there, the appraisal must show a most detailed inventory of minor as well as major equipment. This idea may prove to be a misapprehension. Rapid and inexpensive methods of valuation giving over-all results of substantial accuracy are necessary in many cases — notably for bankers' participation in utility-refinancing schemes and for insurance of manufacturing establishments. The experience in the latter field has been correlated to a notable extent and the accomplishments of such an organization as the Inspection Department of the Associated Factory Mutual Fire Insurance Companies are worthy of careful study by utilities.* Some details of this work

* Mr. J. G. Morse presented the results of his work as Appraiser for the Inspection Department in a paper "Valuation by Approximation" at the

are discussed a little later under the topic " Short Cuts in Appraisal." The intervening remarks apply particularly to current practice in utility rate cases — without constituting a defense of every practice noted.

Preliminary Investigation. — A first step in appraisal is to search out and compile all possible historical data, and all construction and operating accounts of the concern in question, to see if real knowledge of investments can be secured, to find what depreciation compensation has been levied on customers and where such money has been put, to learn what hardships the promoters and investors have endured, to discover possible improper manipulations of capital, etc. Generally, this first step has been productive of meager and disappointing results.

The Inventories. — The second step in appraisal is the preparation of a detail inventory — a listing of the tangible property and related intangible items with remarks on condition of various items and any information affecting worth — dimensions, materials, qualities, design, condition, important specifications, finish, date of installation, repairs, condition, scrap value, contractors' profits, cost of engineering and contingencies. In "inventory" here are included all papers from the first field and office notes to the final summaries.

Really, the building up of a public-utility inventory is in several distinct steps instead of one, as might be thought from the foregoing. There is first an office inventory, based on the preliminary investigation and any information furnished by the company. That inventory can be expected to be little more than a mere listing of equipment which is expected to be found but it facilitates the preparation for the inspectors' efforts. It is often useful, particularly in the absence of the pre-inventory, to study forms devised elsewhere for the field work. A number of complete systems have been published as worked out by various Commissions and private firms. Those in charge of this detailed study must be very familiar with the design and operation of such properties as are under examination.

In mapping out the inspectors' work, only a few main divisions can be made, and these along natural lines, or else there will be so

Valuation Conference of the Utilities Bureau, in Philadelphia, November, 1915; for proceedings of this Conference see the Bureau's " Utilities Magazine," January, 1916.

much property on the borders of several divisions that no force lists it, each one thinking some other division had recorded it. Beyond this, it is not here possible to make detailed rules as to how the inventory must or must not be made. It can be said, however, that as generally successful a plan as any has placed the inspection and cataloging of these major divisions on separate parties (or for small properties on the same party at different times) with instructions to follow a logical or orderly path in their endeavor to get everything of the particular nature then dealt with. Such major divisions of inventory may be for instance; land, buildings, machinery (and rolling stock), service lines (track, wires, pipes, etc.), supplies, furniture and tools.

When a paper pre-inventory has been worked up from records supplied, the inspectors' work is more a checking than an original listing. When blank forms have to be developed it is an aid to follow the standard classifications of accounts in general use as developed by the Interstate Commerce Commission, the several state commissions, the National Electric Light Association, the American Electric Railway Association, etc. Their service consists chiefly in reminding of detailed items.

It has been found well, too, to have the listers or inspectors confine themselves in the field work to mere cataloging of property items and all available information about them. Then they study one grand division of equipment to the exclusion (temporarily at least) of the others and that is the extent of such classification as is worth while by these men. For further rearrangement of items into different groups, pure office help is believed by some engineers to be the best — under technical scrutiny of course.

The property items listed should be complete in every important detail, so as to determine character and probable cost, but pursuit of petty details beyond that point is expensive and useless. This point alone shows the necessity of care, conscientiousness and experience. The "field notes" of an appraisal should be well made and preserved for other possible use, as in court review which is frequently present as a possibility.

In making the field inventory, the inspectors should be familiar with the apparatus they are listing so that, among other things they can form some approximate idea of the amount of depreciation undergone. Before the reports are made use of, however, some of the most experienced engineers in charge generally study at least the important parts of a plant to arrive at an idea of the life and depreciation of the apparatus.

Unit Prices. — Each property item reported as in service or available needs to have its number of property units multiplied by "unit prices" to get the physical cost. These unit prices, it is now generally accepted in finding a present value for rate making, should be prices of today — or the average of the last 5 to 10 years for fluctuating data. Combining present prices and old pieces of property seems to many doubtless to introduce an inconsistency into the whole procedure. Yet sometimes the original charges are no longer procurable, and if the official directions to appraisers are to obtain present cost of reproducing the still existing old property items, then no other procedure is more logical. It has been often argued that it is the height of inconsistency to figure reproduction cost taking into account historical facts of the course of construction and then using unit prices of today. Yet that inconsistency diminishes, or fades entirely, when we see that this is but a labor-saving way of attaining the equivalent present value — instead of reproducing a plant under old unit prices and then adjusting the whole value to present prices in the endeavor to approximate present worth.

Unit prices in but few cases are all fixed by men of such experience that the figures do not have to be selected for a case after careful comparison and consultation of the appraisal staff. Unless care is taken peculiarities may creep in to discredit the appraisal.

Some unit prices, as those taken from contracts, will show a contractor's profit of 5 to 20% and when such units are used this should be clearly expressed so that later the aggregate costs may not be increased by amounts intended to cover contractors' work. In rare cases, the unit prices used may have been changed to show appreciation or depreciation, and the value then secured by appraisal is not simple reproduction cost. Such situations must be guarded against. In some appraisals the inventories and unit prices cover the overhead costs of plant development commonly included under going-concern value. In the Des Moines Gas case before the U. S. Supreme Court this procedure was held to prevent further entrance of going-concern value.

Short Cuts in Appraisals. — Brief mention has been made of the possibility of lowering the cost of appraisals and of the work done by the Inspection Department of the Associated Factory Mutual Fire Insurance Companies. The practice of this organization is based on the argument that it is inconsistent to inventory the material of a building and the machinery in a plant to the last minute detail while only the value of the different standard materials and machines can be as accurately secured, while large costs of waste, labor, erection and contingencies have to be gross estimates, and while depreciation in value is largely guessed at. Therefore the detail to which a given part of a works is inventoried by these insurance appraisers depends on the percentage which that part may be expected to have of the value of the whole works. In such ways large manufacturing establishments have been appraised by a few days work in the field and an equal time in the office. These valuations have been free — being a part of the insurance work — but they have been accepted for cost accounting, etc., by the assured concerns some of whom have compared the results with old-school appraisals. Such rapid valuations have not generally come before the courts, but the methods have been supported satisfactorily in court in a couple of instances.

It is the practice of this bureau first to divide a manufacturing plant into buildings and machinery; elevators, piping and all things that can be removed without altering the building are classed as machinery. The floor areas and type of construction of buildings are noted and valuation made on a basis of square feet of floor area, using the cost tables of C. T. Main * as a basis for the length-width-height relations.

The machinery is subdivided into machine units, shafting, belting, piping, electric wiring, and furniture and miscellaneous equipment. These items are inventoried with notation of only such dimensions and description as show trade sizes and lead to location of unit value. Thus " 1 engine lathe 14 × 6 comp. taper " designates a lathe with 14-inch swing, 6-foot bed over all, screw cutting, no special gearing, compound rest and taper attachment. All modern power machines (engines, turbines, motors, generators, etc.) carry a name plate giving the needed information, except that sometimes speed, cylinder diameter

* Given first in a paper before the New England Cotton Manufacturer's Association, April, 1904; revised to January, 1910, in the article " Approximate Cost of Mill Buildings," *Engineering News*, Jan. 27, 1910 (see Appendix).

and length of stroke of engines and pumps have to be noted. Boilers and piping are appraised by rated horsepower. Standard machines are appraised by current price lists, special machines by experience or quotation. Such prices are increased 5 to 10% to cover transportation and erection. Of the total value of the buildings and contents, the value of buildings and fixed machines amounts ordinarily to more than half so that short cuts based on averaged experience are justified for the minor items.

Lengths of shafting are measured and priced per foot erected and equipped. Main belts are measured by eye; an addition in value of a machine unit for its machine belts is made, there being several groups. Steam, hot-water, and gas piping — for heating and lighting — and automatic-sprinkler pipes are covered by an allowance of so many cents per square foot of floor area. The manufacturing-service piping for steam, water, gas, oil and air is covered by per-machine and per-horsepower charges, cross checked. Electric wiring is valued per light and per motor horsepower, actual figures depending on the type of lamp, and on grouping the motors in size groups.

From the experience of this bureau extending over many years, figures have been made of total costs per main machine unit — per spindle in a cotton mill, per pair of cards in a woolen mill and per square foot of floor space or per producing machine in a standard plant so that still quicker approximation can be had, when necessary.

The bureau's practice in regard to depreciation is to assume that where a building is over three or four years old, is plumb and in good repair and adequate, the depreciation stands constant for several years at 5% of total first value. On machinery 2 to 5% is deducted for each year of a main unit's life. Some special machines have depreciation figured on wearing parts only. Depreciation of shafting is not recognized; $\frac{1}{3}$ drop is allowed on belting as a whole. On piping a total of 10% is the usual limit.

This work has been in industrial works but most of these have water, steam, electricity, or gas plants so that the general applicability of the plan has been tested. It is considered by the department that even less detail than noted would be required in a pure utility plant — owing to the concentration of values in a few large machine units, etc. It is obvious that parts of a plant thus appraised are treated as conforming to the average worth of similar parts in other works — unusual contingencies and extreme peculiarities have no effect. The success of such appraisals depends upon how complete are the appraiser's records of plant costs — upon how closely they represent true averages of present values.

Appraisal of Real Estate. — A fair procedure for land valuation, known as the sales method, has been extensively employed with apparent general satisfaction by the Wisconsin Railroad Commission and is discussed at length in an early case (*State Journal Printing Co., v. Madison Gas and Electric Co.*, March, 1910). Yet it is stated (p. 528), that it is only a valuable aid to the judgment of the experts. A part of the opinion reads:

The sales method may be defined as a plan or process for the systematic collection and comparison of data relating to real-estate transfers for the purpose of estimating true market realty values. It consists in a study of the transfers of neighboring property having conditions or characteristics similar to the land whose value is to be determined and it is intended to duplicate as nearly as may be the mental or judicial processes ordinarily employed by the so-called "local real-estate expert," with a view to arriving at results approximating those which would be reached by such local experts acting without bias or suggestion. Two interpretations of the sales method have been most commonly employed. In one of these, the area and consideration in each sale of similarly situated land is found, the average unit price (per square foot, per foot frontage, per lot, per acre, etc.) ascertained, and this unit applied to the tract under investigation. The other application introduces what, in many cases, is believed to be an additional safeguard, consisting in the use of the average assessed value of adjacent or similarly situated lands in combination with an average ratio representing the relationship of the assessed value of transferred lands to the final consideration paid for such lands — all figures being based on "ground values," exclusive of improvements thereon. In the broader and more flexible applications of the sales method, the expert adopts one or the other of the processes outlined or blends the two in such fashion as to yield the most consistent and trustworthy final result.

In view of the close similarity as to fundamental basis of the sales and local expert methods, particular interest and importance attaches to any specific cases affording a direct comparison of actual valuation results by the two methods made under normal conditions. Fortunately, the results of two such comparisons are available, one involving some 300 blocks, or over 3 square miles, of representative, residential property, in St. Paul; the other of some 500 acres of valuable railway-terminal lands, in Milwaukee.

The St. Paul investigation was made by Mr. T. A. Polleys who conceived of a plan to test the sales method of valuing lands. A district in the westerly portion of St. Paul was selected for reason that the great activity for several preceding years would insure ample sales data and because of the representative characteristics of the territory. The average ground values per foot front was ascertained by a flexible application of the sales method, chiefly by Mr. Polleys personally who then requested some 14 highly qualified real-estate experts to submit their estimates of the same values. To arouse interest in the investigation Mr. Polleys charted his determinations and submitted copies to the experts with the urgent request however, that they should not be influenced thereby. The experts served without compensation, acted independently and were free of suggestion in preparing their estimates. . . . It was seen that the tendency of the sales method was to give deficient results to an average amount of 3.8%.

This result is strikingly confirmed by the valuation of terminal lands of the Chicago, Milwaukee & St. Paul Ry., in Milwaukee, in 1903, under the auspices of the Tax Commission. The lands amounted to upwards of 500 acres, scattered through some 15 wards and having an aggregate valuation of approximately $6,000,000. The market value of these railroad lands was determined by specially qualified local experts under the direction of Mr. F. W. Adams, secretary of the railway company. The state valuation staff, under the direction of Prof. W. D. Taylor, engineer for the state board of assessment, used the sales method on a basis consistent with local conditions. The final results differed by only 3.5%, those by the sales method being lower.

Cost of Condemnation. — It is common experience that the cost of acquiring real estate for an utility concern has been two or three times the preliminary valuation based on market value of contiguous property. This is caused in part by the necessary expenses of searching for most suitable grounds, the destruction of existing buildings, and oftentimes the premium which must be paid to induce sale from persons either not anxious to part with the land or suspecting the purchasers' purpose and desirous of securing maximum advantage from the transaction. If the right of eminent domain be used there still are large additional expenses incurred for engineers and lawyers, for damages to plots cut in two and to various other adjacent lands.

An instance has been cited (1914 Report, Valuation Committee,

Am. Soc. C. E.), of the Wachusett Reservoir of the Boston Metropolitan Water Works. Experts made the preliminary valuation of the 4772 acres with buildings at $697,000. The actual aggregate price of the property acquired was $1,182,000, or 69% in excess, and this was under right of eminent domain. The overhead costs of the takings (estimated at 15%) were not included.

Generally, it seems to be recognized as good practice to pay up to two or three times the common market price of similar but unaffected lands rather than enter upon condemnation litigation and delays. The point is that under either bargaining or condemnation there are items of heavy expense and owners' demands not disclosed by either prior or subsequent examination of the lands. These increments of expected cost are not covered, either, by the ordinary overhead allowances of construction engineering, contingencies, etc.

Where the utilities have not the right of condemnation, as in the case of certain eastern electricity-transmission companies, and the corporation has to rely on its own bargaining, there may be a genuine "hold-up" even for easements. Of course, such excessive costs are legitimate and essential matters for capitalization. But if possible the generation that imposed them on the utility should obliterate them through amortization contributions and a corresponding reduction of the ratio of capital to tangible property.

Denial of Condemnation Cost. — Some consternation has been produced among utilities by the so-called Minnesota Rate Cases (230 U. S. 352; June, 1913) in which railroad terminal·properties in St. Paul, Minneapolis, and Duluth were not admitted to have a value as much above the market value of contiguous property as railroad properties generally are known to cost above market price. However, it is only fair to note that the eminent justice's opinion relates only to the cases in hand where the railways had been long established, the contiguous property largely enhanced by the presence of the railways, and the actual increase of price above original market value so far hidden in the dim past that its study was largely conjecture.

It is interesting to note the language of this decision; it states that railroads have been given the right of eminent domain so that their necessities may not be played upon to secure more than market value of land taken. However, this reasoning must not yet be carried as a precedent too far afield of the specific applica-

tion in these cases; it would be expected that for cases when the
actual cost of taking the land was not mere conjecture, the court
would receive evidence of that cost in a case at hand and in similar
cases. The point to be observed is that where the contiguous
property values rise because of the presence of the utility, then
the rising value of the railroad land cannot be expected always to
outstrip the market value of the contiguous parcels. The miscellaneous items of condemnations — engineering, superintendence, legal expense, contingencies, etc., according to this decision,
are to be regarded as absorbed in the general rise of value if that
has carried present worth very much above original total cost.
The decision runs:

It is clear that in ascertaining the present value we are not limited to
the consideration of the amount of the actual investment. . . . The
property is held in private ownership and it is that property, and not the
original cost of it, of which the owner may not be deprived without due
process of law.

Assuming that the company is entitled to a reasonable share in the
general prosperity of the communities which it serves, and thus to attribute to its property an increase in value, still the increase so allowed,
apart from any improvements it may make, cannot properly extend beyond the fair average of the normal market of land in the vicinity having
a similar character. Otherwise we enter the realm of mere conjecture.

Value of Adaptability. — Special value for land because of
its inherent adaptability for reservoirs, wells, dams, railways,
power stations, etc., has often been claimed and numerous decisions are to be found both for and against such allowances.

The U. S. Supreme Court in the Minnesota Rate Cases has this
to say about such an element of value:

It is urged that, in this view, the company would be bound to pay the
"railway value" of the property. But, supposing the railroad to be
obliterated and the lands to be held by others, the owner of each parcel
would be entitled to receive on its condemnation its *fair market value* for
all its available uses and purposes. If, in the case of any such owner, his
property had a peculiar value or special adaptation for railroad purposes,
that would be an element to be considered. But still the inquiry would
be as to the fair market value of the property; as to what the owner had
lost, and not what the taker had gained. The owner would not be entitled to demand payment of the amount which the property might be
deemed worth to the company; or of an enhanced value by virtue of the
purpose for which it was taken; or of an increase over its fair market

value, by reason of any added value supposed to result from its combination with tracts acquired from others so as to make it a part of a continuous railroad right-of-way held in one ownership.

Other cases like *McGovern v. N. Y.* (130 App. Div., N. Y. 350, 356), sustained by the U. S. Supreme Court on account of the discretion allowed the trial court, indicate that if special value is not recognized until the utility starts its initial proceedings, then it could not be secured on condemnation.

Value for Paving Over Mains. — One of the controversial matters in appraisal is what has already been incidentally noted as "value of paving over mains." On the one hand, there are those who argue that if improved paving has been put down since the pipes, conduits or other underground structures, then the value of the mains has increased according to what it would cost to put them down under the new conditions. The theory by which this is defended seems to be that a strict adherence to the cost-of-reproduction method of valuation necessitates reproducing all such actual conditions rather than giving any weight to former conditions.

On the other side of this question are those who argue that this is unreasonable — even verging on extortion. It is obvious that the company necessarily has been passive, so far as improving the pavements, while the city has presumably been active. The net result is that the more money the city puts into the pavements, etc., the more the citizens have to pay for the same old utility service. One reason for denying this value is discussed under increments and decrements of value above.

Those who contended for maximum allowances for improved paving over mains for years relied on the Supreme Court opinion in the Consolidated Gas Case (212 U. S., 19; Jan., 1909), supporting in general the findings of a lower court which had admitted the cost of new paving over old gas mains in New York City. The precarious nature of this foundation is seen from one paragraph in the Supreme Court opinion.

And we concur with the court below in holding that the value of the property is to be determined as of the time when the inquiry is made regarding the rates. If the property which legally enters into the consideration of the question of rates has increased in value since it was acquired, the company is entitled to the benefit of such increase. This is, at any rate, the general rule. We do not say there may not possibly be an exception to it where the property may have increased so enormously in value as to render a rate permitting a reasonable return upon such increased value unjust to the public. How such facts should be treated is not a question now before us, as this case does not present it.

Those who stood out against excess cost of paving over mains, relied on the Supreme Court in the Cedar Rapids Gaslight Case (223 U. S. 665), which generally supported a lower court in denying excess value but did not specifically mention the topic. The intention of the Supreme Court to sanction including cost of new paving over old mains was denied by the highest New York State court in the Kings County Lighting Case (N. Y. Public Service Comm., First District, No. 1273; *People ex. rel. Kings County Lighting Co. v. Wilcox et al.*; March, 1914). The leading statement runs thus:

The relator is entitled to a fair return on investment not on improvements made at public expense. The case is not parallel to the so-called unearned increment of land. That the company owns. It does not own pavements, and the laying of them does not add to its investment or increase the cost to it of producing gas. On one hand, cost of reproduction less accrued depreciation should not be so applied as to deprive the corporation of a fair return at all times on reasonable, proper and necessary investment made by it to serve the public, and on the other side it should not be so applied as to give the corporation a return on improvements made at public expense which in no way increase the cost to it of performing that service.

The question has been definitely settled by the Supreme Court in the Des Moines Gas Case (438 U. S. 153; P. U. R. 1915 D, 577; June, 1915). The Court did not state any new ideas on the subject but accepted and promulgated the views of the court below and the master in chancery, thus:

As to the item of $140,000, which, it is contended, should be added to the valuation, because of the fact that the master valued the property on the basis of the cost of reproduction new, less depreciation, and it would be necessary in such reproduction to take up and replace pavements on streets which were unpaved when the gas mains were laid, in order to replace the mains, we are of the opinion that the court below correctly disposed of this question. These pavements were already in place. It may be conceded that they would require removal at the time when it became necessary to reproduce the plant in this respect. The master reached the conclusion that the life of the mains would not be enhanced by the necessity of removing the pavements, and that the company had no right of property in the pavements, thus dealt with, and that there was neither justice nor equity in requiring the people who had been at the expense of paving the streets to pay an additional sum for gas because the plant, when put in, would have to be at the expense of taking up and replacing the pavements in building the same. He held that such added value was wholly theoretical, when no benefit was derived therefrom. We find no error in this disposition of the question.

Value of **Franchises.** — Under administration expense has been mentioned the cost of obtaining franchises.

But when nothing is paid for the franchise public opinion is against entering any value for it in the appraisal of worth for rate making. That cannot be said to apply to appraisal for purchase since then the company rightfully could expect to receive compensation for expected profits during the rest of the franchise life. In adding franchise value to rate-basis worth, if at all, the history of the company should be consulted particularly to see if the communities definitely held out prospects of extra profits over interest, risk, etc., on actual investment. More and more the franchises now granted are stripped specifically of such possible value at their granting; but the terms, expressed or implied, in existing grants need to be studied carefully in adjusting rates that unjustified retroactive punishment is not meted out.

This question was recently (June, 1915) decided by the highest New Jersey court (Errors and Appeals) in the so-called "Passaic 90-c. Gas Case." The Public Utilities Commission denied a value to the gas company's franchises, beyond cost and burden, and the state supreme court sustained it. The highest court at first reversed the lower court but on a rehearing sustained it. The concurring opinion of Justice White is an interesting discussion of the idea that a franchise is property but not "used and useful" in service. A part of the opinion is given below:

Taking up the second proposition, that the Company's charter right to charge reasonable rates is in itself a valuable property right entitled to consideration in rate making, I suppose it must be conceded that the franchise to charge as a "reasonable rate," sufficient to yield a net profit of 8% on the value of the Company's property as allowed and established respectively by the findings of the Utilities Commission in this case, is a very valuable property right. Certainly I think it is. That this valuable privilege is the Company's is beyond question. That it is property is undoubted. That the law protects it against confiscation and subjects it to taxation follows as a matter of course.

But that this valuable property right to charge "reasonable rates" should by virtue of its own existence have the effect of converting itself into a still more valuable property right to charge "unreasonable rates" is, of course, preposterous. Presumably the incorporators went into this public utility business because they expected that their charter privilege to charge "reasonable rates" for the gas they were to manufacture, distribute and sell, would be a valuable one, but that fact and the fact that it has become so, cannot have the effect of altering the terms of the contract made with the State.

The mere statement of this proposition is sufficiently convincing, but if anything more were needed, a glance at the absurd practical result of the contrary view would be illuminating. If the franchise to charge ninety cents in order to pay 8% on the value of the Company's property not including the franchise is worth a million dollars and must be included and have 8% paid on it also, the rate would have to be $1 instead of 90c.; but if the Company has the property right to charge $1, the franchise is worth two million dollars instead of one million, and so the rate must be $1.10 in order to pay 8% on this additional million, and so on indefinitely.

That the Company's contract with the State to charge "reasonable rates" cannot be thus evaded, is, of course, quite obvious. The plain fact is that the commercial value of the Company's property right in its franchise can have no effect in fixing the rate it can charge, because by the terms of its contract with the State the stream of its franchise value arises from the spring of its right to charge "reasonable rates," and in the very nature of things no stream can rise higher than its source.

Water Rights Must be Considered. — Greatly varying ideas are prevalent as to whether or not a public utility utilizing a water power can include in the rate-basis worth of its plant any allowance for rights to the beneficial use of water.

This has been denied in a few specific cases, notably by the Public Service Commission for the Second District of New York in *Fuhrman v. Cataract Power and Conduit Co.* (3 N. Y. Pub. Ser. Comm. 2nd D. 670) on the grounds that the federal and state permission to use water at Niagara Falls gave the corporation no title to the water and hence no water right measured by the price of steam power. Other commissions, for instance, like those of California (*re No. Calif. Power Co.*, Calif. R. R. Comm. Rep. 1913) and Idaho (*re Pocatello Water Co.* 1 Idaho Pub. Serv. Comm. Orders 78; 1914) appear to have held at one time that water rights were in the nature of fictitious intangibles and so not admissible as part of rate-basis worth.

Later ideas of both these bodies named (See re *City of Santa Cruz*, Calif. R. R. Comm. 2666; P. U. R. 1915 F 768, and re *Pocatello Water Co.*, Idaho Supreme Court, 150 Pac. 47; P. U. R. 1915 F 437) show a different attitude for in both cases a value for the rights was allowed.

There has existed little doubt anywhere as to the necessity of giving proper attention to water rights since the United States Supreme Court held in 1914, in *San Joaquin & Kings River Canal & Irrig. Co. v. Stanislaus County* (233 U. S. 459), that in spite of a declaration in the California Constitution that water appropriated for sale was appropriated for public use, the benefit was private and the rights thereto should be considered in condemnation and rate cases. Mr. Justice Holmes thus speaks:

But it is said that as the plaintiff appropriates this water to distribution and sale, it thereby dedicates it to public use under California law, and so loses its private right in the same. It appears to us that when the cases cited for this proposition are pressed to the conclusion reached in the present case, they are misapplied. No doubt it is true that such an appropriation and use of the water entitles those within reach of it to demand the use of a reasonable share on payment. It well may be true that if the waters were taken for a superior use by eminent domain those whose lands were irrigated would be compensated for the loss. But even if the rate paid is not to be determined as upon a purchase of water from the plaintiff, still, at the lowest, the plaintiff has the sole right to furnish this water, the owner of the irrigated lands cannot get it except through the plaintiff's help, and it would be unjust not to take that fact into account in fixing the rates. . . . It seems unreasonable to suppose that the constitution meant that if a party, instead of using the water on his own land, as he may, sees fit to distribute it to others, he loses the rights that he has bought or lawfully acquired.

This case is widely quoted as controlling. The question now is not whether any water right is to enter rate basis but how much should be allowed. The hesitant attitude of public representatives as to amount is well expressed by the New Hampshire Public Service Commission when it states (re *Grafton El. Light & Power Co.*, 4 *N. H. Pub. Serv. Comm. Rep.* 178)

The objection of the Supreme Court to the conjectural character of the cost of reproduction method [of valuing property in the Minnesota Rate Cases] applies with equal force to the "saving-over-coal" method of valuing water power. It assumes, what is not proved, that power could be produced profitably by coal, and it assumes, what is not true, that a given amount of power produced by water varying in amount as it will on even the best regulated streams is equal in value to a like amount of power generated by steam, constant and reliable at all times.

We live in a region remote from the coal fields, the cost of transportation is heavy, and the price of coal is higher than in almost any other part of the country. On the other hand ours is a mountainous state with many streams having a large fall and furnishing an abundance of water power, much of which is still undeveloped. . . . A fair value of a water power in New Hampshire cannot be a value which takes no account of our natural resources and makes electricity produced by water as expensive to the public as if produced by coal.

The Vermont Public Service Commission also expressed the same hesitancy in re *Montpelier & Barre Light & Power Co.* (No. 452, 1916; P. U. R. 1916 B 973), as follows:

The Commission, however, entirely disapproves of this method of determining the value of water rights [by direct comparison with steam] because, in our opinion it creates a value which may be largely in excess of the actual value of the rights and because this method, if applied to rates, would entirely deprive the consumer of any benefits to which he is entitled by reason of having these natural resources at hand.

Better Understanding Needed of Water Rights. — The large amount of water-power valuation being made all over the country, the peculiar results being presented by some well-meaning but uninstructed appraisers and the hesitation of Commissions to accept the results make timely a review of defensible procedure in water-rights appraisal. Valuations that can be criticized are those, for example, which set forth the worth of water rights as the "combined intangible and going values of a power development" — locating this as the capitalized possible net annual income. Such a finding has no justification for parading as the value of water rights, although water rights indeed are hidden therein.

At the outset it should be stated that authorities are universally agreed that water rights are property having essentially the nature of real estate — industrial real estate. Therefore, they are valuable in accordance with their power to produce income.

The Idaho Commission in valuing the water rights of a hydro-electric company (*Taylor v. N. W. Light & Water Co.;* Idaho Pub. Util. Comm. Order 297; P. U. R. 1916 A 372) refused to

allow a value where it transpired that the company could purchase cheaper than it could develop power.

But this value of earning power must be separated from the
common intangible values also generally recognized by their
earning power or by investment. Even where such procedure
is followed, the greatest variation is seen in the results of its use
by different persons. The appraiser with sympathies running
in one direction seems apt to make value large enough to compensate the holder for amounts more desired than supported by
fact. The appraiser of opposite sympathies seems to minimize
the value of water rights where these can be construed as depending to any measure on public grants. As is usual on such controversial matters, the actual truth in any specific case generally
resides in a somewhat indefinite middle ground and can be
approximated only by the exercise of good judgment as well as
the study of specific data.

Rights as Real Estate. — If water rights are essentially of
the nature of real estate it would be expected that they should
be valued like real estate by the direct comparison of sales.
However, this method, in simple form, is extremely restricted
for the study of water-power rights; exchanges are extremely
few in number compared with the parcels of land that are
traded every year. Moreover, in comparing the values of real
estate it is essential to take into account transfers of land in the
immediate vicinity of the parcels studied. That seldom is possible in the case of water powers, and in making any direct
comparison of sales the geographical separation usually will be
sufficient seriously to impair the validity of the appraisal —
unless such effects as different cost of development, different
annual return, different market conditions and different probable
net profit are brought into play. But the handicap of geographical separation may be overcome by scientific analysis preceding
the attempt at comparison.

Splitting the Value of Rights. — Water rights, it has been stated
already, exhibit the peculiarities of *industrial* real estate in that
the value depends on utility for special service. Indeed consolidated water rights may be regarded as the enhancement of
value of land well situated for the special use of generating
power from falling water, etc. The enhancement from these
special uses is far greater than the value of the real estate for

all the ordinary uses of land, so that the common value of the tracts is generally neglected as inconsequential.

This enhancement consists of two elements of value, the first depending on the physical conditions which lead to ease or difficulty (measured by expense) of developing the rights. The second depends on the demand for water or power in the locality, and the kind and cost of power that predominates to rule the market. The two values are not wholly independent for where there is competition with steam power, the second element increases with any decrease in cost of development.

These value factors we may call * "constructional" and "regional." In case either factor is zero, the value of the water rights is zero. For instance the many water powers hundreds of miles back from even moderately populous areas have little or no regional value at present, and the value of the water rights is inappreciable in spite of possible high constructional value. The numerous waterpowers of the Adirondack region of New York have no local market and cannot be completely developed to compete profitably with steam power in the metropolitan markets; the regional value is low. If it were sought to dam the Hudson River and develop power anywhere near New York City the regional value would be great but constructional value obviously would be zero, so great would be the legal, engineering and financial obstacles.

Comparing Two Rights. — If an engineer has data in hand on the sale prices of scattered water rights, the unknown value of a questioned private water right can be approximated by increasing or decreasing the known value in proportion to (1) the size of the possible development, (2) the difference in regional value and (3) the difference in constructional value. Much the same sort of scheme would be employed by an experienced engineer, the rights of actual scattered plants taken before for comparison being replaced by those of an ideal normal plant existing in the mind of the appraiser. It might be thought that the problem could be approached also by setting up for comparison a hypothetical plant of the specific local capacity, built under local hydraulic data but under fixed difficulties and at specific cost, and finally having a specific market and specific

* Following the nomenclature employed by Robert E. Horton, Consulting Engineer, Albany, N. Y., in recent cases.

income. For such a plant there could be computed a net income and the water rights would depend on this — being in the nature of real estate which is valued by its earning power. Then the real water rights could be approximated by changing this value to accord with greater or less construction difficulties which developed, and for more or less favorable market conditions which arose. But this last study reduces more or less to a direct appraisal by earning capacity.

Valuation of Rights by Earning Capacity. — Where there is not dependable data for the method of appraisal by sales comparison, it is necessary to fall back upon an earning-capacity study. At the outset it is necessary to start with the query: What sum could an intending purchaser afford to pay for consolidated water rights going with a diversion for power or water-supply, knowing the gross income which the power or water will bring, knowing that certain fixed charges, interest and taxes must be paid on the full investment — including land and water rights and the cost of plant and business development? All the factors entering into the solution of the problem are known but one — water rights — and the answer is therefore ascertainable.

On the basis of earning capacity, the capitalized net profit is equal to the cost of the physical plant and going-concern value (the latter estimated for an undeveloped business by any of the acceptable methods) plus the water rights in question. The net earnings or profit in turn are the gross annual earnings less the annual operating, supervision and repair cost, depreciation compensation, etc., and less the interest and taxes on plant (structural) value, going-concern value and worth of water rights. This is briefly and simply stated * in mathematical symbols as:

$$S + G + W = \frac{P}{N} = \frac{I - O - (S + G + W)(R + T)}{N},$$

whence

$$W = \frac{I - O - (S + G)(N + R + T)}{N + R + T},$$

where

P = annual net profits

W = water-rights value

I = annual gross income

---

* Following the form suggested by Robert E. Horton, Consulting Hydraulic Engineer, Albany, N. Y.

O = annual operating expenses
S = structural cost
G = going-concern cost
N = capitalization rate
R = fair return on investment
T = tax rate.

The warning that needs to be made in the use of the earning-value method is that appraisers have seemed apt to under-estimate the annual operating expenses and so over-estimate the profits and the value of water rights.

Short-Cut Steam-Power Comparison. — The gross annual income of a water-power plant in the East is tremendously affected by the cost of steam power. There are few hydro-electric plants where a considerable proportion of the output does not compete with steam drive directly. Even where the service is for lighting the price is limited to that of possible local steam-plant current. Therefore, there has been used in the East a short-cut scheme of appraising water rights by capitalizing the difference in cost of output between the hydraulic plant and an equivalent steam plant in the same district. This may be permissible at times, but it is not to be universally recommended as it substitutes an extreme hypothetical condition where a closer approach to actuality is possible. Public hostility to it has already been noted. For instance, with utility regulation, even in the East, the tendency of rates is toward cost of service, including therein a reasonable return on physical property employed. The regulated rates are not directly or fully related to the cost of steam power. (The off-peak factory-drive competitive business, however, is secured only by cutting under steam-power costs. The off-peak commercial business operates to reduce the general cost of service by giving more constant utilization of the plant and diluting the over-head expenses with small additional profits.)

The desire to use steam-power costs in the valuation of water rights springs out of the convenience of such comparisons rather than rising from their applicability. The capitalized annual cost of operating and maintaining in perpetuity a profitable steam plant to produce an amount of energy equal to that which can be produced at a given water power, generally will prove larger than the similar figure for a water-power development, the water rights of which are determined by weighted comparison of sales, or by study of actual earning-power. Therefore the value of water rights determined by such steam-power cost comparisons may be expected to be often large enough to prove an embarrassment to the owners in time of protracted business stagnation, financial depression, strikes, war, unfavorable legislation, strict regulation, or poor internal management. When this scheme is or has been employed, care should be exercised to see that the valuation of water rights and plant plus capitalized operation and maintenance costs does not exceed the capitalized sum which would maintain and operate the equivalent steam plant *not continuously but for such portion of the time as the water-power plant could reasonably be expected to operate under the unfortunate contingencies noted.* The necessity for such a scrutiny may be realized when it is recalled that the investment costs, which continue always, are high for the water-power plant and low for the steam plant; the operating expenses which may be curtailed during depressions are small for the water-power development and large for the steam plant.

Value of Rights under **Regulation.** — Many believe that the valuation of water rights in the Western states must be on a different plane from that in the East. There is nothing seen, however, in the sales-comparisons or earning-value plans of appraisal but what can be followed in one section as well as in another.

Some publicists claim that as the water rights came from the public and are used for the public good, no value should be allowed the utility company for those rights. The actual conditions under which public grant of water powers has been made need to be considered, of course. It is conceivable that in some cases the public desired that the company should earn on its investment and activity but not on the fundamental land and water rights. Where that view actually prevails, obviously there can be no water right owned by the utility company. Where such a condition has not been found, the appraiser has to find rights even under rate regulation. This is difficult for he has to avoid a reasoning-in-circle situation. That is, if he takes earnings through rates based on a worth which includes value of water rights, the larger the value of those rights the higher the rates must be; then the larger becomes the value of the rights again and the higher the rates, and so on. The only escape usually is to consider what the water rights would be in private service.

The concern may have obligated itself to serve the public when it might have continued to give private service in large blocks; then the water rights ordinarily should be considered as before the public service became predominant. Surely neither the company nor the public expected that the company would be penalized for furnishing a multitude of users instead of the few. The right to use water for private gain of course is as legitimate as the right so to use land. Care has to be taken to insure that the estimate of earnings on a private-business basis is strictly consistent, that it does not include income-rate enhancement promoted by public assistance marking the change from private to public utility — like occupancy of streets or of power of eminent domain.

There are various ways away from reasoning in a circle when the very earnings to be taken in the earning-power method are under attack as unreasonable. First it must be ascertained what peculiar status any Federal and State legislation may give the water rights; or what specific franchise contracts may affect them so that they may be declared non-existent, existent but partly dedicated to public benefit, or existent and entirely in private possession.

If existent and in private seizure, in most cases, there appears to be no escape from the higher prices due to earnings on water right. A parallel case exists: A state may have given away its valuable mineral land to any who would develop and it cannot but endure the situation as to old land patents, though it can demand a share of the profits in land yet ungranted. It is the same way with water rights in many cases. Legislatures may have the power to cancel the rights by amortization and repayment.

The actual estimation of probable earnings of the rights under purely private industry may be arrived at, in some cases for instance, from the figures available from the private utilization of part of the water rights as leased to others.

Values Appurtenant to Water Rights. — The "value" obtained in the ways and under the conditions noted in reality is more than simply worth of water rights. It has been seen that it includes first of all, the relatively unimportant value of the appurtenant land for common uses. If the plant is already built and in operation, the value may often also include a factor depending on the brains worked into the design, construction and operation.

The separation of the value of the real estate for building or agricultural purposes may be carried out with reasonable simplicity, but the value of applied mentality is very difficult to separate from the water rights. Therefore, it is common to allow all of these accompanying values to remain consolidated with the value of water rights and no case is recorded of resulting injury. Care must be exercised not to admit the same application of mentality in two separate parts of the accounts.

A **Water-rights Fallacy.** — In actual cases, there are marked differences in the opinions and procedure of the different sides. For instance, in condemnation proceedings the owners frequently compute the annual cost of their power so as to include the interest and taxes on only structural investment — purposely neglecting charges on water rights. They then subtract this cost of their water power from the annual cost of some substituted form of power, like steam, and arrive at an apparent annual profit which they capitalize at 8, 6, 5, or 4 per cent. The resultant figure is their contended value of water rights. This procedure is defended on the claim that since they own the water power they are not paying interest on the rights, and it should not be charged against them in comparing the cost of water power *to them* with the cost *to them* of some substitute power.

Obviously such a procedure is most unsound. If the water power were worth all that is shown by such a series of computations, the plant and rights could be sold and the money invested in government bonds to bring by pure interest an annual profit as great as could be secured after undergoing the risks, and giving the attention needed to develop and market the power.

On the other side of such condemnation cases, the would-be seizors claim that the value of water rights cannot exceed a sum which a purchaser could afford to pay if he borrowed all the funds for acquisition of rights and development of plant, and if the enjoyment of the rights enabled him to derive a small, safe profit in return for service in promotion and management, and as a guarantee of permanent ability of the works to afford enough revenue to cover interest and retirance.

The monetary value of the water rights in any specific case for different services, power, municipal supply, irrigation, may not be the same. There are grounds, in many cases, for holding that the true monetary value for all services is governed by the maximum for any service, since in private hands it could be put to its most valuable use.

Valuation of Storage Reservoirs. — A problem now becoming pressing is the valuation of storage reservoir sites. In a few cases, the estimated or experienced total annual gross return from the increase in available power over that of no storage has been capitalized to secure this value (with or without deducting investment charges on the reservoir) on the evident assumption that there would be no increase in size of generating plant or in the operating expenses. It is more conservative, but not wholly satisfying, to capitalize the net annual earnings from the increase in power. A still more rational procedure would be to compare the entire situations with and without storage; then the value of the storage site might be, as a maximum, the capitalized difference in net earnings of the larger works with storage (deducting all operating costs and fixed charges on generating station and storage works complete) and of the smaller plant that would have been built if storage had been impossible. In securing these net earnings it hardly need be noted that recognition must be given to the amounts of primary, permanent, assured or continuous power and of secondary, non-permanent, assured or continuous power and of secondary, non-permanent, unassured or non-continuous power produced under the two conditions of storage or no storage.

Where one reservoir benefits a string of plants scattered downstream, it is common to state that the value of the storage depends on the amount of fall through which the impounded waters may be utilized. As a quantitative statement this may be inaccurate for the general benefits of storage decrease with the distance downstream. This is due first to the fact that the impounded waters form a smaller and smaller proportion of the stream flow as added units of drainage area pour their run-off into the stream. It is due also to the disturbing influence of local-plant pondages below, especially where they do not operate alike at simultaneous hours or where they are not under the control of a single load-dispatcher. The value of the reservoir site then is not the sum of capitalized net earnings of each plant assumed to secure full benefit of the stored water; it would depend upon the somewhat complex and difficultly ascertained difference in net earnings for the entire existing or probable situation of all the plants as a unified system with and without the storage.

Omissions in Inventory. — No matter how complete the inventory seems to have been, nor how well supervised, it is the general experience of appraisers that later some things were noted which had been overlooked. It has been found impossible to insure complete freedom from all omissions, and to secure a closer approach to actualities an allowance is frequently made for them. Some 5% is not unwarranted as an average allowance, though 2 or 3% would seem to suffice for a large property of comparatively few items and 15% may be fair at the other extreme of a smaller property with many and scattered items which are difficult to check up.

Allowances for Overhead Charges. — Anyone experienced in construction knows that the bare cost of fabricating the utility's present physical works is not all of the legitimate and necessary expense. There has been money spent in investigating the possibilities of the particular project; the promoters have earned some reward in financing the development; the cost of the engineers' designs and of the inspection of construction are not to be neglected; various contingencies arise to add to the cost, and evidence of their presence does not persist. Working capital has had to be provided and its interest has been lost. These and similar costs are all items locked·in with the tangible features of the actual plant brought into service. These can be accurately determined, as actualities and not as probable approximations, only if the various accounts have been well kept on approved lines and preserved intact — a combination not common in utilities more than 10 to 15 years old.

Cost of Administration, Organization and Preliminary Investigations. — The very first of development costs covers the expense of preliminary engineering studies, of organizing the corporation, of acquiring the franchises and rights of way, of the numerous legal actions which have to be started.

It costs considerable to work up an effective organization and to get out the detailed plans and specifications. After construction is started, all this corporate activity increases. Items like office expense, legal advice, damage claims, salaries of general officers, clerks, accountants, etc., and interest on the working capital (which has to be kept on hand to pay contractors, engineers, administrative force, purchase miscellaneous supplies, etc.) grow apace.

The engineer's appraisal must report all evidence tending to throw light on proper allowances for overhead items. The appraiser's instructions should state whether or not the engineer is to go farther and fix a reasonable figure for such additions; such determination is valuation by judgment rather than mere appraisal by evidence. What has been found fair in the past is noted in the following few paragraphs, on interest and taxes during construction, contingencies, commissions and discounts, discarded property, promoters' profit, etc.

Interest During Construction Period. — A company, of course, has to pay interest on the funds which it secures through bond issues. Therefore it should be allowed to enter as one of the property-development expenses some proper interest on funds locked up in plant not yet earning. In the first place, it is necessary to find or estimate the sums secured from time to time — whether all in a lump before work was started or in smaller amounts from month to month to pay cost of work completed to those dates.

This analysis also involves study of the time before the plant units become operative and capable of earning. Then too the rate which it is reasonable to assume for such money so tied up must be approximated. It is common recourse to allow 6% but it would appear to be more logical to take the rate which the loaners actually demanded. If money came from bonds then the net bond rate (adjusted to sale price) might prevail; if the funds came from stock sales perhaps nothing since the stock holders may have expected and received no return until the plant is capable of operation and such deficits may enter the business-development cost — which should not be confused with overhead charges on plant. If both bonds and stock were put out then perhaps the desired rate might be the bond rate modified by the ratio of bonds sold to total funds provided. Where temporary paper has to be floated to carry construction and later replaced by bond or stock issues, of course, the actual or estimated note rate is to be considered. Some attempt at reduction of the capitalizable interest may be made also by considering how the funds secured have remained on tap — if on deposit ready for meeting payments. If so, then the depositary frequently allows 2% daily balance.

In many cases perhaps it is sufficiently exact, where definite historical figures cannot be discovered, to take half of the total sums involved and the whole of the construction period. But in some cases the heaviest expenses, as for expensive machinery, come toward the end of the work and it is advisable to approximate closer, say by taking the probable figure of construction cost for each year and computing interest for half a year at full rate or at full rate less 2% as may be thought nearer actual procedure; then from that year to the end of construction the estimated expenditure, the full time and the full rate would be used. Where extensive additions or reconstructions to plant are made then each of the various completed units of equipment goes into whole or partial service without waiting for the others and the interest cost of construction is correspondingly reduced to, say, full rate for half the time of constructing each unit. Interest may increase construction cost from 2 to 10%.

Taxes During Construction Period. — Parallel to interest during construction are taxes on the utility before operation. Of these, a great variety are imposed on utility corporations — corporate, capital-stock, franchise, and real- and personal-property. The process of finding the probable figure is similar to determining interest; the local demands must be ascertained and the property owned at each local assessment date. Taxes during construction may amount to as much as $\frac{1}{2}$ of 1% of the construction cost.

Insurance During Construction. — Closely allied with taxes and interest is insurance during construction. There is, of course, fire insurance, where fire loss is possible. Accident-liability protection is generally carried also. These items may run as high as 2% in certain difficult and hazardous undertakings such as in city subway construction under streets in which traffic has to be maintained. Under ordinary conditions $\frac{1}{4}$ to $\frac{1}{2}$ of 1% on cost of work is believed to be a reasonable expectation for the total of all insurance premiums.

Piecemeal Construction. — Where a plant has really been built up by a succession of additions, the cost is more than as if one big job had been done — that is a matter of common experience and is explained by the comparatively larger amounts of overhead charges per unit of plant on the small than on the large job, by the more favorable prices secured on the larger quantities, etc. When such piecemeal construction has to be made around plant in service there is still more added expense. There are innumerable instances of this in connection with power-plant changes, adding valves and hydrants to water mains, etc. But in an appraisal of physical plant as standing, there is usually little sure evidence of the piecemeal construction so that it is essential to consult whatever history of the utility is available if the concern is to be treated equitably. Piecemeal construction has often added upward of 5% to construction cost, the addition increasing with the difficulty of the new work.

Contractor's Profit. — It is usually more economical for an operating company to employ a construction contractor who, from special knowledge and experience, can usually build better and cheaper than the concern organized for operation. Indeed some operating concerns, which expect construction more or less continuously, have organized a friendly construction company. This scheme has been greatly abused at times and made the means of bleeding illegitimate profits out of a project. The wholly independent contractor's profit may run from 5 to 20% of the cost of materials and work, but a common allowance is 10%. The profit of an allied contractor ought not to be more than for an independent one.

Engineering Design and Inspection. — The charge of a consulting engineer who assumes complete responsibility for the design and advises about construction usually is 5% but rises sometimes to 10% depending on the size and intricacy of the work. The fee would be expected to decrease slightly with the magnitude and increase with the difficulty of the work.

Where concerns have done their own engineering design and supervision of construction, with only the review of prominent consulting specialists, the total cost has turned out about the same — 5 to 10%. For example the reported figures for the several rapid transit tunnels and subways in New York City hover around 6%; for similar works in Boston, the reported figures are 9 to 10%.

Architect's Fees. — In some cases, where extensive buildings enter an appraisal, the above allowance for engineering charges may need increasing to include the architect's fees (6% on particular structures). Sometimes the engineer's fee may cover the pay for architects, etc.

In most such cases where many buildings enter, the grading of the grounds has added an appreciable sum — say from $100 to $1000 per acre depending on the fills, cuts, gardening embellishment, etc. This of course is not an overhead item of engineering and design but rather one of structural cost; it is, however, a matter on which oftentimes no little of the engineer's effort is expended.

Influence of Contingencies. — All sorts of unforeseen events may have enhanced the cost of any work more or less over the estimates for normal conditions — there are floods, conflagrations and all the other "acts of God" to be considered. After the adverse situations are past and a few years have elapsed, the marks are not seen on the physical property to be appraised. A true view can only be secured by access to good accounts and these are rare for the older utilities.

The history of a locality or an utility may well be examined to find evidence of particularly favorable or unfavorable circumstances compared with those prevailing at the date of appraisal. But usually it is necessary to add a per cent or two to the pure physical cost to cover what cannot be detailed item by item, but which experience teaches is always met with. This, moreover, covers excess expense not compensated for as a common business risk. Any allowance for contingencies is commonly lumped in with engineering.

Data on Engineering and Contingencies. — Some very instructive data on actual costs of engineering and contingencies have been collected by the American Society of Civil Engineers Valuation Committee (1914). Notable are the following cases: the cost of engineering for the Boston Metropolitan Water Works was 8.42% on $26,736,000, which was the total cost to 1913 — not including engineering; the cost of engineering for the New York additional water supply (Catskill Aqueduct) was 11.2% on $93,128,000 — the cost to September, 1913, not including engineering; on the Boston Tunnel and Subway, the cost of engineering was 5.48% on $3,623,000, and the general expense was 3.58%; on the East Boston Tunnel, cost of engineering was 6.62% on $2,894,595, and general expense was 5.57%; the Cambridge Subway engineering was 8.05% of the construction cost alone ($1,200,000) and general expense was 5.20%.

The cost of several preliminary engineering investigations is also given by the same authority. For the Louisville sewerage works this was 1.7% on the construction cost ($3,317,000) compared with 10.3% for engineering on design and construction and 2.6% for administration and damage suits.

Some very general idea may be gained in the appraisal as to whether the engineering charges have been heavy or light by the appearance and character of the work. If the designs are very simple with comparatively little elaborate detail, as in some storage-reservoir dams, or if the work is somewhat crude and none too well built, judged by the standards of the day, the engineering costs were probably light. If the design has necessitated a vast amount of detail, as in some power stations and filter plants, and the work shows unusual excellence, then the charges were probably above the average.

Bond Commissions and Discounts. — Over and above the allowances for overhead expense noted before in connection with various items of physical property is the cost of floating the stock and bonds — particularly the latter. With bonds, this expense is covered by a commission demanded by the bond brokers as profit and to recompense them for the expense and risk of sale. As a result, the sum realized is less than the liability incurred and this difference varies from 5 to 50%. The cost of the physical property, overhead expenses, etc., should be increased by some allowance for this. Commission control of financing arrangements tends to reduce brokerage costs; the California board recently noted a cost of less than 1% in one large issue taken locally.

Fairly distinct from the commissions and brokerage expenses just noted are bond discounts which have the effect of increasing the interest on capital actually paid in from the sale of securities. If a $4\frac{1}{2}\%$ bond with a 10-year term sells for 96, then the yield rises to 5.1%. Such discounts are not generally recognized as capitalizable, nor is it sufficient to enter the price secured and the actual yield in fair value and fair return — since the concern has incurred a liability for the full par value of the bonds. Two recent typical opinions bear well on this point.

In the Blue Hill Street Railway case of the Massachusetts Public Service Commission (No. 886; P. U. R. 1915 E, 370; July, 1915) it was stated:

While the $13,750 representing discount on bonds likewise cannot be considered a part of the "capital invested," the company is entitled to have this sum liquidated, or amortized, from earnings during the life of the bonds, and to receive interest upon it to the extent that it is insufficient to provide the funds found by the Board of Railroad Commissioners to be "reasonably requisite" for lawful purposes. The deficiency was supplied through floating indebtedness, and the company is fairly entitled to interest upon this indebtedness until the impairment of capital so caused has been made good from earnings.

In the New York Central Bond case of the Illinois Public Utilities Commission (No. 3629; P. U. R. 1915 D, 1025; April, 1915) one reads:

It is further ordered that all discounts, commissions, and expenses in connection with the approval, issuance, and sale of the said bonds authorized to be issued under this order shall be amortized out of the income of the company before May 1, 1935, by the payment of equal annual instalments so long as may be necessary; or that the said company may charge the amount of such discounts, commissions, and expenses to profit and loss at the time of the issuance of said bonds, or at any time may charge to profit and loss any or all of the unamortized balance thereof.

Any premium realized through the conversion of said debenture bonds into capital stock shall be applied against any unamortized balance of the discounts, commissions, and expenses above referred to.

The Value of Discarded Plant. — The rapid growth of certain utilities, especially those involving the use of electricity, has made vast amounts of equipment antiquated so that it has been replaced by apparatus more modern, more economical or more satisfactory to the customers. It is necessary, in recalling such instances, only to mention such things as cable cars, steam engines, common arc lamps, early telephones, etc. Such obsolete property has had a useful life much less than it was reasonable to expect of it when it was placed in service and therefore there has been insufficient time to repay the investment out of earnings even had the need for replacement expense been as well recognized as it is at this later day.

If the worth to be used as a basis of rates is itself based on cost to reproduce the existing structure without regard to the history of the utility concern, how may the company be fairly treated? In one way this is another aspect of a question already touched upon — whether it was better to strive to secure a formal strict

adherence to an appearance of complete consistency in valuing
property on the basis of cost to reproduce new or to secure a nearer
approach to fair dealing by throwing on this scheme "the light of
reason" in allowing the history (but not a legendary past) of the
works to modify the valuation.

This means that the valuation may include cost of some items
not still existing. Especially does this seem essential in those
cases where the old equipment has been thrown aside by legal
enactment (in which case the Knoxville ruling probably does not
apply) and the superseding property has been paid for by fresh
capital — stock, bonds, or notes, etc. Similarly, the utility
corporations may expect to earn on something which has passed
away, when there has been insistence of the customers for greater
convenience or luxury while the actual necessities and ordinary
conveniences of the public were satisfied by the old property, and
when there was no prospect of a compensating economy by the
change. This opens the door for possible abuse of the historical
modification of reproduction cost new, but surely not in a way that
is beyond the powers of any live regulating commission properly
to curb. To prevent the perpetuation of such debts on a future
generation of stock holders and rate payers, the present generation of customers should amortise such sums by contributions
out of the earnings — above those for depreciation, interest,
profit, etc. Moreover, the records should clearly show when such
old debts have been actually refunded. To many the only logical solution will appear to be to allow the unrepaid costs of discarded equipment to enter the item of business-development
cost.

There seems less cause for including such lost investment in
full in the rate-basis worth, when an unregulated company made
the change wholly, or in large part, with the expectation of securing important operating economies and larger profits. Before
the supplanting installation was made, the concern should have
satisfied itself that the net economies of the new apparatus would
have themselves retired any unrepaid cost of the displaced equipment within a reasonable term — say the length of time before
the older became insufficient, — and paid interest on the new
investment and on the diminishing balance of the old.

There may be cases, where the repayment process is not complete and where full economies are not realized, that the "fair

value" would include the new investment and some part of the old. The annual expenses might also include something to hasten the amortization of the old funded debt which it was desired to have continually diminish. Such rather generous treatment, under fair commission regulation, seems to give a more logical solution of the obsolete-property question than the blind provision of allowing a slight addition to the rate called "fair return" to compensate for another "risk of the business."

Promoters Profit. — Compensation for promoters' services is another overhead expense not listed by any inventory of physical property. It has been allowed in some cases and undoubtedly could have been allowed with justice in many others. Probably this item would have been more easily accepted had the attitude and operations of some conspicuous promoters been more calculated to win public confidence.

Many promoters, perhaps a majority, are men of large outlook and force enough to push through a project where the narrower minded or timid would fail. Ability to win support, and to build in face of great obstacles, or at notably low cost, deserves a good reward, of course.

In the past it has been a common custom for promoters to take their pay for the time they have nursed a project, for hardships, etc., in speculative issues of stock rather than in admitted sums, say of 5 to 10% or more of the cost. Up to a certain point this stock is "brains," not "water." Unscrutinized and speculative rewards in connection with public utilities are not highly regarded now, but condemnation of such issues quietly made in the past are not to be over-severely condemned in all cases today on account of the once general public acquiescence. Yet such a statement is not to be construed as a sweeping approval of promoters' watered stocks, some of which seemingly have been put out with evil intent.

Business-development Investment; " Going-concern Value." — It is obvious that for a case of purchase of an utility, a smooth-running concern in an established locality or a developed territory is worth more than a new development of equal capacity. This has been recognized by courts and regulating commissions generally; for instance, an early important decision is that of the U. S. Supreme Court in the Kansas City Water Works case (62 U. S. Fed. Rep. 853) where we read:

The city steps into possession of a property which not only has the ability to earn but is in fact earning. It should pay not merely the value of a system which might be made to earn but that of a system which does earn.

The fact that this earning condition represents money invested and skill applied makes permissible some allowance for it in the basis of rates, among the intangible values. Great care should be exercised, however, not to include in the rate-basis worth those elements which would enter a purchase price as springing out of adequate rates and good service, and which exist because maintained by annual expenditures.

The term "going value" has been used for years to cover a list of vague and diversified ideas as to certain additions to the total worth of physical property used as basis of rates. Some of the claims seemed to include vague unearned increments in market value and were so problematical and difficult of consistent application that "going-value" at one time bid fair to be only a name for a discredited effort to increase value. But if we give it the very definite idea of the unrepaid extra investment surely or probably made, after operation has started, in bringing the utility up to the reasonable earning power which is associated with successful service, then it will be more generally accepted in rate cases.

Accrued Deficits as a Measure of Going Value. — In the early years of an enterprise, it is necessary to make the prices for service attractive in order to build up the business. But the actual costs, if distributed on the few early customers, would make the charges usually all out of proportion to the intrinsic value of service as fixed by potential competition with other service or product. Then there results a series of annual deficits, between earnings as they are and as they might better be, which in justice to the stockholders must be made up somehow and sometime. If we limit "going value," for rate making, to the cost of the aggregate deficiencies in the rates of the utility, then a simple and practical solution of a troublesome problem has been made — though this plan is not universally accepted by any means.

This practice eliminates the factor of "good-will." Utilities have become largely monopolistic in nature and "good-will" is generally discarded as an asset to be included in the basis of rates, it being argued that the public has to buy from the one concern or suffer the inconvenience of no service. No considerable investment is represented in devices to meet competition. There are, to be sure, certain minor expenses, in the case of a monopoly with enlightened management, for publicity, new business, encouraging the confidence and respect of customers, but these are in the nature of general annual administrative costs — certainly if such efforts are cut off the old attitude of suspicion and unfriendliness returns in a few months. Satisfied customers spend more than disaffected ones, and favorable public sentiment makes it easier to tide over operating emergencies; this is like more or better oil for the machinery. There is then no good reason why the customers should pay for this item year after year through general expenses and then pay interest on it as a capitalized value.

Some will argue that during early years there is expense in fitting the new organization together, in harmonizing all the little details of equipment, in adjusting apparatus. It is true that these are more than mere evanescent effects of administrative expenditure for their good result persists and is transferable. How much money is so spent is very speculative and indeed it is probably distributed in various accounts as general expense, repairs, operation, etc. Then this also has been paid by the customers and so a separate increment in worth should not be capitalized directly.

There is, however, logic in the argument that if expenditures for publicity, new business, internal adjustment, etc., had not been made (neglecting the consequent drop in business secured) there might not have been as large early deficits. If the utility concern is allowed to include in its capitalization the early deficiencies below a fair return, then there will be adequate compensation for expense of knitting the organization together — unless rare and peculiar circumstances can be proved. It seems fair if these early deficiencies in interest and profits are summed up, only temporarily capitalized, and the total gradually repaid out of earnings; this has the added advantage (in cases where the cost of service approaches the ultimate "value" as fixed by potential competition of a rival process) of strengthening an utility's commercial position by not asking the customers forever to pay interest on inevitable early mistakes as well as on full cost of final plant.

Wisconsin Method of Estimating Going Value. — What has come to be known as the "Wisconsin method" of estimating going-concern value or business-development investment, consists in adding to each year's investment the deficiency by which net earnings fail to provide for depreciation, interest and profits, etc. The plan was worked out in the case of *Hill v. Antigo Water Co.* (3 Wis. R.R. Com. Rep. 623), and further explained in the case of *State Journal Printing Co. v. Madison Gas Electric Co.* (4 Wis. R.R. Com. Rep. 580). A few paragraphs from this last report state the method so concisely that they are reprinted:

The plant was charged with the cost of the plant at the beginning of the first year, with the new extensions, interest on the investment, depreciation of the plant and the expenses of operation during the first year. It was next credited with the total gross earnings during the year. The balance between these debits and credits was regarded as the net value of the plant at the end of the year. This balance was then carried forward to the beginning of the second year, and with the extensions, interest, depreciation and operating expenses for this year charged up against the plant in the same manner as for the first year. The credits to the plant for the second year, the same as for the first, consisted of the gross earnings; and the balance was regarded as the net value of the plant at the end of the second year. These operations were performed for each year of the life of the plant, the balance at the end of the last regarded as the value of the plant on the earnings basis in question at the end of the period. Computations of this character must of necessity show the value of a plant at the end of each year on any given earning basis. If the figures that are included in these calculations contain only such items as equitably belong therein, and if the rate of interest and profit that is used is the rate that is fair and equitable to all concerned, then it also follows that the balances at the end of the year are fairly close representations of the reasonable valuation of the plant and its business.

Thus it is seen that early deficits in net earnings below stipulated rates of return increased the cost of the plants and business by that amount; early surpluses above such stipulated return repaid the cost of plant and business. The Wisconsin Commission, at that time (1910), held that when the worth of physical property (by appraisal) was less than the total investment as above determined, the concern was entitled to have at least the difference entered into the rate-basis valuation. If the probable investment figure was equal to or less than the appraised value of physical plant, then no allowance for going-concern value or business-development expense was admitted. The same Wisconsin report above quoted has this further to add about the plan:

For public utilities which, under both the common and the statute law, under normal conditions, are only entitled to reasonable returns on the investment, justice as well as equity appears to demand that the amounts, if any, by which they, under ordinary conditions, have failed to earn such returns, should be considered in fixing values and rates for such plants.   In fact, such consideration would in most cases seem to be absolutely necessary in order to secure the capital required.   For it must be obvious to all, that unless the prospects for obtaining at least a reasonable amount for interest and profit are at least fairly good, private capital will not enter such enterprises.   By this is not meant, however, that deficits from operation can be equitably taken into account in the appraisals or rates regardless of the conditions under which they were incurred.   As already stated, when such deficits are due to abnormal conditions, or when due to bad management, defective judgment, extravagance, lack of ordinary care and foresight, unduly high capital charges and other causes of this nature, it is manifestly clear that they should be accorded little or no consideration in either the valuation or the rates.   This is also likely to be the case for such deficits which were incurred under and borne by others than the present owners, and which have been wiped out in the various transfers of ownership.   That these propositions are, as a rule, sound and equitable, appears to be so clear as to need no further argument.

This plan has been repeatedly affirmed.*   It seems to be approved in theory at least by one old federal-court decision — *Metropolitan Trust Co. v. Houston & T. C. Ry. Co.*, 1898 (90 Fed. Rep. 683).   The plan has been disapproved in a few rate cases — notably *Spring Valley Water Co. v. San Francisco*, 1908 (165 Fed. Rep. 667), evidently (1) in fear that the deficits might be due to waste, extravagance, and mismanagement and (2) because a concern earning well from the start would have no "going value."   It is true that the method fails to show a "going value" in initially prosperous concerns — a value actually acquired but nevertheless one possibly to be regarded as amortized by the consumers through high rates.   No concern jumps into a full-fledged business and the presumption is safe that there will be early deficits or else comparatively high rates.   It should be noted that the denial of

* In the following rate cases: *Racine v. Racine Gas Light Co.*, 1911 (6 Wis. R.R. Com. Rep., 228); *Beloit v. Beloit Water, Gas & Electric Co.*, 1911 (7 Wis. R.R. Com. Rep., 187); *in re Oconto City Water Supply Co.*, 1911 (7 Wis. R.R. Com. Rep., 497); *Janesville v. Janesville Water Co.*, 1911 (7 Wis. R.R. Com. Rep., 628); *Marinette v. City Water Co.*, 1911 (8 Wis. R.R. Com. Rep., 334).

going-concern value to a prosperous utility is possibly a retroactive penalizing for past profits — a procedure apt to be challenged in any high court.

Reproduction of Going-concern Value. — The Wisconsin method of finding going value depends on securing records of original investment, extensions, earnings, etc., and it fails when the basic data are not available. Some other approach to the same end then is desirable. An attractive but laborious method of reproducing the going-concern value has been evolved by J. W. Alvord and Leonard Metcalf (American Water Works Association, June, 1909; Transactions American Society of Civil Engineers, Vol. LXXIII). This method probably appeals strongly to the advocates of a strict consistency in use of reproduction cost of property (unaffected by historical conditions).

Alvord and Metcalf take development cost as the sum of the present worths of the annual excesses in net return available for fixed charges and dividends (excess divided by the amount of $1 at interest to the end of the given time) from the existing plant over the net earnings of an imaginary comparative plant (construction just started) from the date of valuation to the time when the net earnings of the new plant equal those of the old. The comparative plant, which of course is purely hypothetical, is pushed ahead as rapidly as possible, taking up the business of the old as fast as suitable units can go into service.

Obviously many estimates have to be made such as (1) time required for construction of the comparative plant, (2) time required for its net earnings to equal those of the old plant, (3) ratio of installed capacity to actual business for the new plant compared with the old, (4) the gross income of the new plant at various stages of the transfer of business, (5) the various expenses except return available for interest and dividends.

It is evident also that many of the assumptions must be more or less arbitrary. There is also the anomalous situation that complete value of the new plant has to be in hand to start with, including the very going-value sought. However, a tentative value is given from experience and the calculations are carried through. Then, if the actual resultant going-concern value is much different from the assumed, the tentative value is changed and the process repeated until there is no change needed.

This scheme of finding going-concern value has been applied

to condemnation and transfer proceedings rather than to rates, though there is no good reason why it is not so applicable. Some will accept it as they accept reproduction cost based on present physical conditions — in lieu of original cost and investment or knowledge of old conditions; others seeking rigid consistency of reproduction methods of evaluation will accept it in place of the Wisconsin accrued-deficit method. It has been assailed by the opponents of the reproduction-cost schemes of appraisal for what they call its "unreal and fantastic assumptions" — such as starting a hypothetical new plant in a community and taking over as fast as possible the business of the existing plant. Those who assail it most have no more logical substitute and retire to a general denial of value from business-development expense.

Depreciation as a Measure of Going Value. — It has frequently transpired that an utility company, instead of making wise provision against depreciation (usually not realizing the necessity of giving this item careful consideration), has continued to pay dividends more or less satisfactory to the stockholders. In some quarters there is a disposition to hold that the depreciation in value of the plant is then a direct measure of the cost of developing a going concern.

There is merit in this attitude if the management has been honest though short-sighted and if the dividends from the start have been only reasonable — no more or no less. Then the moneys diverted from depreciation funds can have gone only into development of business. The trouble with this measure of going value is that seldom is the proper combination seen of honest management, lack of depreciation provisions, and reasonable return. Such a measure of going value may be expected to be unfair to the utility, rather than to the public, since it is a common result that in the early years the concern is not able to set aside from earnings, either ample depreciation funds or reasonable return.

Amortization of Intangible Values. — While all the plant-development items, discounts, promoter's profits, engineering and contingent allowances, taxes, business-development costs, etc., are to be seriously considered and usually aggregated in fair value, yet they are expenses which the present generation of users should be expected to wipe away so far as it is possible. We may rightfully pass along to our successors total liabilities equal only to the tangible assets and leave their hands free to work out their utility problems under their own strange conditions. They should not start with the burden of our development expenses which, if history repeats, will not prevent development expenses of the future plants.

The common way to attain this end is to lay aside out of earnings, some contributions to an amortization fund for retiring bonds, etc. It is equivalent to this to make extensions to equipment out of earnings or surplus until the worth of tangible property is up to the capitalization and bonds. In the early years, before the business has attained any dividend-yielding status, either course may not be possible but the need for such action is not to be permanently forgotten and the process should be instituted as soon as a way can be found. There is no occasion for amortizing an overhead burden which will be wiped out by the funds provided against depreciation of the underlying property item.

While as a general proposition it seems fair to group the development expenses noted as parts of rate-basis worth, yet it is not to be forgotten that such a practice in rare cases may make the cost of service prohibitive or unattractive in some specific cases and thus hamper a concern's development. Therefore, cases may arise when these sums in part are to be noted as an unearning investment to be retired as described, and as early as possible.

Effect of Good Design or Favorable Location. — After a "fair-value" has been established so far in accordance with the ideas already set forth, then if the plant in question does not stand free from comparison with any similar plant, a final disturbing question arises as to the full propriety of making this somewhat idealized value the actual rate-basis worth. Nearly every engineer knows of some utility plants of such meritorious design and favorable location that they can give good service at less than average cost; other plants have such inferior design and poor location that they can furnish only inferior service and that at higher prices. Shall the same percentage rate of earnings in both cases be allowed on the aforesaid "fair value" similarly obtained for each — supposing that capital is attracted by the same rate in both localities? If so, then the inferior service must cost the customers more than the superior.

There is some ground for arguing that the better situated company should be given still another increment of "fair value" so that the rate-basis worth may include some of the capitalized brains that may have been responsible for the favored condition. But obviously, if inherent natural conditions contribute to the superior service and low cost then the public should reap a proportionate benefit, for it has been settled that an utility is entitled to a fair return on fair value and no more — which surely does not include a return on capitalized opportunity. How then can this be adjusted? The question has not been decided by any court or commission and so may be regarded as in the formative stage. Tentative schemes, however, may here be advanced for future test of propriety.

If the utility works are really able to furnish the superior service at low rates, and there are absolutely no natural endowments which create or foster this situation, then it may be accepted, *prima facie*, that unusual promotion ability must have been manifest and may be rewarded — if any principles akin to "statutes of limitation" do not prevent. The amount by which the "appraised-value" may be increased for the rate-basis worth, is then such a sum as would make the resultant rates approach more or less to the average of many similar localities — or to the average, perhaps of a selected number showing comparatively low rates. This has the effect of increasing the rate of return. Indeed the rate of return may in the end be the real criterion. A good commission ought to be able to estimate the cost of having the work planned by one of the leaders of the industry, then adding this to fair value. A dividing scale also might be devised for the allowable increase of worth corresponding to a given decrease in rates.

If on the other hand, natural opportunities create or foster the favorable rates and service, then there can logically be little or no increase in capitalization and all the benefit may go to the customers. If the peculiar favorability is due say half to the promoters and half to nature, then the utility corporation may secure half the value increase it would have secured if the promoter alone has made the gain possible; and so on.

It may be desired to secure this end sometimes by changing the rate instead of the rate-basis value. Then, the high rate is always before the public where the explanation of its size must be repeated at times. Changes in capital-value are not so easily compared "in the street" as are rates of return and are not so frequently published. There would perhaps be aroused less misconception and misunderstanding by providing for the extra reward in rate-basis worth instead of per cent return; if commission regulation is complete and in good hands the chance of abusing the lack of easy publicity is small.

If the foregoing reward be permitted, then it seems necessary, in the absence of natural obstacles causing inferior service and higher costs, to penalize poor design and construction or lack of promotion brains. If the added cost and inferior service are wholly due to short-sightedness, then the intangible values already noted may be properly reduced until the rates approach those elsewhere for the same service. How far this should go depends on the grossness of mismanagement, extravagance of expenditures, etc.; as to the presence or absence of extreme negligence and gross carelessness, commissions may judge. If natural conditions impair service and lead to the high costs then the public should bear the burden and the concern little or none. Intermediate degrees of shared responsibility may allow proportionate reduction of intangible parts of capitalized values. The various schemes possible for estimating increase of intangible values to cover unusually beneficial promotion can be reversed for computing a decrease.

Sudden Reduction of Value. — The few paragraphs immediately foregoing lead to a possible solution incidentally of another problem which has bothered many. Suppose the favored utilities to have been established for a decade or two and always to have charged rates comparing favorably with those in other localities but bringing an unusually good net return to the company. The securities then have appreciated on the general expectation that the high returns will continue. Shall a new commission with large powers break in, reduce rates to the idealized "fair-value-fair-return" plane, cause a decrease in market value of securities and a corresponding financial loss to recent investors? Certainly if the favored earning condition of the utility is purely the result of promotion brains, such a change would not seem equitable, on the grounds previously noted. If natural conditions produce the favored situation, wholly or in part, then in many cases it may be possible, without great hardship on any one, to reduce gradually the price per unit output and the actual return on appraised value, the time involved depending somewhat on how widespread the distribution of securities has been from the original holders. The aim might well be to let a security holder recover in his super-profits (above a very moderate return on his investment) the final loss of principal to be expected.

Such a situation also somewhat resembles the gas-utility situation in England, public control of which was secured with difficulty. The final outcome was that a lower return was earned by new capital, through limiting dividends or selling shares at auction, and increases of dividends depended on reductions of rates for service. Excess earnings went into a reserve fund (10% of capital) for contingencies, extraordinary renewals; or indicated further reductions of rates.

CHAPTER VII

REASONABLE RETURN; INTEREST; COMPENSATION FOR RISK AND ATTENTION; EXTRA PROFITS

What is a Reasonable Return? — The rate of return which should be secured on the money invested in a public-utility plant has been commonly defined in a general way as that which is sufficient to pay ordinary interest and above this to compensate for the risks of the business. It has also been generally defined, from another angle, as one just sufficient to attract fresh capital to the field. But for the very specific problems of ascertaining fair rates, very definite percentages as to the allowable of return are required, and these are not indicated by such broad statements which are declarations of ends rather than descriptions of means. But by scientific approach one can analyze the judgment of successful men and fix upon quite definite percentages.

It is obvious that capital will flow into a field, if it secures (1) ordinary local interest return, plus (2) compensation for business risks, plus (3) some reward for the actual attention required from the investor, and plus (4) the possibility of more or less profit above these other factors which partake much of the nature of mere wages of capital and capitalists. It should be illuminating therefore to examine these elements in theory and practice, to formulate a basis of judgment as to the rate of return in specific cases. Only what may be called normal conditions will be considered — where the utility can sell its product or service, with profit, at rates which are equal or less than those which customers will pay rather than forego the service. Situations where such is not the case require such special measures that their discussion cannot easily be undertaken in advance of occurrence.

Pure Interest. — Money cannot be secured for any business purpose unless a certain annual percentage be paid for the use of it. In most cases, individual borrowers can exert little or no influence widely to reduce the rates of interest, though it is largely affected by the desires of borrowers as a body. Similarly, an individual lender can seldom exert influence to raise the general rate though the total available funds and the aggregate demands of the lenders may do it.

It is commonly reported at times that 4%, 5% or 6%, say, is the prevailing interest rate because mortgages and notes can be negotiated on that basis. However, other elements than interest, pure and simple, enter in nearly all such cases and the real interest rate is appreciably less. An idea may be secured of the prevailing true interest by the return in the locality on funds put out with practically no risk and requiring practically no effort of the lender to keep risk away and to collect the income. Bonds of stable governments and deposits in some savings banks are fair indicators of unalloyed interest — as good perhaps as are easily examined. The real interest rate corresponding to the 5% or 6% noted as nominal popular figure, is frequently 3 or 4%. The difference compensates the loaner, on mortgage and note for instance, for his need of scrutiny at intervals of the collateral property value, for the greater chance of losing principal or interest, for the effort required to collect the interest, etc.

Compensation for Risk. — The business risk involved in any investment cannot be immediately stated in definite figures — as it can only be estimated rather than measured and as its estimation is, within limits, a matter of judgment. However, it is axiomatic that an individual mortgage is more risky than a savings bank account and the latter in turn more so than a government bond. All admit the respectively increasing uncertainty in manufacturing, mercantile pursuits, railroads, agriculture, mining enterprises, etc. About the nearest approach to a logical scrutiny of the risk in a given public-utility business is to study its organization, stockholders, customers, locality, development, earnings, etc., and to exercise judgment in comparing the risk with that in any local manufacturing, mercantile business, agriculture, railroading, or mining, the returns from which can be found.

Factors Increasing Risk. — The risk of investing in any industrial enterprise may be reasonably held to depend on a few factors such as (1) the soundness of its early organization, financing and management; (2) the honesty and ability of the present management, the present business status of the concern and the present effect of its early history — either good or bad; (3) the possibilities, probabilities and extent of competition; (4) the ability to hold the market and maintain gross earnings, the protection afforded against ruinously low prices, the probability of raising prices or rates parallel with the movement of wages, materials and general expenses, the probability of continued good management or better; (5) the probability of increase in taxes, in prices of materials and in wages of labor, etc.

If in the case of any particular utility, we could study certain other local industrial projects paying good dividends, light might be thrown on the effect of these factors in definite percentages. For instance, take a hypothetical manufacturing concern paying 9% but with its stock hovering a little above par — this would indicate the probable existence of considerable risk to the investors. If local bonds were yielding 4%, savings banks paying 4% and 3½% on small and large accounts respectively; the 5% difference might be largely considered as extra compensation for risk, scrutiny and effort. Suppose study disclosed a variegated past which had not been wholly lived down, although the present management was capable, high minded and well intrenched. Suppose that there was great potential competition to be reckoned with, that taxes had been temporarily set aside by local authorities, prices of wages and materials fairly low but bound to go higher. Assume that our investigation showed the probable weight of these elements of uncertainty as; history (1), competition (3), taxes, wages and material (4). The sum of these weights is eight and corresponds to the added return percentage secured. Then transferring these ideas to the utility in question (having much the same risks), we could add ⅝% for poor history as a money maker, nothing for competition (being a protected monopoly), 2½% for expected rise in cost of taxes, operation, etc. This makes some 3% extra above mere interest for risk and perhaps another ½% could be tacked on for the need of extra attention of stockholders in an enterprise which needed good directors but had once attracted undesirable ones by the opportunities for undue exploitation.

Compensation for Attention. — One difficulty that enters the comparison of a public utility with local businesses, as to relative risks, is the fact that in them all there also enters the variable amount of attention demanded of the investor from time to time.

Before the rise of the modern artificial business individuals — the corporations — investors and managers were more nearly identical. The single man, or the few, who furnished the funds for an enterprise, and carried the risks, also managed the business. But under modern conditions, those who have capital to put out seem to prefer to scatter it among the larger organizations instead of burying it in their own business, and they thereby lose much or all of the direction of the employment of their funds. As stockholders, they still carry the risks of the business and, in theory, while they do not immediately direct the routine, they control the policies of the managers through the directors (whom the stockholders elect). But if a stockholder owns only a small part of the shares outstanding, his voice in the affairs of a concern may be very small unless he agrees with the more powerful interests, or possesses a vigorous personality, or can show illegal acts of other stockholders. The attention to directors required of majority stockholders may affect the return on all stock, and the minority holders get an "unearned increment" — or a return for their slightly greater risk, through lack of voice.

If the investment is in bonds of the corporation, the bondholder has practically no voice in the management of the concern's affairs beyond protecting the security offered for the bond. Naturally if the risk is less than with stock, the rate of return is less. It is less also because the bondholder has less demand on his attention than the stockholder. The larger the proportion of bonds a corporation carries, the greater the risk assumed by the stockholders and the greater amount of attention, correspondingly, both directors and important stockholders have to give to the business and its safety.

It is seen, therefore, that the three variables, interest, risk, and attention, are peculiarly interwoven in any corporation. Any estimation of one or all obviously is so much a matter of personal judgment, that hard and fast rules cannot be made for comparing a public utility with another local business, to see how the returns go along with the degree of risk and attention. Judgment should be based, however, on a logical and scientific scrutiny more or less as indicated.

Prospect of Extra Profits. — In the days of smaller business units, the investor-manager himself supervised that combination of capital and labor that resulted in product or service. He planned the output, superintended the operation, found the market, and collected the revenues. He aimed to secure a fair rate of interest, to insure the risk of loss, to earn the equivalent of an undefined salary, to pile up surplus profits over interest according to his ability as an economizer (an "efficiency expert") or a bargainer. In a corporation with large affairs, the managers are salaried officers whose pay is, or should be, ample to secure the same ability to plan, to superintend operation, to develop the markets and to collect the revenue. The risks of the business, however, are not borne by the managers, for, distinctly as managers, they have usually no financial interest in it. In some cases, stockholders and directors may have transferred their functions largely to the salaried managers, though still carrying the risk of stocks and bonds.

In private business, the sometimes apparently high profits above interest may often include the manager's wage for attention; in the corporation, especially the utility corporation, the wage of management has already entered the operating expense and should not be further considered in demands for profits. The business handled by the corporation manager is frequently more or less speculative — there is some uncertainty of his making a profitable use of labor and money, of the stability of the market he finds, of his ability to collect the revenue. Yet all the salaried manager risks is his situation and pay; the stockholder bears the burden and this is additionally heavy since he necessarily must depend on the skill, knowledge, foresight, tact and honesty of his hired agents. Such situations must be considered in finding what return will attract capital, and in comparing local industries.

There is a certain amount of inherent reduction to these added burdens of risk in corporate business, resulting from the truly monopolistic nature of a few utilities. Obviously greater risks are met in competitive business through ungoverned markets and prices, improvement in competitors' arts, reliance on patent and secret advantages of inherent instability. With utilities there is, to be sure, the menace of potential competition by temporarily outclassed services, but this change is generally so slow that the first art and science has a chance to make compensating advance.

It appears probable that if there is the possibility of earning 1 to 3% on the value of an utility plant as extra profits above interest, risk and attention, capital should be forthcoming in times of normal activity and good business. However, instead of being a blind allowance which any who rush in may secure, such surplus profits should be automatically developed when stockholders and directors show constructive shrewdness, ability to develop at unusual advantage, ability to perform ever more adequate service, ability to improve efficiency of production and to decrease cost of service, willingness to maintain a broad and beneficent public policy, deep-seated desire to win and maintain public confidence, etc.

Super-profits through Infrequent Rate Revisions. — It is not generally well, in fixing a fair rate, that excess profits should be immediately included in the rate of return; in many cases it is sufficient to leave an open door for their development. For instance, where there is expected, more than realized, an unusual ability to perform more and more adequate service and to present more and more beneficent public policies, there may be a tacit agreement that rates will be undisturbed for a considerable period, during which term the company secures the full benefit of its advances in the art and its search for economies.

Dividing Scales. — A plan of dividing the benefit of developments between utility and customer, while strongly encouraging economy and efficiency in operation, is seen in the so-called "London sliding scale" for gas companies. Throughout Great Britain it is common to allow an increase of $\frac{1}{4}\%$ over the standard or base dividend for each penny (2c.) reduction below a standard price. But in Britain frequently only the early issues of stock have been allowed to earn say 10% while later issues of an established concern have been set at 7%, 5%, 3.5% base rate. On the low-rate shares, a common increment has been $\frac{7}{40}\%$ for the 7% issues and $\frac{1}{8}\%$ for the 5% capital. Similarly, in Massachusetts, the Boston Consolidated Gas Light Co. was authorized to pay dividends, increased over 7%, by $\frac{1}{5}\%$ for every 1c. reduction in retail price for gas below 90c. per 1000 cu. ft.

Of course these particular so-called "sliding scales"* seem more or less arbitrary and under them the consumer has often secured the lion's share of benefit. However, it is possible logically to apportion the dividend increment and price decrement so that the benefit is otherwise divided (as early pointed out by the late W. D. Marks in Engineering News, Aug. 26, 1909).

* The term "dividing scale" has been used hereafter in this work as being more truly expressive — especially in view of the common use of the other term to indicate a scale of prices changing with quantity purchased.

Assume, for example, that half the benefit is to go to the company and half to the customers; then half the profit (per unit of service or product) equals the rate reduction. Expressed in mathematical form:

$$r = \frac{p - ma - c}{2}.$$

r = cents reduction in unit price of service or product.

p = standard fair unit price, cents.

c = cost of delivering a unit of product or service (including interest on bonds, preferred dividends, fixed charges, depreciation compensation, etc.), cents.

m = proportional amount of stock (cents per unit of quantity of product or service sold per year) benefiting from the dividing scale.

a = standard dividend rate (expressed as a decimal) on benefiting stock.

Also, the cents increased return on stock per unit of product (m) is equal to the cents price reduction per service unit (r). If we denote by x, the increase of dividend for each cent of price reduction, then

$$mrx = r \qquad \text{and} \qquad x = 1/m.$$

These expressions are very convenient in applying the apportionment to actual cases, it being understood that the "rate" is the resultant of all the actual tariffs and that the further distribution of the reduction is a complicated procedure. Therefore such scales are more easily applied to utilities having a simple rate or charge, like many gas and water concerns and street railways.

The apportionment has been applied to a composite of eight gas companies in Massachusetts selling gas by the thousand cubic feet. From their reports:

$$p = 90 \qquad\qquad r = 4.99$$
$$c = 60 \qquad\qquad x = 0.0055$$
$$a = 0.11 \qquad\qquad a + rx = 0.1375, \text{ or}$$
$$m = 182 \qquad\qquad 13\tfrac{3}{4}\% \text{ new dividend.}$$

Applying to the Cleveland electric railways in 1909, the following figures resulted:

$$m = 18 \qquad a = 0.05$$
$$c = 3 \qquad r = 0.05$$
$$p = 4 \qquad x = 0.0556$$

The standard profit then is $0.05 \times 18 = 0.9c$. per passenger fare compared with the actual of 1c. on the books. But as reduction could easily come only in 1c. steps, such a low fare would be possible only after a large increase in economy and traffic so that "m" and "c" are reduced. For the 1c. reduction to be safe, applying the above expressions,

$$r = \frac{4 - (0.05\,m + c)}{2} = 1$$

and, $\qquad\qquad 0.05\,m + c = 2,$

which would be satisfied if unit cost, $c = 1.8$ and unit stock, $m = 4$; if $c = 1.9$ and $m = 2.0$; or if $c = 1.99$ and $m = 0.2$.

This "dividing scale" apportionment may also provide for the possibility of raising prices above a standard and decreasing dividends in case it is desirable to share with customers the effect of a drop in sales, a decrease in economy or even an increase in cost of labor and material — though it is very questionable whether or not all the last item should not fall on the consumers' prices instead of investors' dividends.

Suppose that in the composite of ten gas companies, it was seen that

$$p = 90c., \ a = 0.11, \ c = 75c. \text{ and } m = 190c.$$
Then

$$r = \frac{90 - 190 \times 0.11 - 75}{2} = -2.95c.,$$

the negative result signifying increase of price to 93c. The dividend decrease would be

$$x = 1/190 = 0.00526,$$
$$a + rx = 0.11 - (2.95 \times 0.00526) = 0.095,$$

or 9.5% instead of the old 11%.

It is by no means necessary that the surplus profits be divided into two equal parts, one going to consumer and one to company. There can be any desired arrangement — say one-third for the company, one-third for the customers and one-third for the local government. Then the expression before given reads

$$r = \frac{p - ma - c}{3}.$$

The total divisible surplus is now $3r$ but if the extra dividends still equal the price reduction, the expression

$$x = 1/m \text{ holds.}$$

What is a Fair Division of Excess Profits. — There is a certain superficial air of fairness about splitting the benefit equally between an utility and the customers, but this plausibility is diminished after noting that the dividend increments ordinarily are cumulative and that the reward for advance made by the company is analogous to an individual's patent. The inventor is allowed to reap his reward only for a period; each generation of utility managers should have to make its own advances rather than continue forever to reap the rewards of its predecessors. The logical expectation would be that each dividend increment should run only for a fair period — say, 5 to 20 years. Greatly reducing the premiums and neglecting the cumulative action, which was the course followed in England, may be regarded as an easy makeshift aimed to secure the same end.

The proportion of the excess profits over a common fair return that should go to the utility customers obviously depends in a measure on the growth of a community, the price of material and labor, and on that normal development of the art in which the local manager has no part; the company part depends all or nearly all on increases in operating efficiency, on extensions of service, on improvement of load factor, and on reduction of capital costs.

In England it is not believed that equal division of surplus profits would have worked as well in the gas industry for either public or companies. It is reported (R. H. Whitten, Appendix to Annual Report for 1913, Public Service Commission, First District, State of New York) that for 18 leading British concerns the ratio of dividend premium to price reduction, both expressed per thousand cubic feet of gas sold, at first averaged 1 : 3.8, but by 1911 had fallen to 1 : 7. The maximum was 1 : 4.6 and the minimum 1 : 20. It is not thought in England that greater economies could have been produced had the premiums been greater — and the aim was to allow only the smallest incentive that would stimulate maximum possible price reduction; too great a premium was considered "easy money" and a hindrance to continual progress. A typical concern (Luton Gas Co.) sells gas for 48c. below the standard price. The premium dividend is 6% on ordinary 10% shares, being a burden of 2.4c. per thousand cubic feet of gas sold. This is $\frac{1}{20}$ of the price reduction.

Freedom from Lax Management. — Willingness to allow a concern to develop surplus profits by unusual attainments in service, economy, contributions to public welfare, etc., should not degenerate into giving special rewards for freedom from lax management, or from mere failure to drop beneath common standards as to adequacy of service, cost of supply, or public policy. The public utility may be regarded as being under constraint to live up to reasonable standards without claim for surplus profits.

Except in the matter of dividing scales, no standards have been set as to how much surplus profit should be allowed for super-standard service, etc. A commission wishing to make utility investments in its state attractive to capital (without injustice to public and customers) could without much serious difficulty make up tentative and flexible standards of management, public policy, welfare work among employees, etc., and give some rough estimate of how improvement would be measured quantitatively and how far judgment of profits would be affected thereby.

Surplus Profits as Compensation for Early Inadequate Return. — It is common to read in utility-commission reports that the latter-year returns have been examined to see if they make up for the deficiencies of early years. So far as has been seen there has been no scientific or logical comparison of return in these periods — nor is one easy. For instance a report may state that "the net earnings recently have been 8% or 9% (or more) on the present value of the property and that this should compensate for the 3% and 4% (or less) of much earlier years." Generally data is not complete for definitely formulating the extra return that should come today truly to compensate the stockholder for lean years at the start; it seems a more accurate process to include deficits in business-development costs.

Official Burdens not a Basis for Profits. — One plea for higher dividend rates of public utilities which has been heard in various parts of this country runs as follows:

"This industry is by no means a pleasant one for those engaged in it. It is fraught with annoyances, unpleasantnesses and extraordinary hazards. If we are to be limited to .6 or 7% as a maximum earning after bearing all these hazards and annoyances and after going through the lean years necessary with all new enterprises, then I would rather go into other business."

Such arguments indicate a subtle, though probably unconscious, attempt to throw an undue burden on customers. Of course, as already emphasized, there should be due compensation to investors for attention, use of money and risks of investment. But the trouble and grief of the officers is not an excuse for larger income to the stockholders. The fallacy in such arguments as that quoted is not so plain if the officers have not completely separated their relations as employees and stockholders of the corporation. It is the function of the officers to bear the annoyances and unpleasant features of the business. Salaries are, and properly should be, affected by the conditions under which these men labor; but there has not yet been pointed out any reason for increasing the rate of return to stockholders on that account.

CHAPTER VIII

DEPRECIATION AS IT AFFECTS UTILITY RATES

Liability for Retirement. — Where maintenance and repairs are well cared for, obviously for a long time the plant suffers no reduction in ability to render service. Its service ability (called by some "service value") is 100%. Of course, the time must come, in a more or less foreseen number of years, when repairs no longer can suffice to maintain service, and retirement becomes advisable or absolutely necessary.

But such wear-deterioration is not the only effect to be noted as causing retirements. When the demands for service from a popular and growing utility outstrip the designed capacity of the system, then the extra service can be performed, if at all, with various sacrifices of efficiency and quality. Too small electricity, gas, water and sewer mains, and too small street cars for the crowds that try to board are common examples.

Differing from the simple inadequacy described are the conditions which arise with an old plant when advances in an art or science have made the service of the given equipment less safe, less economical, or less attractive, though still adequate. For example, it is only necessary to cite the replacement of cable and horse-car lines by electric tramways, the use of tungsten-filament lamps in place of carbon, underground electric cables for overhead wires, steam turbines for reciprocating engines, steel railway cars for wood, etc.

Beyond wear-deterioration, inadequacy, supercession and antiquation, there is a natural dilapidation which arises merely from age, though in practice not easily distinguished from that irreparable deterioration which springs from continued wear and tear. Structures corrode, shrink, crack, or rot on mere exposure to the elements without use; the insulation of electrical equipment grows weak; pipe lines rust and clog and leak, and a variety of phenomena can be traced solely to the ravages of time.

The responsibility for making changes in equipment on account of these actions is a contingent liability of the operating concern. If it should sell out, the purchasers would have to assume the burden and therefore would demand a deduction from a full-cost price. If the business could cease at the retirement period for the first investment, then the concern would suffer the loss of its early funds unless it had received very large dividends, had retired its indebtedness, had accumulated a proper reserve, or had spent for other equipment an equivalent sum out of the receipts beyond all the normal expenses and reasonable profits. Therefore, there must be a certain growing reduction in the value of the parts of a plant with the passing of the years of service, even though that service might continue to be given at 100% of original quantity and quality. This loss of value is "depreciation," in the most generally accepted meaning of the term — though so many other uses of the word have sprung up that endless confusion usually arises in discussions participated in by several persons.

"Depreciation" Too Loosely Employed. — The meanings which have been given to the term "depreciation" are seen to fall into two general classes: (a) losses in value of physical property, and (b) sums secured from earnings to offset loss in value of property.

The first group of definitions of "depreciation" is further divided into: (1) aggregate actual or estimated loss in value from all causes, (2) the loss in value due to wear- and age-deterioration as distinguished from the loss of value from liability of obsoletion or inadequacy, (3) the loss in value due to loss of ability to render full service or to decreased efficiency.

The second group of definitions is seen to be split into: (4) an annual accounting figure representing the depreciation for the year, or any other given period, deducted from gross earnings in computing probable true net earnings; (5) an annual sum used in making up the amount of necessary income to be secured by the rates. This last is often an annual amount to be set aside out of the earnings to help create a reserve which will equal the cost of the several items of plant when they are retired from service, and will pay for the renewals to the extent of the cost of the items retired. It might well be a direct repayment out of earnings of investment, equal to the annual loss in value of property due to depreciation. There is a final observable definition of depreciation as (6) various aggregates of the annual sums secured from time to time to compensate for loss in value through depreciation.

The various shades of meaning indicated in these definitions explain the extreme confusion which has been introduced into discussions of depreciation and the need of greatly restricting the use of the term. Language is not so impoverished that it is necessary to use the single word in so many senses.

"Depreciation" Properly Used. — The first definition — as the aggregate loss in value from wear-deterioration, inadequacy, supercession, antiquation, delapidation, etc., — is probably the most used and the original one. This can well be adhered to, and a few available terms employed to carry the other meanings given.

The idea involved in the second definition makes a most useful distinction which should be preserved, but it is more definitely indicated by "wear-deterioration," "age-deterioration" or "wear-and-age deterioration" according to the precise shade of meaning needed.

The third definition — loss in value due to diminished power to function or decreased efficiency — has no real place in depreciation discussions, for mere ability to render the original service does not indicate lack of depreciation, and percentage of service ability (which is not the "serviceability" of the dictionary) alone does not measure value. (It indicates relative value only when the duration of that percentage of service ability is considered; if one machine can yield certain service for 10 years and a second machine can yield the same service for 20 years their real values are not equal.) Instead of speaking of this loss of service ability as depreciation it should be called "service-ability drop" or some equivalent.

The fourth definition has sprung up to give a short expression equivalent to "deductions for depreciation expense," or something like that. If there were not so many definitions in the field needing weeding out, its abbreviation to "depreciation" would be excusable; but, because of the confusion this induces, the longer phrase should be reverted to.

Similarly in the case of the fifth definition it is advisable to say "allowance for depreciation expense," or more briefly "depreciation allowance," and not merely "depreciation." Between speed of speech and accuracy of expression there should be no question of choice. Depreciation-allowances correspond to what some engineers call a "theoretical depreciation" in contrast with what they designate as "actual depreciation" (meaning wear-deterioration) found by examination.

Definition five conveniently reduces to "renewal allowance" and for further simplicity to the coined word "renewance" which the author has found generally understandable. . The first and the fifth definitions are perhaps the ones most used, so that it is a great advance to agree to speak of "depreciation" as the actual lost value, and "renewance" as one year's part of the compensation therefor.

However, it is little more than a convenient fiction to speak of building up reserves for renewals, since those funds have no relation to the amounts spent for the new equipments. Electric railways have been known to scrap their generating stations and purchase power from central-station companies (notable examples being the Cleveland, Ohio, Railway Co., and the Third Ave. R.R. in New York City). In general, replacements are made with radically different equipment. What the business must be made to yield, in line with the Supreme Court's dictum, is full compensation to the utility concern for the loss in value of property from all the various causes already outlined. That is to say, the rates must cover the liability for retiring plant rather than the cost of renewing it. "Retirance" therefore has been substituted for "renewance." Retirance then is the annual amount to be repaid the corporation to compensate it for each year's depreciation. Retirance is a definite factor in rates and in its nature is a repayment of invested capital. Unit retirance may be spoken of as a subdivision of retirance as it has been apportioned over rates. Wear-retirance, age-retirance, obsoletion-retirance, etc., become useful special terms which can be accurately employed. The place of aggregate retirance is obvious.

By such a restriction as outlined on the employment of the terms "depreciation," "wear-deterioration," "depreciation-allowance," "retirance," etc., discussion is not appreciably encumbered and a fundamental cause of exasperating confusion is removed.

Retirance a Repayment of Lost Investment. — Whether or not the retirance money secured out of rates can be regarded as a repayment of investment is one of the most debated points that has arisen. Careful consideration of the question (keeping in mind the fundamental idea that loss of investment, impairment of capital, or assumption of liability for renewal must be compensated by the customers in whose service the loss, impairment or assumption arose) will seemingly leave little doubt that the retirance collected is a restoration of balance between physical assets and incurred liabilities (including stocks and bonds). That looks like repayment.

However, retirance cannot be a direct repayment when it is purposely made smaller than the annual depreciation with a view to placing it in a sinking fund and obtaining the normal amount through accumulations of interest. In this case the retirance is not free capital which the owner of the property may put in service to swell his income; all the earnings must be retained to complete the retirance fund which can be drawn on only when an item has reached its assumed length of life.

Subdivision of Retirance. — It has been stated already (p. 24) that in some (but not all) rate-making problems it is useful to keep retirance in component sums and to apportion them among the customers according to the fundamental peculiarities of the several services. It is not necessary to repeat here the reasons for different apportionments but it is useful perhaps to note that, where any division of depreciation and retirance is logical, it is wear-deterioration that follows the hours of plant service, and wear-retirance that may be assessed like operating expense on quantity units; it is antiquation, obsoletion, and inadequacy that depends on the years which pass, and age-retirance, etc., that may be assessed, like investment-costs, on the demand units.

All action leading up to the retirement of utility property can be put into these two groups — the "wear" or the "age" classes. Even hastened decrepitude (like the racking of street-car bodies) which some regard as a distinct action, is seen on analysis to be essentially the same as the unrepairable wear-deterioration of machinery — about which there is no question.

Expected length of life, considering only wear-deterioration must be based on early experience with apparatus worn, or wearing down, to the discarding point. Expected life, considering only obsolescence, etc., is based on the experience of older apparatus (and the probability of newer) becoming less economical than that available, or less attractive to customers, or less adequate for growing needs, etc.

Relations Between Depreciation and Retirance. — It is the actual depreciation which in the long run affects real profits — considering actual values preserved as well as net earnings secured. But it is retirance which determines the computed, and approx-

imated; profits and possible dividends from quarter to quarter
or year to year. The annual increment in actual depreciation is
not necessarily the same as the annual retirance sum which is
intended to cover it, though that is the ideal sought. The most
that can be said is that the aggregate of retirance accumulated on
an item of property plus the scrap value should equal the total first
cost when the item is discarded — no sooner, no later. Few can
estimate so happily as to have their first estimate of retirance continue to the end without readjustment. If an examination of a
piece of apparatus showed that the aggregate of contributions
made against its retirement is going to be too large, then they
might be decreased to such an amount as will probably complete
the return of cost at the end of the useful life of the item, except
that the rates should be held steady rather than fluctuating. The
reverse adjustment would be necessary if the aggregate of allowances for a number of years proved to be less than the actual decrease in worth shown by examination. This adjustment affects
dividends and surplus rather than stable rate schedules.

The exact eventual return of cost through retirances can be
simply secured with the sort of accounting required by the Interstate Commerce Commission. In following its rules monthly
charges against depreciation are made, based on expectation of
life. If an item lasts longer than anticipated, the retirance
charges stop when 100% of its cost has been reached. If the life
for any reason is shorter than expected the unreturned balance is
used to swell the depreciation-expense account for the year, or
for large sums, the balance is put into a suspense account and
spread over several years.

Relations Between Appraised Value and Retirance. — It
must not be expected that the valuation figures of a property,
even though based on a good appraisal, plus the aggregate of all
retirance moneys secured out of rates, will any more than roughly
approximate the reproduction cost of the property or the legitimate investment historically established. The reasons are fairly
obvious. Among other things the value may be based on changing
unit prices; appreciation of property may enter. The retirement
allowances, as assessed on customers, are weighted composites for
the various items that make up the whole plant. With uniformity
and stability of rates over a given short period of time, the annual
retirance at first would usually accumulate faster than *observable*

composite depreciation would accrue. The deterioration of machinery seems to become more obvious in the last years of its service than in the earliest; and part of the retirance covers an antiquation which descends swiftly and, though impending, may not be seen by the appraiser.

Failures to Collect Retirance. — Where retirance money has not been collected, through the error and oversight of officials or neglect to charge sufficient rates, then according to the Knoxville case decision the company still is entitled to earn only on its depreciated value of property. This view has been assailed by many prominent engineers and the hope has been cherished by them that the Supreme Court would reverse itself. It is of interest therefore to examine this part of the decision in question (*City of Knoxville v. Knoxville Water Co.*, 1909; 29 Sup. Ct. Rep. 148) to find its basis in law and economics.

The company's original case was based on an elaborate analysis of the cost of construction. To arrive at the present value of the plant large deductions were made on account of the depreciation. This depreciation was divided into complete depreciation and incomplete depreciation. The complete depreciation represented that part of the original plant which through destruction or obsolescence had actually perished as useful property. The incomplete depreciation represented the impairment in value of the parts of the plant which remained in existence and were continued in use. It was urgently contended that, in fixing upon the value of the plant upon which the company was entitled to earn a reasonable return, the amounts of complete and incomplete depreciation should be · added to the present value of the surviving parts. The court refused to approve this method and we think properly refused.

A water plant with all its additions begins to depreciate in value from the moment of its use. Before coming to the question of profits, the company is entitled to earn a sufficient sum annually to provide not only for current repairs, but for making good the depreciation and replacing the parts of the property when they come to the end of their life. The company is not bound to see its property gradually waste without making provision out of earnings for its replacement. It is entitled to see that from earnings the value of the property invested is kept unimpaired, so that at the end of any given term of years, the original investment remains as it was at the beginning. It is not only the right of the company to make such a provision, but it is its duty to its bond- and stockholders, and in the case of a public-service corporation, at least, its plain duty to the public. If a different course were pursued, the only method of providing for replacement of property which had ceased to be useful

would be the investment of new capital and the issue of new bonds or
stocks. This course would lead to a constantly increasing variance between present value and bond and stock capitalization — a tendency
which would inevitably lead to disaster either to the stockholders or to
the public, or both. If, however, a company fails to perform this plain
duty and to exact sufficient returns to keep the investment unimpaired
whether this is the result of unwarranted dividends upon over issues of
securities, or of omission to exact proper prices for the output, the fault
is its own. When, therefore, a public regulation of its prices comes under
question, the true value of the property then employed for the purpose
of earning a return cannot be enhanced by a consideration of the errors
in management which have been committed in the past.

This statement is seen to be based on the proposition that for
every dollar by which the property has depreciated, the company
is entitled to earn a dollar above interest and profits. When this
is done each item is repaid as it is retired and existing depreciation
is made good each year. If it should not be done, in the course
of time replacements would have to be made out of entirely new
capital and that would be an economic sin against the next generation.

This is a statement of general principle evidently intended as
broadly applicable — since there are no references to the effect
of peculiar conditions disclosed by the evidence in this case. So
it must have been well considered before given form and stated
without exceptions. It is hard to find grounds therein for ex-
pecting its reversal *except* for those cases where the company has
been constrained by local government or regulating commission
to make rates that did not fully provide "for the replacement of
its property out of earnings." Requiring a company to base
rates on depreciated value of property in such cases would seem
to constitute confiscation. The same unfortunate result would
be attained if the regulating authority had applied and continued
to use the sinking-fund annuity in determining rates together with
depreciated value of property. The sinking fund is not free capital;
it brings the company no dividends by its investment and the
concern gets no return on part of its investment where the equivalent of full value is not retained in the rate basis.

If rates have been based on full value and retirance has been
secured by sinking-fund annuities, the regulating authorities could
follow two courses. First, they could continue to risk using the

sinking-fund annuity for retirance and full value of property on
which to figure return; or they could follow the Knoxville dictum
and use depreciated value provided retirance was made fully equal
to computed annual depreciation henceforth; the accumulated
sinking fund properly handled would equal the depreciation up to
that time and would then become free capital.

The last sentence quoted from the opinion lays stress on the
errors of management which cause or permit insufficient rates.
It is not to be assumed that the same interdiction applies to the
many cases where the business could not have struggled along in
its earlier stages had the charges been large enough to satisfy
this demand — customers would have been driven away instead
of being encouraged to increase to the point when the same rates
yielded all the proper sums without being burdensome. Error
and incompetency, not mere force of circumstances, are to be
penalized, if a strict sense of equity is to be preserved — and that
surely was what the court sought. Therefore, the inclusion of
deficits between the actual returns and what would be proper to
cover depreciation may be retained in development expense or
"going value."

Computing Annual Depreciation and Retirance. — Depreciation computations depend first on past experience as to future
expectation of life. With some utilities wear-deterioration,
natural delapidation, or antiquation may fix the probable time
when various parts of plant will have to be retired from service,
as already noted. Once the term is fixed, and the apportionment
made as quantity or demand charges, how shall the amount be
distributed as to years? How close may the annual retirance be
made to follow the annual increment of depreciation? Some of
the schemes followed are outlined below in answer to these queries.

Maintenance Plan. — The oldest and the simplest attempt to
saddle renewals on customers was by charging them for all the
repairs and renewals of the year. This had the unfortunate
effect in some cases of placing an extreme burden of retirance on
some years and practically none on others, with the result that
rates were too far below true cost at the start and the company
was in financial straits at the end. This was apt to be the situation particularly in those utilities where the property items were
long lived — like water and gas works. It has worked out best
in the case of utilities whose plant was composed of a multitude

of parts of short life — like telephone systems and some railroads, though the latter have to resort to "expedients" when expensive long-lived fixtures like stations and bridges give way.

It is hard to distinguish between upkeep of old property and new extensions, so that one result of the direct-replacement or maintenance scheme in some cases has been to make additions out of earnings. A certain amount of such manipulation often may be sanctioned, but too much of it hides the true cost of service and may cause a company's stockholders to earn unduly on property which the customers and not the investors paid for.

The actual value of an established property in equilibrium administered after this scheme is only from 60 to 85% of the investment (plus appreciation). This 15 to 40% depreciation is lost to the company, according to the Knoxville decision, through neglect to collect. The plan gives no adequate knowledge of the annual depreciation and it is assuming less and less importance each year.

Appraisal Plan. — A second plan that has been tried is the subtraction from earnings of sums which an examination of the property shows to represent the loss in value. This is better in theory than in practice — due to certain human limitations and to one inherent defect. Changes due to depreciation are not well disclosed by annual examinations because of but slight changes in appearance from year to year — differences which however become more noticeable as the period between appraisals lengthens. Then, the mind of the appraiser may change from year to year, or, more likely perhaps, the appraisers themselves may change and bring a radical change in standards of comparison.

This sort of a depreciation levy must be dangerous, in view of the Knoxville decision. It gives weight largely to superficial evidence of past deterioration, while the worth of the property, from the point of view of the integrity of investment, has been further impaired by the accrued liability for renewals on account of probable obsoletion. It will not do to say that the "depreciation" allowances secured from rates relate absolutely to the past decay — to what can be seen to have definitely happened. Retirements of obsolete equipment must come in the future, it is true, but when they do come they must be paid out of past earnings or future economies, to accord with the Knoxville decision. This means that the utility has an increasing liability each year for obsolescence and that each year something must be secured to compensate for the annual increment.

Straight-line Scheme. — The most obvious way of distributing the burden of retirement over the life of service is to divide the cost by the years of life and set out the resultant quotient from each year's earnings. Such money can be held by the utility owner as he sees fit against the day of replacement. If the accumulated reserves and the time passed be plotted as a mathematical graph or "curve," the form will be a straight line of course — hence the engineers' term "straight-line scheme" which has mystified most laymen and some attorneys.

One difficulty is that in spite of a superficial plausibility in the straight-line plan, there is no logical reason to expect that simple depreciation necessarily accumulates in direct proportion to the age — that the value of a machine is half gone at half its expected life. Indeed when property having a very long life, like cast-iron pipe which is good for 60 to 100 years, is considered the value is seen to be not inversely proportional to the age. In fact the pipe at 30 years is worth 80% instead of 50% — because of the importance of interest element in affecting worth. Moreover, during the early period of operation, the load is apt to be light and the unit costs high anyway so that the development of the business would be hampered by large retirance factors in rates.

However, on the other hand, if the utility property largely consists of a great number of short-lived items, as is the case with most telephone systems, railroads, and some electric railways, then the straight-line scheme has an attractive simplicity and the discrepancy between actual depreciation and retirance secured cannot be appreciable. Straight-line schemes here have an advantage over the actual-renewal or maintenance basis for utilities whose properties may not show equilibrium between depreciation and maintenance.

Sinking-fund Plan. — It is desirable that annual retirances should closely approximate annual depreciations. The most popular scheme of computing the annual depreciation of a property item is to consider that it follows the growth of a sinking fund sufficient to extinguish the cost at the end of the probable life. Now, as is well known, a sinking fund grows through the payment to it of an annuity or annual contribution and by the investment of the sums so contributed, so that there is an annual sum for interest which is retained in the fund. The annuity or annual contribution is made of such size that it will, if invested at compound interest, with the interest accumulations, equal the cost of the property item after a given number of years, representing the life of such item. Therefore, in order that the annual retirances which must come from the rate payers may closely approximate the annual depreciation increments, they must in each year equal *the annual contribution to a sinking fund plus the accumulations of interest,* and this furnishes the basis for the equal-annual-payment plan, subsequently described. The general practice, however, is to include directly in the sums to be earned as retirances only the annuity or annual contribution to the sinking fund, which is a much smaller sum, and if the discrepancy were not provided for in the earnings somehow, a great injustice would be done the owner, for it is only through the rates that the entire depreciation can be made good and the investment kept unimpaired. This discrepancy between annuity and required retirance, in practice, is compensated for by allowing the owner of the property to include in rate-basis worth the undepreciated value of the property — even though it may have lost considerable value through depreciation. Part of what should have been accounted for as direct retirance is recovered in increased interest.

It is a serious defect of the sinking-fund-annuity plan, in view of the principles underlying the Knoxville decision, that it is necessary in order to preserve equity to use the undepreciated value of property contrary to the requirements of law as interpreted in this famous case. There is danger that the law, as it stands interpreted so far, may prevail against equity for the older utilities working with sinking-fund annuities as pseudo-retirances. The injustice will come to those concerns which in good faith have used sinking-fund annuities to provide retirance. The situation is brighter for those who have been constrained by government to form sinking funds, for they may charge that confiscation has begun, unless they employ full value. The remedy for these dangers seems to be the abandonment of the sinking-fund annuity as the measure of retirance and the substitution of the larger sum equivalent to a sinking-fund annuity plus the interest accumulations of the year.

A good part of the popularity of the sinking-fund-annuity plan has possibly been due to a vague feeling that somehow the depre-

ciation was being cared for adequately at much less expense than
by any other scheme.   Such a view savors a bit of the old "some-
thing-for-nothing" ideas that are so persistent and so often attractive.   A good example is furnished by the following remark of one
of the best known utility commissioners in the country:

Without going into details, it can be said that the sinking-fund method
employs a more efficient use of the reserve [than the straight-line plan].
Because of such use, the amount the consumers will have to contribute to
cover depreciation is less than under the straight-line method.

Where the amounts so provided have been used for necessary and
proper renewals and for the accumulation of a reserve for covering the
accrued depreciation of the property still in use, no reduction from the
cost new, because of depreciation, should be made in determining the fair
value for rate making and certain other purposes.

Obviously, what is not paid in as retirance is covered by interest on nonexistent plant value — a palpable trick in words or
bookkeeping.

This plan carries with it, in some cases and always in some
people's minds, the implication of a distinct reserve fund invested
in outside securities.   However, in the great majority of cases
seemingly, the allowances so secured are put into the property in
place of money that would have to be raised from outside sources.
Investing reserve funds inside the business complicates the scrutiny
of accounts and operating results, but it tends to reduce slightly
the cost of service or product — something which is desirable.

No matter whether the retirance funds are invested inside or
outside of the business, for the scrutiny of rate facts it seems
essential to remember that reserves made up of sinking-fund
annuities must earn for their own aggrandizement in order to
provide full amortization.   Therefore they are not to be regarded
as free capital in studying the business, no matter how the owner
chooses to handle them in the interests of daily operation.

It needs to be emphasized perhaps that in the great majority
of concerns, up to the present, the sinking-fund method of figuring retirance in rates has been merely an attempted process of
arriving at a fair and proper burden on the customers.   Unless
the degree of regulation is severe, there is not apt to be dictation
as to how the retirance moneys shall be invested.   The public
is protected when the utility uses these repaid moneys in well
defined and safe ways.

Modified Straight-line Schemes. — The complication and confusion of thought introduced into the scrutiny of utility business by the "sinking-fund" plan has led some to go back to the scheme of directly apportioning the cost of an item over the expected years of life, but not uniformly as in the regular straight-line scheme. Instead they have variously decreased it in the early years and increased it toward the end of the expected life period of the piece of equipment in question. Usually this has been done arbitrarily and empirically.

Annual Cost of Service and Actual Depreciation. — It is not mere age, nor yet service ability drop that discloses annual depreciation; nor is it general appearance. But it is reasonable to expect that there should be some fairly logical basis of computing the probable annual real decrement. If the annual depreciation be assumed to start high, then the early retirance must be heavy and in the later years light; the fair value (rate basis, Knoxville-Case standard) of an item would be low in later years and the fixed charges (interest and retirance) would greatly fluctuate. If now operating costs have not risen (excluding the effect of rise in price of labor and materials) and the service is well maintained, steady fixed charges may be regarded as a normal economic phenomenon. Fluctuation of service cost would be due to fluctuating cost of labor and supplies. That is to say, given a probable life of equipment where the fixed charges are large in proportion to the operating costs and where the deterioration or inadequacy will not seriously change the operating costs until very near the expected time of retirement, the real annual depreciation is such that the fixed charges (interest and retirance) continue steady year after year.

For example, assume that a water pipe costing new $1000 and having an expected life of 50 years had been in use 25 years. The interest at 6% and retirance would be for the first and 25th year, by the straight-line plan:

1st year interest.........................	$60.00	
1st year retirance.........................	20.00	
1st year fixed charges.......................		$80.00
25th year value...	500.00	
" " interest.........................	30.00	
" " retirance.........................	20.00	
" " fixed charges.....................		$50.00

If it were assumed that there was no depreciation up to 25 years, as the pipe was giving good service, the comparison would be:

1st year interest..............................	$60.00
1st year retirance.............................	0.00
1st year fixed charges.........................	$60.00
25th year value...............................	$1000.00
" " interest............................	60.00
" " retirance...........................	40.00
" " fixed charges.......................	$100.00

Following sinking-fund computations the same pipe would show these figures:

1st year interest..............................	$60.00
1st year retirance.............................	3.44
1st year fixed charges.........................	$63.44
25th year retirance aggregate..................	$188.97
" " value...............................	811.03
" " interest............................	48.66
" " retirance (on $811.03)...............	14.78
" " fixed charges.......................	$63.44

It is obvious that the $80 and $50 given by the straight-line plan for fixed charges during the first and 25th year, and the $60 and $100 given by the inspection plan are extremely abnormal and uncommercial, while the $63.44 for both years by sinking-fund computations is economically and reasonably desirable.

Where the operating expenses go up materially due to the deterioration of the equipment, then the depreciation increases more rapidly than otherwise and may approach the straight-line basis, as shown later.

" Equal-Annual-Payment " Scheme for Computing Retirance. — This plan is really a convex-curve modification of the straight-line scheme and is, with its developments, the most ingenious and the only scientific modification which the author has seen. It was developed by Frederic P. Stearns for his engineering practice and the simpler elements were discussed in 1914, in the progress report of the special Committee of the American Society of Civil Engineers on Valuation for Utility Rate-making. The annual allowances were not arranged arbitrarily but were fixed in such a way that the aggregate of dominant factors in rates would tend to be constant year after year.

The calculations leading to equal annual fixed charges in the preceding example were spoken of as "sinking-fund computations." They follow the standard sinking-fund tables as to the amount of depreciation in the property at the beginning of the 25th year, but the amount of retirance adopted for the 25th year is not the sinking-fund annuity but the increase in the amount of the sinking fund during the year, consisting of annuity plus interest accumulations. When the sinking-fund computations are used in this way, the equal-annual-payment scheme of compensating for depreciation is evolved. As each year's retirance by the equal-annual-payment plan is equal to the annuity under the sinking-fund plan, plus the amount of the interest accumulations of the sinking-fund during the year, the larger sum thus represented by the equal-annual-payment plan is the sum which the company is entitled to earn as an offset to the depreciation of its property items in order to keep its investment intact.

It may seem at first sight that the equal-annual-payment plan, providing as it does a larger retirance for each year after the first than the annuity of a sinking fund, would be opposed to the interests of the rate payers and would give larger earnings to the company. This, however, is not the case when both systems are applied in an equitable manner. The company should be permitted to earn a retirance equivalent to the amount of depreciation, and if the retirance is figured to be the inadequate sum represented by the sinking-fund annuity alone there must be a further allowance from the rate payers to cover the interest accumulations of a sinking fund during the year. As shown already, it commonly masquerades with interest on full undepreciated value of plant. The assumption, contrary to the facts, that the property has not depreciated in value, is wholly for the purpose of making up for the inadequacy of the retirance when it is assumed to be equal to the sinking-fund annuity.

By the equal-annual-payment plan substantially the same results can be secured as with the sinking-fund annuity and full-value scheme — but quite in harmony with the Knoxville decision. The equal-annual-payment plan will be seen to be the simplest case of what the author has called for convenience a group of "convex-curve" plans all closely related to it and all springing out of complicated practical conditions discussed in a later paragraph on the effect on depreciation of rising cost of operation.

Retirance, figured by this plan, is declared not to be in any sense a reserve. It is an immediate and direct compensation for property value lost by deterioration and by liability incurred for retirement of equipment. The retirance is immediately available for canceling obligations or, what is equivalent, for reinvestment in replacements, additions, improvements, etc. When retirances are so reinvested they enter rate-basis worth on a par with extensions paid for by fresh accessions of capital.

Interest is allowed only on the diminished worth (unreturned investment) of each item; where the retirance sums are reinvested those new property items so purchased earn like all the other items and retirance is collected each year for them also. Obviously, the annual interest on unrepaid investment in each item of property goes down steadily but the retirance aggregate goes up correspondingly. The annual payments for retirance and interest on continuing investment then can have a constant annual aggregate when the rate of interest and rate for retirance computations are the same.

Objections to the Equal-Annual-Payment Plan. — The Stearns plan has been criticised for making the retirance (and the computed annual depreciation increment) change with the selection of an interest rate at which the hypothetical sinking fund is compounded, whereas the actual depreciation obviously is independent of the rate for the calculations. The answer to this objection is that there is but one definite rate for compounding the hypothetical fund to satisfy the economic criterion already applied — equal annual fixed charges. That proper interest rate is the same as the allowed rate of return on the property — so long as there is no change in operating cost or capacity through depreciation. The effect of such changes is traced in a later paragraph.

This plan would seem to allow great flexibility of management in public utilities, but it has not been universally accepted. In the first place, many railroad men have shown themselves hostile to anything which suggested "basing rates on cost of service" — having in mind, however, not "rates" but "tariffs" and forgetting that a "rate" for a railroad at present means a sort of unit gross revenue, a weighted average of all the detailed "tariffs" — which admittedly are affected by many things besides cost of service, as noted under special problems of specific utilities.

Other utility officials have been hostile to this plan because it followed the dictum of the Knoxville Water case (that the rate-basis worth must be a depreciated value of property used and useful, irrespective of former investment). But the method includes in "property," the reinvestment of retirance, development expenses, early deficits, etc., so that the objections were not so much against a principle as a policy. It has been argued by some objectors that to admit that a depreciated value could ever equitably be used (in the absence of official misconduct) in figuring rate basis, would result in a clamor for use of depreciated value irrespective of the treatment of retirance.

Depreciation Under Increasing Operating Costs. — Where the cost of operation goes up materially because of the deterioration of the equipment, then of course the equalization of annual fixed charges alone is not a proper criterion. Rather it would appear to be proper to hold that the sum of fixed charges and of operation-cost increase should remain constant. Under these conditions the real depreciation may more nearly approach the unmodified straight-line apportionment. It may disclose a depreciation more rapid than that given by the straight-line scheme for the length of life first assumed to hold.

For instance, take the case of a small water-works pump. Suppose that it was a new departure in design and was expected to have a life of ten years; suppose that in service it was found that slip and increased friction increased the cost of operation $4 each year. (This is a hypothetical condition purposely taken to illustrate the depreciation action involved.) Assume that the scrap value only equals the cost of removal.

To find the actual depreciation under these conditions the capitalized excess cost of operation is deducted from the figures for nominal value and considered as repaid to the investor. The remaining value is repaid during the ten years according to equal-annual-payment plan; the depreciation (and the retirance) is the sum of each year's capitalized excess cost and the other annual factor. The computations are shown in the accompanying tables, the simple plan for unchanged operating costs being presented first.

When the output has decreased with age, the unit cost has increased. The multiplier is the reciprocal of the decreased capacity — if the output is only 0.9 of the initial, then the unit cost is

I. Annual Retirance and Fixed Charges by the Equal-Annual-Payment Plan

End of Year	Diminished Value	Interest	Annual Retirance (or Depreciation Increment)	Aggregate Retirance (or Depreciation)	Interest plus Retirance
0	$1000.00	....	....	....	....
1	924.13	$60.00	$75.87	$75.87	$135.87
2	843.71	55.45	80.42	156.29	135.87
3	758.46	50.62	85.25	241.54	135.87
4	668.10	45.51	90.36	331.90	135.87
5	572.32	40.09	95.78	427.68	135.87
6	470.79	34.34	101.53	529.21	135.87
7	363.18	28.26	107.61	636.82	135.87
8	249.10	21.79	114.08	750.90	135.87
9	128.18	14.95	120.92	871.82	135.87
10	....	7.69	128.18	1000.00	135.87

II. Annual Retirance and Fixed Charges for Equal Fixed-and-Excess Costs: Rising Operating Expense or Decreasing Capacity

End of Year	Excess Operating Cost	Total Capitalized Excess Repaid	Sinking Fund Increment	Annual Depreciation or Retirance	Aggregate Retirance or Depreciation	Diminished Value	Interest on Value	Retirance Interest and Excess Cost
0	......	......	....	......	......	$1000.00	.....	......
1	$4.00	$66.67	$25.29	$91.96	$91.96	908.04	$60.00	$155.96
2	8.00	133.33	26.81	93.48	185.44	814.56	54.48	155.96
3	12.00	200.00	28.42	95.09	280.53	719.47	48.87	155.96
4	16.00	266.67	30.12	96.79	377.32	622.68	43.17	155.96
5	20.00	333.33	31.93	98.60	475.92	524.08	37.36	155.96
6	24.00	400.00	33.85	100.52	576.44	423.56	31.44	155.96
7	28.00	466.67	35.88	102.55	678.99	321.01	25.41	155.96
8	32.00	533.33	38.03	104.70	783.69	216.31	19.26	155.96
9	36.00	600.00	40.31	106.98	890.67	109.33	12.98	155.96
10	40.00	666.67	42.73	109.40	1000.07	−0.07	6.56	155.96

III. Annual Retirance and Fixed Charges for Equal Fixed-and-Excess Costs: Increasing Operating Expense with Decreasing Capacity

End of Year	Excess Cost	Total Capitalized Excess Repaid	Annual Depreciation (or Retirance)	Aggregate Retirance	Diminished Value	Interest on Value	Retirance Interest and Excess Cost
0	......	......	......	......	$1000.00	......	......
1	$8.00	$133.34	$133.34	$133.34	866.66	$60.00	$201.34
2	16.00	266.66	133.34	266.66	733.34	52.00	201.34
3	24.00	400.00	133.34	400.00	600.00	44.00	201.34
4	32.00	533.34	133.34	533.34	466.66	36.00	201.34
5	40.00	666.66	133.34	666.66	333.34	28.00	201.34
6	48.00	800.00	133.34	800.00	200.00	20.00	201.34
7	56.00	933.34	133.34	933.34	66.66	12.00	201.34
8	64.00	1066.66	66.66	1000.00	0.00	4.00	134.68
9	72.00	1200.00	....	....	....	0.00	....
10	80.00	1333.34	....	....	....	....	....

1.11 times the initial value. The total cost of the original output, if the deficiency was made up by other machines of similar type, would be increased by use of the same multiplier; that is, an excess cost results which can be studied exactly as was the extra cost of operation. If the annual operating expense of the hypothetical pump already noted was say $800, a gradual drop of capacity, without increase of gross operating expense, to 95.3% in these ten years would mean an increase in excess cost of 5% or $40. Table II therefore applies to this case.

Should the two actions be combined then the result would be as in Table III. The only change over Table II is that caused by doubling the excess cost, and capitalized excess cost. This amounts to the original cost of the $1000 item by the 8th year so that there' is no need of attempting to retire the item by introducing any equal-annual-payment plan factor.

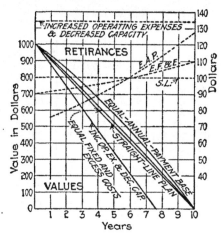

VALUE AND RETIRANCE CURVES FROM
TABLES I, II AND III

In theory the excess costs may rise more rapidly than shown but attempts to find how they go probably are no closer estimates than assuming a uniform increase.

The Supreme Court on Retirance Methods. — There are no high court decisions dealing specifically on the questions of sinking funds actually maintained to offset depreciation and cover retirements. The nearest approach probably is the Knoxville water case, noted before. This opinion clearly points out that a company should earn enough to cover the depreciation of all its property, and pay the running expenses, fixed charges, etc., but it holds that depreciation must be deducted from cost in arriving at the rate basis — "fair value." Beyond that there seemingly are no specific and inflexible demands in the Knoxville case opinion completely in favor either of setting up true sinking funds, or of putting the annuities into productive extensions of the plant, or of returning to the investor his annual impairment of investment for him to put back into the business as fresh capital if he chooses. Yet the Knoxville-decision has been greatly feared as a breeder of injustice because it demands a return only on depreciated value whereas with the true sinking funds set up, as required by some state commissions, the equivalent of a return on undepreciated value is needed.

It is reasonable to expect that the court will recognize the unjust constraint and provide the remedy — admitting the equivalent of undepreciated value of plant in rate-basis worth. The reasoning which the court might be expected to follow is not difficult to trace:

The retirance comes from rates and only from rates. If the annual retirances have been held down by state regulations to less than the annual depreciations, some equivalent of the difference must have been made available to the company or confiscation has resulted. Numerically this has been accomplished by the bookkeeping fiction of using undepreciated value in the rate basis. It is incidental that the retirances have been ordered tied up in a reserve fund — for the earnings of that fund, which equal the return on the false element of value, prevent confiscation by providing return on enforced reservation of capital. The final results have been equitable and the methods of computation may be neglected as to the past. For the future, however, retirance should not masquerade as interest on a false value and the rate-basis worth should not be increased by any non-existent elements.

Lower Courts on Sinking-fund Retirance. — There are various lower-court decisions favoring and disapproving the sinking-fund-annuity method of figuring retirance elements in rates. But none of the lower courts have ·objected to the sinking-fund-annuity plan on the vital grounds already noted; their opposition seems to be due to a misapprehension of the mathematical basis of computation. Possibly this is because some courts have been led by the quotation of average percentages for composite depreciation on the whole property to think that the sinking-fund method necessitated tying up the whole of the concern's renewal funds until the average life of the assembled equipment was reached. That, of course, is not the intention by any scheme of proportioning the retirance and the quotation of average lives and aggregate percentages is but· a convenient form for some discussions and comparisons. In every case the aggregates can be resolved into their components, when it is seen that the funds for retirement of each and every item is complete at the end of its estimated life. Reinvestment of a completed retirement item does not affect the growth of other and incomplete items. Replacement of an item can be paid for at the expiration of its life out of the fund — up to the stated cost-less-salvage.

Typical of the adverse court decisions noted above two may be cited. The first is the New York case, *People ex rel. Manhattan Ry. Co. v. Woodbury* (203 N. Y. 239; Oct. 1911). The opinion of Judge Haight runs:

"The Special Term in this case, however, adopted a plan of amortization upon which an annual sum was authorized to be set apart as a sinking fund, which, by compounding the interest thereon for a period equal to the life of the structure, tracks, engines, machinery and rolling stock, would at the end of that period create a fund sufficient to replace the property. The difficulty with such holding is that railroad corporations do not reconstruct their railroads and rolling stock in that way. In order to afford proper protection to the public they are required to maintain a high state of efficiency both in roadbed and rolling stock. The relator's railroad has been in existence already for about thirty years and some portion of its property has already suffered from decay and use to such an extent that portions thereof have to be reconstructed and made new each year. Old ties have to be removed and replaced with new ones; old rails that have become worn and battered have to be removed and their places supplied with new rails and so the work of reconstruction progresses from year to year. It is not the waiting forty or sixty years to reconstruct, during which time the amount set apart as a sinking fund may be doubled many times over by compounding the interest, but it is the annual expenditure for reconstruction which is to be paid for at the time that the construction is made. To illustrate: Suppose the average life of the tangible property of a railroad, outside of the land itself, to be sixty years and the cost of reconstruction to be sixty million dollars, it would follow that one million dollars would have to be used each year in reconstruction, and that amount would have to be annually used for that purpose; but under the plan adopted in this case, instead of deducting from the gross earnings the amount necessarily expended for that purpose, a small fraction of that sum, viz., $4200, only is allowed to be deducted, a sum which, with the interest compounded for the next sixty years, would amount to a million dollars. Under such a plan the company would be practically prohibited from annually constructing a portion of its road and thus prevented from keeping it in that state of efficiency which the public demands. Of course the necessities of reconstruction vary from year to year; some years it may be greater than others, but the assessors each year can easily ascertain the sum required for that purpose. I think, therefore, that we should adhere to the rule sanctioned in the *Jamaica* case, and that a gross sum should be deducted annually for the purposes of reconstruction."

Two things are seen by reading this with the preceding discussions of "depreciation" and "retirance" in mind. The first is that the court did not grasp the possibility of the component items in the aggregate of the sinking-fund allowances maturing at different periods and being thereupon available for making a replacement. The second point is a palpable arithmetical slip; the cost of reconstruction is stated as sixty million dollars, yet the aggregate retirance is stated as one million. If the $4200 applies to only this one million, then the allowance for full retirance which should have been made is $252,000. Computing the annual contribution at 4% compound interest for 60 years and sixty million dollars gives $252,000 also. It may be said that even this is only a quarter that needed for annual renewals; the reply must be that the needed replacements cannot reach that million average or equilibrium figure for many years and that in that time there has been a heavy fund accumulation which, being distributed over the remaining years of the 60 and added to the annual amounts will give the million and over needed thereafter. This must necessarily result if the aggregate renewance figure is made up, as it should be when this plan is followed, of component factors properly figured on the several property items and their life as experienced under similar conditions.

Similar misunderstanding of the underlying mathematical basis is seen in the so-called Louisville Telephone Case decision of Judge Evans (*Cumberland Tel. and Tel. Co. v. City of Louisville*, 187 Fed. Rep. 637; April, 1911), often quoted as adverse to sinking funds:

Of course our estimate could not be based upon the proposition that the per centum set apart to cover depreciation would be deposited in bank or loaned out from year to year so as to accumulate and be on hand at the end of 14 years, and to be then used to construct an entirely new plant, and so on from period to period. In such a case the public

would not only have a service that would progressively grow worse until
its operations ceased altogether, but it would thereafter get no service
at all until a new plant replacing the old could be completed and put into
operation. The question rather has been; What does experience show
to be the proper average per cent of annual earnings which the company
should expend in order to insure that its plant at the end of 14 years will
be as good as it now is, and in the meantime render to the public that
good service which its duty to the public requires?

Choice of Retirance Plans. — Some engineers rest their confidence in one scheme of getting retirance out of rates, and others
in another — each contending that his is better than any other.
Each may be justified in the light of his own experience, and as
that changes so may his views on this point. It serves no good
end to be dogmatic in opinions on any one plan, for under special
conditions some shine to better advantage than others. Often
the differences to a large extent indeed are matters of definition.
It can be said, however, that with careful study some plan or other
can be selected which will simply meet peculiar needs, remain
within the spirit of the highest court decisions and protect all
continuing investments.

This may result in use of two or more plans in combination;
however, the one should not require undiminished value and the
other depreciated value. For instance in a telephone plant, there
is a vast number of property items each comparatively small
and of comparatively short life — from obsoletion. The history
of the art is so filled with rapid changes that it is difficult to make
more than the roughest estimate in the hope that it will cover
the renewals as a whole. But it is seen that there has been a
steady growth of the more permanent plant, like buildings and
underground conduits, on which one can approximately fix the
life and therefore provide reasonable retirance by the straight-line
or convex-curve plan as may be required. Then when these
items have lived their useful life, the owners will have their equivalent in hand. But for the multitude of instruments, switchboards
and various pieces of more or less small equipment it may be
necessary to set aside out of earnings the actual annual cost of
replacements. That alone will not do in fixing rates, however,
and it may become necessary to estimate the most probable average as shown by the cost of such replacements in the past. The
two factors then may combine into an aggregate annual sum

which may enter rates. Since the equilibrium value of the telephone system (excluding buildings, conduits, and other long-lived items) will be found 10 to 20% under investment the difference should be repaid somehow and this is easily done by spreading the amount over several years in a suspense account.

The inaccuracy, the inadequacy and the expense of the "valuation" plan of providing retirance seem to be valid arguments against the universal employment of this plan. The valuation study has some usefulness, however, as already noted, in being applied at intervals of five or ten years to correct any false trend taken by the other more easily applied annual schemes based on estimates of probable life.

The Famous Hen Argument. — One argument, advanced against use of depreciated value of physical plant in rate bases, which has captivated many hearers is the now well known hen story of counsel for the Consolidated Gas Co., in the famous 80c. rate case (*Willcox v. Consolidated Gas;* 212 U. S. 19). His argument in brief was that toward the end of the hen's career while she was still laying vigorously but apt to stop, the price of the eggs should decline with the value of the hen if the depreciated-value basis were followed, until perfectly good eggs would be sold at a ridiculous price.

That illustration, as generally used, is extremely fallacious. A moment's careful thought shows that the cost of the eggs should be unchanged — with a steady market price of chicken feed. The factors entering in (besides daily food) are (1) interest on depreciated value of hen, and (2) annual retirance; as (1) goes down (2) correspondingly goes up, if the problem be looked at from the standpoint of the straight-line or equal-annual-payment plan, and the aggregate repayment for the years past has been available for the owner to put into other hens or equivalent earning property (since he undoubtedly had more than one hen). If the sinking-fund annuity plan is followed, equity is established only by admitting the fictitious undepreciated value of the hen to make up the required retirance. This hen argument is hesitantly reviewed here, but these few words have been added because the hen story has found too ready acceptance and has a certain popular appeal.

Other Depreciation-computation Plans. — The schemes discussed already are not the only ones that have been proposed for finding the retirances to be secured out of rates. Some of the others, however, do not satisfy the economic criterion of stable fixed and excess costs. One of their chief faults is that the early-year charges are excessive.

One of these plans is the "reducing-balance" method, by which a definite percentage of the diminishing value is considered as each year's contribution. Its illogical status is obvious.

Another is the "simple-annuity" scheme by which an equal annual sum is found which will include a given percentage interest on the remaining investment and reduce the investment to zero at the close of a given period. This is in contrast with the equal-annual-payment plan by which retirance is made to include the interest of an accumulated hypothetical fund and, incidentally, therefore on the lost value.

There is finally to be noted the "unit-cost" method which aims to secure the same results as attained by the "convex-curve" schemes developed from the equal-annual-payment plan — equal annual costs of service. The total cost of operation, the amount of repairs, the sinking-fund annuity, the output old and new, etc., enter a complicated but logically developed formula:*

$$\frac{Q + P + F + iV}{Y} = \frac{q + p + f + iv}{y},$$

$$v = \frac{y}{x+i}\left(\frac{Q + P + XV + iV}{Y} - \frac{q+p}{y}\right).$$

V = cost of new substitute machine; v = diminished value of old machine; F = sinking-fund annuity to amortize V in N years; f = sinking-fund annuity to amortize v in n years; Q = average annual operating expense of new substitute machine, excluding repairs; q = average annual operating expense of old machine, excluding repairs; P = annuity to meet repairs on new plant; p = annuity to meet repairs of new plant; i = interest rate; U = average unit cost of output from new machine in N years; u = average unit cost of output from old machine in n years left; Y = average number of output units per year from new machine working for N years; y = unit output from old machine for n years left; X = sinking-fund annuity to accumulate $1 in N years; x = sinking-fund annuity to accumulate $1 in n years.

* Detailed by E. A. Saliers, "Theory of Depreciation," Ronald Press, N. Y., 1915.

The plan accomplishes no more than the convex-curve scheme and has one great weakness which that scheme has not — depreciation and retirance are assumed to be equal to sinking fund annuities, and not to annuities plus interest accretions.

The "unit-cost" scheme was developed by equating a supposed unit cost of output of both old and new substitute machine. But the cost of production for both old and new machine is understated, since retirance is taken as the sinking-fund annuity and not annuity plus interest accretion. The underestimate amounts to only 10% in the case of the old machine but is nearly 50% in the case of the new, with the result that the computed value of the old unit is too low.

CHAPTER IX

MISCELLANEOUS PROBLEMS INDIRECTLY RELATED TO RATE-MAKING

Problems Old and New. — Some of the problems that confront public utilities (including both privately and municipally owned works) seem to change from decade to decade. In the past, the more pressing problems have been technical and more or less peculiar to each utility. Gas works once faced potential calamity until central-station electricity supply found its field and the two divided their services according to the intrinsic advantages of each. Water-supply men sought, among the various methods of improving available but polluted supplies, some universal scheme until they found the conditions under which each plan should be favored. Light railways had to change from animal to cable traction and again to electric. Trunk railroads found lines and equipment of insufficient capacity.

Each utility has similar new problems today and they have, in addition and in common, a new one of paramount importance — public regulation. It has been but a few years since utilities ran as best they could, and with no complete public oversight; they charged what they could get and figured their profits (or their losses) after, instead of before, a given period of operation. Even municipal utility departments seldom rendered an accounting of their stewardship that was more than a hopeless jumble of arbitrarily chosen figures. Now utilities are constrained to take the public into confidence and are warned that they are to meet the public's desires for service so far as the customers are willing to pay for it — and so far as a fair profit can be earned for the investors (in the case of privately owned utilities). This broad problem of regulation brings a complication of intricate questions, only a few of which have been discussed in the preceding pages and then as they directly affect rates. There are others of less direct influence which may be lightly touched upon, however. These problems are commonly spoken of as "economic" but they are to a larger extent political — using that term in a broader and less popular meaning than usual, to signify a close relation to matters of local government.

The Future of Regulation. — Rate-making is necessarily most intimately connected with the whole scheme of public supervision and regulation but the plan of supervision itself is a problem.

Utility regulation is not a new departure in the American political situation, although the tremendous development of ten years somewhat obscures the earlier steps. Indeed in the early common law descended to us there have been various restrictions on some industrial efforts closely related to the public life, though these impositions were designed solely to protect the people from real or fancied oppressions. For example, various attempts to lay hold of American transportation facilities can be discerned through the past. Indeed, it was the pressing need of facilitating commerce between the colonies that made possible the amalgamation of the states of the American Union and the adoption of the federal constitution. Political and economic differences of opinion prevented fusion until the needed freedom of a fettered trade over-rode all obstacles. Therefore the utility regulation now beginning to flower is deeper seated than many persons are ready to admit and it does not appear like a transitory fad likely to be cast aside soon for some other political bauble.

At the same time, however, it is common political experience that such movements have pendulum-like swings and some abatement of popularity must be foreseen. Such a temporary reversion may be expected when the tide seems to be running toward governmental operation, or when increased demands are evident for "home" rule of our cities, or when the cost of detailed supervision becomes more oppressive than the burden of unsupervised monopoly. The net effect of all these political and economic tendencies is probably to be a state of more or less equilibrium where benefits generally balance the burdens and where departure either toward or away from deeper regulation brings greater burdens of one sort or another than benefits of any kind.

Avenues of Regulation. — Whether general regulation is by state or municipal body, the powers of supervision are limited to the powers of the legislature and the latter always has the paramount authority, fixed by state and federal constitutions and restricted by valid contract rights which may have come into existence and may continue even perhaps with public injury.

Thus there are six possible avenues of regulation (1) direct congressional, (2) by federal commission, both of these applying to interstate matters and to intrastate only in the absence of state legislation and effort, (3) by direct state legislation, (4) by state commission, (5) by municipal-council supervision, (6) by local commission. Regulation by direct congressional act, state legislation, or even municipal ordinance, cannot hope ever to cover more than most general instructions, and any details of application necessitate long continued industry beyond the power of the legislators and necessarily are thrown upon organized employees. A commission seems to be required whatever the plan followed.

The existing popularity of the state board at present seems to spring from certain real advantages such as (1) regulation at lower relative cost the greater the scale, (2) probable wider outlook and experience of state over city commissions and (3) absence of local prejudices.

Common Powers of a Commission. — It is a common principle of American jurisprudence that a legislature cannot delegate broad powers, yet public-utility commissions are ordinarily spoken of as enjoying delegated powers. Where is the fallacy? The courts have held that the legislature is not delegating its powers when it decrees, for instance, that the rates shall "yield a fair return on fair value" and lays upon a subordinate body the work of filling out the details which depend on investigation and computation.

Commissions usually cannot enforce contracts — a function of existing courts; they have to call on the courts to enforce their own orders. Findings and orders of the commissions are reviewed by proper courts though presumption of facts established by a commission is recognized. These bodies have limited judicial and executive functions but such are subordinate and auxiliary to the main functions of a legislative subcommission.

Public Regard of Franchises. — A "franchise"* has been

---

* The term "franchise" in this work, and in this section particularly, is used in a broad sense as applied to utility operations and not in the restricted way some legal minds employ it. Thus some would specifically limit the term (see paper by W. M. Wherry, on "Franchise Values," before the American Electric Railway Association, October, 1913) to (1) general rights to be corporations and (2) such special rights to occupy public territory as are legal private property — "incorporeal hereditaments," vendible and transferable,

variously called the delegation of municipal functions to private individuals or corporations for the furtherance of public welfare, a license to do business and, again, a mere inducement to invest money and undertake service. The confusion arising from many definitions of a franchise and many attitudes toward franchise holders cannot be removed unless in the course of time, all such enterprises should be placed on approximately equal footings, and all have then come under a wise public control.

Franchise Value in Rate Basis. — The older franchises are largely of the type responding to the tests of value as private property. They have, perhaps unwittingly, been given a value then which cannot be taken away without "due process of law" and are apt to enter the rate basis. The grantors in very many cases desired to hold out, to the existing generation, chances for unusual profits but it seems improbable that they contemplated holding up all the future generations of customers for payment of the same profits to heirs or assigns of the promoters.

An important case of this sort is now pending before the U. S. Supreme Court — the Passaic (N. J.) 90-cent gas rates. This has already been noted (page 65) in regard to the decision of the highest New Jersey State Court, in concurring with which one justice pointed out that franchises were property to be protected by the government, but were not property used and useful in the public service since their value depended on the service and rates. The franchise value sprung out of a contract to "furnish services at reasonable rates" and since the "stream could not rise higher than its source," the reasonable rates could not depend on the value of the contract.

Franchises can be drawn which raise no such disturbing questions but which still are equally fair to the utility and advantageous to the public. They may deny perpetual rights but allow maximum development by making an indeterminate life with compensation for seizure. They may deny the chance for large speculative

bestowing unimpairable enjoyment or earning capacity on physical possessions. Having thus all the attributes of private property such a franchise is held to have a value not related to its cost but determined by its marketability, by its ability to increase profits, and by all unearned increments attached to itself and to the accompanying property and business. It has already been noted that franchises have been held in court to have a value springing out of service and hence not to be property "used and useful" in the service. See page 65.

rewards but they can insure moderate profits. The commercial success of companies under these measures explains why some concerns have relinquished franchises of some monetary or market value in order to secure added privileges necessary for the further growth of their service.

Other Regards of Franchises. — The franchise, to a certain extent, may be regarded as an appointment to office with the corporation as a "public servant" — and like other public officials subjected to public scrutiny and criticism of motives, ability and results. Those who would push the agent analogy to an extreme, however, are apt to fail to give adequate consideration to certain characteristics of the utility corporation which prevent its completely being so treated. For instance, (1) money has been invested to give to the public a service corresponding to the privilege conferred on the corporation; the concern, therefore, has certain property rights of managing the public utility as a business and these are not to be lightly invaded. (2) It is entitled to secure high-priced expert employees if they promote efficiency and adequate service. (3) Finally, the investors are entitled to compensation, above mere rates of interest, for risk and attention, while for notable skill, zeal and broad public policy, it may be sometimes advisable to allow other added profit.

If the franchise is purchased, perhaps at open sale, the agent or public-servant characterization fails still further and there is better ground for holding the franchise as a license to do business — especially if the franchise be not completely monopolistic. A franchise may properly be regarded as in the nature of a license to do business and not at all a badge of office when a general need for the particular product or service has not been felt. Under such a pioneer condition, the people, not being dependent upon the company for comfort, convenience or reasonable cost of living, endure no hardship through irregularity or cessation of a service that is regarded as a luxury. The rates may be fixed in a general way by the ordinance, otherwise any charges may be valid which the company can impose and still get business. If such a license-franchise confers a monopoly, then it may be regarded as a privilege given to induce the recipient to develop the city and to give him some notable reward for early efforts — a cheap grant serving the same end as special town bonds, tax rebates, etc., which have often been made for private business, particularly railroad projects, in the hope of eventual gain to the public.

Naturally, when the private service company develops into a true public utility and becomes a necessary part of community life, the public regard in which the franchise is held may change and it may become more a mark of public function assumed than of mere license or inducement to transact a desired business. This changed attitude may be seen in a few rate cases when, in the early days through high rates or inferior service, the promoters had already earned their reward for pioneering or if failure to do so is traceable to lack of industry, skill or honesty.

In case the promoters have not secured a justifiable reward, then rates may still be fairly adjusted to permit this tardy recompense even though the regard of the early franchise has changed as noted. In recognition of the changed status it may usually be advisable to begin to pay off some of the accumulated deficit, capitalized franchise value, or "good will" which may have been floated in the days of private industry. · This writing off and retiring of stocks or bonds (or any equivalent increase of assets) may be regarded as a return to those who early risked much in the hope of reward or to secondary holders of stock who purchased with these hopes in mind.

This leads up to the proposition that even when a license-franchise or an inducement-franchise is hereafter given for early development of a private business, if there is any fair chance that it may develop to a true public utility, we can see that the promoters should not be able to make the development with an absolutely free hand but should have to bear in mind the effect of early policy on future status. If this proposition be admitted, then the contention still made by some utility officials that they may seek the pioneers' reward by permanent excessive capitalization, or variously as they see fit, is not harmonious with present tendency of public policy and corporate conscience. But harsh incrimination, against those men who have sought their reward in that fashion in the past, should not be made — for it must be admitted that the condemnation of such action springs from a growing public consciousness, or from an expanding horizon, or from improving ideals — however one desires to express it. In earlier days, when promoters generally sought legitimate rewards for large risks of unknown undertaking in ways not now approved, it was hardly called reprehensible — or even undesirable — except perhaps by the most advanced students of public policy. Then, too, there is now an increasing willingness to include in capitalization, the promoters proper rewards — which, however, are to be more openly paid as straight fees.

Short-term Franchises. — A few years ago there was an evident desire in some quarters to try the short-term franchise as a cure for the unfair entailments of unlimited-term and unrestricted grants. The franchises themselves may cost considerable sums and require the annual expenditures of large sums unproductively. Before money will be put into such ventures, investors must be assured either (1) that the rates will allow the amortization of the investment, above scrap value, during the life of the franchise or (2) that the percentage return will be large enough to cover the risk of not being able to sell the business at a fair price to some successor, when the franchise expires.

Short-term franchises would seem to discourage the most efficient and permanent installation for the widest geographical distribution of service or product and to encourage a rather temporary sort of organization with loose business methods. All such results, of course, are detrimental to adequate service and low rates. The public, in adding to the cost of franchises in this way, must then be willing to bear proportionately increased rates or inferior service — one or both of which may be necessary to guarantee a "reasonable return" on capital.

Indeterminate Franchise. — A remedy for the evils of both short-term (or limited-term) and unrestricted franchises seems possible in a development of the indeterminate franchise, like the non-expiring "operating agreements" provided for in the Wisconsin public-utilities law, coupled with wise supervision by a proper public-service commission. Under this law public-utility concerns may surrender their old franchises for "operating agreements" which hold good during the good behavior, so to speak, of the concerns. Provision is made for continuation of service and purchase of plant when the company is forced to transfer operation, so that the liabilities may be discharged. Some important sections of the Wisconsin law follow.

Section 1797t-3. The term "indeterminate permit" as used in this Act shall mean and embrace every grant, directly or indirectly from the State, to any street railway company, or power, right or privilege to own, operate, manage or control any street railway plant or equipment or any part thereof within this State, which shall continue in force until such time as the municipality shall exercise its option to purchase as provided in this Act or until it shall be otherwise terminated according to law. Ch. 578, 1907.

Section 1797t-2. Every license, permit or franchise hereafter granted to any street railway company shall have the effect of an indeterminate permit subject to the provisions of this Act, and subject to the provision that the municipality in which the major part of its property is situated may purchase the property of such street railway company actually used and useful for the convenience of the public at any time as provided herein, paying therefor just compensation to be determined by the commission and according to the terms and conditions fixed by said commission. Any such municipality is authorized to purchase such property, and every such street railway company is required to sell such property at the compensation and according to the terms and conditions determined by the commission as herein provided. Ch. 578, 1907.

Section 1797t-3. Any street railway company operating under an existing license, permit or franchise shall, upon filing at any time prior to the expiration of such license, permit or franchise, with the clerk of the municipality which granted such franchise and with the commission, a written declaration legally executed that it surrenders such license, permit or franchise, receive by operation of law, in lieu thereof, an indeterminate permit as provided in this Act; and such street railway company shall hold such permit under all the terms, conditions and limitations of this Act. The filing of such declaration shall be deemed a waiver by such street railway company of the right to insist upon the fulfillment of any contract theretofore entered into relating to any rate, fare, charge or service regulated by Sections 1797-1 to 1797-38 of the statutes, as amended. Ch. 578, 1907.

Section 1797m-74. (1) No license, permit or franchise shall be granted to any person, copartnership or corporation to own, operate, manage or control any plant or equipment for the production, transmission, delivery or furnishing of heat, light, water or power in any municipality where there is in operation under an indeterminate permit, as provided in this Act, a public utility engaged in similar service, and no telephone exchange for furnishing local service to subscribers within any village or city shall be installed in such village or city by any public utility, other than those already furnishing such telephone service therein, where there is in operation in such village or city a public utility engaged in similar service, without first securing from the commission a declaration after a public hearing of all parties interested, that public convenience and necessity require such second public utility. . . .

All licenses, permits and franchises to own, operate, manage, or control any plant or equipment for the production, transmission, delivery, or furnishing of heat, light, water, or power in any municipality, heretofore granted or attempted to be granted to any public utility by or by virtue of any ordinance pending or under consideration in the municipal council of any municipality at the time of the obtaining of an indeterminate permit by any other public utility operating therein, are hereby validated and confirmed and shall not be affected by the provisions of subsection 1 of Section 1797m–74 of the statutes. Ch. 499, 1907; ch. 546, 1911; ch. 14, 1911 (1).

(2) Any existing permit, license or franchise which shall contain any term whatsoever interfering with the existence of such second public utility is hereby amended in such a manner as to permit such municipality to grant an indeterminate permit for the operation of such second public utility pursuant to the provisions of this Act. Ch. 499, 1907.

(3) No municipality shall hereafter construct any such plant or equipment where there is in operation under an indeterminate permit as provided in this Act, in such municipality a public utility engaged in similar service, without first securing from the commission a declaration, after a public hearing of all parties interested, that public convenience and necessity require such municipal public utility. But nothing in this section shall be construed as preventing a municipality acquiring any existing plant by purchase or by condemnation as hereinafter provided. Ch. 499, 1907.

(4) Nothing in this section shall be construed so as to prevent the granting of an indeterminate permit or the construction of a municipal plant where the existing public utility is operating without an indeterminate permit as provided in this Act. Ch. 499, 1907.

Section 1797m–75. No license, permit or franchise to own, operate, manage or control any plant or equipment for the production, transmission, delivery or furnishing of heat, light, water or power shall be hereafter granted or transferred except to a corporation duly organized under the laws of the State of Wisconsin. Ch. 499, 1907.

Section 1797m–76. Every license, permit or franchise hereafter granted to any public utility shall have the effect of an indeterminate permit subject to the provisions of this Act, and subject to the provision that the municipality in which the major part of its property is situate may purchase the property of such public utility actually used and useful for the convenience of the public at any time as provided herein, paying therefor just compensation to be determined by the commission and according to the terms and conditions fixed by said commission. Any such municipality is authorized to purchase such property and every such public utility is required to sell such property at the value and according to the terms and conditions determined by the commission as herein provided. Ch. 499, 1907.

Section 1797m-77. Every license, permit, or franchise granted prior to July 11, 1907, by the State or by the common council, the board of aldermen, the board of trustees, the town or village board, or any other governing body of any town, village or city, to any corporation, company, individual, association of individuals, their lessees, trustees or receivers appointed by any court whatsoever, authorizing and empowering such grantee or grantees to own, operate, manage or control any plant or equipment, or any part of a plant or equipment within this State, for the conveyance of telephone messages, or for the production, transmission, delivery or furnishing of heat, light, water or power, either directly or indirectly, to or for the public, is so altered and amended as to constitute and to be an "indeterminate permit" within the terms and meaning of Sections 1797m-1 to 1797m-108, inclusive, of the statutes of 1898, and subject to all the terms, provisions, conditions and limitations of said sections 1797m-1 to 1797m-108, inclusive, and shall have the same force and effect as a license, permit, or franchise granted after July 11, 1907, to any public utility embraced in and subject to the provisions of said Sections 1797m-1 to 1797m-108, inclusive, except as provided by Section 1797m-80. Ch. 217, 1911 (1).

No franchise heretofore surrendered by any corporation of this State in the manner and within the time provided by Section 1797m-77, and no indeterminate permit based thereon, shall be declared invalid by reason of any defect, irregularity, or invalidity in such franchise whatsoever, provided that such franchises shall not have been obtained by fraud, bribery, or corrupt practices; that when such franchise was granted no officer of the municipality granting the same was directly or indirectly interested in such franchise or in the corporation obtaining same; and that the corporation having the same shall have prior to the surrendering of said franchise in good faith purchased or constructed any street or interurban railroad, water works, gas or electric light plant, or other public utility or any part thereof by such franchise authorized; and subject to the foregoing exceptions, every such franchise and permit is hereby legalized and confirmed. Ch. 499, 1907; ch. 180, 1909; ch. 596, 1911.

Section 1797m-78. Any public utility accepting or operating under any license, permit or franchise hereafter granted shall, by acceptance of any such indeterminate permit, be deemed to have consented to future purchase of its property actually used and useful for the convenience of the public by the municipality in which the major part of it is situate for the compensation and under the terms and conditions determined by the commission, and shall thereby be deemed to have waived the right of requiring the necessity of such taking to be established by the verdict of a jury, and to have waived all other remedies and rights relative to condemnation, except such rights and remedies as are provided in this Act. Ch. 499, 1907.

The Interference of Public Utilities. — A tendency is seen, in recent court decisions, not to demand an absolute freedom from injury to the plant of one public-utility concern from the operation of another public-utility service, if such freedom from injury would place prohibitive expense or great risk of accident on the concern complained of. Where two different utilities are maintained in a given territory, say an electric railway and a water supply, or an electric railway and a gas supply, or an electric railway and a telephone company, a certain minimum burden of damage may be caused by the mere juxtaposition of the two service plants, and this minimum in cases may not be eliminated without such restriction on the operations of one or the other utility as would amount to excessive expense and prohibitive rates.

Following the decision of the U. S. Circuit Court in the case of the Peoria (Ill,) Water Works Co., against the Central Railway Co.* (to restrain the latter from so operating its electric-railway system that damage to the pipes of the water company was possible), then the greater part of the burden of preventing and limiting damage would seem to fall on the concern last to enter the field (the "junior company" in legal parlance) whether complainant or defendant. At the same time, every reasonable coöperation to lessen the total burden of damage is made still encumbent on the utility company first in the field (the "senior company").

Similar reasoning is seen in the decision † of the Illinois Superior Court in the case of *Postal Telegraph-Cable Co., Western Union Telegraph Co.* and *Lake Shore & Michigan Southern R.R. Co. v. Chicago, Lake Shore & South Bend Ry. Co.*, to prevent the operation of a 6600-volt, single-phase railway line on account of certain electrical interferences with adjacent telephone and telegraph lines.

Where no negligence, malice or unskillfulness, on the part of a dependent public-utility concern, can be shown it would seem that the unavoidable minimum injury is, to use the legal phrase, *"damnum absque injuria"* — that is "damage without injury," as in the case of an accident for which no one is responsible. Neither utility can put the other out of business; the situation is to be considered from the standpoint of total public benefit, not mere convenience of the earlier concern.

* Engineering News, Nov. 17, 1910.
† Noted in Engineering News, Dec. 8, 1911, p. 631.

Cost of Changes to Avoid Interference. — Two rules have been proposed for dividing the expense of changes made in utility plants to avoid interferences, so that the prior company bears no burden of expense for the mere change, but is assessed for the cost of improvements.* The first rule is simple and reads as follows:

Charge the second company with the net cost of the new equipment not to exceed the capacity of the old amd make no credits for recovery value of material removed.

The second rule is more elaborate but possibly more generally applicable:

Charge the intruding company for all material, labor, supervision, etc., for the change, and credit it with all material recovered. Charge the intruding company an amount equal to the present worth of the future recovery value of the old plant if no changes had been made. (This will be a credit if the recovery value is a liability.) Credit it with an amount equal to the present worth of the future recovery value of the new plant. (This will be a charge if the recovery value is a liability.) When the new unit is of larger capacity than the old, these rules apply to amounts not exceeding the charges and credits for a unit of the same capacity, since that is the extent of the intruder's responsibility.

Improper Activities. — That conduct of certain utility corporations which has been most widely condemned (except possibly the evil of discrimination) is the exploiting of the public service by loading down the project with huge speculative promoters' profits in the shape of watered stock. In some cases there has been a direct and immediate extortion from the customers through earnings in excess of reasonable returns or through high rates for poor service. Investors have suffered from association with managements which have let plants run down.

For rank overcapitalizations no adequate excuse has been offered, though the offenses of years ago are perhaps mitigated by the general lack of condemnation of such practices. Possibly the extortions have arisen largely from failure of concerns to change their policy when their business was freed from the risks of pioneer days and strenuous competition, and when perhaps they tried to

* Discussed at length by H. H. Shearer and D. F. Norton in Engineering News, Mar. 23, and June 1, 1916.

recoup too many fold their earlier losses. Perpetuation of lax managements may be traced in the last analysis, perhaps to the eagerness of the investors to secure high rates of return without scrutinizing the conduct of promoters and managers who promised much; the investors failed to recognize the reasons for returns above ordinary interest and to realize that attention is a necessary safeguard.

Undue Discrimination. — The improper activity most closely related to rate making is broadly covered by the term *"discrimination."* Since an utility serves all comers, the several customers are entitled to the same equitable treatment. Lower rates to one customer under the same conditions, or any rebates to that end, are contrary to the spirit by which it is agreed that a quasi-public corporation should be governed. When customers are attracted by public convenience or necessity (rather than by commercial advantages) the rates become more and more based on cost of service, and less and less on what the traffic will bear. This view would indicate that there should be no change of rate, no discrimination, according to the ultimate use of the product, such as still prevails in some places where the same gas is sold at different prices for lighting and heating. Special conditions, however, may render this sort of discrimination equitable from a broad point of view sometimes. For instance, electricity for heating may be sold in some places at reduced rates and yet there may be no discrimination against lighting users because of the different hours of use and because of the great benefit to all in spreading the service over the greatest number of hours, and keeping the equipment busy day and night. The benefits of such discrimination should be open to all comers.

There may fairly be different rates to customers of the same size but under different working conditions. Thus a factory securing electric power from central stations, but only in times of lightest station load, is a more profitable customer than one taking power at all times and contributing to the peak load. There is little investment charge in the rates that may be made for real nonpeak load and the rates may be very low and still not be discriminatory or in conflict with "cost of service" principles. However, in building up a non-peak business, the public-utility corporation is only remotely performing a public service and is dependent on the industry and business ability of its officials or directors. It is incumbent on the corporation then, if ever, to charge all that the non-peak customers will pay; it is its legitimate concern to make the rate for non-peak customers sufficiently attractive to get the business. The general obligation to the public is to furnish no off-peak power below cost, i.e., at a loss which must be repaid by peak-load customers. Yet there may be rare cases where the initial off-peak business is carried for a very short time at a small loss more than made up as this sort of business is increased.

A broad policy on the part of any utility management would dictate, in making new rates for non-peak service, giving equal opportunities to all its customers — or at least not enabling one to secure through the service rates an undue commercial advantage over another. For instance, if the cost of off-peak service to one customer is reduced to secure certain new business, then the rates for such service to other customers of the same class should be reduced to the same level.

Many persons believe that in any one case uniform rates to customers of all types should prevail, on the theory that a public utility must not expect to make every customer or every class pay an equal profit. But, at the present, as the cost of service is usually not the same to different classes of customers and in effect varies largely with amount of service given, it seems like a mild form of discrimination to force the heavy-service class to furnish the profit on a small-load class.

Utilities in Politics. — Political domination and highwaymen's methods of preventing competition need little comment here. They have had their local effects of altering rates and of securing more business at first while alienating public respect and confidence and ultimately losing business. In the train of such actions comes a magnified public demand for abolishing such things as secrecy of accounts, protection of contracts, private selection of employees, and everything which tends to bring public officials under undue influence of the corporation.

Preventing Overcapitalization. — A company will be in strongest position, and unhampered in meeting any local competition which it may desire to head off legitimately, if its stocks, bonds and other evidences of indebtedness represent only tangible elements of physical property. In a young utility, of course, there has not been time to secure out of earnings funds to amortize plant-development expenses, while business-development and all the other intangible elements in worth are still being established. Even in many of the older utilities, this amortization has not yet been possible and, the accumulated deficits between actual and reasonable returns on investment remain in the "going value" of the concern.

The attitude of commissions in general has not yet gone as far as to insist on a complete eventual amortization of intangibles. While that is not impending at the moment, yet, considering the interests of future generations and the impossibility of our comprehending their unknown problems, it would seem advisable to reduce so far as possible the burdens they will inherit.

Prominent bankers, in laying down the requirements which must be satisfied before utility bonds can be carried as a safe investment and in discussing the causes of their past financial weaknesses, have emphasized the necessity of eliminating high capitalization — which is indirectly advocating the complete amortization of intangibles.

High capitalization tends to obscure, to the general public view at least, the size of the true return on actual investment in service, making it seem small when in reality it is large. On such accounts, there is a marked tendency to pay no attention to return on stocks and other securities, but to consider the return on a probable legitimate investment or "fair value."

Looked at from another point of view, it is reasonable to demand that the promoters and directors furnish a considerable proportion of the funds needed for the work they propose to control. Any man is most careful of his own money. Moreover, in corporate organizations the liability of a stockholder for the concern's debts is limited by the size of his investment so that the combination of large bond issues and small amounts of stock offers greater encouragement for mismanagement.

In direct contrast, it seems to be generally regarded as more economical to use, up to the safe limit, funds secured from bonds rather than from stock on account of the lower interest rate sought by the former. There may be a certain amount of fact behind this belief, but seemingly the benefit has been somewhat overestimated. The smaller the proportion of capital stock to total investment the greater the risk of losing it all in case of foreclosure by bondholders and the greater the per cent return that would be demanded. Also, the greater the preponderance of bond money, the greater is the risk of not realizing the face of bonds on foreclosure, and therefore the higher the probable bond interest. The common proportions of a utility's capitalization spoken of today are 40% stock and 60% bonds; stated another way the face of the bonds is 150% of the par value of stock — which sounds much different. This ratio, however, is a most variable condition, and is fixed by judgment rather than definite analysis.

Broad Public Policy. — The most successful public-utility corporations of the future seemingly will be those who hold to a very broad public policy as to what constitutes adequate service, reasonable profit and local obligations. There are some utility concerns today which are dominated by men attempting to run their affairs in the light of such a policy, but suffering still from public misapprehension and suspicion which prevent the best service and greatest profits. Eventually they must approach their desired status if they have sincere convictions and patience, though they may first pass through many storms of abusive misunderstanding. There will always be a disgruntled minority in any community to serve as a thorn in the side of the management, but this can only have a healthy effect in the realization that every lapse will be recorded, every move scrutinized and every motive searched. Meritorious effort and unimpeachable character can stand such opposition.

By broad public policy is meant no mere ostentatious display of solicitude for the "dear people" but a deep-seated willingness to pursue certain aims all unseen and unapplauded. For instance, directors and their hired officials will not only court and kindly receive criticisms but really sift them to the bottom and impress the originators with some definite result rather than mere agreeable assurances. Further, any increase in return which they think reasonable, they will discuss frankly before the public and meet and disarm criticism rather than seek to crush it out. Increased profit they will seek as the result of securing new economies in operation rather than increased rates. New economies are impossible, declare many utility managers; but the arts progress and some bright man stumbles on a neglected point every few years that makes a new equilibrium possible at lower costs.

An Utility Should Relieve Public Burdens. — Where there is any question about the extent of obligation of a franchise holder, it would seem in wise accord with a good policy to concede the rights and privileges of the public if a burden is actually placed on that public in any way by the exercise of franchise rights, though the cost of such burdens may well be charged to operation. For instance, the presence of street-railway tracks in a street may be destructive to a pavement ordinarily adequate; then it might be fair to require the company to put down and maintain a higher class paving between tracks and for a foot or two on both sides but the costs thereof should go against capital and operation. The electric railway may stir up such a dust as would not rise under vehicle traffic, whereupon the company might be required fairly to sprinkle its tracks and perhaps the street beyond.

If profits are fairly high, then the acceptance of cost burdens which unduly and unfairly burden the public would in most cases cause hardly appreciable reduction in profit and this probably would be overcome by extra business turned to the utility through the good will of the public. Such a situation if properly aired should tend to win public confidence and thereby be worth more than the cost. If profits should be appreciably reduced a wise regulating commission would place the burden on customers rather than stockholders.

Reduce Company Burdens. — The ready assumption of burdens properly laid on an utility as noted above is not to be advertised as a piece of generosity on the part of the corporation toward the public, for the disturbance occasioned to ordinary municipal maintenance by the utility is the basis of the burden. On the other hand there is an equal counterpart obligation on the part of municipal officials not to demand questionable obligations where no real burden is placed on the municipality and when an increase in rates or decrease in earnings is the means of relieving the people of ordinary tax burdens. Where such a demand is made on the public utility it can more successfully be resisted if the concern has been following a comprehensive policy of publicity and has received public confidence. Various events have repeatedly demonstrated that the public as a whole will demand fair play and will follow any strong leader, public or private official, in demanding security against political oppression.

Secure Full Publicity. — Publicity of accidents, plans, statistics is a feature of a broad public policy that may almost be called a local obligation and, if made to cover everything not legitimately

detrimental to business practice, is generally conceded best calculated to win public confidence and to prevent charges of improper activity of officials or subordinate employees.

Competition or Monopoly. — It is known that, up to a certain point at least, there is a possibility of increment in profits
by a combination of similar or competing businesses. This is a
great cause of monopoly, along with those prospects which stimulate men to strenuous and continued effort. But this is not the
only recognized cause of mergers. There seems to be an inherent
desire, on the part of men responsible for certain results, to prefer to do things continuously in an easier and more efficient way
and the useless duplication of plant and effort must always appeal
to them as wasteful. Moreover, where the utility is one of communication like the telephone or telegraph the more completely
it unites all possible people who may ever desire to get into communication, the better it performs its function. Competing communication systems segregate the peoples, making access more
difficult and expensive, and oppose the motive of the invention.

Turning aside from what possibly may seem academic views
of monopoly, into actual practice, it is a common experience that
low rates for adequate and satisfactory service have not resulted
from direct competition in the long run. In theory, and under
well established rate regulation, there seems little justification
for competition if an utility lives up to its opportunities. Where
the utilities duplicate equipment so that neither is used to the
extent that one alone could be, there is at least a condition tending toward inefficiency, high rates, poor returns and instability
of enterprise. The logical result is failure of one or the other
enterprise or, before that happens, a consolidation which carries an
extra burden of early investment that must be liquidated out of
earnings, repudiated by the present generation of directors, or
saddled upon succeeding generations of customers.

Some Results of Monopoly. — We might be led to expect that,
with the suppression of competition under regulation, we would
lose a powerful stimulus for progress in an art. But "regulation"
implies that an utility would not be stimulated to continue in
antiquated fashion for it would be allowed to earn money for
renewing obsolete and worn-out machinery and should be encouraged to earn constant or growing super-profits' only by the continual attainment of new economies and improved services.

Technical progress in the arts and sciences involved is not actually lost by suppression of competition for there still will be seen many manufacturing concerns striving to secure the monopoly's trade in cars, motors, generators, engines, turbines, rails, wire, poles, ties, pumps, pipe, meters, etc., and apparatus of conspicuous merit will win its way.

In the telephone industry there seems to be a closer approach to universal monopoly, for the largest holding company of local exchanges is the great toll-line owner and in control of the largest manufacturer of such apparatus. Yet there has been a steady improvement of equipment and service together with a reduction in cost of service of fully half in 20 years. There is evidence that it is impossible to so monopolize the manufacturing business but what an outside idea of conspicuous and radical merit will batter its way in. In the case of the telephone industry, the monopoly's allied manufacturer goes out after the business in private and isolated equipments, which brings such direct and immediate competition that stagnation cannot obtain.

Lessons from Competition. — There are many cases where utilities have reduced rates under stress of competition (particularly the competition of municipally owned plants) and when there was strong presumption that it would not have been done otherwise. These have occurred under no regulation, with reduced dividends and where for one reason or another the company had not maintained a broad policy of reducing its dead capital and putting itself in trim to give voluntarily the service and rates which competition forced. These cases teach many lessons. It is wise even where there is no regulation to secure depreciation, obsolescence and retirement compensation out of rates. Where the earnings in early stages in utility development do not permit profitable rates, if business growth is to be secured it is necessary that the public be frankly informed of the defaulted retirance and amortization and the necessity of carrying dead capital and accumulated deficits a little longer. If all this is done there will be no great danger from unfair competition for the private utility is in good shape to meet it.

Potential Competition a Constant Restraint. — While uurestricted direct competition in public services has signally failed to be as broadly beneficial as wise public regulation and has usually resulted in ultimate consolidation and return to higher rates, yet indirect competition still prevails to limit rates or to fix quality of service. Thus with electric lighting the combined factors of cost and convenience have to equal the cost-convenience rating of common gas, acetylene, or petroleum lighting. Central-station electric power has to meet, on such a basis, power from individual gas, gasoline, oil or alcohol engines, from isolated plants that use cheaper fuel, than do the central stations, under boilers or in gas producers, or from nearby water powers. Local electric transportation, should it become unattractive or unduly expensive, would be supplanted by motor busses, motor cars, boats or even horse vehicles, and for short distances more people would walk than ride.

Lighten Future Burdens. — At times in the preceding remarks, mention has been made of the tendency to impose conditions on future generations which make life and business more burdensome than is fair. The idea therein is that even if our present depredations of stored natural resources were wholly justifiable, the most we should do is to consume. We should not waste or mortgage the future. We should not saddle on the future generation the discharge of our obligations for machinery and improvements which will be non-existent or obsolescent when the burden of debt is discharged.

Some persons contend that the bonds of public-utility concerns, secured by property and rights in public ways, should be counted in with municipal debt in any estimate of the burden placed on the next generation for public improvement. Such contention seems hardly justifiable if depreciation of equipment, retirement of bond issues and cancelation of intangible values are provided for simultaneously from earnings — as by trust and sinking-fund or retirance safeguards. A concern so protected is not a mere legacy of debt to posterity, since the investment may be returned to stock- and bondholders. The menace of debt comes when the obligation to pay is not balanced by actual cash or tangible property in hand, assets which in fact, as well as in theory, can be traded to discharge the obligation. Then the mere existence of interest-bearing public-utility bonds or other evidences of investment seems hardly a menace but rather an evidence of capital at work. If the obligation is discharged the capital will not long stay idle. The owner will seek for it a new activity — new investments and new obligations but with the same old burden of interest on society as a whole.

As an example of a real and common debt menace, there may be cited those cases where a state or city issues 50-year bonds for improvements (roads and pavements, for instance) that will last only ten years. Then, ordinarily, the material and labor literally are frittered away (as in dust) while the city or state has failed to collect more than a fifth of the sums really due — leaving on a future generation the burden of our pleasures and follies.

No Call for Industrial Legacies. — On the other hand, it seems hardly justifiable, with our ignorance of the great developments of science and industry 25 or 50 years hence, to conduct our public utilities so that plants without proper counterbalancing obligation equal to immediate tangible value, may be passed along to succeeding generations as a pure industrial legacy from our own times. Each generation works under peculiar conditions, and aid which an earlier people thinks advisable may have to be thrown aside by their successors. Each generation should pay for the equipment it makes obsolete.

It also seems probable that in the future public sentiment will demand that inroads into limited natural resources for public utilities be accompanied by economical consumption, the complete utilization of waste products and the substitution of unlimited supplies of other materials where possible without greatly increased cost — as in the case of alcohol (from vegetation) for petroleum, solar heat and water power for coal, portland-cement concrete and clay products, for timber, etc.

The Vicious Cost Spiral. — Beyond all the problems recalled above, there is another very different in nature but equally momentous. The same problem, as it hits the great mass of people, is known as that of "the high cost of living." It is a fact that living expenses, in America at least, have risen extraordinarily in the last two decades. Even discounting the greater present-day comforts, the more exacting tastes of all classes of people, etc., the cost of living under the old standards would be much greater today. Naturally, this fact has been the basis of demand for increased wages at various periods. Their justification to a considerable extent under existing industrial and economic conditions has been generally recognized and reasonable advances have been made. But all these advances in wages have increased the cost of production. There has resulted a vicious spiral of high prices and high wages, higher prices and higher wages, still higher prices and more wages yet. This is an unstable process that continues indefinitely until a panic or some catastrophe disorganizes production, throws labor out of employment, and sends prices of material and labor tumbling down, but only to be started on the upward path again.

Preventing Higher Costs. — How is this unfortunate course of rising costs to be checked? Not by mere legislative enactment, for the laws of industry and human nature are extraconstitutional and inexorable. If a rising cost of food and necessary living supplies is the cause of the demands for larger wages and in turn later are increased by higher wages, then it would be a logical step to increase the efficiency of labor, to increase the production of raw materials, and to lessen the cost of manufacture into supplies. The improvements that can come in these ways require such a fundamental readjustment of existing schemes, that progress will be slow. Increased production is secured by the medium of higher prices through the market relations of supply and demand; supply manufacturers will have to compensate for this by improving their methods and details. The efficiency enthusiasts have seen here their opportunity and are, some of them, vociferously proclaiming the wonders that can be performed.

Utilities are, for the most part, the great general exceptions among industrial enterprises, in that the cost of product or service to the consumer has gone down continually. This is more true in gas and electricity works than in water supply for instance, due to the importance of machinery and the development of high-speed or large-size low-output-cost apparatus in the two first cases and the large investment in watersheds, aqueducts, mains, reservoirs, dams, filters, etc., in the third case. Railways and electric roads perhaps have an intermediate place because of the great costs of labor, particularly in electric railways where it may amount to 50% of the total annual expenditures.

Reduce Unit Labor Costs. — All this emphasizes the need of making labor more effective, for in those utilities where cost of labor is a large factor in cost of service, the limit is about or quite reached below which cost of service to patrons cannot go (without marked decrease in wage rates). Reduction of wages may be expected only if the cost of family supplies drops. Securing a greater productivity of labor alone is a difficult and delicate problem. Here enters study of the extent to which welfare work, coöperative buying and insurance, medical supervision, etc., are economical propositions. Here enter the labor union, the uniform wage scale, the closed shop, the stifling of personal effort, etc.

Every man of the utility force, from the president down, can well ask himself if he is really giving the effort contracted for and paid for. There would be great good from such a decided quickening of the conscience of every man in utility circles — from highest to lowest. "Economy" needs to be a watchword with each of these thousands of persons; all-around economy is most important in arresting the upward trend in the cost of labor and supplies. The "dignity of labor" has been often stated; we now need to hear more of the dignity of economy. However, expenditures in securing true economy are not to be cut off by a mere penny-wise policy which saves today but penalizes tomorrow.

Cause of Inefficient Labor. — Why is much labor less effective in this country today than once? Perhaps it lies in the very evident discontent of labor, and if so the question resolves itself into these: Why is labor discontented? Is there good reason? Can contentment take its place?

There is some evidence that the large degree of political liberty attained, and the advancement of broader human rights, has not been accompanied by increasing industrial freedom. Speaking of conditions in this country alone, it is not debatable that workers very largely are more dependent than ever before on large and impersonal organizations for employment, wages, necessities of life, transportation, and even pleasures. This is a condition notoriously and naturally depressing and in great contrast with the situation a half century ago and less.

To promote satisfaction in daily work, there are certain easily recognizable aids which may to a large extent offset the depressing effects of employment by massive organization, and of the present extreme division of labor with its monotony in repetitive tasks automatically performed.

Satisfactions of Labor. — The first of these aids is complete personal industrial freedom of the worker to select his occupation and employer (within the limits of his own skill and the willingness of some one to use it), freedom to earn all that his skill and efforts can command, freedom to advance in his trade or occupation, freedom from any tyrannical dictates of other workmen which may hold him down to average performance and pay.

A second aid is increased pleasure in the daily tasks of livelihood — through the sense of power that comes from exercise of muscle and mind to some definite end, through a knowledge of enough elementary science to see a reason for each process. It is generally supposed that the monotony of repetitive tasks, as in a modern factory system, is death to this pleasure. For some types of minds this evidently is the case but it is not so for others, as psychological research has begun to show. The square peg should not be in the round hole.

More or less allied with the aid of a suitable occupation to greater satisfaction in and effectiveness of labor, is the pleasure of completed accomplishment. There seems to be more appeal to an inherent creative faculty if the daily tasks are such that some definite thing is seen to be made or some definite part completed of a larger task on which many are employed. It is this appeal that makes the higher professions attractive fields of labor. Some of the extremes to which labor has been divided in mass production under modern factory organization are commonly credited with preventing a workman's vision of a completed creation, but there is little real knowledge of the soundness of this theory. Possibly the studies of practical psychologists and sociologists, noted above, may illuminate this matter also.

A fourth play of the usually unrecognized emotions, tending to greater interest in daily tasks, is a sense of competition and co-operation — contest and team work. It is another, and less openly exhibited manifestation of the world of sport — the zest of a foot race or of a broad jump on one hand, the thrill of a ball game on the other hand. Here, again, it would seem as though an extreme division of labor, as in the factory, would keep team work to a minimum though perhaps would not stifle the sense of competition. The contribution of each worker toward the ultimate completed machine or other marketable product may be lost in the general assembly so that, while many work to a common end, each knows not what the other has contributed.

Not last in this or any list, which one would draw up of the intangible elements in employment that promote mental satisfaction and personal efficiency are risk and adventure. The sea has always lured many to its occupations, the army and navy recruits greatly increase on intimations of international difficulties. An adventurous occupation must involve risk or it ceases to be adventurous and becomes merely varied. The danger must be such that there is a gambler's chance of escaping it and some compensation in pay, or glory, or in sport. The appeal of business is much the same; there is the chance to win or lose, to make or break.

Utility Labor in an Enviable Position. — There may be various other elements which can be set down, but with one exception enough has been said to show some important lines which may be scrutinized. This last is possibly dependent on the existence of most of the other elements outlined and it arises from their appeal. These are pride and loyalty — pride in the trade or occupation or profession, loyalty to fellow workers, and to employers. If a gainful pursuit yields most of the higher satisfactions already noted there must be some sense of pride in such a livelihood. And least of all, there can be a just pride in being an independent self-sustaining citizen — a supporter of organized government, not a beggar from the hand of charity. Any employer in whose works the various satisfactions of the workers are cultivated, even though modern business dictates that it is a physical impossibility to know each man in the organization, must find loyalty in the men — to the extent that he probably has earned it.

All the public utilities are in an enviable position, among industrial organizations, for increasing the contentment of employees. The tasks are not often as repetitive as in a factory and there is a maximum of play for muscular force and judgment. The tasks are complete in themselves and the toiler sees his work as needful and creative. There is no end of possible competition between fellow workers to do better than each other. All see easily how their function is added to all the others to make the service real, and frequently the coöperation is hand to hand and mind to mind under the stimulating stress of emergency. Few lines of public service are without some danger and some adventure; few can be so hedged as that it is not necessary to strive for greater safety to all, for larger gains to employer and employee, and for better convenience to the customers.

The utility concerns should recognize the inherent advantage they have and seek to perpetuate it. The advantage is real but it can be neglected and finally wasted.

Higher Rates or Greater Economy. — Marked evidence is seen among many utility officials of more or less organized effort to increase rates all along the line. Of course, if their business is well organized, if scientific study of avenues of economy in materials and of productivity of labor is maintained and in spite of all advice they can see no improvement, there is every justification of educating the public and persuading the regulating commissions that higher rates are needed. But there have been some cases of vociferous demand for higher rates to prevent calamity, where equal energy applied at home to the study of organization of men and use of materials and labor would go a great way toward the desired goal of larger dividends.

Scarcity of Funds for Investment. — At various times there has been a manifest difficulty in finding the money at satisfactory rates of interest for new industrial enterprises of any sort. Particularly has this been true off and on since 1907. The cause of this is closely linked with the cause of higher cost of living (or the cost of higher living perhaps) and the course suggested as the logical attack of the one will automatically bring relief from the other. For instance, if the efficiency of labor is increased by better organization of the men and their work, by increased satisfaction in working, and by more conscientious effort from all, operating costs will go down and a surplus will be available for extensions or the better dividends needed to attract capital.

The capital that any one man can invest in gainful enterprise is necessarily the surplus of his earnings over his expenses; the more economical he is the more capital he has available. A nation is made up of such individuals and the total capital available for new enterprises and extensions of old ones is the sum of the surplus of all the individuals great and small. This is often disregarded by those who discourse on the evil times which they hold prevail.

Just why there is such a close relation between lack of individual savings and industrial stagnation, may be seen from another view of conditions which exist when the people largely live up to their income. The more money there is spent in unnecessary living expenses the more people there are engaged in supplying these fancied needs, and the fewer there are available for work of industrial extensions — as well as the less money available for investment. Under such conditions labor tends to become high-priced and inefficient. "Easy-money" and "sure" jobs cultivate further extravagant expenditures and small surplusses. The evil effects pyramid up. The dignity of economy needs to be accentuated now and humility in labor for each and all, high and low.

Better Public Relations. — Very few of the public utilities of the country enjoy the confidence and approval of the public which they serve, to an extent which both managers and customers would like. In a few cases, the hostility or coldness is perhaps absolutely unmerited; but the author has come in personal contact with the service of a few companies where there was every reason to expect harmonious public relations on account of good engineers, well-known managers, good earnings, welfare work for employees, etc., etc., but where the services were irregular and inadequate, the employees in contact with the public uncivil, the result of complaints unseen and the whole ultimate effect disappointing — not to say exasperating.

This experience has been duplicated by others in various quarters, and naturally the question arises "How is it possible?" Perhaps it is due to an earlier unsavory history kept alive by petty grievances. Perhaps, in spite of the men of prestige (or is it mere self-advertisement?) in the offices, there is a lack of company loyalty, or a lack of opportunity for leaders to rise out of the ranks, and other matters of short-sightedness and mismanagement.

Better Ideas of Service Needed. — Surely in many towns it is seen that no one there has learned the meaning of the word "service"; the mayor seems to regard himself as a political sun around which the municipal constellation moves, instead of considering himself only the first servant of the people; the policeman seems to think that he is there to keep the citizens out of mischief more than to help them preserve organized order, safety, and government; the street-car motorman and conductor give the impression that the customers exist only to keep the cars running and to furnish a job; the electric-station and water-service meter reader comports himself with the air of one who is dispensing great favors rather than making a necessary intrusion to keep the service up.

The American people from top to bottom could well be schooled to greater humility. All are servants of one another, and life is happy and successful in proportion to the service given others. Service and humility are not degrading; indeed they are attributes of the noblest characters, while selfishness and arrogance mark the person of inferior ideals. Such remarks are ordinarily very trite, but are repeated here for behind them are lessons that countless utility officials and employees may well learn.

CHAPTER X

PROBLEMS OF RAILWAY RATES

Problems of Specific Utilities. — In attempting the application of the preceding general discussions to particular utility fields, and in reviewing certain specific problems of the different services — with which these studies will be brought to a close — attention is naturally first directed to the railways. This is logical, for the railroads of the country were among the earliest of the present great public utilities and today constitute the largest group. The legislation aimed to effect their proper regulation has been to a large extent the prototype of all American utility-regulation acts, and the oldest and most representative general regulating bodies grew out of " railroad commissions." The leading expositions of the Supreme Court now broadly applied to various utility cases were — with a few notable exceptions — given in railroad litigation.

In spite of railroad regulation furnishing the foundation for the present structure of utility control, much less has been done in establishing a logical arrangement of rates, in place of the old inherited complication of transportation charges, than in setting up scientifically-adjusted prices for water, gas, electric and other services. The following paragraphs will show the reason for this; in brief, tremendous difficulties arise to the arranging of any logical scheme at all, on account of the infinite number of different services rendered the shippers of freight.

This discussion of matters affecting railroad rates is not intended as a complete exposition of how railway rates are or should be made. There are plenty of works on that subject without adding to the number now. But enough can be shown, in comparatively small space, to demonstrate to men in all other utility fields the sort of complications that enter because of the larger areas and more diverse communities served in a multiplicity of peculiar ways.

Magnitude of the Railway Industry.* — There were, in 1915, 257,569 miles of railway line in the country, and the total trackage had risen to 391,142 miles. There were in service 65,099 locomotives (14,700 in passenger service) and 2,507,997 cars (55,705 in passenger service). The securities behind this property totalled $21,127,959,078. The total number of revenue passengers per year was 976,303,602 (32,384,247,563 carried one mile) and the tons of revenue freight were 1,802,018,177 (276,830,302,723 carried one mile). These figures are of such great magnitude that, standing alone, they become nearly meaningless; their significance is shown only by comparison. For each 1000 persons in the country (total population taken as 100,399,000) there were about 3.9 miles of track, 25 cars, and $210,000 in nominal property. The average number of rides per capita had risen to 10.5 per year and the tons of freight moved per capita per year had mounted to 18. The total income was $2,956,193,202 or $29.50 per capita; the operating expenses $2,088,682,956 or $20.80 per capita. (The passenger and freight business in this year, 1914–15, was slightly less than in 1913–14.)

Beginnings of the Railway Industry. — The vast industry, whose outstanding size has been lightly touched upon, is about 90 years old. The first American line, the Quincy " Granite Road " was a mere horse tramway laid down in 1826 for getting granite for the Bunker Hill monument from Quincy down to a wharf on the Neponset River.† But the franchise was purchased in 1871 by the Old Colony R. R. Co., and eventually entered the New York, New Haven & Hartford system.

The South Carolina R. R. (a stock concern) was formally opened in Charleston, Jan. 15, 1830. Pennsylvania had a road in 1827, and Maryland and South Carolina followed in 1828. A part of the New York Central, the Mohawk Valley R. R., from Albany to Schenectady, was chartered in 1825. On it a steam train had a trial trip Mar. 5, 1831 with the famous locomotive " De Witt Clinton." Stimulated by the success of the British

---

* Deduced from the 1914–15 annual "Statistics of Railways," of the Interstate Commerce Commission.

† See "Railroads, Their Origin and Problems," New York, 1878, by C. F. Adams, Jr. For other early history read, "Railroad Transportation," 1886, by A. T. Hadley.

steam-traction experiments, the Boston & Lowell, Boston & Providence, and the Boston & Worcester roads were chartered, built and operated in 1830–1835. These were all opened about the same time and were the beginning of the present New York, New Haven & Hartford system.

The whole railway development in these early years and since has been in private hands; in 1915 the Federal government built its first railroad line — the Alaskan Ry. — though in 1905 it purchased the Panama R. R. as a construction adjunct to the Panama Canal. It happened that at the time when the practicability of steam locomotion became demonstrated, and the possibilities in a new transportation service began to be dimly foreseen, sufficient public funds could not be raised for railway construction and organization. A certain amount of public construction and operation was tried at the outset and did precede the general organization of the industry in private hands. For instance, the Michigan Central and Michigan Southern were started as state lines but the financial depression of 1837 forced their sale. The notable Western and Atlantic line from Atlanta to Chattanooga was started by the State of Georgia. Public initiative was not strong enough to override the first financial barriers, but public aid was not hard to obtain; private enterprise was stimulated by obvious opportunities for grand profits. The resulting unsavory history of early railroad promotion was but a repetition of the old country-wide scandals in canal building prior to 1835.

Development of Governmental Regulation. — A fundamental public interest in railways has always been assumed to exist, though in the early days apparently it was not held to be a matter of prime importance. Public regard for railways first was like that for the previous " common carriers " — with such later limitations to the use of independent vehicles as were found necessarily to go with faster transportation, special track and a more complete network of lines. That railways, by depending on the public for business and offering their facilities to the general public, thereby take their property out of the class of private property and relinquish the right of complete control, was a principle of common law unmistakably enunciated by Chief Justice Waite in the historic case of *Munn v. Illinois* (94 U. S. 113) early referred to in these pages.

Power of Eminent Domain an Early Mark. — The evidence of
public interest in railways goes back much beyond 1876, the date
of the Munn case, for the public nature of the business was early
recognized. It was seen to be essential to the development of
land transportation lines that the power to condemn and appro-
priate property be invoked. The railway right of way had to
be a continuous strip of land carved out of hundreds or thousands
of smaller parcels — else the owner of any one parcel could delay
or kill a project by refusal to sell. If more than a few held out
for extortionate prices the prospective first cost — and annual
fixed charges — on the proposed line became an excessive burden
on the public. But under American constitutional principles,
the right of eminent domain conferred on railroads was a mark
of sovereignty — a public function possible only for definite
public good. If the state did not choose to condemn the land
and build the carrier line, it could delegate this power to a concern
created by it for public purposes — and only to such.

All such matters show that the right of public supervision
of railways, though long unemployed effectively, has been regarded as inherent, fundamental, inalienable. This principle was
enunciated by the courts in the cases of railways as highways and
common carriers; it has been applied by analogy to any utility
service taking on public interest — the degree of control depending on the extent and depth of public concern. This may develop
the possibility of a closer public dictation of railway management than is lawful in utilities where no rights of condemnation
and appropriation have been conferred — like most gas, water
and electric-transmission-line companies.

Early Beginnings of Public Regulation. — Public control of
railroads was not a live matter for about a quarter century after
railway expansion really started. The great aim was to get the
roads built. The public then did not realize the magnitude of
the systems that might develop nor did it quickly appreciate the
power of natural monopolies. Competition, " the soul of trade,"
was popularly regarded as the complete and satisfactory regulator of all business, although it had been pointed out abroad that
" where combination was possible, competition was impossible."

The awakening came nearly simultaneously in America and
Europe. The British Parliament had felt for years that there
was something indefinitely ominous hanging over the country

because of the growth and consolidation of the country's railways. Finally in 1872 a Parliament committee reported that the bogey was only a natural consolidation of lines which once it had been supposed would continue to compete. It was judged that consolidation was inevitable and required only the safeguard of some public supervision over the railways. In 1873 a board of commissioners was created to guard the rights of private persons, to prevent trouble between roads, to insure interchange of traffic, and to prevent discrimination.

In America the early years of pioneer development were succeeded by a period (from about 1860) of destructive competition and oppressive discrimination. The flagrant injustice meted out by arrogant railway officials, who openly declared themselves to be above public scrutiny, stimulated two quite different plans for regaining the upper hand for the public.

In the one case there was ready at hand a vigorous organization of farmers known as the " Grange," * whose members were revolting at the treatment afforded by the railways.

The Grangers' vitriolic attacks on railway officials broke open the situation in the West and secured the enactment of drastic laws interfering with the asserted rights of common carriers and subjecting the roads to the control of state commissioners. The early laws were crude and the first commissioners were necessarily inexperienced; both laws and men were pitted against organization, wealth and brains. Looking back, it is phenomenal that any considerable success was attained. Possibly the roads overreached themselves in their first arrogant independence — for after they finally bowed to the Supreme Court's affirmation of the right of state control they proved more formidable in attack than ever before.

---

* The "Order of Patrons of Husbandry" or the "Grange," as it was commonly called, was founded in 1867 by O. H. Kelley, of the (then) U. S. Bureau of Agriculture. It was the most successful of several attempts of farmers to organize for mutual benefit. The society's greatest development was from 1872 on, in Iowa where 100,000 members were enrolled in two years. In 1875 there were a million members in the country. Later its power waned with the rise of the more political "Farmers Alliance." The aims of the Grange were social and technical as well as political. It aimed to disseminate good technical information about crops, cultivation, markets and transportation. It hoped also to organize the farmers for coöperative buying and selling, to oppose monopolistic railways, banks, implement makers and produce speculators.

Meanwhile things were working out differently in the East. For instance, Massachusetts organized its "advisory" commission in 1869 * and gave it but one weapon — publicity. To support itself before the public, careful study had to be made of any complaints and a report stood on its merits. In 1876 the Massachusetts publicity measure was completed by the imposition of uniform accounts and complete reports — a development toward which the railways materially coöperated.

The two movements gradually consolidated. It began to be realized that it was an exaggeration of fear which the Grangers had had for the " money barons," the " eastern sharks," and the " bloated bondholders," — to quote common epithets. In 1877 the Illinois Commission began to adopt the advisory and conciliatory tactics of the Massachusetts Commission; that year Iowa replaced its Granger law with one more of the Massachusetts type. From then thè influence of publicity was widely recognized; the more speedy action secured under some conditions by commission interference, however, was not forgotten.

The Interstate Commerce Commission Established. — State regulation of railways has necessarily been of comparatively minor importance as by the commerce clause of the Federal Constitution, all transportation of persons and goods from one state to another, or going abroad, is under the exclusive control of the Federal Government. This clause arose from the impelling necessity of facilitating commerce between the colonies freed from England. Indeed it was the pressing demands for unfettered commerce that drew the constitutional convention together when the local interests and jealousies threatened to override the other grounds for unification.

The more or less successful attempts at state regulation of railways only emphasized the need of Federal supervision if effective control was to be secured. There was undoubtedly great direct influence toward Federal regulation exerted by the Granger agitations. The Interstate Commerce Act was not

---

* Although the Massachusetts Railroad Commission made the greatest impression, it was not the earliest; Rhode Island had one in 1836—but it died of inanition,'— New Hampshire in 1844, New York in 1850, Connecticut in 1853, Vermont in 1855, Maine in 1858, Ohio in 1867, etc. See F. Hendrick, "Railway Control By Commission," 1900; B. H. Meyer, "Railway Legislation in the U. S.," 1903.

passed, however, until 1887, 13 years after first introduced, and then after persistent efforts of Representative Reagan, of Texas, and Senator Cullom, of Illinois. The original act prohibited unreasonable and unjust rates, rebates, and discriminations, and required the publication of rates and detailed financial statements. Pooling, and greater charges for a shorter than a longer haul under similar conditions were prohibited. A commission was established and its orders were to be enforced by the Federal courts, to whom also appeals might be made. This imposition of court control in the end emasculated the law. The first result was that the courts really decided the cases which merely originated before the Commission — an expensive and time consuming procedure. In 1890 the Supreme Court decided that witnesses could not be compelled to answer questions in the commerce cases. In 1897 it held that the Commission could not adjust rates — in the absence of express authority of Congress. The court ruled also that the Commission had no authority even to decide the relative reasonableness of charges between different cities — thus killing the long-and-short-haul section. By this time the Commission was well stripped of power; but a series of congressional acts effectively restored its authority. In 1906 it received definite power to determine and prescribe reasonable rates, the burden of proof on appeal being upon the carriers. Free passes were prohibited and railroads were forced to give up other lines of business like mining. In 1910 the Commission was authorized to suspend new rates of carriers, pending investigation. Then the long-and-short-haul section was restored to effectiveness. Jurisdiction was extended over pipe-line, telephone and telegraph, cable and power-transmission companies.

This is not all of the legislation affecting the Interstate Commerce Commission. The enforcement of the Railway Safety-Appliances Act of 1893 was given to it, and it was charged with the investigation of accidents. The inspection of all locomotive boilers has been added.

The Railway is a Service-type Utility. — A moment's consideration shows that while the railways handle products they themselves are only giving a service, as are electricity-supply or telephone concerns. One test of this is their peak loads and their inability to manufacture or acquire the essential elements of their service in times of light demands. Passengers require to be carried when they present themselves. They can effect little adjustment to off-peak loads — they want to travel on holidays, days of college games, etc., and must all be carried at once or not at all. For instance * in Nov. 13, 1915, at the time of a Yale-Princeton football game in New Haven, 20,232 passengers were taken into New Haven during four hours; 13,277 came from New York City and 6950 from Boston and other points, all in 22 regular and 23 special trains. When the tide turned, 19,678 passengers were carried out in two hours by 22 regular and 20 special trains.

Thousands of workers in urban districts must be taken from suburban districts in two early morning hours and carried back in three evening hours, with comparatively light travel at other hours. Crops have to be moved to the markets quickly if at all.

There is a slight, almost inappreciable, storage capacity given to railway lines by their receiving depots, but freights cannot be allowed to congest at a shipping transfer or delivery points beyond a certain minimum, or else the service is retarded, if not finally stalled. After the slight storage capacity of terminals is once reached, extreme steps have to be taken to prevent the receipt of freight — even embargoes are declared by the roads, as in 1907 and 1915.

Difficulty of Applying " Cost of Service " to Rates. — Even in the local utilities where the different kinds of service and classes of customers are comparatively few, the exact proper apportionment of costs as fixed charges and operating expenses is not very easy. In railway transportation, where the kinds of service — local, joint-route, long-haul, short-haul, fast-freight, slow-freight, flat-car, coal-car, refrigerator-car, heater-car, regular passenger, excursion-trip, commuting, etc. — mount up to the dozens and the groups of shippers run into the hundreds (for there are now some 85,000 separate tariffs in force on American railways, and that is a forced reduction from over 220,000 in 1907 †) the difficulties of logically determining the costs of each service are obvious. Where a few allocations of joint expenses have been made the apportionment has been partly by judgment. When the study of railway costs is carried out, a survey on different lines is needed from that used on local utilities; the aim

* See Engineering News, Nov. 18, 1915, p. 1005.
† For details see " Railroad Rates and Regulations," W. Z. Ripley, 1912.

is to find terminal expense and carriage expense for each service. In each of these expenses of course both fixed and operating costs enter.

It is a common assumption of railway men that terminal costs — loading and unloading — cost 50¢ per ton on the average and that ½¢ per ton mile is a good guess at cost of haulage, the combination of the two factors resulting in the cost rising less rapidly than the distance. But such a charge for service could be successfully applied under existing commercial conditions only as a basis of departure — modifications being made above or below to accord with the value of the product, competition of water routes and other rail lines, and all the points exemplified later in the citations of actual cases.

Expenses Independent of Traffic. — Railway and commission statisticians seem to agree that about two-thirds of a road's annual expenditures are nearly or quite independent of traffic — they would continue if traffic dropped nearly to zero. It is generally estimated that one-third of the annual expense covers fixed charges on investment — interest and retirance — and a third goes into maintenance of way, of structures and of rolling stock, into operating the trains (empty or loaded) and for paying for the general administration. That leaves only a third to rise and fall closely with the tide of shipments and travel.

It may be argued that interest depends on amount of equipment and that in turn on traffic. That is not true, however, in considering a road with given equipment and fluctuating traffic — the common situation. Deterioration of structures and roadbed on the whole is caused by weather far more than by wear and tear of traffic, though in special situations that may not be true. Deterioration of rolling stock alone depends mostly on the amount of its use — but even here, in times of idleness, there is a depreciation due to the attack of weather. Maintenance of the roadbed, structures and rolling stock is affected by, or is independent of, traffic in much the same way as is deterioration. Sometimes added tracks are required to take slow traffic off congested high-speed tracks to prevent congestion of service. Then the new construction may not be self-supporting for the traffic over it, but the improvement in the capacity of the older tracks would more than compensate.

Thus the more the railway service is studied the more it is

seen how, even with the ideal condition of traffic of a single uniform quantity and quality day by day, it has been very difficult to arrange convincingly all the expenses according to (1) amount of equipment required by a given service, (2) the operating cost of haulage, (3) the proportionate use of terminal facilities by a given service and (4) the proportion of overhead charges for management. Add the complications of dividing the cost of tracks, yards, terminals, and rolling stock between freight and passenger service (and this has been seriously tried by railroads and commissions but more often with inconsistent and sometimes absurd results which sprung from the highly arbitrary assumptions which had to be made) and an idea of the incomplete reliability of the results begins to be gained. Further, take the amounts assessed as the cost of the freight business and try to split it up for shipments of coal, stone, timber, fruits, meats, groceries, machinery, wagons, clothing, ores, explosives, oils, beverages, medicines, and what not, and the immensity of the problems of scientific rates are realized. (There has been of late, however, a revival of confidence in the possibility of a limited segregation of costs, as noted later.)

"**Law of Joint Costs.**" — The inter-dependence of costs already mentioned is an exhibition of what economists have long called the "Law of Joint Costs." It means, translated into the terms of this case, that so many of the expenditures are unaffected by the presence or absence of traffic and are so inevitable if the road is to be operated at all, that no apportionment is wholly rational. Then, it is argued by many, rates have to be adjusted to what the shippers are willing to pay — modified by the provision that always the rate system as a whole must yield a "reasonable return on the fair value of the property used and useful," if the road is to live and grow.

There is, finally, a crucial test for a value-of-service rate — will it upset an existing equilibrium of traffic? Will it throttle transportation so that the net result is loss of revenue, or will it boom a carrier's business. This is solely a question of record, experience and judgment, except perhaps as to those vital living supplies which must flow unabated anyway — coal, grain, and salt for instance.

"**Law of Increasing Returns.**" — The economists' "Law of Increasing Returns" has been much discussed by writers on railway problems. But it is essentially the same action seen in local-utility operation, though it is little spoken of there under its formal and formidable title. The " law " may be stated in two ways: (1) The operating cost of an utility does not go up as rapidly as the volume of business; (2) the unit cost of service decreases and the profits increase, under fixed rates, as the volume increases.

The first statement emphasizes an effect evidently more pronounced in railway operation than with local utilities. It is more heard of in railway problems because of the lack of control over it. Each hundredweight of freight added to a partly loaded car adds less to cost of haul than a hundredweight of the original load. Each car added to a train, up to the capacity of the locomotive, costs less to transport than one of the cars first coupled.

Similarly, in an electric central station all the extra energy furnished by an underloaded generator costs less per unit than the output before the increase. But the local electric station, however, may adjust its rates to the unit cost under full-capacity output, and failure to earn its legitimate return is but a temporary loss as this may go into the cost of developing the business and affect the rates. Not so the railroad; the rates so far have been generally fixed by considerations beyond the absolute cost of service. If the legitimate return on the investment as a whole is not earned still the roads cannot easily raise the rates for fear of discouraging traffic. It does them little good to throw deficits into intangible property value (such as " business-development investment ") so long as cost of service is not the accepted criterion of railway rates.

The alternative is always to secure the maximum amount of traffic which can be handled and this explains the time-honored struggle of all roads for more business. Traffic is carried on night and day; cars and engines are worked intensively; trains are spaced as close together as safety permits. American traffic officials have always sought to develop business to keep up this rush; they have taken new traffic at a small profit above the bare increment in cost brought by the added traffic, and it is only when fresh competition between localities and industries is kindled that serious contention has arisen — such as has been seen over the cheap transportation of Pacific Coast fruit into the markets of Southern and Eastern growers.

Renewing Separation of Operating Expenses. — From 1888 to 1893 the separation of operating expenses was required by the Interstate Commerce Commission in the reports demanded of carriers. At that time expenses not directly chargeable to freight or passenger traffic were divided on a basis of proportionate train mileage. In 1894 the practice was discontinued owing to the few directly assignable items and the uselessness of the train-mileage derivatives. By 1913, however, the Commission became convinced that sufficient progress in railway accounting had been made to make the separation serviceable. Some roads were already making it — perhaps somewhat arbitrarily — in studying efficiency of operation. It was judged possible to separate two-thirds of the operating expenses satisfactorily, the remainder being divided on some basis which measured the use which either service makes of common facilities. The general and long-term statistics of separated expenses were held to be much more reliable in rate cases than any special short-time studies made for specific cases.

In the testimony taken at hearings on *Advances in Rates — Western Case* (20 I. C. C. 307), one railroad official testified that some 51% of operating costs could be directly apportioned, 29% divided with practical accuracy and 20% arbitrarily placed; this was interpreted to show that a statistician's estimate of service cost would be within 5% of actual. The practice on the Burlington and Santa Fe lines was concretely cited.

After conferences the Commission's scheme of division was approved by the railroads and the Commission issued governing rules. The only disagreement seemed to be as to whether maintenance of way and structures should be divided in proportion to " engine-ton-miles " or " gross-ton-miles." Both schemes are being tried out. The reported separations are according (a) solely to freight service, (b) solely to passenger or allied services (baggage, mail and express), (c) in common to freight and passenger services, (d) to neither service.

It is of interest to note briefly how some of the items are apportioned. Thus in maintenance of way and structures only cost of superintendence, upkeep of roadway buildings, paving and roadway machines, a part of track work, and shops and engine houses, are reported common and undivided. Maintenance of yard tracks is segregated by record or estimate and joint costs are apportioned according to switching locomotive miles. Expenditures on station and office buildings, grain elevators, storage warehouses, power plants, and injuries to persons are divided according to the facts. Expense of signals, interlocking plants, telephones and telegraphs are apportioned on a basis of transportation train miles. Water and fuel stations are divided in proportion to the division of engine fuel.

Under maintenance of equipment, only the cost of keeping up work-train equipment is undivided. Expense on locomotives is placed directly as for freight or passengers or divided according to the locomotive-ton-miles given in each service. Expenses on car equipment, of course, can be assigned directly. The other items like cost of superintendence, shop machinery, power plants, floating and miscellaneous equipment, and injuries to persons are apportioned according to the freight and passenger proportions of the aggregate of the primary accounts mentioned.

The expenses of getting business (Group III, Interstate Commerce Commission Accounts) are assigned directly where possible and the remainder divided in proportion to the aggregate of directly assigned items.

Under the rail-transportation group of operating expenses, train labor, fuel, water, lubricant and supplies are assigned directly as far as possible; for mixed trains these items are divided on a basis of car miles in each service. Yard labor, fuel, supplies, etc., are assigned directly or divided in accordance with the switch-engine-miles in each service. Cost of dispatching trains, signal operation and crossing protection is apportioned on a basis of the transportation train miles (or by special study); mixed-train costs are divided on the basis of car miles. Engine-house expenses are split according to the number of engines handled for each service, with an arbitrary multiplier for engines hard to handle. Cost of weighing, inspection and demurrage bureaus, of coal and ore wharves, express and sleeping-car service, clearing wrecks, damage to property, lost or damaged freight, lost or damaged baggage, injuries to persons, etc., are assigned directly. Most other items like superintendence, station employees (in part), drawbridge operation, telegraphs and telephones, floating equipment, stationery, insurance, etc., are divided in proportion to the aggregate of the divided primary accounts of this group already mentioned.

How Freight Charges are Figured. — A local railway agent
settling with a shipper ordinarily computes a two-part charge.
From the " classification sheets " furnished the agent, is found
the class (1, 2, 3, 4, etc.) in which fall the goods shipped.   From
the "tariff-sheets" are taken the lawful charges per hundredweight for this class between the shipping point and destination
over the route specified.   The actual weight multiplied by this
tariff gives the charges to be imposed — unless there are extras
for storage, switching (on carload shipments), transfer, lighterage, refrigeration, etc.

Classification of Freight. — In the classification sheets, mentioned above, all possible articles are put into various numbered
classes depending on value, bulkiness, quantity, risk of damage,
similarity to previously classified items and the relative cost of
carriage.   Prof. W. Z. Ripley has very aptly described * the
classification sheets:

Imagine the Encyclopedia Brittanica, a Chicago mail-order catalog and
a U. S. protective tariff law blended in a single volume. . . . Such a classification is first of all a list of every possible commodity which may move
by rail, from Academy or Artists' Board and Accoutrements to Xylophones
and Zylonite.   In this list one finds Algarorilla, Bagasse, Pie Crust —
Prepared, Artificial Hams, Cattle Tails and Wombat Skins; Wings,
Crutches, Cradles, Baby Jumpers and all; together with Shoo Flies and
Grave Vaults.   Everything above, on or under the earth will be found
listed in such a volume.

There are three important groups of freight classifications in
the United States, known as the Official, the Southern and the
Western, made up by committees of all the railways in those
respective territories.   In the Official Classification (applying
to the northeastern quadrant of the country) there are six regular (numbered) and three special classes; in the Southern (applying to the Southeastern quadrant) there are six numbered and
seven lettered classes; in the Western (applying in the territory
West of the Mississippi River) are five numbered, and five lettered
classes and a few special cases where the maximum class rating
has been multiplied or discounted.   Many commodities shipped
in carload lots (designated " C. L.") are given a lower classification than the same commodities moved in less than carload

* "Railways: Rates and Regulation"; 1912, New York.

lots (" L. C. L.'). The "exception sheets" going with the classification used by any road show special products given a different classification within a restricted locality because of peculiar local conditions.

Moreover from each important shipping point neither classification sheets nor exception sheets may apply to certain commodities since the need of special low rates (usually on the coarser products) to cause movement has led to the publication of so-called commodity rates, applying only to specified localities and products.. There seems to be a general effort after given traffic has moved a few years under commodity rates to substitute regular classifications and tariffs but there is great difficulty oftentimes in retiring a favor once granted. It is commonly reported that as much as 75% of the tonnage of American roads moves under these exceptional rates. Grain, coal, oil, lumber, wool, cotton, live stock, dressed meats, and some of the products of these staples, are the most favored commodities.

Trunk-Line Rate System. — The trunk roads in self-protection built up a logical rate system for traffic between the Middle West and the Atlantic seaboard which antedates by 15 years the Interstate Commerce Act and embodies, in a general way, many essentials of a cost-of-service plan. This system has not been directly presented to the shippers but exists back of the tariffs — a guide for railway officials (see *Pratt Lumber Co. v. C. I. & L. Ry.*, 10 I. C. C. 29).

In trunk-line territory the charges for a given locality are proportioned to the length of haul, the shortest line from Chicago to New York (920 miles) being the basis. In fixing the proportion, to illustrate, for Columbus, from the Chicago rate, say 25¢ per 100 lb., the fixed charges on both ends of the haul (6¢) are deducted and the remainder (19¢) reduced in proportion to the reduced distance to New York (70%). The haul charge therefore is 13.3¢; to this is added the terminal charges to get the total rate 19.3¢ — which is 77.2% of the standard. This basis was not strictly applied to every intermediate point; rather it gave the rate from points common to two or more carriers, the local stations having to stand a small arbitrary addition to the nearest common point, but the long-and-short-haul prohibition being observed. One result has been the establishment of percentage zones which have been slightly stretched here and there to meet railway competition at junctions, by the presence of independent cross feeder roads, and by commercial competition between localities.*

Zone Rates for Transcontinental Freight. — Of interest in comparison with the trunk-line rate system, but not intimately related to it, is the system of class and commodity tariffs which have been evolved by the transcontinental roads and the Interstate Commerce Commission from 1910–1915 in making certain allowed exceptions to the long-and-short-haul provisions of the revised Interstate Commerce Act.

For instance, a $3 base rate once prevailed for Class 1 goods for the Pacific Coast cities from anywhere in a broad belt between Denver and Boston, but the rate to the intermountain points east of the coast was this figure plus a local back-haul — though the freight was merely stopped off at the proper point on its transcontinental trip. This practice came under the prohibitions of the long-and-short haul and the Commission, in effect, was asked to allow it to continue, on the score of water competition through the Panama canal governing the coast rates but not the intermountain. The Commission reaffirmed the principle but found the difference too great and the origin zone too broad. So they adopted certain zones then seen on existing schedules and graduated the transcontinental class rates from New York, Buffalo-Pittsburgh, Cincinnati-Detroit, Chicago, and from Denver. The intermountain rates were made, for example in Class 1 on shipments to Reno and points east to Utah, $3.50 from New York City, and all the others correspondingly higher than the coast-terminal rate. (See *R. R. Comm. Nev. v. S. P. Co.*, 19 I. C. C. 238; *Transcontinental Rates From Group I*, 28 I. C. C. 1.) The commodity rates were studied separately from the class rates and a somewhat similar system of zones worked out (*Commodity Rates to Pacific Coast*, 32 I. C. C. 611). Zone 1 included the states west of Minnesota, South Dakota, Nebraska, Kansas, Missouri, Arkansas and Louisiana; but for traffic to the Northwest the east line of Zone 1 was drawn west from Missouri to Kansas and New Mexico. Zone 2 extended some 400 miles to the east of Zone 1; Zone 3 had its eastern line running from Buffalo and Pittsburgh down the Ohio

* Details may be studied in "Railroads: Rates and Regulation," by W. Z. Ripley, 1912.

River; Zone 4 included the North Atlantic group and Zone 5 the Southern and South Atlantic states.

Higher rates, generally, on certain commodities which constituted the water-borne Atlantic-Pacific business were allowed out of Zones 2, 3, and 4 to intermediate points than to the coast; the excess however was limited to 7% from Zone 2, 15% from Zone 3, and 25% from Zone 4. Similar carload rates on chemicals, and metal products were allowed but the excess was limited to 15, 25 and 35¢ per 100 lb. from Zones 2, 3 and 4. Coal was allowed to have an excess of 5 mills per ton-mile. The arrangements in their entirety are not as simple as here noted and the decisions themselves must be consulted for details.

Southern Basing-point System. — In great contrast with the trunk-line rate system is the so-called Southern basing-point system. The existence of this scheme depends on certain characteristics of the Southern carriers not pronounced in other parts of the country. First is the general high level of freight charges — due both to tariffs and classification. A second prominent difference is the comparatively sparse population in the territory served and the small amount of local traffic. A third difference is shown by railway maps where the important cities and towns are seen to be centers from which railways radiate, rather than junction points on parallel trunk lines where cross lines are met.

Rates from the more distant origins of traffic are made up of a through rate to some of these centers, plus a local to destination. The basing points first were historic trade centers at which cotton and tobacco (typically) could be concentrated for grading; Savannah and Montgomery are examples of old centers which enjoyed the benefits of water competition, and here the arguments were frequently accepted about the impossibility of charging minor towns as low rates as were given places where competition flourished.

Other great centers sprang up where no water competition was found but rival roads met. Finally the gateway idea was extended by the carriers to certain minor junctions — resulting in many local discriminations. There has been experienced more trouble from this third class than from the others.

The basing point system as constituted is inconsistent with the distance basis so satisfactorily employed in the trunk-line scheme and the gradual change of basic characteristics of transportation in the South is expected in many quarters to point to the eventual elimination of the plan.

Early Interstate Commerce Commission Rates. — It is of no particular value here to examine into the basis of interstate railway rates before they came under the control of the Interstate Commerce Commission. It is of passing interest to note, however, that the interstate rate situation had become deadlocked and unresponsive to changing commercial conditions (although the situation in a few states had improved). The Lincoln (Neb.) Commercial Club case (13 I. C. C. 319) illustrates this. Once the general supplies for Lincoln came from east of the Missouri River and had rates greater than to Omaha. But with industrial changes, the lumber, coal, salt, glass, sugar, etc., were produced nearer to Lincoln than to Omaha but rates could be changed only by unanimous action of the companies, and this could not be secured. Individual action would have started a rate war.

The nearest approach to principles that can be found in early railway tariff tinkering (it hardly merits the term "rate making") were necessity of securing traffic and general expediency. When the newly created Interstate Commerce Commission sought to make order out of the chaos which it found, it was soon confronted with the need of deciding whether the cost of a given service or its value should be the fundamental basis. They accepted the latter and while there have been notable departures and modifications — especially toward the end that a railroad's whole rate system should give a reasonable return on a fair value of the transportation property — yet the value-of-service theory still appears to be the dominant factor considered by the Commission. The declaration of this has been repeated at intervals, notably in 1910 in the general case of returned (rejected) shipments which take a low rate (19 I. C. C. 409).

The Interstate Commission has always apparently been a little troubled in finding a logical way of defining and determining the value of a given specific service. Many of the findings in their own analysis palpably reduce to "what the traffic will bear" — being proportional to the difference in prevailing prices at shipping and receiving points. This has proved to be reasoning in a circle since the prices at the receiving point are fixed by prices at the shipping point and the charges for transportation. While the early commissioners may have sincerely believed that they were applying the value-of-service criterion, yet a careful study of the important decisions * shows the substitution of such bases as relative values of goods shipped, relative risks, relative distances and costs of carriage, natural advantages of localities, general public interest, maintenance of competition between producers, preservation of vested interests, etc. The Commission evidently realized that certain necessities of life once made to flow must continue nearly independent of the price of carriage so that " value of service " alone is an undesirable basis. It is in such cases where the other standards were brought in, and before long they rivaled the fundamental standard in importance. In the actual cases the employment of several criteria are generally seen. A few selected cases have been noted in the following paragraphs to show how railway freight rates have been shaped in practice; the review of cases is not attempted to be complete and especially in the years 1908–1916 are the gaps large, for in these years the cases were mostly affirmations of earlier work.

Effect of Value of Commodity. — In a variety of cases the Interstate Commission allowed a higher rate on finished goods than on raw materials or intermediate products. Thus: wheel-hub blocks went cheaper than wheels in *Hurlburt v. L. S. & M. S. Ry.* (2 I. C. C. 122); chair materials than chairs, *Murphy, Wasey & Co. v. Wabash R. R.* (5 I. C. C. 122); unfinished furniture than finished, *Potter Mfg. Co. v. C. & G. T. Ry.* (5 I. C. C. 514); lumber products than lumber, *Eastern Wheel Mfg. Assoc. v. A. & V. Ry.* (27 I. C. C. 370); hatters' fur than hats, *Myer v. C. C. C. & St. L. Ry.* (9 I. C. C. 78); live stock than packing-house products, *Chicago Board of Trade v. C. & A. R. R.* (4 I. C. C. 153); *Chicago Live Stock Ex. v. C. & G. W. Ry.* (10 I. C. C. 428); *Sinclair & Co. v. C. M. & St. P. R. R.* (21 I. C. C. 490); grain than live stock, *Grain Shippers Assoc. v. I. C. R. R.* (8 I. C. C. 158); cotton waste than cotton goods (12 I. C. C. 388; 22 I. C. C. 293); cotton seed than its products (20 I. C. C. 37); salt in bulk than salt in packages, *Gottron v. G. & W. R. R.* (28 I. C. C. 38).

This idea has been a straightforward proposition generally acceptable to shippers. Oftentimes cost of service has indi-

* Such as may be found in "Railway Rate Theories of the Interstate Commerce Commission" by M. B. Hammond, 1911, or in the "B" Appendices to the annual reports of the Interstate Commerce Commission to Congress.

rectly entered through consideration also of reduced risk and care demanded for rough stocks.

Effect of Market Price of Competing Products. — A few cases are on record where competing or substitute products were allowed to carry rates differing roughly according to general market prices. For instance: soap powder and soap, *J. Pyle & Sons v. E. T. V. G. Ry* (1 I. C. C. 465); anthracite and bituminous coal, *Coxe Bros. v. L. V. R. R.* (4 I. C. C. 535); envelopes and cheap paper bags, *Wolf v. Alleghany Ry.* (7 I. C. C. 40); concrete and steel vaults, *Van Camp B. V. Co. v. C. I. & L. Ry.* (12 I. C. C. 79); wheat and corn (12 I. C. C. 418).

Similar in theory are several cases involving products nominally not competing: Patent medicines versus beers and ales, *Warner v. N. Y. C. & H. R. R. R.* (4 I. C. C. 32); toilet versus laundry soap, *Andrews Soap Co. v. P. C. & St. L. Ry.* (4 I. C. C. 41); petroleum versus cottonseed oil, *Rice v. C. W. & B. R. R.* (5 I. C. C. 193).

Different tariffs for differing products of similar value have been disapproved in several cases, notably: Ties and lumber, *Reynolds v. W. N. Y. & P. Ry.* (1 I. C. C. 393); raisins and other dried fruits, *Martin v. S. P. Co.* (2 I. C. C. 1); celery and other green produce, *Tecumseh C. Co. v. J. & M. Ry.* (5 I. C. C. 663).

Closely connected with the idea of market value of products is the quality of use for them. Where transportation places goods for high-value service, higher rates have been allowed than for similar carriage of goods intended for low-value utilization. For instance: cow peas as fodder instead of fertilizer, *Swaffield v. A. C. L. R. R.* (10 I. C. C. 281); electrical equipment as scientific apparatus or mechanic appliances, *Scheidel v. C. & N. W. Ry.* (11 I. C. C. 532).

Changing tariffs to agree with considerable changes of market prices (of the coarser materials in general demand) have been sanctioned on the excuse of public benefit. One case covered hay, *Nat. Hay Assoc. v. L. S. & M. S. Ry.* (9 I. C. C. 264); others concerned iron and steel, *Colo. Fuel & Iron Co. v. S. P. Co.* (6 I. C. C. 488), *Proposed Advances in Freight Rates* (9 I. C. C. 382); still others involved grains, *Alleged Excessive Rates on Food Products* (4 I. C. C. 48), *Evans v. U. P. Ry.* (6 I. C. C. 520), *Delaware Grange v. N. Y., P. & N. R. R.* (4 I. C. C. 588).

It should be noted that in 1914 the Interstate Commission de-

clared (*Bd. R. R. Comm. Montana v. B. A. & P. Ry.* — 31 I. C. C.
641) that unreasonableness of rates (on grain) could not be
wholly gaged by inability of shippers with depressed market
conditions profitably to market their products under existing
rates.

How Cost of Service Has Been Used. — The opinions of the
Interstate Commission make frequent reference to the cost of
railway service but this is seen to be very largely in regard to
the relative cost of two services — which is much more easy to
scrutinize than absolute cost of either. (Indeed throughout
the Interstate Commission reports, it is seen that in the majority
of cases two rates are being compared — one which it is desired
to charge and one which is taken as a convenient standard for
comparison.)

Cost of Carrying Competing Products. — Where two services
have been compared in studying the reasonableness of one, the
transportation has frequently been of what may be termed
competing products such as raw or finished materials. Thus
there was competition between live hogs and dressed pork for the
Eastern markets in *Squire & Co. v. M. C. R. R.* (4 I. C. C. 611);
a lower rate for hogs was allowed but largely on considerations
of cost (through value of service entered). Similar considerations were seen in *Chicago Board of Trade v. C. & A. R. R.* (4
I. C. C. 153) and *Chicago Live Stock Exchange v. C. & G. W. Ry.*
(10 I. C. C. 428). Other cases involved strawberries versus
potatoes, *Truck Farmers Assoc. v. N. E. R. R. of S. C.* (6 I. C. C.
295); peaches versus common freight, *Ga. Peach Growers Assoc.
v. A. C. L. R. R.* (10 I. C. C. 255); lumber dressed in transit
compared with simple through shipment, *Farrar v. S. Ry.* (11
I. C. C. 632); berries versus oranges, *Perry v. Fla. C. R. R.*
(5 I. C. C. 97); beans versus tomatoes, *Rea v. M. & O. R. R.*
(7 I. C. C. 43); corn products versus corn, *Bates v. Penn. R. R.*
(3 I. C. C. 435; 4 I. C. C. 281), *Kansas R. R. Comm. v. A. T. & S. F.
Ry.* (8 I. C. C. 304); live stock compared with general freight,
Cattle Raisers Assoc. v. M. K. & T. Ry. (11 I. C. C. 296).

Geographical Comparisons of Cost. — Relative cost of service
has been deduced by the Interstate Commission in a few instances by comparing an attacked rate with rates for similar
service elsewhere. Thus carriage of cotton from Meridian, Miss.,
to New Orleans was compared with shipments from Shreveport,

in *N. O. Cotton Exch. v. C. N. O. & T. P. Ry.* (2 I. C. C. 375);
wheat over a short and a long route, *Newland v. N. P. R. R.* (6
I. C. C. 131); cotton goods to Denver and to San Francisco;
Kindel v. B. & A. R. R. (11 I. C. C. 495) (the last two cases involved route competition also); fruit in refrigerator and ordinary
cars, *Waxelbaum v. A. C. L. R. R.* (12 I. C. C. 178).

Under prevailing customs of making separate charges for haul
and for refrigeration on fruit shipments, it has been held (*R. R.
Comm. Calif. v. A. G. S. R. R.*, 32 I. C. C. 17) that a " theory
of differential costs " should be adhered to in judging of reasonableness of charges; the refrigeration charge should cover cost
of hauling the ice carried in the car and the extra cost of switching.

Effect of Carload Lots on Cost. — The Interstate Commission
has often compared the cost of transporting goods in carload
and less-than-carload lots, supporting a lower tariff for the
former because of less labor in loading and unloading at transfer
points, a single bill of lading and collection for the whole carload,
better utilization of cars, etc.   Among the cases to be noted is
an early one involving oil in barrels, *Schofield v. L. S. & M. S.
Ry.* (2 I. C. C. 90); another involved groceries, *Thurber v.
N. Y. C. & H. R. R. R.* (3 I. C. C. 473).   The Interstate Commission in 1912 declared that where a shipper asked for cars of
certain recognized capacity and they were not furnished, the
carload rates should be based on requested capacity. *Lindsay
Bros. v. L. S. & M. S. Ry.* (22 I. C. C. 516).

On mixed carload lots the rate and maximum charge applying
to the article of highest rate prevails so as to give the carrier the
earnings it might have for an entire carload of that commodity;
Florida Fruit and Veg. Shippers Assoc. v. A. C. L. R. R. (17
I. C. C. 552).

Effect of Distance on Cost of Transport. — The distance of
carriage obviously has some effect on cost of service in railway
transportation, and therefore may be expected to have been
considered in rate making.   The relation between distance and
cost of service were discussed in early cases; *Lincoln B. of T. v. B.
& M. R. R.* (2 I. C. C. 147); *Farrar v. E. T. Va. & Ga. Ry.*
(1 I. C. C. 480).   Class rates from Sioux City, Iowa, to points in
southwestern Minnesota were reduced to equal those from St.
Paul and Minneapolis for equal distances; *Traffic Bureau of
Sioux City C. C. v. C. & N. W. Ry.* (22 I. C. C. 110).   Tariffs

from points on the Louisville & Nashville R. R. to Louisville were ordered to be no higher than to Cairo for equal distances; *Norman Lumber Co. v. L. & N. Ry.* (22 I. C. C. 239). Conversely, distance permitted larger rates on cotton from Texas points to New Orleans than to Texas ports; *Re Texas Cotton and Linters* (23 I. C. C. 404).

Equal or greater charges for a shorter than a longer haul on the same line were generally disapproved for the first years of the life of the Interstate Commerce Commission, as shown in *Re Louisville & Nashville R. R.* (1 I. C. C. 31); *Commercial Club of Omaha v. C. R. I. & P. Ry.* (7 I. C. C. 386). But the Commission's power in this matter was reduced in 1892 (*Osborne Case* — 52 Fed. Rep. 912) and practically lost by 1897 (*Board of Trade of Troy v. Alabama Midland R. R.*, 6 I. C. C. 3, 168 U. S. 144; and the *Chattanooga Case*, 10 I. C. C. 111, 181 U. S. 1). The power of the Commission, however, was restored in 1910 by a revision of the Commerce Act. The Commission may expressly permit the use of greater charges for the longer haul in specific cases; a long list of such permissions is given in *Fourth Section Violations in Southeast* (30 I. C. C. 153; 32 I. C. C. 61), *R. R. Comm. of Nev. v. S. P. Co.* (19 I. C. C. 238), *Commodity Rates to Pacific Coast* (32 I. C. C. 611), and others.

In making rates bear some relation to length of haul, the longer or shorter distances did not have to be over the same line necessarily, as shown by *Freight Bureau Cincinnati Cham. of Comm. v. C. N. O. & T. P. R. R.* (7 I. C. C. 180) involving carriage from Cincinnati and Louisville to points south. Similarly the service from Eau Claire and La Crosse, Wis., to the Missouri River was covered in *Eau Claire B. T. v. C. M. & St. P. R. R.* (5 I. C. C. 264). Shipments from Great Falls and Pipestone, Minn., to Chicago were covered in *Morse Produce Co. v. C. M. & St. P. Rys.* (12 I. C. C. 485).

Risk as a Factor in Rates. — A high explosive less dangerous to handle than dynamite was afforded a generally lower rate (by classification) in *Masurite Expl. Co. v. P. & L. E. R. R.* (13 I. C. C. 405). In *Va.-Carolina Chem. Co. v. St. L. Swn. Ry.* (16 I. C. C. 49) rates were lowered on fertilizer as a low grade traffic requiring " no special service," having less risk than other business, and also of service as an auxiliary producer of other traffic.

Sum of Locals Gives Maximum Through Rate. — There are repeated instances where the sum of local rates has been taken as the maximum reasonable amount which a through rate may be. This is typically outlined in *Porter v. St. L. & S. F.* (15 I. C. C. 1), where emigrant outfits were involved. The same idea was applied for shipments of steam boilers in *Lindsay Bros. v. M. C. R. R.* (15 I. C. C. 40), and *Lindsay Bros. v. B. & O. Swn. R. R.* (16 I. C. C. 6). In this connection is of interest the case *Laning-Harris v. Mo. P. Ry.* (13 I. C. C. 154) wherein it was held that there could be but one lawful rate for a given shipment between two points — the local rate if on one road, the joint rate if on two agreeing roads, the sums of two locals if on two non-agreeing roads.

A qualification to this principle was recorded by the Interstate Commission in *Humphreys-Goodwin Co. v. Y. & M. R. R.* (31 I. C. C. 25). The fact that the joint (through) rate exceeded the sum of intermediates, it was noted, raised a strong presumption of unreasonableness but this could be rebutted by evidence.

Federal Versus State Rates. — In 1907 the Interstate Commerce decided, in *Hope Cotton Oil Co. v. T. & P. Ry.* (12 I. C. C. 265), that a state-made rate " has no greater sanctity than a rate established by a railroad company " and while entitled to respectful consideration could not be accepted in fixing an interstate rate. The same declaration was made in *Saunders v. So. Ex. Co.* (18 I. C. C. 417), in *Cobb v. No. P. Ry.* (20 I. C. C. 100) and in *Trier v. C. St. P., M. & O. Ry.* (30 I. C. C. 707). When state rates are reduced the effect on interstate commerce must be considered, reports the Interstate Commission in *R. R. Comm. of La. v. St. L. Swn. Ry.* (23 I. C. C. 31). Here rates from Shreveport, La., to points in eastern Texas were ordered made similar to those from Dallas and Houston, Tex.

The Effect of Water Competition. — The effect of the real or potential competition of water routes with railway lines has long been a recognized factor in making freight rates. For instance sugar from San Francisco to Humboldt, Kan., was given 30% higher rates than to Kansas City, in *Lehmann, Higginson & Co. v. S. P. Co.* (4 I. C. C. 1). Lower rates on oil from Pennsylvania and Ohio were given the Standard Oil Co., than to competitors at intermediate points because of water and pipe-line competition which the Standard Co. had but the others had not;

(*Rice v. A. T. & S. F. R. R.* 4 I. C. C. 228). Lower rates to Memphis and Nashville than to Chattanooga were permitted because of water competition (*Chattanooga B. T. v. E. T. V. & G. Ry.*, 5 I. C. C. 546, and *Chattanooga C. C. v. S. Ry.*, 10 I. C. C. 111). For the same reason lower rates from the Mississippi River to the Pacific Coast were allowed in *Spokane v. Mo. P. Ry.* (15 I. C. C. 376). Lower rates on flour from New York City to Boston than to Readville, eight miles nearer, were allowed to stand because of the Boston water route (*King & Co. v. N. Y., N. H. & H. R. R.*, 4 I. C. C. 251). Brick machinery from Lockland, Ky., to East St. Louis, Ill., took a higher rate than that from more distant Louisville on the same line (*Durham v. I. C. R. R.*, 12 I. C. C. 37).

A recent declaration of the Interstate Commission (1912) was to the effect that a road could not discriminate against a city unless transportation forces (water competition) were brought into force in one place and not in another (*Re S. P. Co.*, 22 I. C. C. 366, 24 I. C. C. 34).

After the New York, New Haven & Hartford R. R. had consolidated the rail and water lines between southern New England and New York City, a competing boat line broke in, but the other railroads would not make joint rates with the new concern. The Interstate Commission ordered the joint rates on grounds of fostering competition (*Re Discriminations against Enterprise Trans. Co.*, 11 I. C. C. 587).

Railway Route Competition Still Affects Rates. — While rate wars are a thing of the past and governmental regulation has supplanted destructive competition, yet competition, real and potential, has left an indelible mark. In many cases where "local advantages" have been preserved these benefits are shown to be the results of competition in rail transportation. Roads have been allowed to lower their rates to meet short-line competition but the Interstate Commerce Commission has maintained that a road cannot be compelled to do so, and that a mere reduction furnishes no evidence of the unreasonableness of the older rate. See *Ottumwa Bridge Co. v. C. M. & St. P. Ry.* (14 I. C. C. 125); *Commercial Coal Co. v. B. & O. R. R.* (15 I. C. C. 11); *LaSalle Paper Co. v. Mich. C. R. R.* (16 I. C. C. 149).

An increase of rates on lumber going from southern states to Ohio River points, the after effect of consolidation, were disapproved by the Interstate Commission because competition was favored by law and the old rates were fixed by competition (*Cent. Yellow Pine Assoc. v. I. C. R. R.*, 10 I. C. C. 505).

In some of the early cases of the Commerce Commission railroute competition was held not to be sufficient ground to warrant lesser charges for a longer than for a shorter haul over the same line but this was overruled by the Supreme Court in the *Troy Case* (6 I. C. C. 3; 168 U. S. 144) and the Commission's authority was restored only by special legislation in 1910. Route competition has long been recognized by the Supreme Court as one of the factors entering freight rates, see *Social Circle Case* (162 U. S. 184). Presence of water competition between terminals has been judged excuse for permitting a greater charge for a shorter than a longer haul; *Re Lumber Rates from South to Ohio River* (25 I. C. C. 50) is typical of the many cases involving this idea.

Raw wool went 50% cheaper from Fort Wayne, Ind., to Philadelphia than in the reverse direction due to competition for steady traffic eastbound which did not exist westbound (*Weil Bros. v. P. R. R.*, 11 I. C. C. 627). Similar grounds did not hold in *A. J. Phillips, v. G. T. W. Ry.* (11 I. C. C. 659). Higher rates were allowed east from Fenton, Mich., to Winooski, Vt., than from Winooski to Detroit — owing to empty cars going out (*Phillips & Co. v. G. T. W. Ry.*, 11 I. C. C. 659).

Rates to St. Cloud, intermediate between Duluth and St. Paul, were held unfair unless sharing in a general reduction of the through rate made to compete with a shorter through line (*Tileston Millg. Co. v. N. P. Ry.*, 8 I. C. C. 346).

In *McLean Lumber Co. v. L. & N. Ry.* (22 I. C. C. 349) a carrier was allowed to transport a shipment at a rate fixed for a route of a competitor specified by the shipper but the competitor's lower rate not accepted as evidence of unreasonableness of carrier's regular rates.

Limits to Route Competition. — Some cases are to be noted where no particular natural advantages were evident but old railway rates had given a locality certain business assistance which was preserved. Thus Wilmington, N. C., was losing jobber's distribution business to Norfolk and Richmond by virtue of a change in existing rates. The Interstate Commission restored the handicap (*Wilmington Tariff Assoc. v. C. P. & Va.*

R. R., 9 I. C. C. 118). Yet in contrast there are cases where the advantages of trade centers, due to old railway rates, were not perpetuated, the Commission ruling that the competition of merchants in smaller places could not any longer be shut out by discriminatory rates; see *Payne, Gardner v. L. & N. R. R.* (13 I. C. C. 638). Railroads cannot longer adjust rates (in order to increase revenues) so as to constrain shippers to send to one market on one line rather than another market off that line (*Milwaukee C. C. v. C. R. I. & P. Ry.*, 15 I. C. C. 460).

Competition of Seaports. — One of the most important grouping of interstate-commerce cases that can be made would cover those involving competition of seaports, the efforts of railroads to overcome peculiar port advantages, and the willingness of the Interstate Commission to foster such competition. Helping the port of Boston to compete with New York City has already been noted (*Re Export Trade of Boston*, 1 I. C. C. 24; *Boston Cham. Comm. v. L. S. & M. S. Ry.;* 1 I. C. C. 436). The long-discussed differentials on freight for export in favor of Philadelphia and Baltimore, and against New York City, were allowed to stand on first examination as the Interstate Commission concluded that they were the result of the competition of various carriers to get a part of the export business and had existed for forty odd years without " untoward or unnatural influence on traffic." The differentials were reduced however (*N. Y. Prod. Ex. v. B. & O. R. R.*, 7 I. C. C. 612).

Lower rates on grain for export than for domestic sale were allowed after a general study of export rates because of competition of routes to foreign markets, because the Interstate Commerce Act was intended to foster competition, and because the Supreme Court had ruled that competition of carriers might be reason for lower charges to a distant than to a nearer point. Export grain rates came up again when the trunk lines leading East tried to justify a proposed increase from 17½ to 20¢ per 100 lb. The Pennsylvania and New York Central roads had bought up some of the earlier competitors and believed that the 20¢ rate could be returned to. The Commission did not sanction the raise — on the grounds that the lower rate was not below the cost of service, had been dictated by ancient competition and was not unfair (*Proposed Advances in Freight Rates*, 9 I. C. C. 384).

The same differentials came up again in 1904 and the figures as reduced in 1899 were upheld on the grounds of preserving competition between great railway lines and ports. The differentials for export, under import, freight through Philadelphia, Baltimore and New York City were again adjusted in 1912 (*Cham. Comm. of N. Y. v. N. Y. C. & H. R. R. R.*, 24 I. C. C. 55). Newport News, Va., was given old through routes and joint rates, the same as for Norfolk although the carrier lines did not go to Newport News (*Cham. Comm. of Newport News v. S. Ry.*, 23 I. C. C. 345).

Yet in spite of allowing all these differentials, the Commission has repeatedly declared that " differentials diminish with increasing distance and vanish when the mileage on which the differential is based becomes inconsiderable in proportion to the total mileage from basing point to destination " (*Williams Co. v. V. S. & P. Ry.*, 16 I. C. C. 482; *Norman Lumber Co. v. L. & N. R. R.*, 29 I. C. C. 565).

Competition of Private Producers. — While the Interstate Commerce Commission has several times refused to assume the right to foster an industry, no matter how desirable such action might be, on the grounds that it was not a rule of transportation (see *Bults Milling Co. v. C. & A. R. R.*, 15 I. C. C. 351), yet there are some cases closely approaching such action. For instance in *Schumacher Milling Co. v. C. R. I. & P. Ry.* (4 I. C. C. 373) carload rates applying to a single grain were not allowed for a car of mixed grain when it was shown that only one producer could ship mixed grains in such amounts, and that his carload rate would enable him to kill off competition. A similar situation arose in *Proctor & Gamble v. C. H. & D. Ry.* (9 I. C. C. 440) where meat packers shipping a mixed carload of soap and meats were not allowed to secure the highest carload minimum tariff when soap makers had to pay more. Local carload rates on eggs, lower than on the " less-than carload " tariff, were denied by the Commerce Commission on the ground that it would throw all the egg business into the hands of a few great concerns (*Brownell v. C. & C. M. R. R.*, 5 I. C. C. 638). This stand was taken in spite of a showing of reduced cost of service for carload shipments. Similar cases were *Paper Mills Co. v. P. R. R.* (12 I. C. C. 438), and *Milwaukee-Waukesha Brew'g Co. v. C. M. & St. P. Ry.* (13 I. C. C. 28).

This stand also contrasts with the general attitude of the Interstate Commission that mixed carloads are to be liberally provided for (*Re Western Classification*, 25 I. C. C. 442).

The same disregard of cost of service was shown in the case of *Glade Coal Co. v. B. & O. R. R.* (10 I. C. C. 226), where lower rates were denied for coal loaded from a tipple than on coal loaded from wagons or sleds; the Commission held that this differential would reduce the number of shippers and shipping points whereas Congress intended that all persons desiring to ship goods should have a reasonable chance.

The Commerce Commission has repeatedly refused to blanket the central-creamery industry in order to encourage the small local creameries; for a typical example see *Beatrice Creamery Co. v. I. C. R. R.* (15 I. C. C. 109). A low rate on cotton goods from Texas to Wichita, Kan., was once ordered (equal to old secret rates) so that local jobbers could compete with Kansas City firms (*Johnston-Larimer D. G. Co. v. Wabash R. R.*, 12 I. C. C. 51). Other discriminations between Kansas City and Wichita, on mixed-car rates, were removed in *Wichita B. Assoc. v. A. T. & S. F. Ry.* (30 I. C. C. 374). One railroad was not allowed arbitrarily to charge more on a product from one mill on its line than others and to prevent the one from competing in certain markets while assisting the others (*Texas Cement Plaster Co. v. St. L. & S. F. R. R.*, 12 I. C. C. 68).

Vested Interests Protected. — Delivery of oil tank cars to a Brooklyn, N. Y., railway terminal was ordered restored — partly on grounds of plant built up on the old rates and partly to enable a competition of refiners (*Preston & Davis v. D. L. & W. R. R.*, 12 I. C. C. 114). There are various cases on grain differentials which have been largely decided for the industries built up on them (*Bates v. P. R. R.*, 3 I. C. C. 435; *Kaufman Mill'g Co. v. Mo. P. Ry.*, 10 I. C. C. 35; *Howard Mills Co. v. Mo. P. Ry.*, 12 I. C. C. 258). A furniture concern which had been given special rates to enable it to compete in certain markets, and which had therefore gone to much expense in order to manufacture for the new market, was judged entitled to hold the rates specially established (*New Albany Furn. Co. v. M. J. & K. C. R. R.*, 13 I. C. C. 594). This policy was again declared in *Green Bay B. M. A. v. B. & O. R. R.* (15 I. C. C. 59).

Even where the cost of service gave rates above those formerly prevailing, a road was not allowed to impose charges that would destroy a business and investment (*Mt. Ice Co. v. D. L. & W. R. R.*, 15 I. C. C. 305). Splitting up single-rate territory into districts, with different rates which resulted in loss of business to concerns in one district fostered by the old rates, was disapproved in *Ind. Steel & Wire Co. v. C. M. & St. P. Ry.* (16 I. C. C. 155).

Some Rates Fixed by General Public Interest. — There are many miscellaneous cases where the Interstate Commission's " theories of transportation " have been overridden for what the Commission has considered " a general public benefit." For instance higher rates on Missouri and Kansas flour going to Texas, than on wheat, were allowed as they protected the Texas milling industry, the existence of which had a beneficial effect on price of wheat in all three states (*Kaufman Milling Co. v. Mo. P. Ry.*, 4 I. C. C. 417; *Wichita v. Mo. P. Ry.*, 10 I. C. C. 35).

In the days before Los Angeles had grown down to the seacoast and become a port, the eastern carriers were giving the same rates as enjoyed by San Francisco — which were fixed by water competition. This preference over other Southern California cities was contested in *Holdzkom v. M. C. Ry.* (9 I. C. C. 420) but was allowed to remain on the excuse of creating lower prices throughout Southern California by making Los Angeles the distributing center in place of San Francisco.

A number of cases established, or re-established, joint routes and rates " in the public interest " — not in detail defined. For instance, regarding cattle coming out of Texas, see *Am. Nat. Live Stock Assoc. v. T. & P. Ry.* (12 I. C. C. 32); *Birmingham Packing Co. v. T. & P. Ry.* (12 I. C. C. 29). The Commission has held, in *Loup Creek Co. v. Va. Ry.* (12 I. C. C. 469), that a through rate over two or more roads may be greater than would be reasonable over one road, and that through routes and joint rates are not required in all cases — only where there will be public benefit or promotion of justice. In contrast with this is a case decided shortly after, *Cardiff Coal Co. v. C. M. & St. P. Ry.* (13 I. C. C. 460), where it was held that a merchant or manufacturer having goods to be moved and ready to pay a reasonable rate is entitled to have through routes and joint rates established regardless of the fact that his competition with distant concerns may unfavorably affect the revenues of the railroad in question.

Rates not Allowed to Overcome Natural Advantages. — Localities under a commercial handicap compared with more favored places naturally employ every influence to offset their natural disadvantages, and, to this end, discrimination in tariffs have been no mean tool. The railroad position has been one of trying to equalize rates over all routes between any two competing points, so that goods may move freely everywhere to market. By this old order of things all products moved under flat rates largely, irrespective of distance. The Interstate Commerce Commission, however, has constantly frowned on most such practices and endeavored to have installed more natural and logical rates.

The natural advantages, aside from water routes, which are preserved depend (1) on naturally lower transportation costs or shorter distances from one shipping locality than another to the same market, (2) on water-route competition and in some instances all-rail competition; or else (3) group, blanket, or zone rates are involved. There has naturally been a limit to the protection afforded natural advantages and this appears to have been set so that one locality could not develop a trade monopoly, or so that relative costs of service might be followed. Indeed, the list of cases touching on this point shows that the " natural advantage " idea is largely a second aspect of the cost-of-service plan. An early case was *Imperial Coal Co. v. P. & L. E. R. R.* (2 I. C. C. 618). A more recent case is *Enterprise Mfg. Co. v. Ga. R. R.* (12 I. C. C. 131 and 451); low rates were there denied southeastern cotton mills to San Francisco as the advantage of water carriage from New England was offset by southeastern mills' proximity of supply.

Boston enjoys certain long standing concessions over New York City on western freight for Europe but these differentials have not been allowed on domestic traffic for which New York's natural advantages are preserved; *Boston Chamber of Commerce v. L. E. & M. S. R. R.* (1 I. C. C. 436). The advantage of Eau Claire, Wis., for making lumber for Missouri River towns, which had been overcome by rates favoring La Crosse and Winona, were restored in *Eau Claire B. T. v. C. M. & St. P. Ry.* (5 I. C. C. 264).

Certain rates, of eastern and western roads running to southern markets, which had favored the east for various manufactures and the west for certain natural products were changed so that the manufacturers in the close Middle West might enjoy the advantages which they had developed (*Freight Bureau of Cincinnati v. C. N. O. & T. P. Ry., Chicago F. B. v. L. N. A. & C. Ry.*, 6 I. C. C. 195). The advantages of Ludington and Manistee, Mich., over Detroit in procuring salt for Missouri River points (advantages of distance, competing routes, and manufacture) were protected in *Re Transportation of Salt* (10 I. C. C. 148). Similarly the advantage of distance possessed by Kansas salt makers, supplying Texas, over Michigan were protected by low rates (*Anthony Salt Co. v. Mo. P. Ry.*, 5 I. C. C. 299).

Pueblo, Colo., as a steel center possessed great advantages of nearness to far western markets and eastern steel rates were not allowed to overcome the advantage (*Colo. F. & I. Co. v. S. P. Co.*, 6 I. C. C. 488). Rates on milk for New York City from points 25 to 335 miles from the city were changed from flat to zone basis for 40, 100, 190, and 335 miles out so that nearby producers should not be forced out (*Milk Prod. Prot. Assoc. v. D. L. & W. R. R.*, 7 I. C. C. 92). The Interstate Commission refused to make rates from Indianapolis to Wisconsin, Minnesota, and Michigan points as favorable as from Chicago or St. Louis to these places, on the score of shorter routes, competition of carriers and natural advantages of location for Chicago and St. Louis (*Indianapolis Freight Bureau v. C. C. C. & St. L.*, 16 I. C. C. 276).

Equalization of advantages of milling in transit possessed by Bangor and Lewiston, Me., over Washington county towns was not granted in *Quimby v. Maine Central R. R.* (13 I. C. C. 246).

A declaration of lack of power of the Interstate Commerce Commission "to equalize advantage, to place one market in competition with another, to treat all railroads as part of one great whole," etc., was seen recently (1912) in *Ashland Fire Brick Co. v. So. Ry.* (22 I. C. C. 115).

Competition of Localities Fostered. — There are on record a number of cases where the Interstate Commission has helped commercial competition between localities which showed no peculiar advantages one over the other, by removing railroad discrimination. Thus, an arbitrary charge of 5¢ per 100 lb. for mills off the line of the Missouri, Kansas & Texas Ry. was held unjust as prohibiting the off mills from selling along the line (*Blackwell Millg. Co. v. M. K. & T. Ry.*, 12 I. C. C. 23).

In *Black Mt. Coal Land Co. v. So. Ry.* (15 I. C. C. 286) it was held that, where one carrier serves two districts which by location, output and distance from markets are under similar conditions, a carrier cannot prefer one to another. Sioux City petitioned to be put on an equality with Omaha, Kansas City and Minneapolis for purchasing, milling and distributing grain; while it was held that certain competitive conditions did not prevail in Sioux City, as in the other places, and the full equalization could not be made, yet partial relief was granted by requiring more reasonable local rates for collecting grain (*Sioux City T. E. Co. v. C. M. & St. P. Ry.*, 23 I. C. C. 98). Buffalo millers were enabled to continue in competition with Minneapolis by preserving old differences in rates to New York City and New England (*Banner Milling Co. v. N. Y. C. & H. R. R. R.;* 13 I. C. C. 31).

There have been a long list of cases before the commission charging the effect of simple discrimination against one city over another. In general the policy has been to adjust rates so as to equalize advantages in the absence of causes for differences already mentioned. Recent cases were *Paducah B. T. v. I. C. R. R.* (29 I. C. C. 583 and 593); *Re Tropical Fruits From Gulf Ports* (30 I. C. C. 621).

Railway Passenger Rates. — Greater simplicity exists among the railway passenger rates of America than in the freight rates. This is only to be expected because of the comparatively few different passenger services rendered.

For years the division of railway revenues has been about constant — in the vicinity of 70% freight, 25% passenger (mail and express), and 5% minor — the passenger revenues including those from hauling parlor and sleeping cars, etc. The average revenue per passenger mile was 2.35¢ in 1889, 1.93¢ in 1909 and 1.98¢ in 1914. The total travel was 472,171,000 passengers in 1889, rose to 891,472,000 in 1909 and 1,053,139,000 in 1914. The passenger miles in the same periods were 11,553,820,445, 29,109,323,000 and 35,258,498,000.

The classic rate is 2¢ per passenger mile though lately there has been a widespread movement permitted which substitutes 2¼¢. For instance see *Railroad Passenger Rate Case* (Mass. P. S. C. Nos. 805, 673, and 698 — 1915; P. U. R. 1915 B. 363). The 2¢ or 2¼¢ rate is intended to apply to extensive traveling and therefore is effective through the sale of coupon books. Where strictly local tickets are sold the rate may rise to from 3 to 6¢ per passenger mile depending on the scarcity of local travel, the difficulties of local operation, etc. It may rise above 6¢ under extremely unfavorable conditions.

For example in *Arkansas v. M. & N. A. R. R.* (30 I. C. C. 488) local fares of 6½¢ were found reasonable over a mountain line. Mention should be made of special-excursion fares which are seen in seasons of light travel and which are intended to make idle property produce some small profit. Special fares less than normal rates are permitted but cannot be required; and they may be accompanied by any lawful non-discriminatory regulations (see *Eschner v. Penn. R. R.;* 18 I. C. C. 60).

Commutation service between residential districts and business centers needs special mention, since here the rates are phenomenally low and the service peculiar. Many rates around New York City are below 0.4¢ per passenger mile.

These passenger rates are for first class travel — which is practically the only class in America. There are a few second-class tickets sold but these may be regarded as special provision for immigrants, etc. First-class travel is comfortable, not to say luxurious; second-class passengers are required to travel in smoking cars or frequently on special trains.

The unit cost of travel is increased by special services furnished many passengers — parlor and sleeping cars, fast express service between important cities. But, with all these additions to the passenger-rate system, all the schedules which may be found are comparatively few and simple.

It is generally accepted that railway passenger and freight business each should pay its own way, though each may not contribute the same profit (see *Buel v. C. M. & St. P. R. R.,* 1 W. R. R. Rep. 324; *Five Per Cent Rate Case,* 31 I. C. C. 351 and 32 I. C. C. 325). The idea is difficult to apply on account of the difficulty of apportioning large items of expense — as already referred to. But apparently the Interstate Commerce Commission hopes to make progress here.

Commission Control of Passenger Fares. — The Wisconsin Railroad Commission started out to administer control of the railway passenger service of the state as carefully as the freight. However the legislature soon imposed a flat 2¢ fare on the more prosperous roads and all carriers accepted the change. That has relieved the Commission of passenger cases to a great extent. The Interstate Commerce Commission has had many passenger-rate cases in the aggregate though the percentage would be small of the whole dockets.

In many ways there has been merely a transference of ideas expounded in freight cases. For instance discrimination between places has been stopped as in freight rates; in one typical case, *Beach v. Ann Arbor R. R.* (26 I. C. C. 40), week-end excursion rates were required to all resorts in a locality where some were favored. Party tickets must now be sold to all applicants meeting the numerical requirements, whereas once they were available only for theatrical troupes, athletic teams, etc. (see *re Party Rate Tickets*, 12 I. C. C. 95, and *Koch Secret Service v. L. & N. R. R.*, 131 I. C. C. 523). Commutation tickets for school children were similarly thrown open to all children (see *re Regulations Governing Sale of Commutation Tickets*, 17 I. C. C. 144).

Other examples: The federal disregard for state-made rates is shown in passenger traffic; in *Arkansas v. M. & N. A. R. R.* noted above, it was held that interstate fares, of one road higher than another in the same general territory and higher than intrastate fares fixed by state laws, are not evidence of unreasonableness; the aggregate of intermediate fares, fixed by state laws, being less than the through interstate fare is not a violation of the · long-and-short haul legislation. But where such conditions do not prevail through tickets are to cost no more than the sum of locals (see *Kurtz v. Penn. R. R.;* 16 I. C. C. 410).

Route competition may permit of advantages to one place over another. Thus New York has lower tariffs to the famous resort Atlantic City, N. J., than has Baltimore (*M. and M. Assoc. of Baltimore v. A. C. R. R.;* 23 I. C. C. 129).

Rates depending on value of service given under the same conditions and at identical costs were made when the prices of upper berths in sleeping cars were cut to 60% to 80% those of the lowers — see *Loftus v. Pullman Co.* (18 I. C. C. 135; 20 I. C. C. 31).

Appreciation and Depreciation of Railroad Property. — There is a certain peculiar appreciation of railway track and roadbed which can be recognized — aside from the increments of value of real estate due to general rises in value of contiguous lands. This appreciation is variously known but may well be covered by what has been called "adaptation, solidification and seasoning." Its value is due to its effect in reducing the annual maintenance expenses of unseasoned and unsettled roadbed and reducing the cost of wear and tear of trains passing over an uneven track.   There is a small element of value due to the possibility of more safely running trains at higher speeds.   A large part of any solidification value has been paid for by heavy maintenance expense in early years to compensate for settlement of fills, consolidation of ballast, etc.   According to the Washington Railroad Commission, this appreciation amounts to 10% in the first five years (*Findings of Fact in the Valuation of Railroads*, p. 164).

Railway officials generally claim that there is no depreciation in a composite property like a railroad's plant.   They admit that there may be a certain depreciation of each of the individual units that make up a road's property — such as rails, ties, switches, cars, locomotives, buildings, bridges, etc. — but they strenuously and unitedly deny the existence of depreciation in the aggregation of these individual items which makes up the working railroad.

The argument back of this stand apparently is simply the old one that full capability of service is present and that the annual maintenance work provides sufficient annual renewals of the more decrepit individual items of property so that full service ability or efficiency is held to.   The railways deny that there is any relation between depreciation and what they call " deferred maintenance " or " accrued deterioration " (meaning what has been termed in this work " retirance " or " renewance ") — contributions secured out of earnings to offset increasing liability of property having to be taken out of service and new equipment substituted.

Outside of railway circles there has not been a ready acceptance of the carriers' protests that their property is the great exception to all other property actively employed by man — in that it does not depreciate.   It may be that the railroad man's attitude is influenced by his fear that railway credit may be impaired if the usual deductions for depreciation be made in ascertaining present value of physical plant.

Depreciation and retirance do not play nearly the important part in railway rates that they do in other utility charges, since the property units are so many and so diversified, and annual maintenance aggregates such a large sum that there is not much unbalancing of each year's expenses if the renewals and replacements are charged directly year by year instead of being equalized by predetermined annual payments. There is a certain unbalance apt to occur in certain years, however, when large and expensive items like whole routes and large structures are superseded. In these cases " expedients " are resorted to — often suspense accounts are set up or temporary reductions of surplus are made; reductions of dividend are not to be expected — if, happily, the road is paying a return and has a surplus.

There is real ground for the claim of railway officials that they will not be equitably dealt with, if their credit is forced to depend solely upon depreciated value of plant — seeing that railway rates have not been adjusted to repay the roads the capital lost through depreciation — lost in the event of official government valuation result being stated as depreciated cost. In such a case it would seem that equity could be preserved by placing the uncompensated depreciation in the department of business-development expenses, along with any other deficits which may be fairly included. This subtraction of physical value and addition to intangibles is, of course, only paying from one pocket into another, but it has the great advantage that everything is properly labeled and if it ever becomes possible to amortize the intangible items their proper figure is known.

The Interstate Commission has made provision for retirance (under the name " depreciation ") in its uniform accounting plans but it has not required the roads to accept it to very great extent. The roads have not used the strong claims that reside in retirance for increased revenues and rates to compensate for constant impairment of capital invested.

The Valuation of American Railways. — The difficulty if not the impossibility of finding the real cost of each individual service performed by the railways of the country has not prevented a keen desire to find the value of the several carriers' property. The argument has been that it was impossible to know whether the rates of a road as a whole returned a reasonable percentage on a fair value — somehow defined. It is possible that, in the event of a valuation showing insufficient earnings, rates as a whole might be raised over a given system or territory, though any such effect would be expected to be more or less incomplete owing to the necessity of holding many schedules down in order to make certain traffic flow at all.

From its inception the Interstate Commerce Commission has advocated the making of a general physical valuation of railroad property, and finally in 1910 Congress authorized the project. The Act as adopted specifically called for the detailed listing of all railway property, the original cost to date, cost of reproduction new, cost of reproduction less depreciation, intangible elements of value, the original costs and present values of lands, rights of way and terminals, cost of condemnation, damages, excess purchase price, etc., the original cost and presentation of property held for other than transportation service, the history and organization of the road, increases or decreases of securities in reorganization, money received from sale of securities and expended. The valuation is required to be detailed by state areas, so that there will be finally state valuations making up the federal. The best estimates that could be made at the time the Act was adopted allowed five years and $10,000,000 for the task. But as the organization of the valuation work was completed the early estimates had to be raised, both in point of time and money to be expended. It is now confidently predicted that the task will be finished in ten years after it was started (1913–1923) and at a cost of $50,000,000 ($15,-000,000 to the Commission and $35,000,000 to the roads). A very considerable part of this increase has been due the requirement that the original construction cost, etc., should also be established historically as far as possible. In some cases it has been noted that the cost of the historical studies alone has mounted to $133 per mile of line.

Organization of the Federal Valuation. — One of the members of the Interstate Commerce Commission resigned to become Director of Valuation. One of the first steps was to divide the country into five geographical districts, and group the organization likewise. The appraisal of physical plant, aside from land, is under five members of an Engineer Board, one man for each district. Under him is a district engineer, and in turn under the latter one or more senior field engineers who inventory only track and roadway, a senior structural engineer having jurisdiction over bridges, a senior architect for buildings, a senior signal engineer for signals and interlocking plants, a senior mechanical engineer for rolling stock and equipment, a senior electrical engineer for electrical apparatus.

The Valuation Director has with him also, besides counsel, a Supervisor of Land Appraisals, and five land attorneys — each in charge of a district. There is similarly a Supervisor of Accounts and five valuation accountants; this bureau has the investigation of history, organization, and financial arrangements, and the determination of original cost to date. A Cost Bureau is collecting data to make up unit prices for applying to the inventories. The five district land attorneys form a Land Board, and the five district accountants form an Accounting Board for the country. There is also a General Advisory Board of engineers, economists, publicists, lawyers, etc., which confers with the Valuation Division on the more important questions that have to be settled.

The valuation act requires the railways to coöperate in the work of valuation besides furnishing information, maps, contracts, reports, etc. The roads organized a " Railroad Presidents' Conference Committee " of 18 members to be the buffer between the Valuation Division and the carriers, and this committee in turn has appointed law, engineering, land and accounting sub-committees to confer with the Valuation Division.

The government put out field parties to make an inventory of the various railway properties, the roads furnishing maps, inventories of terminals, etc. The federal parties were accompanied by a company " pilot " (a representative of the road who was intimately acquainted with the present construction, history, etc., and could point out obscure and hidden property like foundations, subsided roadbed, etc., and check computers). After the work was well under way an average accomplishment was the inventory of some 4000 miles per month. As already noted the roads are necessarily put to great expense in the aggregate because of the appraisal. Valuation departments have been created, records have been assembled and in some cases preliminary private inventories have been made — all so as to be in proper shape to coöperate in the government's studies, or to be prepared to controvert any undesirable tendencies shown.*

* For typical details of the government and corporate activities necessitated by this valuation work see: "Chicago & Northwestern Ry. Valuation Work." Engineering News, Oct. 28, 1915, p. 843; "Railway Valuation Office System," by H. J. Saunders, Engineering News, Nov. 4, 1915; and "The Federal Valuation of the Boston & Maine R. R.," by F. C. Shepherd, Boston Society of Civil Engineers, November, 1915.

Suggested Economics in Railroad Operation. — In 1914 the Interstate Commission made a very careful study of rates and service east of the Mississippi to judge of the reasonableness of a flat 5% increase in freight rates (*Five Per Cent Case;* 31 I. C. C. 351; 32 I. C. C. 325). Some advances were allowed at first but not the scheme as a whole until 1915. An elaborate presentation was made of the ways in which operating revenue could be legitimately increased and expenses cut down. For instance (1) the general increase of passenger fares in New England was cited and carriers urged to work for repeal of low-fare statutes in the Middle West; (2) freight-rate schedules were recommended to be overhauled to weed out many individual items which had become unremunerative under ancient and fierce competition; (3) more logical charges for special services, like time allowances for loading and unloading, collecting and delivering, storing, refrigerating, switching, lighterage, etc.; (4) reducing travel on passes — which had been shown to be over 10% of total passenger travel, in spite of the Federal anti-pass laws — and allowing fewer free private-car services for minor officials and families of major officials; (5) intensifying the use of freight cars which in a typical case were moving loaded in trains only two days a month and then carrying 58% of their capacity; (6) reducing the coal consumption — which on one road had been cut 9.5% through greater knowledge and care of employees; (7) greater effectiveness of labor and elimination of penalties for infraction of commerce laws, the latter aggregating $814,000 in three years; (8) sale of property not used in transportation service; (9) purchasing supplies and contracting for construction only from concerns in which the officials of the paying railroad have no interest; (10) revision of sleeping-car and railway-mail contracts.

CHAPTER XI

PROBLEMS OF EXPRESS TRANSPORTATION RATES

THE fast carriage of small railway freights, combined with house collection and delivery, now universally known in America as "express service" is a peculiar American institution which has grown up superimposed from the first upon the regular railway services — instead of being here, as abroad, developed as an integral part of the railways' business. The failure of the government early to adopt a parcel post was an important factor in the growth of the express companies, since for decades they gave the only means which any shipper had of quick transfer of goods, and were the sole reliance of all who had more than a letter or a paper or a few ounces of merchandise to send away.

, The first express service was instituted some 65 years ago — by a messenger with a big carpet bag traveling between Boston and New York City, paying his regular railway fare. The business has grown by natural steps — and practically out of the profits of the business — until there are now 11 concerns operating over practically the entire mileage of railway line in America. These companies are the Adams, American, Wells Fargo, National, Southern, Great Northern, Northern, Western, Globe, Canadian and Canadian Northern. These are by no means all the companies that have flourished — they are the successors and assigns of many smaller companies, some of which bore the same names.

Relations of Express Companies. — While all these are distinctly separate companies, and to a certain extent are competitors, yet the strongest community of interest appears. Indeed the whole express system has been called a family affair, so interlocked is it by the stock ownership of a few persons. The Adams and Southern companies are affiliated; the National is subsidiary to the American, and the American is the second largest stockholder in the Wells Fargo. The largest stockholder in the United States company (now out of business) was

201

also the largest in the Wells Fargo. Large stockholders in the country's trunk railways are stockholders and directors of various express companies. The Great Northern, Northern and Globe companies are owned and controlled by the railways over which they principally operate.

For many years the country was geographically divided among the important express companies and they did not seriously press beyond their limits. For instance, Wells Fargo kept west of the Mississippi River and the others east — but now in the Central States the Wells Fargo, Adams, and American appear in active competition. The Southern dominates the South from Washington to New Orleans, although the American has broken in. New England is still the home of the American (and the affiliated National) and the Adams. The Northwest is served by the Great Northern, Northern, Wells Fargo, and Western. The American company operates over a central route (Union Pacific) to the coast, as does the Globe (over the Denver & Rio Grande). Wells Fargo reaches the Pacific through the Southwest also, but this territory has been opened by all the companies except the Southern and those in the Northwest. The Canadian companies named operate mostly within the Dominion but enter the states of Maine, New Hampshire, Vermont, New York, Michigan and Minnesota where Canadian railway lines operate.

Worth of Express Companies. — The property owned and used by the express companies is worth somewhat over $27,000,000 including horses and wagons, motor trucks, office equipment, safes, trunks, etc. — out of which probably not more than $1,000,000 represents original investment of outside capital. The vital assets of the companies, however, are the contracts with the railways by virtue of which the latter provide the engines, cars and railway terminals, and haul the goods for the express companies, which are but an auxiliary arm of the railway service. These contracts have formed to a considerable extent the basis of capitalization as disclosed by history. There is reported some $63,500,000 in stock, $36,000,000 in funded debt, and $59,000,000 in undivided profits.

Recent Improvements in Express Rates. — The whole fabric of express rates was recast in 1913 by the Interstate Commerce Commission and put into effect Feb. 1, 1914. The change put the service on a cost-of-service basis and arranged the charges as though all the companies together formed one grand concern covering the entire country with a unified system. The quick shift to cost-of-service was feasible because the factors causing departure from it in the case of railway freight tariffs — like water-route competition, protection of vested interests, etc. — are of less consequence when the size of each shipment is as small as in express service, and the number and variety of shipments to any one important receiver is so large.

The Old Express Rate System. — Under the practices which prevailed up to 1914 there were two main classes of express shipments: (1) "merchandise" and (2) "general-special" — the latter covering articles of rougher character and smaller value, generally food and agricultural products, which nevertheless needed to be moved under express service though they would not support the rates of more valuable goods.

The old "merchandise" charges were proportioned per pound according to a tariff for 100-lb. shipments, lesser weights taking higher graduated charges per pound when the hundredweight tariff was under $2. When the base tariff was over $2 the higher graduated charges were applied only to shipments of less than 50 lb. The graduations bore heavily on the small-shipment business — the pound rates for 10 lb. running to three or four times the pound rates on a hundredweight. Multiple graduation was also used; for over 7-pound weights where there was only one company in the place of destination and two companies shared the carriage, the base tariffs were graduated before addition, raising the final charge over that from a single graduation on the aggregate of base tariffs.

The express agent in figuring charges for a customer had tariff sheets, giving the 100-lb. rate, and graduation tables giving the actual charges for a given weight and base tariff.

The "general-special" goods were billed by the pound according to 100-lb. rates which were from 60 to 80% of the merchandise rate. A 35¢ minimum charge was commonly imposed, though where two companies had part in the carriage each collected a 25¢ minimum. Where a single shipment comprised several packages, charges were on the aggregate where the average weight was over 20 lb. Insurance charges for declared valuations of over $50 (or 50¢ per lb. on over 100 lb.) have ranged from 10 to 20¢ per $100, according to the tariff for carriage.

Upon this simple base all sorts of special schemes had become grafted, and these were used for various favors and discriminations to shippers who understood the loopholes. Such were the notorious "Sections A, D and E" and "Scales J, K, L, M, N, O and Z." The three "sections" were created to meet postal competition. "E" was confided to manufacturers and large shippers; any merchandise package marked "Value not exceeding $10," unsealed and prepaid, went to any express office in the country for 16¢ per lb. — which was to be compared with 25 to 40¢ under the ordinary rates. "Section D" was intended for large advertisers and was for printed matter; packages marked with a designation of contents and the legend "Value not exceeding $10" were carried at ½¢ per ounce with a 2¢ discount on packages of 50 ounces or more. "Section A" carried the same goods at merchandise pound rates which were lower than "Section D" rates where a package weighed over 4½ pounds — for any tariff under $8 per 100 pounds.

"Scale J" made a carload rate on horses about half the railroad freight rate; "K" made a rate of 60 to 80% merchandise rates on beer and temperance beverages — with a 30¢ minimum charge; "L" applied package rates to crated berries — 5¢ to $12, depending on size of crate and length of haul — in place of the 100-pound berry rate which was 60 to 80% of the merchandise rate; "M" gave a case rate for eggs of 14¢ to $3.30; "N" covered the "general-specials" noted before; "O" let live poultry in crates pass at 74 to 80% of merchandise rates; "Z" gave cheese 60 to 80% merchandise rates with 25¢ minimum.

The tariff system was so complicated that experts could not surely compute the possible rates — which numbered over 600,000,000. No relation prevailed between railway freight and express rates — except that the express charges were not (with rare exceptions), and properly should not have been, lower than the railway-freight charges. Many of the operating contracts between express companies and railroads provided that express charges should be not less than 1½ times the freight. In many cases the express was some three times the freight though up to six times had been noted.

The Interstate Express-rate System. — The rate system evolved by the Interstate Commerce Commission was much like what some of the express-officials had been working towards for many years, but which they had been unable to put into effect in spite of the marked community of interests inside the small group of men who controlled all the express companies of the country.

All goods have been reduced to a simple classification of three groups — merchandise (Class 1), articles of food and drink (Class 2) and very small packages (Class 3). Class 1 is the standard, the rate for which is multiplied on risky, valuable or bulky articles — two times for crated marble, scenery, typewriters unboxed, etc., three times for camels and elephants uncrated, eight times for airships unboxed. A very few articles, like fruit-basket material and newspapers, go for half first-class rates.

Class 2 rates in general are 75% of first class — with a minimum of 25¢. Empty containers, crates, boxes, etc., are returned at specified sums running from 10 to 50¢. Third-class rates are 1¢ for each 2 ounces or fraction thereof — with a minimum of 15¢ — but not to exceed Class 1 charges. Where two or more packages form a single shipment, with an average weight of 10 pounds per package, the charge is based on the aggregate weight. Where the average weight is under 10 pounds per package, the charge is to be figured upon 10 pounds per package.

The receipts, waybills, etc., of all the companies were improved and made uniform, and chances of double charge eliminated. The ordinary insurance liability of a company was limited to $50 per shipment of 100 pounds or less; excess value carries an extra charge varying from 25¢ per $100 where the Class 1 rate is $1, to 50¢ where the Class 1 rate is $8 or over. On live stock 1 to $2\frac{1}{2}$% is charged above fixed sums.

Rates Made Between Geographical Blocks. — The greatest innovation of the Interstate Commission's order was in the system of computing specific shipper's charges. This is built up as though one great express company served the whole country — there are no multiple graduations, etc. The country has been divided into geographical blocks, bounded by parallels and meridians, and rates computed for carriage (including pick-up and delivery) from each block into every other block where interstate commerce can occur. Every office in the block takes the same rate. By duplication and approximation all these charges reduce to 294 base rates applying to 100-pound shipments. By having 294 graduation tables for weights of 1 to 100 pounds the scheme is completed.

The way these charges ran is seen from the following extracts from the scales as first announced:

Weight, Lb.	Rate Scale No. and Charge						
	1	5	25	50	100	200	294
1	0.21	0.21	0.22	0.23	0.26	0.31	0.35
5	0.22	0.23	0.28	0.34	0.46	0.71	0.95
10	0.23	0.25	0.35	0.48	0.73	1.23	1.70
25	0.29	0.34	0.59	0.90	1.52	2.77	3.95
50	0.37	0.47	0.97	1.60	2.85	5.35	7.70
75	0.46	0.61	1.36	2.30	4.17	7.92	11.45
100	0.55	0.75	1.75	3.00	5.50	10.50	15.20

To give fair rates between offices in the same or adjacent blocks, each block has been divided into 16 squares and rates computed from each square into every other square in the same and adjacent blocks.

The rates, shown in the table just given, were based on three factors, (1) a charge of 20¢ per shipment for collection and delivery, (2) a charge of 25¢ per 100 pounds for railway terminal charges, and (3) a sum depending on weight and distance of carriage. This latter the Commission stated it varied for different localities according to the density of traffic and population therein and the cost of operating railroads, the country being divided into five zones. Zone I was north of the Ohio and Potomac Rivers and east of the Mississippi; it is the corner of the country having densest population and lowest freight and passenger rates. South of this region was Zone II. Zone III lay to the west, roughly between the 92nd and 105th meridians but including also northern Wisconsin and Michigan, above 43°. Zone IV spread west to the Sierra Nevada Mts. and Zone V was the strip between mountains and ocean.

There was still apparent wide variation in the rail factor inside a zone — in analyzing the rates in Zone I, for instance, about $1 per 100 miles on 100 pounds may be seen over some routes and in others only 40¢. The variations are best seen by analyzing the rate tables, which are given *in extenso* in *Re Express Rates* (24 I. C. C. 381, 28 I. C. C. 131 and 35 I. C. C. 3).

While the Commission had authority over interstate commerce only, the companies affected took hold of ·the plan with ready coöperation and adjusted their intra-state business upon the same plan, in order to give the scheme a fair trial. Even the contracts with the railways, by which the latter used to receive from 35 to 60% of the express revenues, were modified in view of the showing that nothing was due the roads from what the express companies collected for pick-up and delivery.

Tentative Scheme Inadequate. — After two years' trial of the system and rates outlined in the foregoing paragraphs, the case was reopened by the Commission on complaint of the companies that they were not securing adequate revenue. The number of shipments was shown to have increased from 191,644,891 in 1914 (2 months under the old plan and 10 under the new) to 193,870,819 in 1915; the average charge fell from 75.6¢ to 67.7¢. In these years the operating expenses of the companies decreased $4,111,992. The gross transportation revenue in 1915 was $131,173,670. $66,470,551 was paid the railways, $67,084,013 went into operating expenses, taxes, etc., leaving $2,380,894 deficit from operation. An increase of 3.86% was asked — amounting to $5,062,634; this was what · it was estimated would be secured by interchanging the 20¢ collection-delivery allowance and the 25¢ rail-terminal charge. This increase was seen to bear heaviest on the small-package business — which was a desired effect since the heaviest cuts in the new system over the old had been in that field. The effect on the charges is shown in the following extracts from the modified scales, comparable with the table already given:

Weight, Lb.	Rate Scale No. and Charge						
	1	5	25	50	100	200	294
1	0.26	0.26	0.26	0.28	0.30	0.35	0.40
5	0.26	0.27	0.32	0.39	0.51	0.76	1.00
10	0.28	0.30	0.40	0.52	0.77	1.27	1.74
25	0.32	0.37	0.62	0.94	1.56	2.81	3.99
50	0.40	0.50	1.00	1.62	2.87	5.37	7.72 .
75	0.47	0.62	1.37	2.31	4.19	7.94	11.46
100	0.55	0.75	1.75	3.00	5.50	10.50	15.20

CHAPTER XII

RATE PROBLEMS OF STREET AND INTERURBAN RAILWAY TRANSPORTATION

Rise of City Transit. — While industrial tramways, with iron rails on cross sleepers or stone blocks, were used abroad as early as 1770, such a railway in city streets for urban passenger transportation seems to have originated in 1831 with Stephenson's Bowery line in New York; the cars were practically horse-drawn omnibuses. The road was reported not to be a great success. Cars more like the present type appeared in 1845, and about 1855 came the prototype of the present track construction — $1\frac{1}{4}$ by $2\frac{1}{2}$-in. strap-iron rails spiked to a stringer on cross ties. The ballast was the excavated material, in a few cases topped with beach or field stone. By 1870 most of the important cities in America had some form of horse railway. The system of cars hauled by a cable driven through a small under-track conduit by a stationary steam engine appeared in New York in 1869, in San Francisco in 1873, and in Chicago in 1881. The scheme was technically successful and only the development of the more flexible electric traction caused the abandonment of the cable.

Surface cars were seen to be necessarily slow in busy streets, so that with the growth of American cities, the need of urban rapid transit became gradually pressing. The elevated road with stations say each five blocks was the first improvement, and construction was undertaken on a considerable scale in New York from 1878 on. Operation with steam locomotives was seen until 1901 when a third-rail electric-traction system was found successful, employing motor-equipped passenger cars.

From as early as 1835 various attempts to propel vehicles by electric motors had been attempted, but no great progress was possible until engine-driven generators and the distribution of power over extended conductor systems became feasible. The first successful commercial line was opened at the Berlin

Exposition in 1879; in 1881 this was developed into a public line at Lichtenfelde. In 1883 a .light third-rail line was operated between Saratoga Springs and Mt. McGregor (N. Y.) — some 10 miles. In 1884 a conduit road was opened in Cleveland and also a line in Kansas City with an overhead contact or trolley wire. The line in Appleton, Wis. (1886), is commonly considered the first commercially successful American electric railway. By 1888 F. J. Sprague had completed the Richmond (Va.) installation where were laid the foundations of present practice — separation of car body and motor trucks, the under-running trolley, flexible motor suspension, etc.

In 1886 there were 3268 miles of street railways and only two electric lines. In 1889 there were 5285 miles of street railways and 70 electric lines. By 1907 there had come to be 25,547 miles of line (34,382 miles of track) with 70,000 cars, 580 power houses of 2,520,000 kw. capacity — representing in the aggregate with auxiliary equipment $3,774,772,000. By 1912 (the last U. S. Census of this industry) there were 30,438 miles of line, 41,065 miles of tracks (only 256 miles of which were not operated by electricity), 76,160 passenger and 7790 freight cars, 500 power houses of 3,665,000 kw. capacity — representing in all $4,708,568,000.

Some Technical Features. — Street, suburban and interurban lines have general technical features much alike — the chief differences being mechanical, on account of the progressively heavier cars and higher speeds required for attractive suburban and interurban service. All roads are alike in that they generate electric energy at a central station and transmit it over a system of feeders and running conductors from which the cars derive their power (except of course those few lines which are satisfactorily served by self-propelled gasoline-engine or storage-battery cars).

For street railways the preferred running conductor is a bare copper wire about $\frac{1}{2}$ inch in diameter strung on insulating hangers over the center of the track from cross wires or brackets. The trolley wire hangs in a series of drooping curves which are none too sightly where conspicuous, and not very serviceable if high speeds have to be attained. For fast running, a more expensive overhead construction — known as the catenary type — is employed: A steel messenger cable takes the place of the trolley wire between main supports and hangs in more pronounced curves; from the messenger in turn the trolley or running wire is supported at frequent intervals by hangers of such length that the running wire is practically parallel with the rails.

Every layman even is familiar with the construction, if not with the function of the trolley-arm collector — the long pole carrying a small deep-grooved bronze wheel running underneath the trolley wire. An insulated cable rings the current from the pole to the controller and motor whence it returns to the station or substation *via* the running wheels and track. Departure from the trolley-pole equipment is seen on a number of high-speed interurban cars which have pantograph frames with sliding bows or rollers to make contact.

In a few important cities where traffic is heavy enough to warrant the expense (notably New York and Washington) the running conductors are steel T-rails, placed in a slotted conduit open to the street; suspended from the car trucks are plows which carry slippers in contact with the conductors.

For elevated or subway rapid-transit lines, the running conductor commonly is a steel third rail supported on insulators at one side of the track. The current collectors are then short hinged arms, or shoes or slippers, on brackets carried by insulated frames on the sides of the trucks. The collectors on such urban lines commonly slide along on top of the contact rail, though an under-running design has been found satisfactory in heavy railroad electrification (New York Central Railroad metropolitan zone).

The most common power-supply schemes involve the use of direct current at 500 to 600 volts. In recent years this has become a combined alternating- and direct-current system, since the primary supply is from three-phase generators and this is transmitted at high voltage to rotary converters located at favorable feeding points along the railway system.

Cars are controlled and operated by a motorman while a conductor is in charge and collects fares. On account of the inconvenience of the conductors passing back and forth through crowded aisles of city cars, because of fares missed, and on account of greater chance of accidents when the conductor is away from the entrance, a new type of car has been evolved to remedy these evils. This is the " prepayment " or " pay-as-you-enter" design, with separate entrance and exit; the conductor has a fixed post at the entrance and collects fares as passengers pass into the body of the car. "Pay-as-you leave" cars are also used.

Recently, to meet the competition of motor-busses, light one-man cars have been successfully put into extensive service in a large number of the smaller cities. One man serves as both motorman and conductor, the passengers entering and paying at the front vestibule. This cuts the labor costs in two, and, the lighter cars being smaller, appreciably reduces energy and maintenance charges. A frequent fly-away service with fewer stops is furnished which seems to be the attraction of the motor-bus.

Depth of Organization. — While the platform labor — conductors and motormen — is what the public comes most in contact with, yet it should be remembered in studying rates that there are other needed organizations of size and importance, and expense. The tracks, wires and rolling stock have to be repaired day by day; there are a certain number of service inspectors, dispatchers, switchmen and flagmen; there are the firemen, enginemen, oilers and switchboard attendants in the power plants and substations; the funds collected by the conductors have to be received, the men paid, the company's purchases audited. All this demands an important system — but one which the public rarely touches. Then over all and gathering together the several departments in a concern of size there have to be a number of general executive officers; and the satisfaction of the public depends to a marked degree on the calibre and ability of these men.

Reasons for Nickel Fares.* — The universal fare on the early

* Before these notes on fare problems of electric-railway transportation were completed, the official manual on street-railway traffic, costs and fares of the American Electric Railway Association had appeared — "Cost of Urban Transportation Service" by F. W. Doolittle, Chief of the Bureau of Fare Research. That book makes use of many of the same important published papers referred to in this section and it covers the economics of costs and fares in much greater detail. Although to some persons it necessarily must appear as a partisan discussion, yet it will be seen to be broadly based on data and studies of regulating commissions as well as of officials of supporting railways. Its appearance has made possible the omission of some detail originally covered in this section.

horse railways was a nickel — from convenience in collection
and from belief that patrons would yield that sum quite as
willingly as any smaller one. As city lines were first extended
the five-cent fare was adhered to by managements partly from
the overestimated inconvenience of making penny change, partly to encourage travel and partly knowing that a dime was too
great a sum for the service. But with the growth of suburban
lines the necessity of extra fares for the longer hauls became
appreciated and nickel zones grew up.

Growth of City Systems. — The expansion of cities and the
absorption of outlying municipalities within city limits has
brought very serious problems to electric-railway companies, for
in many cases extensions have been governed by new franchises which fixed the fare limits and frequency of service
without adequate consideration of what it would cost a company.

To see the growth of cities and some of the burdens thrust
upon the street-railway systems a few scattered typical cities,
for which data have been collected, may be cited. Thus Detroit in 1870 had only 11 square miles within city limits, but this
area has jumped to 13.7, 20.2, 27.3, 39.7 and 41.8 square miles
— a gain of 300% in 45 years. The population served had risen
from some 80,000 in 1870, to 465,766 in 1910, and 674,000 in
1915. The maximum length of single-fare ride had gone to
12.5 miles in 1901, and 13.5 in 1910, and 13.5 in 1915. In these
years the car-miles (number of cars times miles of trips) had
jumped from 14,614,000 to 22,847,000 and 33,696,000, and the
revenue per car-mile from 17.78¢ to 23.20¢ and 25.81¢.

Milwaukee, Wis., rose from an area of 10.3 square miles in
1870 to 25.9 in 1915 (35.40 inside first-fare limits), while the
population grew from 14,000 to 425,000 (455,000 inside first-
fare limits). Tracks extended from 25 miles to 136. In 1890
the longest single-fare ride was 4 miles; in 1910 it was 12.1
miles; in 1915 it was 10.8 miles. In these years the car-mile
record shifted from 8,395,000 to 13,813,000, and to 14,323,000;
the earnings per car-mile went from 22.04 to 27.42¢ and 27.31¢.
Milwaukee is of special interest because of the zone system recently installed, giving fares based on cost of service in the
different districts as noted more in detail in a later paragraph.

Memphis, Tenn., had only 2.8 square miles area in 1870 but 19.3 in 1914 — a total growth of some 560%. Meantime the population rose from 40,226 to 155,000. In 1906 there were 68.6 miles of street-railway track and in 1910 it was 110.4 miles; in these years the maximum single-fare rides were 9.6 and 16.1 miles respectively; in 1915 it was 15.7 miles. The car-miles of 1906 were 6,221,000; in 1910 they were 6,895,000, and in 1914, 7,966,000. The passenger-car-mile revenues in these years were 22.96¢, 26.14¢ and 25.09¢.

Birmingham, Ala., gives a remarkable case of territorial extension. In 1870 the city area was about ½ square mile, which has jumped to 50.1 (in 1915) — although only 20 square miles has a typical city development. The early population was insignificant — about 1000; in 1910 it was 132,700; and in 1915, 198,000. By 1890 the system had 81 miles of track and in 1910, 133 miles. In 1900 the longest single-fare ride was 7.3 miles; in 1910 it was 13.6, and in 1915 it was 14.9. In 1902 about 3,519,000 car-miles were recorded, in 1910, 6,195,000 and in 1915, 8,044,000. The passenger earnings per car-mile were 20.74¢ in 1902, 26.32 in 1910 and 19.8 in 1915. This city has imposed single-fare limits coincident with the city boundaries; beyond this the company has several 5¢ zones.

Early Departures from Nickel Fares. — Probably few people realize that there was a general small-unit rise in fares on horse-railways toward the close of the Civil War when Congress saw fit to impose a revenue tax of ⅛¢ per passenger. This, coincident with increased cost of labor and supplies, caused most companies to increase the fare from 5 to 6¢. Indeed in 1865 Congress expressly authorized such a move.

In New York City * it was 1880 before all the lines had gone back to 5¢. In Brooklyn, the 5¢ was made 6¢ in 1865–1870; 8 and 10¢ was charged beyond city limits up to 1895 when 5¢ became the universal unit. In Boston the original 5¢ fare was made 6¢ in 1866 and held there until 1880; thereafter 5, 10, 15, 18 and 20¢ were collected on the longer lines. But after consolidation and electrification the nickel fare again became universal. In Philadelphia the street (horse) railways started about 1858 with 5¢ fares but raised them to 6¢ in 1864 and to

* F. R. Ford, in Report of Committee on Basis of Rates, and Fares, American Electric Ry. Assoc., Oct., 1911.

7¢ in 1866. In 1877 a reduction to 6¢ was made, exchange and transfer tickets remaining 9¢. Between 1877 and 1887 the city councils made 5¢ fares a condition of extensions.

Electric Traction has not Prevented Congestion. — Many early sociological students expected that quick and cheap transportation, afforded from the environs of a city or town of industrial importance, would automatically prevent all undesirable congestion of population. Undoubtedly it has materially modified and checked the congestion that would have accompanied modern commercial and manufacturing developments had easy transportation not been available (assuming the questionable position that this industrial development could have been possible at all without the growth in transit facilities). It has, however, only enabled those workers who preferred rural environment to secure it — those whose tastes or income dictated living in crowded districts have remained in such numbers that the tenements have not disappeared.

Natural Step to Suburban and Interurban Lines. — It was a simple and natural matter to extend the strictly city line out into the thinly settled areas. This was welcomed by the real-estate promoters, and it greatly encouraged the development of residential districts but it is doubtful if the railway people realized their dreams of profitable traffic in any case as quickly as they were led to expect.

The successful transmission of power over long stretches of territory, and its easy conversion into forms of current suitable for street-railway operation, probably suggested continuous lines of electric railway from town to town. The early promoters cherished the illusion that light tracks along highways, with sharp curves and heavy grades, abolition of locomotives and expensive passenger stations, etc., would result in greatly decreased investment, operating costs and fares, over those for steam railways, and in grand profits. But it became necessary to carry baggage, and then express and package freight and mail were taken on. The necessity for heavier track construction and reduced grades and curves began to be felt; better schedules, train-dispatching systems, safety devices, terminal and way stations, and private rights of way had to be provided. The economies over steam road operation began to diminish.

Financial Status of the Industry. — According to the 1912 U. S. Census of this industry there was outstanding $2,324,224,000 in bonds or equivalent and $2,384,344,000 in stock. For 1912 the average return on stock was but 2.65% and on bonds 4.90%. According to the Census reports there is basis for the claim that the fair value of street railway property was not less than the stocks and bonds — $4,708,568,000.

Of course this poor showing was caused by the companies which paid little or no dividends. In Wisconsin where the average rates of return are as good as anywhere in the country — with probably fewer extremes, only 44% of the lines declared dividends — the rate averaging 5.55%. In Massachusetts the average dividend over a period of 20 years was 5.28 and the average divisible net income was 5.68%.

The investment in a normal electric street-railway property is apparently of the order of $4 for each $1 of gross earnings — for both large and small companies. This would be on the basis of present values, including intangibles, and would neglect the effects of large sums lost in obsolete items like cable roads. It would not apply to unusual conditions where, for instance, an expensive underground conduit line was required, as in New York City and Washington.

This figure is borne out by figures presented by H. G. Bradlee in 1912.* Nine companies having gross annual receipts of over $1,000,000, had investments of respectively $3.03, $3.15, $3.25, $3.30, $3.90, $4.00, $4.40, $4.97, $5.55 per $1 of gross receipts. One company of between $750,000 and $1,000,000 gross receipts had $3. Two concerns of gross earnings between $500,000 and $750,000 showed $3.00 and $3.90 respectively. Four railways having between $250,000 and $500,000 gross had unit investments of $3.80, $4.20, $4.40 and $4.40 respectively. Four companies having annual gross earnings of less than $250,000 had investments of $3.70, $3.70, $4.20 and $4.50. The average of all these 20 companies was $3.92.

Peculiarities as an Utility. — In considering the application of general discussions of utility problems to electric-railway service, it becomes obvious first that here is a service-type utility

---

* Appendix B. 1912 Report of Committee on Proper Basis of Fares, American Electric Railway Association; "Actual Figures of Existing Street Railways," H. G. Bradlee, of Stone and Webster, Boston.

and not a product dispenser. The service of most roads has the pioneer-day feature that all the customers are put in one big class and all charged a single flat-rate fare, though there is an evident desire to break away from this by the use of several small-fare zones which serve to classify customers by length of journey. It has apparently been considered to be of little or no use to cultivate off-peak classes by special rates which might be permissible — since the service is such an intimately personal matter that the equity of such discrimination between persons and classes would not be recognized and the differences would be resented. Moreover, the people who seek preferential treatment — like workingmen's tickets — seek it on social grounds unrelated to the railway business, and for peak-load periods when oftentimes the real cost of added facilities rises faster than the added income at full rates.

The load factor on city lines is perhaps the lowest of all the public utilities — about 33% of the traffic is handled in four hours of each day. This arises of course from the desire of workers to travel morning and night — or morning, noon and night. Sharp peak loads are produced by such a concentration of traffic, and it is short-hour concentration which excuses strap-hangers — for it may be a physical impossibility to operate cars enough to give seats for all who attempt to board at once. In many cases — possibly in most — to order a company to furnish rush-hour cars up to the absolute limit of ability to run them over a given line may cause unremunerative operation.

Obviously various data can be used in comparing the concentration of traffic on one line with another, and in one hour or another; the "concentration factor" employed by the Fare Research Bureau of the American Electric Railway Association is the ratio of number of passengers who would be carried in 24 hours at maximum peak figures to the actual number in 24 hours.

What is called "diversity-factor" in other utilities does not enter electric-railway operation as such, for a person either rides or does not ride; there is no quarter or half load so far as one customer is concerned. There is used, however, a figure which is indeed called "diversity factor," and it needs to be carefully distinguished from the diversity factor of other utilities. The street railways' diversity-factor (according to the use of the American Electric Railway Association Fare Research Bureau) shows the difference of traffic carried by consecutive cars over a given line in a definite interval. Numerically it is the percentage ratio of average number of passengers per car to maximum for the period and place selected.

The costs of operation in different cities, expressed for the units most nearly comparable, like car-hours, car-miles, passengers, passenger-miles, etc., have been found to vary extraordinarily even when each company under discussion is operating as efficiently and satisfactorily as possible under its local conditions. This means simply that even after giving consideration to the usual evident conditions there remain so many variables undisclosed that direct unweighted comparisons are untrustworthy. In many cases certain units of operation may, on careful scrutiny, be valid bases of study; but these same units may lead to wild results in other cases. Each case is to be judged largely by itself in ascertaining proper and reasonable fares — or, better expressed for most cases, the limitations to be placed on travel for a single fixed common fare.

The commonly seen units on which roads have been compared are, for example, operating and fixed cost per passenger, per track-mile, per car-mile and per car-hour. Each may be of use at times but they should not be held up as universal indices. Number of passengers alone gives unreliable results since the length of travel varies from place to place, line to line, season to season and hour to hour. Passenger-miles comes nearer to wide application but again here curves, grades, schedules and peak loads materially alter the showing. Moreover, the length of a passenger's trip is not easily ascertained, special counts having to be made over typical periods and the results taken as applying to continuous operation.

Tests for Fixed Charges, Etc. — The tests for fixed charges previously outlined perhaps need special interpretation for application to electric-railway studies. Peak-load distinctions in fares are not practicable so that apportionment of fixed charges on that basis is usually out of the question.

Fixed charges may be grouped by scrutinizing and dividing the annual expense accounts as fixed, operating and customer's in accordance with such test questions as: "Is this most concerned with merely providing equipment?" "Is this item dependent on amount of ultimate service given?" "Is this item caused by dealings with individual customers?" It can be seen that there are a few small customer costs but their close determination is difficult and they are generally allowed to merge with fixed and operating costs.

It is seen that some items of expenditure are to be split between fixed and operating charges. This should be done in accordance with any real knowledge of the proper proportions — such as in regard to retirance for weather- and wear-deterioration, and expenses of the engineering department. But where definite knowledge of proper apportionment is lacking it is often sufficient to split the aggregate of such items — like costs of administration, general office expense, working capital, amortization of intangibles — according to degree of utilization of plant. This can be done according to the ratio of actual passenger-miles to possible passenger-miles with the cars as run, or it can be done by dividing in proportion to the ascertainable fixed and service charge. But the use of such a segregation is not so obvious as with most other utilities where peak loads .fix participation in fixed costs.

Fixing the Fare. — One way of looking at the fare problem considers that there is a potential service available to every customer — a readiness to serve, the charge for which is the total of fixed charges as above determined divided by the number of passengers the system is expected to carry without more equipment. This is a sort of minimum charge which must be collected from every customer and to which would have to be added, of course, the other-customer costs if any. If a zone system were in effect, the shortest possible ride should yield this sum at least. Some might expect that these fixed costs should be divided among the passengers actually carried rather than the passengers for which the equipment is sufficient as it normally flows; but to divide it among actual customers is like dividing all the fixed charges in a water or electricity works among the units of actual peak-load instead of units of peak-load capacity of equipment — which at once is recognized to be inequitable and to place a premium on careless over development. However, on account of the inflexibility of street-railway fares and fare zones, greater latitude may be allowed in the calculations.

Then the second group of expenses, rising closely with the

number and distance of passengers carried, expressed say as an average cost per passenger-mile would give the additions to the minimum charge for each unit length traversed. For example it might turn out that each customer should yield up 3¢ minimum plus 1¢ per mile carried. Then in a central zone of 2-mile radius from the transportation center — or such distance out as studies showed resulted in an average of 2 miles per trip — there could be the usual 5¢ fare and for each mile or two miles beyond there could be the collection of 2¢ more.

No case is recorded of precisely this sort of rate fixing but the New Jersey Commission once indicated (*So. Englewood Imp. Assoc. v. N. J. & H. R. Ry.;* Dec., 1911) that a scheme somewhat resembling it might have to be put into effect.

Wisconsin Idea of Fares. — A somewhat different apportionment of expenses designed to secure the same ends and leading up to a zone system of fares was worked out very carefully by the Wisconsin Railroad Commission in 1914 (*Milwaukee v. T. M. E. R. & L. Co.*, 10 Wis. R. R. Comm. Rep. 1). The fixed costs were defined as those which would exist if there were no traffic — which is seen to be another way of stating "expenses of providing equipment" — covering most of interest on investment, the compensation for depreciation due to the elements alone, a part of the maintenance and repair costs, and the part of power costs usually assessed on demand. These were called "terminal" costs.

Because a certain minimum amount of car service was required on definite schedules in spite of very light traffic in some hours, the expenses of conducting transportation, the output costs of the power plants and the part of maintenance and depreciation caused by wear were held to be part "terminal" and part "movement" in their nature. The exact division of this group was made according to the ratio of average carload to "comfortable" carload. (It would seem to have been more logical to make the division according to utilization more strictly — say inversely by the ratio of actual passenger-miles to possible passenger-miles for the cars as run.)

Certain expenses were held to vary directly with the traffic — items like cost of injuries, and part of conducting-transportation expense, and these were considered to be purely "movement" charges. Certain other expenditures, as for general administration, could not be definitely allocated and so were divided according to the proportions of the ascertainable terminal and movement costs.

The terminal costs were assessed by the Wisconsin Commission on the probable number of passengers to be carried as a minimum charge and the movement costs were distributed as cost per passenger-mile in fixing the width of traffic zones.

Apportionment of Standard-account Items. — After running through the uniform system of accounts prescribed for electric railways by the Interstate Commerce Commission, and adopted by the American Electric Railway Association, the following division into fixed and movement costs has been made as showing the probable results of applying the ideas already noted as acceptable. Obviously this cannot be an accurate indication of what would be found advisable for each account of every railway. In a specific case the actual accounts studied in the light of the Interstate Commerce Commission recommendations * will indicate the proper division. One practice of this commission has been followed in this illustrative tabulation — dividing accounts not directly scrutinizable according to the division of aggregate related accounts. (See "Rules Governing Separation of Operating Expenses between Freight and Passenger Service on Large Steam Railways," Interstate Commerce Commission, 1915.)

* Bulletins: "Uniform System of Accounts for Electric Railways," "Decisions on Questions, Uniform Accounts for Electric Railways, Interstate Commerce Commission.

TABLE ILLUSTRATING TYPICAL APPORTIONMENT OF ELECTRIC-RAILWAY EXPENSE ACCOUNTS AS FIXED OR TERMINAL AND VARIABLE OR MOVEMENT CHARGES: FOLLOWING INTERSTATE UNIFORM SYSTEM OF ACCOUNTS

Account Number	Description	Fixed %	Variable %
Income Accounts — Debits			
215	Taxes	100	
216	Rental, leased lines	100	
217	Miscellaneous rent	90	10
218	Miscellaneous taxes	90	10
220–1	Interest on funded and unfunded debt	100	
222	Amortization, funded debt	100	
224	Maintenance of organization	100	
225	Miscellaneous	90	10
Operating Accounts — Expense			
1	Superintendence, way and structures	According to division of Accts. 2–25	
2	Ballast	90	10
3	Ties	80	20
4–6	Rails, fastenings, joints and special work	10	90
7	Repairs, underground, construction	90	10
8–9	Track and roadway labor and miscellaneous expense.	According to division of Accounts 2–6	
10	Paving	90	10
11–12	Cleaning and sanding track, removing snow and ice	100	
13	Repairs, tunnels and subways	100	
14–15	Repairs, elevated structures, bridges, trestles, culverts	90	10
16–18	Repairs, crossings, fences, signs, signals, interlocking, telephones and telegraphs	100	
19	Miscellaneous way expenses	According to division of Accts. 10–18	
20–22	Repairs, electric-line poles, conduits, distribution system.	100	
23	Miscellaneous electric-line expenses	100	
24	Repairs, buildings and grounds	70	30
25	Depreciation, way and structures	60	40
26–27	Balance, expense chargeable to way and structures.	According to division of Accts. 2–25	
29	Superintendence, equipment	According to division of Accts. 30–43	
30–31	Repairs, revenue cars	20	80
32	Repairs, service cars	40	60
33	Repairs, car electric equipment	10	90
34–37	Repairs, locomotives, floating equipment, shop equipment; shop expenses.	According to division of Accounts 30–33	
38	Expense of vehicles and animals	According to division of Accts. 20–37	
39	Miscellaneous equipment expense	According to division of Accts. 30–35	
40–41	Depreciation and retirement, rolling stock	20	80
42–43	Balance, operating expenses chargeable to maintenance rolling stock.	According to division of Accounts 30–41	

TABLE ILLUSTRATING TYPICAL APPORTIONMENT OF ELECTRIC-RAILWAY EXPENSE
ACCOUNTS AS FIXED OR TERMINAL AND VARIABLE OR MOVEMENT CHARGES:
FOLLOWING INTERSTATE UNIFORM SYSTEM OF ACCOUNTS. *Continued*

Account Number	Description	Fixed %	Variable %
45	Superintendence, power...............	According to division of Accts. 46–62	
46	Repairs, power stations and substations..	80	20
47–48	Repairs, power station and substation equipment.	10	90
49	Repairs, transmission system............	100	
50	Depreciation of power plants, substations and transmission system.	30	70
56 and 58	Power plant and substation supplies......	10	90
52–57	Power plant, fuel, water, oil, labor........		100
59	Purchased power......................		100
60–62	Balance, power exchanges, etc..........	According to division of Accts. 52–58	
63	Superintendence, transportation........	According to division of Accts. 64–78	
64	Platform labor, passenger car service.....		100
60–67	Miscellaneous car service, labor and expense.	60	40
68–69	Passenger station labor and expense......	80	20
70–71	Carhouse labor and expense.............	20	80
72–73	Operating labor and supplies; signals, interlocking, telephones and telegraphs.	100	
74	Labor and expense, passenger marine equipment......................	100	
78	Miscellaneous transportation expense...	According to division of Accts. 64–74	
79–80	Solicitation of traffic advertising........		100
81	Parks and resorts.....................	Where admissible	100
82	Miscellaneous traffic expense..........		100
83	General officers, salaries and expenses....	80	20
84	General office clerks, salaries and expenses.	70	30
85	General office supplies...................	60	40
86	Legal expenses........................	100	
87–88	Relief department expenses; pensions...	According to division of total labor and salaries	
89	Miscellaneous general expenses.........	According to division of Accts. 83–86	
90	Valuation expense.....................	100	
91	Amortization, franchises.................	100	
92	Injuries and damages...................		100
93	Insurance............................	90	10
94	Printing stationary, tickets, etc..........	20	80
95	Storehouse expense....................	100	
96	Garage and stable expense..............	According to division of Accts. 20–37	
97	Rental, tracks and terminals............	100	
98	Rental, equipment.....................		100
99	Balance, miscellaneous operations......	According to division of Accts. 83–98	

Substituting Car Unit for Passenger. — Instead of using passenger-miles in the foregoing studies of fare limits, the more easily obtained unit, the car-mile, may be used. The fixed charges do not depend on ultimate service — length of car trip — but can be apportioned to the equipment in service — shown by number of car trips. The service charges do depend on ultimate quantity of service and hence are apportioned on car-miles. If the average revenue per car trip is known, deducting the fixed charges per trip will leave a sum which divided by the car-mile operating cost gives the length of haul possible with profit. The effect of a change in fares on number of passengers should be studied and possibly a modified calculation made of earnings.

Effect of Peak Loads. — The effect of high or low load factor — that is, of travel in off-peak or in rush hours — is reflected in the fixed costs to be carried by a passenger, through the division of some important items according to utilization of equipment. It is also reflected in the operating cost per passenger- or per car-mile through spreading the arbitrarily split expenses over more units. The ultimate effect of good load factor is thus made similar to the case of utilities where peak loads directly determine participation in fixed costs. In the general case the minimum or ready-to-serve charge is reduced and the unit operating cost is improved; and for the street railway the length of profitable haul, or the width of single-fare zones, is increased.

Reasonable Length of Trips on Individual Lines. — In the foregoing all the lines have been aggregated and the results as to length of haul, etc., apply as an average over the system. In many cases this is sufficient but in others — notably larger cities and suburban lines — it is desired to treat each line on its merits. To do this the costs for the line must be found. Where possible the accounts, of course, will be drawn on for the apportionment, but this is more apt to be possible on the suburban and interurban lines. For cities it is more often necessary to approximate the costs by applying to suitable construction and service units, the fixed and variable costs for such units applying to the whole system — for instance, multiplying a line's miles of track by the system's fixed costs per track mile, and the actual line's car-miles by the system's service cost per car-mile, or using whatever units best fit the local conditions.

Having located the fixed and service costs for a line, and knowing the number of passengers and passenger-miles on the line, makes it possible to treat the line as was the system. That is, the minimum charge for the shortest possible ride is found; and the difference between this and the unit fare, divided by the movement cost per passenger-mile, gives the length of ride, or average width of zone.

Practical Fixing of Zone Fares. — An extension of the ideas involved in the scrutiny of profitable haul on individual lines has been developed * for fixing actual and workable zone rates. Briefly sketched, the process starts by fixing the length of zones, arbitrarily or otherwise, and apportioning the fixed and service costs on the basis of track- and car-miles respectively, or by passengers and passenger-miles after a traffic census, or by car trips and car-miles on the record. Then various rates of fare (a fixed-cost factor plus a mileage unit) are computed which would meet the cost of service. These are applied to the traffic found in the zones to see how nearly they make each zone pay its own costs. Finally such practical changes are made as are needed to present the most convenient and acceptable provisions.

Traffic Surveys. — The need in any rate case of specific data, beyond those yielded by the ordinary records of the company, have been evident throughout the foregoing discussions — information for instance on passengers boarding and alighting all or typical cars at various points from hour to hour, passengers on each car at maximum load points, length of passenger travel, etc. The questions of adequate service are so ultimately connected with fares and costs that most surveys of notable value have been much more comprehensive than the cost data alone would require — covering number of persons standing, number of empty seats, occupational classes of passengers, delays and their causes, effect of weather, of municipal events and of street vehicles. How these studies may be made suggests itself by a survey of local conditions but may be understood by scrutinizing such reports as those of B. J. Arnold on transportation problems in Chicago (1902-'06-'08-'10-'11-'13), Pittsburg (1910), Providence (1911), San Francisco (1912-'13); of Ford, Bacon and Davis on Philadelphia (1911); of A. M. Taylor on Philadelphia (1913); Wisconsin Railroad Commission

* Doolittle, "Cost of Urban Transportation Service," 1916, p. 256-263.

on Milwaukee (1912 and 1913); Barclay Parsons and Klapp on Detroit (1915).

Constitution of Good Service. — The several city-transit reports named, and other similar ones, review what was judged to be adequate and reasonable service for the place and time — within the ability of the people to support it. In New York City sufficient cars are required in any 15-minute period to provide 10% excess capacity (or failing that 25 cars per hour in each direction); and no less than 6 per hour in each direction during the day or night.* In Milwaukee † a headway of 10 minutes in non-rush day hours was required, with 20 minutes at night; in rush periods during any half hour seats must be provided for 67% of the passengers offered and for 133% in each other half ,hour. In Providence for non-rush hours it was recommended that each 20 minutes should see as many seats as passengers; for rush hours, seats for 50% of the offered passengers.‡

The reasonableness of demands for a particular degree of service cannot be wholly judged on the comfort and convenience of the riders, for this may depend largely on the location and practices of industries, local customs and topography, city plan, etc., — matters beyond the control of a traction company. Any study of reasonable service must include the cost effects. For example if it were physically possible to operate over a system's tracks cars enough to provide seats for all rush-hour passengers it might cost so much more that the company would face a serious deficit. The motormen and conductors would all have to get pay for a full day's work, and some cars would not be needed but an hour or two out of the day; both fixed and movement costs per car trip would be too great for the traffic to support.

Contrasts Between Old and Present Costs. — In place of the light track construction already described for the early days of street railways, today the rails weigh from 70 to 120 lb. per yard and are laid on heavy ties, 6 × 8 in. × 8 ft., 2 ft. apart and ballasted with rock or gravel or bedded in concrete. In

---

* N. Y. Public Service Comm. First Dist., Rep., 1908-10.

† *Milwaukee Suburban Fares*, 13 Wis. R. R. Comm. Rep. 245.

‡ B. J. Arnold, "Traction Improvement and Development in Providence District," 1911.

streets, paving between rails and for 1 to 2 feet on each side is required — of granite, brick or wood block. The whole cost today is in the order of $15 to $20 per yard compared with $3 to $6 at first.

The cost of a bobtail horse car and horses was some $2500, while a modern electric car runs from $5000 to $12,000. The cost of light track alone, where no paving or similar street improvement is involved, runs to $25,000 per mile; in cities it may be $40,000 — in both cases without rolling stock, power plants, etc. According to the 1912 U. S. Census of the industry, the average cost per mile of equipped American electric railways has gone from $48,000 in 1890 to $96,000 in 1902 and $113,600 in 1912. This rise has been due not only to the heavier equipment but to increased cost of work in streets due to pipes, sewers and conduits, grade crossing elimination on interurban lines, etc. There has been some effect too on the census data from expensive subway work in Boston, New York and Philadelphia.

There has been a marked tendency for taxes on electric railways to increase; according to the 1912 Census the taxes on operating and lessor companies in 1902 was 4.8% of gross earnings and 5.6% in 1912. This is due probably to the continuation of a movement which antedates the now popular commission regulation and which aimed to secure for the public a share of the profits of public monopolies. It was in effect an attempt at regulation — which however has now no place alongside commission supervision.

The growth in taxation has been nominally about 16% but actually the effect has been greater, for the operating expenses of the roads have climbed meanwhile, and the unit fare has remained the nickel. Longer rides, more transfers, greater interest rates on bonds, etc., have conspired to heighten the actual burden of taxation on net income.

Wages of trades most involved have risen some 35% over the figures for 1890–1900 * keeping pace with the cost of family living. Prices of materials of repair by July, 1916, had gone up over the average for the 1890–1900 decade approximately as follows: 10% for metals, 11% for paints, 13% for building materials, 16% for tools, 50% for coal, and 57% for lumber.

* A more detailed study of various authorities on such points is given in Doolittle's "Cost of Urban Railway Transportation."

Depreciation of Electric-railway Property. — The sacrifice of investment in street-railway properties experienced up to 1900 was perhaps more by obsolescence than by deterioration — and unfortunately the need of making good this loss out of the current earnings was realized too late. From 1900 to 1910, there was still some loss by obsolescence but a greater part by deterioration. Since 1910 there has been comparatively little change in the industry as a whole and, consequently, only small loss by pure obsolescence.

Prior to 1900 there was the progressive scrapping of horse cars and light railway track, cable cars and conduit, and all the early experimental electrical equipment before standardization set in. In the decade 1900–1910 the obsolescence was due to discard of medium-weight track and single-track cars in those localities where heavier traffic developed — or was hoped for. In this period, too, came the prepayment-type of car and the greater use of steam turbines in place of reciprocating engines for prime motive power.

A well-kept modern electric railway — city, suburban or interurban — should show on examination that its physical property is worth about 85% the first cost of all the several items which can be inventoried. That takes no account of big works which have been discarded and disappeared from the sight of the appraiser.

There is some chance that where adequate records have been kept of the companies' investments and supersessions of apparatus it may still be possible to recover some of the money spent in good faith but unproductively. Such treatment is to be seen in the bond issues of the Binghamton company approved in April, 1916, by the New York Public Service Commission, Second District. Out of a total of $1,000,000, some $100,000 went for improvements and the rest to fund a floating debt — which funded debt, however, is to be carried in a suspense account with at least $7500 paid back to bondholders each year. But for the most part all such developments expenses are now pure conjecture and more than apt to be ruled out by commission and court, on the argument also that the early ventures were largely speculative — the early investors taking great risks and expecting great profits.

Securing Retirance. — In the street-railway industry at the present moment it does not seem feasible to establish any one single way of treating depreciation of properties and its compensation — what has here before been called retirance. A combination of methods seems desirable — though they may all be regarded as of the direct-repayment type discussed before (see Chapter VIII). First a study of the property, records and accounts may establish satisfactorily the accumulated losses due to obsolescence, inadequacy, etc., which have never been made good out of earnings and which properly may enter the capitalization, or rate-basis worth, as part of the business development — unless that element has been computed in such a way that this brings duplication. It may, in many cases, prove better to put such losses of capital into a suspense account which is reduced by contributions out of earnings, as in the Binghamton case already noted.

Then there is a second element of depreciation to be observed — an annual wear-deterioration that is made good by the replacement in course of general maintenance — of wires, supports, rails, ties, poles, paving, and the other small units which exist in great quantities in all stages of life. This variety of retirance is well covered by the cost of maintenance and at the present time in most cases there appears no necessity of complicating the records by separate accounts. (It should be noted, however, that some parts of trackwork like special work in cities which is heavy, expensive and not duplicated, or like granite-block paving on concrete foundations, may require little renewal from year to year but will demand replacement in large amounts after few years. This sort of retirance then is better cared for as noted in the next paragraph.)

There is finally that sort of depreciation and retirance which have been most discussed among utility men — those on large important items slowly wearing out or become antiquated. This retirance is to be secured by one of the sanctioned plans which deducts proper sums from the earnings — preferably the concave-curve scheme or straight-line plan, depending on the extent to which depreciation causes an increase in operating cost or a decrease in capacity and efficiency. In this class is the retirance on cars, power plants, barns, shops, stations, etc.

In a few roads of normal condition and history where retirance is handled on some such basis, there is a direct repayment equal to some 4% of the gross annual earnings. Retirance covered up in maintenance and repairs may amount to 6 of the 10% of gross earnings needed for this item. The item of compensation for old obsolescences, or reductions of a suspense account, may reasonably take 3% in good years if it can be secured. Expressed in terms of physical property value — not necessarily full rate-basis worth — the 4% of gross earnings becomes some 1.0%, the 6% becomes 1.5% and the 3% becomes 0.75% — the total amounting to 3.25% — of the physical value. This would appear to be an altogether too small sum to accord with experience in other utilities as to what constituted safe financing; that some of these companies are safe is due to other appropriations going back into the property — extensions, surplus funds, etc., amounting to another 1 or 2% in good properties.

Because of the great changes in the technique of street-railway construction and operation in the various decades up to 1910, it is obvious that life-experience tables of electric railway apparatus are of much less value in the study of depreciation and retirance here than the life-experience tables which may be used in some of the other utilities which have become more stabilized technically — water-works particularly. The divergences of experience and conditions like climate, degree of maintenance, adequacy, quality of labor, public demands, earnings, etc., are marked, not only between different companies but for a single company * so that no conclusions can be drawn. On the other hand there is the quoted experience of bodies like the Wisconsin Railroad Commission's Engineering Department that their life tables, carefully handled and regarded more as bases for departure in specific cases, are most useful.

Rapid Transit and Rates. — As cities grow and develop more or less extensive districts of concentrated business, the appearances of traffic congestion multiply and the time of transit between homes and places of work lengthens. Then the more thoughtful citizens begin to consider the possibility of subways — the appeal of elevated lines at present not being great in the absence of experience with heavy masonry (concrete)

* Reports of Joint Committee on Life of Railway Physical Property, American Electric Railway Engineering and Accountants Associations, 1911-12-13.

viaducts and rock-ballasted tracks on steel structures. If they are well advised they soon see that the feasibility of a rapid-transit line or system of lines depends on the fares which the riders are willing to pay for the saving in time or the personal convenience. They find that it is only in the places of greatest population or with peculiar geographical arrangements that rapid transit is possible for surface-car fares or that the city's commercial development is hampered by the lack of a rapid-transit system. The citizens have to realize soon that common-fare operation becomes possible only where the density of traffic probably will decrease the operating cost per passenger trip enough to make up the interest on large investment. How much this saving must be is seen after noting that the cost of a rapid-transit line will be from $60,000 to $2,500,000 per mile more than an ordinary city surface line (experience showing the order of costs as $40,000 per mile for the surface line, without rolling stock; $120,000 for the steel elevated line; $330,000 for the concrete viaduct; $220,000 for an open-cut railway; $400,000 to $1,200,000 per mile for the subway — depending on the difficulty of excavation and the interference with traffic; and $2,700,000 for subaqueous tunnels). To make a $500,000-per-mile rapid-transit line pay (including return on extra investment in rolling stock and other necessary operating equipment) would require 4300 passengers per working day for each mile of line.*

The principles of rapid-transit planning have been well summarized in the following seven paragraphs.†

1. Locate rapid-transit lines in general along direct routes where the congestion has become too great for surface lines to run at fair speed and properly to take care of the traffic; the main object of rapid-transit lines in a unified system is to supplement the surface car service by removing therefrom a large part of the passenger traffic and placing this traffic above or below the street level where, being free from interference with other traffic, much higher speed can be maintained and larger and heavier trains operated.

2. Construct each line in progressive steps, completing the most

---

* From figures in "Provision for Rapid Transit in Cities," a paper by J. V. Davies before the National Conference on City Planning; see Engineering News, June 11, 1914.

† W. S. Twining, "The Problem of Passenger Transportation in Philadelphia," a report to the Select and Common Councils, March 29, 1916.

urgently needed section first and adding extensions or branches only as their necessity or feasibility is demonstrated.

3. Plan the system as a comprehensive whole conforming to the ideal plan as nearly as local conditions permit and with the underlying idea of operating all trains on the principle of through-routing as far as possible, as this is now universally conceded to be the proper method of operation. Avoid the so-called " looping " method of operation wherever possible.

4. Construct the minimum amount of subway line, as this is the most expensive form of construction and hence carries the highest interest charge per mile. As a corollary of this, subways should be built only where no other form can be used or accepted on account of high property damages resulting from the use of any other form, or for esthetic reasons, or where some special or peculiar conformation of the streets makes a subway imperative.

5. Construct rapid-transit lines to only such points in the outlying districts as will provide sufficient traffic to load the lines to an economical amount. Beyond such points the traffic should be carried by either surface lines or by other cheaper forms of high-speed construction.

6. Locate rapid-transit lines in the business district so they will act as channels through which the main traffic flow between the residential and business districts may be conveyed without confusion or congestion, and so as to require a minimum of transferring to reach the rider's destination.

7. Utilize existing surface car facilities to the fullest extent possible and supplement them by high-speed surface extensions into the suburbs, located on wide streets or private right-of-way so as to provide economically for the development of the territory adjacent or tributary to the rapid-transit lines.

It is true in general that before subways are profitable every resource of police power for the regulating and routing of traffic will have to be exhausted. After that, it is probable that comparatively short elevated or subway routes for surface cars across congested districts will prove the economical first step in reducing the delays and operating costs. The revision of the Newark (N. J.) lines of the Public Service Ry. is an example of this action.* Here very short subway and elevated lines lead to a three-deck exchange station. The first cost of a railway terminal (which, as a rule, is too heavy a burden for economy) is here diminished by the superposition of a much-needed huge office building on the terminal structure.

* See Engineering News, Oct. 7 and 28, 1915.

The Transfer Problem. — The extensive use of transfer tickets
enabling passengers to complete their journeys over various routes
for the original fare has become one of the pressing problems of
street-railway operation. The transfer ticket was at first highly
regarded by street-railway managers (as the proceedings of early
conventions of street-railway men show) as a device which continued the attractions of a multiplicity of old single-fare through
routes without the necessity of continuing an expensive and
complicated schedule of tortuous trips after the consolidation of
several lines. It was believed that the use of transfers would
stimulate traffic — and undoubtedly it had and still has a certain effect. But with the increasing costs of electric-railway
operation the transfer came to be more and more frowned on
by railway officials as a device that strings out the ride beyond
the ever shortening length that a nickel will profitably cover,
and in many cases that gives one fare when two would otherwise be yielded. The possibilities of abuse too have proved
considerable.

Yet a considerable part of the hostility toward free transfers
has been due to its statistical effect — which perhaps exagger-
ates its economic disadvantages. If a "passenger" is considered as any person who boards any car at any point, irrespective of origin, destination, route or length of ride, then it is
obvious that the total cash fares collected divided by the aggregate number of "passengers" will result in showing an average
revenue unit or fare of less than a nickel — 4¢, 3¢ or even less.
Such a statement is naturally alarming to a manager and ought
to be at least significant to an intelligent public. Its harm and·
exaggeration arises from its lack of significance standing alone
and the distraction it induces from the main issue — cost of
carrying a passenger. Such a diluted average fare becomes
significant only when stated beside the cost of the average trip
taken by the "passenger." If the fare is diluted by dividing
the cash collection by total number of boarders it is obvious that
the cost per passenger trip should be also diluted, the terminal
costs being distributed over more persons and the movement
costs being divided a greater number of shorter rides. This
dilution of cost figures is apt to give a misconception of unit
cost per paying passenger for it is logical to assess each paying
passenger with fixed costs only once — whether he transfers or not.

The transfer problem then should not be a distinct problem; it should be another phase of the vital problem of making the average ride over the system, or perhaps on each line thereof, approximately not greater than the profitable distance.

Attempts to cut off transfers, instead of general equitable restriction of trip length over all routes, is sure to arouse greater hostility and to result in an irritating impression of a discrimination whereby passengers on through routes are to be carried further for a single fare than those who have to suffer the inconvenience of change in order to get to their destination. The actual curtailment of transfer privileges in many situations is apt to cause a demand for multiplicity of through routes which may not be economical.

One significance of a heavy statistical dilution of unit fares by transfer "passengers" is that there may be a heavy transfer movement which could be economically handled by through routing of some cars or revising the main trunk route. Such a reduction of transfers reduces expense through delays, stops (which affect minor repairs and renewals), injuries, etc.

Jitney-bus Competition. — No other one phenomenon in electric-railway operation has raised any such tempest as has the competition of the small motor cab or bus — the "jitney." Crazes for jitney riding seem to have possessed large parts of the riding public in some cities for a time, and distracted railway officials have seen ruin staring out of their shrunken gross earnings. At this early date, when the jitney is only a couple years old, it is not possible clearly to foresee its future position; however, as far as costs show, the jitney may be expected to be more of a short acute attack than a chronic continued disease. Such cost figures on the operation of light automobiles as are commonly available leads to the expectation that a free-lance owner-driver will have an actual cash expenditure so nearly approaching his maximum possible revenue that he can earn only a motorman's wage for a long day's work — and that after neglecting interest on his small investment, depreciation, etc. Where a company operates, say 50 to 100 jitneys, the stated costs rise above the expenditures of the free-lance, for hired men do not work as long hours, the repairs are made by a special force, and interest is not neglected. Jitney companies are not inviting prospects and the continuance of this type of service seems to depend, each year, on a fresh crop of enthusiastic owner-drivers — each with an investment of a few hundred dollars which he may sacrifice.

The appeal of the jitney bus comes from its fair-weather advantages under light traffic — smoother carriage, better air, higher speeds, and fewer stops. It is obvious that if a two-mile trip is made by an automobile with four passengers and a 40-seat filled car, there may be up to ten times as many stops by the car as by the auto — a matter affecting the comfort of the longest riders, and the speed of the journey.

Cleveland 3¢ Fare Campaigns. — The street-railway system of Cleveland, Ohio, is unique among American roads in its operating arrangements and no review of street-railway rates and services would be complete without calling attention to it. The events of 1903–1910 leading up to the change have become historical and only the briefest review is needed to show the development of the present plan.

One Tom L. Johnson was elected in 1903 on a platform of 3¢ fares, competing railways, universal transfers and eventual municipal ownership. Immediately there started a most tangled series of moves on the part of every interest involved. Some of the franchises of the old concern, the Cleveland Electric Railway Co., were expiring, and renewals and rights for extended lines were desired. In response to the mayor's appeal the company tried 3¢ and 4¢ fares without transfers on several lines and reported the earnings insufficient. A rival enterprise, the Forest City Street Ry. Co., and its successor, the Municipal Traction Co., had secured franchises but the courts prevented any great utilization of the rights granted. There were proposals and counter-proposals, injunction suits, spectacular attempts to secure possession of streets, contempt-of-court proceedings, etc. No real progress was evident, however.

In 1907 Johnson ran for office again — and on a 3¢-fare platform — winning the race. Shortly after, the old company agreed to certain of his proposals, became the Cleveland Railway Co., and leased its lines to the Municipal Traction Co., under a 6% guaranteed dividend. A city fare of 3¢ with 1¢ for transfers was put into effect. Consequent reductions of service caused such dissatisfaction that the whole arrangement was upset again, the Municipal Traction Co. going into receivers' hands.

By court orders the maximum fares allowed in the franchises were put on — 5¢ on some lines and 3¢ on others. Suburban fares remained at 5¢. Various attempts were made to force the Cleveland Railway Co. to accept a franchise providing for 4¢ fares, a revaluation of property, arbitration of disputes, right of city to name a purchaser, city control of operation, appointment of a city railway commissioner to be paid by the company. The company balked at some of these steps but negotiations proceeded and finally the troublesome points — maximum fare and valuation — went to Judge Tayler of the U.S. Circuit Court, as arbitrator. While the arbitrator was considering the case, Johnson was defeated in his third campaign for the mayoralty, but the arbitrator's report was made, the ordinance was passed in December, 1909, and accepted before the new administration came in. It was approved by referendum in February, 1910.

Cleveland City-Control Ordinance. — The 1909 settlement ordinance (commonly known around the country as the " Tayler Ordinance ") was designed, in the language of the statute, to

secure to the owners of property invested in street railroads security as to their property, and a fair and fixed rate of return thereon, at the same time securing to the public the largest powers of regulation in the interest of public service, and the best street-railroad transportation at cost consistent with the security of the property, and the certainty of a fixed return thereon, and no more.

The railway company by this scheme operated the property and the City prescribed the service through the Council and the Railway Commissioner. The fare was started in the middle of a sliding scale at 3¢ cash with 1¢ for transfer without rebate. Revenues were credited to an "interest fund" established at $500,000 to start with by a company payment. The company was allowed for maintenance, depreciation and renewals, 4¢ per car mile in January, February, March, April, May and December; 5¢ in November; and 6¢ in June, July, August, September and October. For operation the allowance was 11.4¢ per car mile. Interest on funded debt was allowed as paid. From the interest fund, each month a proper portion of 6% per year on the valuation was drawn. If, after 8 months' trial, the interest fund rose to over $700,000, a lower rate of fare was to go into effect and if the fund sank below $300,000, a higher rate was to be permitted. The sliding scale of fares was as follows:

(a) 4¢ cash, 7 tickets for 25¢, 1¢ transfer, no rebate;
(b) 4¢ cash, 7 tickets for 25¢, 1¢ transfer, 1¢ rebate;
(c) 4¢ cash, 3 ticket for 10¢, 1¢ transfer, no rebate;
(d) 4¢ cash, 3 tickets for 10¢, 1¢ transfer, 1¢ rebate;
(e) 3¢ cash, 1¢ transfer, no rebate;
(f) 3¢ cash, 1¢ transfer, 1¢ rebate;
(g) 3¢ cash, 2 tickets for 5¢, 1¢ transfer, no rebate;
(h) 3¢ cash, 2 tickets for 5¢, 1¢ transfer, 1¢ rebate;
(i) 2¢ cash, 1¢ transfer, no rebate;
(j) 2¢ cash, 1¢ transfer, 1¢ rebate.

The first eight months (to Nov. 30, 1910) showed an increase of $50,000 in the interest fund so that the first fares (at e in the sliding scale) were held to. In May, 1911, the Railway Commissioner found the interest fund $200,000 high, and the Council decreased the fare by one step (to f). This continued up to Sept. 1, 1914, when fares were raised.

Meantime the allowances of the ordinance for operating expense, and for maintenance and renewals had proved insufficient so that deficits had been created in these departments in spite of a growing interest fund which called for lower fares. The City, nevertheless, demanded still lower fares and, under a wise provision of the ordinance, the dispute went to a board of three arbitrators. These men reported after due deliberation that, in the three years' operation to Feb. 28, 1913, there had accumulated a necessary over-expenditure of $259,593 for operation, — 2.63% on an allowance of $9,860,816. The over-expenditure for maintenance was $323,597, — 7.8% on $4,155,459. The arbitrators recommended that the operating allowance be increased from 11.5¢ to 12.1¢ per car mile. The accumulated operating deficit they recommended should be taken from the interest fund at once. No added annual allowance for maintenance was granted, although the deficit had included no figure for retirance on long-lived property. The maintenance deficit was to be cared for by such occasional drafts on the interest fund as would not draw it down below $400,000.

There had accumulated surpluses in the accounts for insurance and for injuries and damages amounting to $63,049 and $152,954. The arbitrators found that unexpected balances of allowances for insurance and injuries and damages should have been annually credited to the interest fund.

The several findings of the board were put into effect by the City Council, the Railroad Commissioner and the company. The low fare of 3¢ with 1¢ for transfer has been continued through an unusual coöperation of Council, people and company to keep costs down, although the service is better than in many other cities of the country. The topography and arrangement of residential districts is favorable. Shortened routes are permitted, to concentrate crowds for longer distances and to increase car intervals on longer lines. Cars do not stop at all streets, which, together with use of trailers and special loading methods, gives some 20% faster schedules than seen in other American cities. The speedy loading is secured by running cars so far as possible on a pay-as-you-leave scheme outbound and pay-as-you-enter coming back. Special rolling stock favors such operation. Police control of vehicular street traffic is strict. All of the lines (16) radiate from the commercial center of the city and most cars go around some one of several loops in this district.

Objections to the Cleveland Scheme. — Electric-railway men outside of Cleveland who have examined the operation in detail are not satisfied that it should be copied elsewhere. The arguments of the rest of the industry to it are: (1) rigid specific allowances for operation and maintenance are insufficient, (2) there are no damage and insurance reserve funds, (3) depreciation is not cared for adequately, (4) the fixed rate of return (6%) is too small to attract capital, (5) the extension of lines is checked, (6) the service is below the Wisconsin Commission's standards, etc.

Milwaukee Zone System. — For two years a well-planned zone system of fares has been in force on the lines of the Milwaukee Electric Ry. and Light Co., apparently working well, and certainly better than the old rate system before in effect. Before the new system became effective there had been 5¢ zones of 0.99 to 7.17 miles length depending on boundaries fixed by franchises or concessions. Various overlaps had been established to meet local demands.

In the system there were some 404 miles of tracks — 175 in the city of Milwaukee, 20½ in Racine, 60 miles suburban and

16½ miles interurban. Under the old plan, 5¢ cash fares were collected going in, into and across each zone. On some suburban lines 7½¢ commutation ticket books were sold. A few reduced-rate round-trip tickets were sold to some interurban parts. With such a field of discrimination over which the company had no control, it was inevitable that a flood of complaints should have come to the Railroad Commission, newly endowed with broader powers. By mutual agreement the Commission undertook the study of the fare question in Milwaukee in August, 1913, and in January, 1914, recommended a new zone system. There were provided seven zones, outside the central city district. This last was 9 miles long and 6 miles wide — roughly semi-circular (for Milwaukee is on the shore of Lake Michigan). The first-fare district extends out from the center of gravity of traffic from 2.7 to 5.8 miles — roughly corresponding to the then city boundaries. Surrounding this are the other zones each about 1 mile wide but shifted reasonably to important traffic points.

Inside the central district a single 5¢ fare is charged and the usual transfers are given. For a ride from the central district into or across each zone 2¢ is collected in addition to the 5¢ fare. For local traffic outside the central district 2¢ is collected for each zone traveled in, the minimum being 5¢, however, for a single ride. On the interurban lines beyond the suburban zones 2¢ per mile is charged, except that where the lines pass through important towns a single 5¢ fare is provided within that municipality's limits in place of the 2¢ per mile. For through interurban service the central-district part of the fare is made 4¢. The fare between any two outlying towns on the same interurban line is equal to the difference between the through rates to these places. Children under three years of age are carried free; children of three to ten years at half fare.

The Commission in its opinion * establishing this zone system, noted that the actual costs justified rates that would yield about 2.75¢ per passenger-mile but placed the fares below such a basis in hope of encouraging traffic to such an extent that an adequate return would be gained over all expenses. The weighted average over-all earning per passenger-mile for the city and

* *Re Application of T. M. E. R. & L. Co. for Reasonable Rates*, 13 Wis. R. R. Comm. Rep. 475.

suburban system was reported * to be 1.18¢ before the change and 1.50¢ after.

Milwaukee Ticket System. — The collection of fares on the zone system described has not been insuperably difficult, although considerable study and experimenting has been needed. The city and suburban cars are of prepayment types and a light portable fare box is used. The first problem was the handling of small zone fares. A 2¢ zone ticket was provided, marked with a conspicuous red band across it, and sold in quantities. These have eliminated trouble in collecting pennies; the conductors carry no more change than under the old system.

The second pressing problem was to show the zones into which each passenger had paid to travel. The transfers from central district to suburban lines were changed so that the zone to which fare had been paid could be punched. On the longest line, with seven 2¢ zones, a special receipt is issued because of lack of space on the transfer ticket. As outbound passengers may pay the city fare first and zone fares later, the conductor goes through the car at the first zone, carrying the portable farebox, collecting the extra fares from those who have not paid through and issuing special or transfer receipts. When passengers leave they surrender the receipts — and if the amount paid has been too small the difference is then collected. In the case of inbound passengers no receipts are given except on the longest line; the passengers deposit through fares to destination.

This collection system is reported to work satisfactorily, not causing delays or congestion. On special occasions when crowds are presented at definite points for loading, extra collectors are put on for as long periods as needed and the cars (prepayment type) are loaded at both ends. Rapid loading is also helped by setting up portable ticket booths at suburban resorts.

* For detailed figures and notes on the system here described see " A Zone System of Fares in Practice," by R. B. Stearns, of Milwaukee, before the American Electric Ry. Assoc., October, 1914.

CHAPTER XIII

PROBLEMS OF WATER RATES

Development and Magnitude of Industry.* — The first American water-works probably was that in Boston in 1652 — having a 12-foot tank near Dock Square supplied by pipes from springs and used for both fire protection and domestic supply. It was not until 1796, when the population was 21,000, that an "Aqueduct Corporation" was formed to bring in water five miles from Jamaica Pond. This private system was relied upon until 1848 when the first steps toward the present system were taken.

Bethlehem, Penn., appears next (1754) with its 5-in. lignumvitæ pump, log-pipe line and wooden reservoir. In 1762 the town installed three 4 × 18-inch iron pumps which were in service for 70 odd years.

The earliest New York City project was a municipal one and started in 1774 when the city had 22,000 population; there was to be a reservoir and well east of Broadway, 1½ miles above the Battery. The Revolution prevented completion of the system. In 1799 the City, then having a population of 60,000, took stock in the Manhattan Corporation which built a tank of cast-iron plates and pumped from a well by two 18-hp. engines. By 1823 there were 25 miles of pipes and 2000 taps. In 1830 another well and reservoir were built further uptown. About this time the city built its own works for fire service, which rapidly grew and developed into the Croton River system launched in 1835.

In 1791 the Morristown, N. J., Water Co. began collecting and distributing water from the local hillsides. Up to 1798 Philadelphia, with 80,000 people, had drawn its water from wells; then it started a municipal supply project which was com-

* See a series of papers on the History and Statistics of American Water-Works, in Engineering News, 1881 to 1887. These studies led to J. J. R. Croes' "Statistical Tables of American Water-Works," and M. N. Baker's "Manual of American Water-Works," the last edition of which appeared in 1897.

pleted in 1800, using water from the Schuylkill River. Here were (for America) the first big steam water-works pumps, the first cast-iron water mains, the first successful municipal water-works development. The first prominent advance in American water-works engineering was the construction of the water-power pumping station at the Schuylkill River, 1818–1822. (A log-crib dam gave a head of 1 to 7 feet for three breast wheels driving large double-acting horizontal force pumps; turbines were later substituted.)

In 1798 Worcester, Mass., and Portsmouth, N. H., started water-works; in Albany, N. Y., a private system was started in 1799. The first works of magnitude in the several New England states appeared as follows: New Hampshire, 1798; Massachusetts, 1801; Vermont, 1820; Connecticut, 1832; Maine, 1851; Rhode Island, 1876. The development in important and typical cities is shown by a few cases: New Orleans (founded in 1718) had no water-works until 1836. Buffalo (founded in 1801) had none until 1852; Chicago (laid out in 1833) had water service in 1840; Cleveland (settled in 1810) waited until 1853; San Francisco (settled in 1776) had no works before 1857.

In 1800 there were 16 water-works in this country and in 1850 there were only 83. In 1890 the number had grown to 1878, and in 1897 there were 3196. At the present time there are perhaps 6000, complete figures not having been collected in recent years. In Canada there were 528 works in 1915.

In 1800 only one of the 16 existing water-works was municipally owned. In 1835, 28% had come under the local governments; in 1855 the figure had risen to 45%. In 1875, 54% were owned by the public but the addition of many private works in the next few years brought the figure down to 43% in 1890. However, it rose to 54% in 1897, and today is probably above 70%.

In 1888 there were 1666 water-works serving a population of 14,858,000 and having an investment of $432,226,000. The revenue was $39,363,000. No accurate figures are available at the present moment for the whole industry in spite of the great activity of the United States Census Bureau.*

* Attention should be called to the very complete data for 1915 on service equipment and rates in cities of over 30,000 population, in "General

What meager evidence there is, however, points to a total investment of $1,500,000,000 in the 6000 plants already mentioned as existing, to a population served of about 40,000,000, and to an annual revenue of $115,000,000. But of course such estimates can only be "educated guesses." It is greatly to be regretted that as accurate a survey of the development of this most important of all utilities has not been kept up as has been in the case of the railroads, electric railways, electricity-supply works, and telephone companies. This will be changed undoubtedly, as the necessity is more completely recognized of placing water-works under the same regulation as other utilities.

Water-works as Utilities. — A complete works for the distribution of a supply of potable water to inhabitants of a community may be, as to its general place among public utilities, either a service or a product type — as earlier defined. If it captures a surface supply of water and impounds it for conveying by gravity in aqueducts and mains to the consumers, obviously it is of the product type for the magnitude of its works depends on the total quantity supplied during some operating cycle more than on the peaks of demand, maximum rates of draft, etc.* If, however, it pumps from an underground or low-level body into the supply mains and the supply and pressure are pump maintained, then much investment in plant is fixed by the peak service and the water-works becomes a service-type utility to which the principles of demand,· quantity and customer costs may apply to greater or less extent. These principles would apply here without reservation if it were not for the superimposition of fire-protection; the physical plant developed for the combined services is not what it would be for either alone. Notwithstanding the complication of fire service,

---

Statistics of Cities, 1915" issued in 1916 by the U. S. Bureau. Information on the personnel, equipment, treatment, service and rates of a large percentage of American water-works is to be found in the 1915 "Water Works Directory" of the McGraw Publishing Co., New York City.

* Speaking of the ordinary consumer's requirements only, and not including the effect of municipal fire service which may be regarded as superimposed on the domestic-supply service (or *vice versa*). For the first approach to a study of water-works rate-making, the domestic-supply and fire-protection works may be considered as superimposed departments, the functions and technology of which may be discussed separately, leaving the effect of the superimposition on rate-making to appear later.

the demand, quantity and customer costs may be assessed on a consumer fairly in accordance with his maximum demand, diversity factor, quantity furnished and the number of customers supplied.

Regulation of Water Utilities. — The regulation of rates, service, capitalization and development of water-supply utilities and projects has been caught between various regulating bodies so that there are in some cases uncertainty and inconvenience for the utility, and, in other cases, general lack of that control which the public may fairly and reasonably exercise. There is as yet only a tendency to escape this condition by a more logical development of state supervision, ·though it is plainly evident that such is the best course.

Every state has a department of health of greater or less effectiveness, depending on its authority, personnel, and appropriations; and to these boards sanitary control over the water-works — private company or municipal department — is commonly given, so widespread is the knowledge that the lives of the people at large depend on the quality of the water. The best, and a considerable number, of these boards have well-equipped and well-manned laboratory and field-engineering departments so that their control of water-supplies, along with the parallel matters of sewage disposal and disease control, is highly intelligent, efficient, effective and beneficial. The approach to this situation has been gradual and fairly logical.

Alongside the boards of health have sprung up the state public-utility commissions exercising more or less complete supervision over character of service and size of rates for various public services. Legislatures have apparently hesitated to give utility commissions the same powers over water utilities that they exercise over railroad, gas, electric and telephone companies. They have evidently realized the health menace that would result by transferring sanitary control from an experienced and equipped department to a green organization; they have seen as well the intimate relation between sanitary control of water-works and general public-health work. Legislatures have hesitated to put the financial operations under utility commissions, perhaps because of the great preponderance of municipally owned works — 2 to 1. In few states has as complete oversight over municipal as over private utilities been secured. In only one known case — Massachusetts, for private companies, only — was rate control placed in the health board's hands, presumably because of the apparent remoteness of rates from matters of public health. But nevertheless the control of water-works service, as to pressure, fire protection, adequate and safe structures and the scrutiny of rates, has continued to grow steadily as an utility-commission function.

There is no reason why this bifurcated supervision should not continue to give good results, though such division of governmental function in general is hardly to be encouraged. If there should arise any tendency to friction or deadlock, it can be eliminated, without the sacrifice of prestige on either side, by following the course taken in 1915 by the Wisconsin Railroad and Industrial Commissions in regard to safety of electric circuits; they sat jointly and produced a single code of rules under which either or both may act with full knowledge that no one will escape the provisions of the law by litigation over respective jurisdictions.

Between the sanitary and financial supervision exercised by health and utility commissions there has sprung up in a few states the control of water-shed acquisition and development by a third body commonly styled a water-supply commission. Apportionment of water between rival claimants also has been settled by such boards. This may be regarded as a non-permanent development not apt to extend greatly and then only for special conditions. The work of a water-supply board is in some ways closely analogous to the valuation and rate-making activities of an utility commission, and in any event the engineering and legal departments of the latter are in an excellent position to handle all the matters which the water-supply commission could take up.

Better regulation of water utilities is one of the greatest needs of present-day public-utility service. By leaving water companies and municipal departments — the latter particularly — too much to themselves, there have been encouraged widespread continuance of unfair rates, unintelligent accounting, and inefficient and inadequate service. With all these there is a surprising narrow-mindedness of managing officials as to the place of a water-works among the other utilities and as to the occupancy of streets, the assumption of fire-protection duties, etc.

The ease with which a fair supply is distributed through a community, the inherently simple and almost fool-proof nature of many moderate-pressure gravity-supply works, and the wide discrepancy prevailing between the cost and the value of water service, have conspired to keep knowledge of this situation from spreading widely. Had the shortcomings of municipal water departments been fully investigated the opponents of municipal ownership of public utilities would not have lacked campaign ammunition; and they would not have sidestepped the issue in the water-supply field or excused municipal ownership here on the ground of close public interest in matters like public health and fire protection.

Varied Requirements for Good Water. — There are a multitude of services for which the supply of a local water-works is drawn on that most people do not realize. The ordinary domestic consumption and the fire-fighting supply are obvious but few of the others are. The requirements defining a good water differ widely and few indeed are the supplies which are ideal for all the purposes to which they are put. Water is needed in large quantities, particularly for feeding steam boilers, for paper and pulp mills, textile-finishing works, food-product factories, for soap, glue and chemical works, etc.

Many of the waters supplied, by companies and municipal departments alike, contain considerable dissolved lime, magnesia and iron, being then called "hard." Such burdens do not affect the healthfulness of a supply, though for steam-power plants and some manufacturing processes its use is very undesirable. There is an appreciable money loss even for ordinary domestic consumers on account of the greater amount of soap used in washing. Hard waters interfere with the treatment of fabrics and waste the chemicals used in breaking up wood fiber and in finishing paper. In steam boilers the hard waters let down a precipitate which incrusts the heat-transfer surfaces and leads to pitting and overheating, besides giving a direct loss of efficiency of evaporation. Iron is a particularly undesirable content for manufacturing plants on account of the discolorations produced on papers, textiles, foods, etc. Inert suspended matter is objectionable for similar reasons.

While stain, turbidity and taste are not entirely pleasant in a potable water they are seldom really unhealthful. It is bacterial content which at present is the common criterion of quality in a domestic supply. Stimulated by state and local boards of health, great attention is paid to removing bacteria from municipal supplies. In a few cases hard waters are softened at the water-works and in many cases by manufacturing customers. Where iron is carried there ultimately develops a demand for its removal.

Water-works Technology. — The water company or municipality which has a " gravity " system usually owns or controls an elevated drainage area on which there is preferably little or no population. It collects part of the run-off in impounding reservoirs, holding the needed supply, and lets the rest waste over the spillways. The all-important question about such a supply is the matter of sewage pollution. Prevention of pollution is sought by sanitary control of the drainage area, though this does not necessarily require depopulation — control of wastes may be sufficient, but purification may be needed.

For municipalities on low plains or above possible reservoirs, the use of pumps ordinarily becomes imperative, to lift water from low-lying surface bodies or from wells tapping water-bearing strata, and to maintain pressure on the distributing pipes — often with an elevated tank or tall standpipe to equalize small flow and pressure fluctuations or to carry through the night when little water is required.

The supply mains from reservoirs, or the force mains from pumps to distributing lines, may be of steel plate, cast iron, reinforced concrete or wood staves, depending on the pressures, local conditions and preferences, etc. The distributing mains in a large majority of installations are of cast-iron pipe, though there is some welded steel pipe and a little cement-lined iron- and steel-plate pipe still used. The latter was popular up to about 1885. The service lines branching off to the consumers' premises are commonly of small galvanized or lead-lined iron and steel pipes. Many are of lead.

So far as public appreciation has shown itself, clear and wholesome ground water rising from considerable depths is the preferred supply for domestic consumption. The supply next in favor seems to be a surface water from distant unpopulated or very sparsely settled mountain drainage areas. Ground waters which have to be softened or otherwise improved, or surface waters which have to be purified seem to occupy the rear place in popularity.

The use of water unpolluted as originally captured is desirable and it inspires public confidence. But the use of a supply that is contaminated as first taken, is safe so long as the management of the water-works is in the hands of competent technical men, for the art and science of water purification have been carried to a certainty of results that may well beget public confidence. Whereas with a good water low rates and adequate service depend on keeping the evils of politics out of the water department, on the other hand if the source be polluted, the very lives of the people may depend on freedom from political dictation.

The incrusting substances precipitated in a boiler by the effect of heat are the iron, calcium, aluminum and silicon oxides, and the calcium and magnesium carbonates and sulphates. Acids that pit boiler shells may be released by the depositions of these compounds, or they may come from organic matter. Foaming may be due to concentration of sodium and potassium salts which remain soluble. Blowing off some of the boiler water and replacing with a fresh supply is the common remedy for foaming; loose precipitates are also swept out in the blowing down. The softening and removal of scale-forming salts may be done cold by a chemical precipitation (commonly with lime and soda ash) and settlement or screening, or it may be done by heating, dosing and rapidly filtering. Also the use of artificial and natural zeolites has been seen; these are peculiar sodium-aluminum silicates which possess the property of exchanging their sodium for calcium and magnesium as hard water flows over them. The material is crushed and placed in filter tanks, and after the exchange of sodium is completed a solution of common salt is allowed to flow through slowly when the reverse restoring exchange is effected. The calcium salts are then washed out of the zeolite bed by a reverse current of water.

The removal of both suspended matter and bacteria is commouly secured by filtration. This may be by the "slow" process of percolating (at a rate of 2,000,000 to 4,000,000 gallons per acre per day) through 3 or 4 feet of sand overlying coarse gravel and drain tiles; or it may be by the more rapid "mechanical" filtration where a coagulant like alum (aluminum sulphate) is added, to form a flocculent precipitate and enmesh the coloring particles and the bacteria, 3 or 4 hours before forcing through small beds of graded sand on strainers — at rates of 100,000,000 to 120,000,000 gallons per acre per day. In the slow-sand filters when the top is fouled the beds are drained and about a half-inch is scraped off and washed for replacing when the beds have been scraped down 20 to 25 times. In a few places a little coagulant is used with slow sand filtration to bring down temporary burdens of clay. When the rapid filter is once clogged, the water flow is reversed and the sand agitated by mechanical raking or by blowing in air. Purification plants add greatly to the investment in and operating costs of a waterworks; they demand skilled attention and unharassed management.

When water has to be pumped continually the lowest-duty unit commonly permitted is the compound non-condensing duplex pump. It is satisfactory for small works because of its simplicity of operation and ease of maintenance, but it is relatively low in economy (50–60 million foot-pounds per 1000 pounds of steam) compared with more expensive equipment. The first step above is the use of a condensing type of compound duplex pump. This introduces only the complication of a condenser and raises the duty to 70–80 million foot-pounds per 1000 pounds steam, increasing the station economies somewhat more than indicated by engine figures alone. Where constant use of good-sized pumps is needed, it pays to go to double- or triple-expansion crank-and-flywheel units for here the heavier costs are spread over such large quantities furnished that the best of mechanics, attendants and works engineers can be afforded. These units have got up to duties of over 200 million foot-pounds per 1000 pounds steam (though the use of superheated steam makes the apparent gain greater than the actual, as disclosed by the more scientific comparison of foot-pounds per million heat units in the steam).

Electric-motor or steam-turbine driven centrifugal pumps are becoming more and more formidable competitors of all the older water-works engines. They can be had already in designs showing 80% of the duty records of the best reciprocating machines and their first cost is sufficiently less to make the total cost of pumping as low or lower, in the majority of cases.

An important part of the water-works equipment from the standpoint of rates is the consumer's meter. The types in most extended use are the positive-action and inferential. The first named are largely miniature rotary-piston engines having either a spur pinion rolling around on a larger internal annular gear or else a disk wabbling around between two conical frustums placed peak to peak in a spherical chamber. In lesser use are the inferential meters which measure the flow by the impact of the flowing supply on buckets or vanes of a wheel. In all types the moving parts actuate a counting gear train, the pointer or numbered disk of which shows on an indicator-dial.

Water Consumption. — A community's draft has marked peaks which may become of importance in finding the capacity required for a system having no fire-protection provisions. There has not been much done in finding this draft of water from hour to hour. It can be approached however from the studies made for sewerage.* The domestic service rises from about 75% of the average during the early morning hours to a sharp peak from 5–9 (125% of average), a drop to 110% at 10 a.m., a peak of 120% at 12–1 p.m., a drop to 100% at 4. p.m., another peak of 115% at 5 o'clock and a slow return through the night. A city having a number of industrial works drawing water, besides the residence drafts from hour to hour as shown, would be expected to have the peak rise to some 140% of average, sustain itself for 2 to 4 hours and steadily drop down to a minimum of 50–60% at 1–4 a.m. Between such cities are those which rise from 70–80% of average between 1 and 4 a.m., and sustain a peak of 120–130% of the average from 7 a.m. to 3 p.m. and then steadily drop off. On Sundays both quantity and peak drop off. On Mondays (washday?) both total amount and height of peak increase. .

The figures quoted are deduced from the flow of sewage at outlets, the corresponding flows of sewage coming about two hours later than the stated water drafts. In studying peak loads of water draft, *via* the sewage, it must be remembered that in specific locations and instances there may be an inleakage of ground water and discharge of industrial-plant water

* Metcalf and Eddy, "American Sewerage Practice," 1914, pp. 187–206.

originally drawn from private wells instead of the water-works system. The sewage flow of Cincinnati, however, for instance, shows in a residential district (Ross Run Sewer) a rise from 5 to 9 A.M. of 50% to 179% of the average, slowly and steadily decreasing for the rest of the day and night, showing that the noon and evening peaks may sometimes be suppressed. The corresponding heavy water draft comes probably from 3 to 7 A.M.

There would not be expected to be any great difference in peaks or totals for summer and winter — such as exist in electric and gas service unless the place has a summer or winter increase of population like some resorts.

Fire Service or Domestic Supply First? — The discussions of water-works officials show that in some places fire protection is regarded as the primary service for which their works were instituted; others regard this as incidental, even though of extreme importance, to the domestic supply. Which view prevails or should prevail in any given case may decidedly affect the rates for fire-protection service. The extreme comes when the charges are based on what a plant solely for the given fire protection would cost and this may approach the cost of the given system — less purification works, service pipes, etc., and with less expensive lower-efficiency pumping equipment where pumps are used. At the other extreme, where the fire service is considered as grafted upon the domestic supply, the minimum burden may be considered as the enlargement of the physical works demanded by the fire protection over that sufficient for adequate domestic and manufacturing supply. If such a view prevailed, as it will in perhaps the majority of instances, it might be necessary to burden the fire service with the larger purification works needed to meet the possible drafts of water in case of a conflagration, the larger pumping units, mains, etc., as discussed in detail later.

A good fire stream requires about 250 gallons per minute at a pressure of 50 to 60 pounds per square inch at the hydrant, though both quantity and pressure may reasonably drop to 150–200 gallons and 40 pounds in purely residential areas. The number of streams possible to be concentrated on any point should depend on the character of the locality — as to population, density and height of buildings, width of streets and factors fixing the dangers of conflagration. The number of streams which it is conceded * need to be available at once runs from 3 in a 1000-population town to 12 for 10,000 people, 15 for 20,000 people and in proportion up to 30 for 100,000 population.

In the congested districts two-thirds of these streams should be concentrated on any square or on each important hazard with a minimum of 10 streams; the hose lengths should not be over 250 feet. Six-inch pipe mains are commonly held to be the safe minimum for good fire pressure whereas 4-inch often would do for ordinary supplies.

Charges for Fire Protection. — It is only in very recent years that intelligent study has been made of the proper charges for the fire-protection service afforded a community by its water-works — for what commonly is called "hydrant rental." It is now seen that in a large number of cases an appreciable injustice has been done on the one hand to the water company or municipal department, or on the other hand to the customers as contrasted with the taxpayers. Where a community has long paid, say, $10 a year per hydrant, it is loath to pay $50 when it realizes that comparatively little water is drawn and few hydrants are opened at all. Some large measure of responsibility must be assumed by the utility managers for the widespread failure of the public to realize that there is a considerable investment in hydrants and hydrant connections, and in larger mains, reservoirs and pumps, which would not have been made if fire protection had not been considered.

Reduced to its fundamental terms the way is simple to find out what charges ought to be made for fire-protection service, or "hydrant rental" as it is inadequately termed. It is assumed of course that the company is to secure a return covering the actual cost of rendering the fire service plus a reasonable return on the investment required for this alone. The question of super-profits to induce maximum economy and superior service usually disappears as most water-utility managers realize that fire protection acts to insure the uninterrupted continuance of each customer's service and payments and is to be encouraged in every way. The community should pay a reason-

* J. R. Freeman, "Arrangement of Hydrants and Pipes For Protection of a City Against Fire," Journal of the New England Water-Works Association, Vol. 7.

able return (including retirance) on the difference in the value of the plant as it exists and as it would be if no fire-protection service were given; the community should also pay the actual cost of maintaining the hydrants, hydrant connections, extra pumps and reservoirs and in most cases the excess cost of maintaining the mains and supply lines over what would be required for the domestic system alone.

The actual determination of the extra investment in the several parts of any specific water-works is properly the work of an engineer and is to a certain extent a matter of judgment as well as of computation. The allocation of maintenance costs is a matter of proper accounting and scrutiny of records. Each case should be studied by itself, but there are various comparisons which may be made to afford a general check on the reasonableness of the results obtained.

The Delusions of "Hydrant Rentals." — Not only is the use of the term "hydrant rentals" unfortunate in its inadequate public impression of what is back of water-works fire protection, but also the term has no logical or consistent relation in different localities. That is to say, the cost of fire protection divided by the number of hydrants is not necessarily the same in two places of the same size. It depends on the character of the city (residential, industrial, etc.), the configuration of the town-site (long and narrow, circular, square, etc.), the extent of congestion in business and population, the peculiarities of business and of building construction, the history of the water-works, and other factors. The costs of fire protection, figured on the hydrant basis are of service for comparison only when the effect of such matters is taken into account.

The use of hydrant-rental figures, in spite of their uncertain basis, is largely seen in statements of fire-protection charges. The figures range all the way from $10 per year to $100 with the majority running between $30 and $60 (see accompanying tabulation of rates from a study of 315 towns and cities, printed in the Journal of The American Water-Works Association, June, 1914). The results of rate investigations in a few cities give rise to the expectation that in few cases will the actual annual cost per hydrant fall below $40. This is confirmed by a study of the number of hydrants in American cities, as reported by the U. S. Bureau of the Census, in connection with the experience

of per capita cost of fire protection in cities of various classes *
as follows:

Population Group	Aggregate Population	Number of Hydrants	Cost of Fire Protection per Capita	Annual Cost per Hydrant
Above 300,000	12,375,463	133,068	$0.60	$56
100,000–300,000	3,285,351	55,053	0.75	42
50,000–100,000	2,364,110	40,865	1.00	58
30,000– 50,000	1,543,286	34,700	1.25	55

Lump-sum Charge for Fire Protection. — Since the proper
amount to be received by a water company or department from
any community depends so much on local conditions an equitable lump-sum charge may be fixed in each case which was
reasonable on a given date. To this from year to year should
equitably be added the fixed charges and operating expenses of
new hydrants, new hydrant connections and excess size of new
mains. In places where the annual determination of these additions by engineering methods demands unwarranted expense,
an approximate substitute should be figured out beforehand, based
on number of new hydrants, miles of new line or even increase
in population.

Effect of Fire Service on Water-works Costs. — It has been
one of the classic statements of water-works men that half of
the cost of the entire equipment was made necessary for fire
protection. Experience of many engineers shows that this is
more or less true in very many cases, and is probably based on
conditions which prevail in cities of 25,000 to 50,000 population.
But that figure is not necessarily true in any one city, so influential are the special local conditions. It has been stated
by well-known experts † that the cost of that part of the physical water-works plant required for fire protection over domestic
and commercial service probably ranges from 10 to 20% in the
largest cities, and 20 to 30% in cities of about 100,000 population,
to 60 or 80% for places of 5000 or less.

Quantity of Water to be Provided for Fire Service. — There
have been several investigations of the amount of water which

* "Reasonable Return For Public Fire Hydrant Service," by Metcalf,
Kuichling and Hawley, Proceedings of the American Water-Works Association, 1911.

† Metcalf, Kuichling and Hawley; 1911 Proceedings, American Water-
Works Association, p. 66.

should be provided for in the design of mains and supply lines to insure adequate fire protection. One of the earliest is that of J. R. Freeman;* this was followed by one by Emil Knichling,† one by Allen Hazen ‡ and one by Metcalf, Kuichling and Hawley, § making use of reports of the National Board of Fire Underwriters for data of requirements in 143 cities. The re-

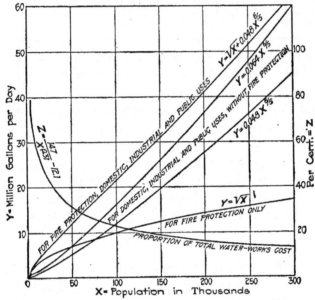

WATER REQUIREMENTS AND FIRE-PROTECTION COSTS

sults obtained by all these men are in fair agreement and are sufficiently represented by the simple Kuichling curve given in the accompanying diagram (which curve has the equation $Y = \sqrt{X}$). The maximum flow due to domestic, industrial and public consumption, without fire protection, is also plotted for two conditions — one on the assumption that the fluctuations of domestic, industrial and public services require a carrying capacity of double the average daily rate, and the other on the assumption that a capacity of $1\frac{1}{2}$ times the average flow is required. These curves have the equations respectively of $Y = 0.064 \, X^{\frac{6}{5}}$ and $Y = 0.048 \, X^{\frac{6}{5}}$. In both cases the consumption

* Journal, New England Water-Works Assoc., Vol. 7, p. 49 (1892).

† Transactions, American Society of Civil Engineers, Vol. 38, p. 15.

‡ "American Civil Engineers Pocketbook," 1911, p. 947.

§ "Determination of Reasonable Return For Public Fire Hydrant Service," Proceedings American Water-Works Assoc., 1911, p. 67.

is computed on the basis of 50 gallons per capita per day for a place of 100,000 population, 80 gallons for a place of 100,000 and 100 gallons for one of 300,000.

The maximum draft then to be provided for is the sum of the domestic and fire-protection demands. The fact should be taken into account that the enlargement of plant for fire service helps the domestic service requirements except in brief times of emergency, when diminished domestic service becomes of secondary importance. This is done by adding to the fire-protection requirements the domestic needs based on a maximum of $1\frac{1}{2}$ times the average instead of the larger figures which would otherwise be expected. The curve of total maximum quantity to be provided is plotted on the same diagram (and is represented by the expression $\sqrt{X} + 0.048\,X^{\frac{2}{3}}$). The ratio of the difference in capacity between the systems with and without fire protection to the capacity of the system with fire protection is then

$$\frac{\sqrt{X} + 0.48\,X^{\frac{2}{3}} - 0.064\,X^{\frac{2}{3}}}{\sqrt{X} + 0.48\,X^{\frac{2}{3}}} = \frac{\sqrt{X} - 0.016\,X^{\frac{2}{3}}}{\sqrt{X} + 0.048\,X^{\frac{2}{3}}}.$$

In the case of mains this ranges from 50–80% for small cities to 10–20% for the largest. The same studies obviously are to be applied to the pumping and various reservoir services.

These engineers after reviewing their experience and that of others as to division of cost of water-works. plants among supply, pumping, reservoir, distribution, filter, real estate and rights, organization and interest during construction conclude that the portion of total cost of water-works necessitated by fire service is as shown in the accompanying curve — for the equation

$$Z = \frac{147}{X^{0.31}} - 12.1.$$

These curves are to be regarded as showing the experience of these men and are of value in indicating only in a very general way what may be expected in specific cases.

Per Capita Cost of Fire Protection. — Messrs. Metcalf, Kuichling and Hawley, in the paper referred to, have used the figures already shown to estimate the probable per capita cost of fire-protection service which it is reasonable to expect may prevail in most ordinary cases. Their results are best shown in the accompanying table, which is self-explanatory.

ESTIMATED APPROXIMATE ANNUAL PER CAPITA COST OF WATER-WORKS
FIRE-PROTECTION SERVICE

	Towns of 5000 Pop.	Cities of 50,000 Pop.	Largest Cities
Per capita value of works *..............	$20	$30	$35
Percentage charged to fire service........	77	32	15
Per capita value charged to fire service...	$15.40	$9.60	$5.25
Annual operation and maintenance charges †.............................	0.30	0.28	0.21
Annual retirance and interest (8%) on value charged to fire service............	1.23	0.77	0.42
Total annual charges per capita..........	1.53	1.05	0.63
Annual charges for fire service in per cent of value of water-works................	7.6	3.5	1.8

* Value here indicates reproduction cost, including engineering, contingencies, organization, interest during construction, and business development.

† For the towns of 5000 population, 10% of annual gross income which is 15% of total value — or 1.5%; for cities of 50,000 population, 7.5% of gross income which is 12.5% of total value — or 1.0%; for largest cities, 6% of 10% — or 0.6%.

Any such a table is to be used with great caution and in a specific case has little weight against a careful determination by a competent engineer. The most it should be taken to show is that the annual cost per capita of water-works fire-protection varies in round numbers from $0.40 to $1.75 and the total annual cost to the community may be expected to be, say from 1.5% to 10% of the value of the entire water-works.

What is the Value of Fire-protection Service. — At the outset these notes on rates for fire-protection service were predicated on the cost-of-service idea. In some cases it may be worth while to find out what the value-of-service idea discloses, for probably there is something grossly wrong with the water-works where the cost of the fire protection is above the value.

The reports of the National Board of Fire Underwriters show insurance rates varying from 2.46% in Nevada to 0.53% in the District of Columbia. Probably at least half of this difference is due to the protection afforded by adequate water supplies — and the other half perhaps to organized fire-fighting forces and fire-resistant construction. If all the combustible property in a community with excellent water-works protection were insured (and here is a measure of the cost of fire risk) according to the above figures about 0.95% of the insured value would represent the total annual saving in cost of insurance over no adequate fire protection. This same amount may be directly compared with the aggregate annual payment made by the community to the water department or company. Thus in New York State about $6,000,000,000 of fire risks are underwritten and this is probably close to the total value of combustible property. The average rate for the State is 0.82%, which gives a saving of 1.65% over Nevada — 0.82% being probably due to good water-works fire protection. The 0.82% of $6,000,000,000 is $49,200,000; and for a population 9,000,000 represents $5.50 per capita. This is to be compared with about $1.00 per capita cost of water-works fire protection.

Charges for Private Fire Protection. — The charges which it is proper for a water company or department to make against a customer for private hydrants or hose or sprinkler connections remains one of the most troublesome problems of water-works rate making. In most communities the number of private fire-protection connections is comparatively small and the amount of water drawn (for legitimate purposes) will always be negligible. In most cases it will be advisable to put on a detector meter to prevent surreptitious drafts or to show up mistaken connections.

Some utility men have urged that rates for this service should be based on what it would cost the private consumer to furnish equivalent protection himself. Others advocate a charge based on the saving in fire-insurance premiums that can be traced to the fire-protection facilities connected to the water-works system. But neither of these schemes can be universally recommended for in the great majority of cases such a procedure is a most undesirable resort to " all the traffic will stand " without regard to the cost-of-service principle which, especially in such a public benefit as fire protection, is a proper basis.

Where the private fire-service connections are numerous and large enough to increase the size of mains over requirements for ordinary domestic or manufacturing supply and street-hydrant pressure, they may well be studied as a distinct superimposed fire-protection system and the proper charges may be figured as already noted in connection with the municipal street-hydrant service. Once a gross lump sum is determined it can be distributed according to number and size of connections, etc.

In many places it may prove to be equitable to consider the public and private fire-protection facilities consolidated into a single system for finding the extra plant required prior to determining a gross fire-protection charge. The division of this charge between the municipality and the private group also can be fairly approached through some basis of number and size of connections. The further distribution of the gross sum applicable to the private group can similarly be apportioned; in some cases it may appear more logical to apportion this gross sum according to the importance of the private connection — measured perhaps by number of hose lines or number of sprinkler heads connected, though these ought to be reflected in the size of the fire-service connection.

If it should be regarded, as it may properly be in many cases, that no charge should be made against the private fire protection for any part of the largest mains required to satisfy the public fire department (the argument being that sprinklers, etc., are more effective fire protection than hose lines from public hydrants and materially lighten the fire department's burdens) then the fixed charges that can be assessed are only those on the extension from existing mains, the safety shut-off valves, detector meters, etc. All the operating expenses that can be fairly levied then cover inspection, maintenance, meter reading and related items. Private fire protection figured on such a basis will be relatively very inexpensive.

Distributing Costs of Comprehensive System. — Obviously when a large water-supply system supplies several communities in a given district, as does the Boston Metropolitan Water Board, a pressing problem arises as to the fair division of the fixed and operating charges. What was done by this board is of interest in this connection. It was first provided that in general the assessment on a town should be in proportion to its tax valuation and its population; water consumption was later substituted for population. Boston's share was laid in proportion only to the ratio of its valuation to the total valuation of the district, towns not applying for water or obtaining a supply from their own sources being entered at $\frac{1}{6}$ their full valuation. The remaining costs were apportioned among the various communities $\frac{2}{3}$ according to valuation and $\frac{1}{3}$ according to consumption.

It has been suggested * that a water company would be

* J. W. Alvord, Journal of the Am. Water-Works Assoc., 1914, Vol. 1, p. 95.

stimulated to keep up a proper fire-protection equipment if the lump sum found equitable, as already noted, should be apportioned over the company's mains as an annual charge per " inch-foot " of main — feet of length times inches in diameter (plus a nominal sum per hydrant).   This has the advantage also of providing easy adjustment of annual compensation where the system is still extending.   Probably for a rapidly growing plant it would be advisable to revise the inch-foot charge about once in five years.

Cost Accounting **for Water-works.** — The need of more complete regulation of the water-works of the country, irrespective of their having private or public ownership, is well shown by the lack of comparable data on operating costs around the country, and in the lack of a generally accepted or generally imposed uniform system of accounts such as are used by practically all other utilities.   Much work has been done inside the water-works industry, and the U. S. Census Bureau in 1908 outlined a desirable system based on the work of water-works associations, etc.*

There is little or no difficulty in assembling from such a system of accounts all the various information needed in computing the cost of service for the various classes of customers in accordance with the general scheme previously set forth.   Inability to secure the necessary information can be traced generally to lack of that proper system of service and financial accounts which enables the managers to comprehend what their works are actually doing.

Assuming, however, that the account books are ample for such studies as may be needed in rate studies, only a few hints as to handling specific items are necessary.   For instance, it should be known how much water is supplied to the municipality itself, and what revenues are paid over to the water-works definitely for the water supplied and the fire protection afforded.   It may be necessary also to know how much water is furnished free to charitable institutions, and how much is required inside the water-works for purification and other operating processes. All costs met out of the general city treasury must be given in

* M. N. Baker, "Appendix B, Uniform Accounts and Reports of Water-Supply Systems"; Special Report of U. S. Census Bureau of Statistics of Cities of over 30,000 Population, 1908.

order to allow intelligent rate study, but it is probably impractical to try to cover such overhead items as allowances for service, time and office expenses of a mayor, councilmen and their subordinates. Office facilities in a public building, etc., ought properly to be taken account of even though it involves no cash rental. Where the city comptroller, or equivalent officer, devotes an appreciable part of his time to the water-works department, that should be covered both for him and his office force. The same applies to the city engineers and bacteriologists if they assist the works superintendent.

Special attention will often be required to see that cost of repairs and cost of renewals are fairly differentiated. The matter of depreciation is also apt to be troublesome. (U. S. Bureau of Census used 10 years' life for horses, carriages, autos, laboratory fixtures, meters; 15 years for office furniture and general equipment; 20 years for boilers, steam lines, filter apparatus; 25 years for pumping machinery; 50 years for masonry, cribs, iron water mains, hydrants, standpipes and buildings; 100 years for aqueducts, reservoirs, tunnels; 50 years for a system as a whole.)

Whether taxes are to be included for a municipal plant is a debated point to be decided as a local issue; in any event, taxes are seldom entirely escaped for a municipality may pay taxes indirectly to some higher civil division on water-works bonds, etc.

Preventing Water Waste. — Before meters were as much used as now, the most extravagant claims were made about the reduction of water used in cities — through prevention of waste when customers had to pay for it. This was a pretty theory but after 20 years of meter use it was found * that the consumption in a large number of important cities had not been checked.

The high per capita use of water is in most places affected by other uses than that of immediate personal consumption or domestic use, and, in all of these, great chances for waste exist that are not caught by ordinary customers' meters. These other services are (1) for fires, street flushing, fountains, public schools, and various municipal consumption; (2) leakage from mains and service pipes, and seepage from storage reservoirs; (3) for manufacturing plants. Moreover, it is now realized that

---

* "New Facts on Effect of Meters on Consumption of Water," by W. S. Johnson, New England Water-Works Association, March, 1907; Engineering News, March 28, 1907.

the small steady leaks in ordinary domestic plumbing are, more often than not, just small enough so that the meter is not operated by that flow.

It is now recognized that where the water supply is not of the best, as regards color or taste, the users are sure to let their taps run in hope that the trouble is local to certain service or house pipes. Moreover, the trend in residences is to the multiplication of outlets — more bath rooms, hot-water systems, lavatories, toilets, laundry tubs, quick-opening faucets, etc., even in modest homes. It is a common experience in all utility service that the more convenient the facilities for service the greater the use, though of course in this case it is not directly in proportion to the increase in number of outlets. Various cities show the influence of this. Thus Richmond, Va., had a record of about 170 gallons per capita per day in 1890 and as the per cent of meters rose from zero to 25 in 1898 the per capita daily consumption dropped to 118 gallons. But the movement did not continue steadily; in 1905 it had climbed back to 150 gallons though the percentage of metered services was 45. Attleboro, Mass., in 1894 had a record of 32 gallons per capita per day with 60% of services metered; in 1906 it ran 48 gallons and 100% metered.

The truth evidently is that the extreme waste will be reduced if there is a meter on every outlet from which water can be drawn, except hydrants, and if excessive and unreasonable drafts by non-revenue consumers, like schools, hospitals, public buildings, etc., are persistently checked. In such ways the per capita daily consumption probably can usually be brought down from 300–700 gallons (found in Burlington, Vt., with 680 gallons and $87\frac{1}{2}$% of taps metered; Portland, Ore., with 325 gallons and 24% of taps metered; and Sacramento, Calif., with 318 gallons and 100% of taps metered, as may be seen in the accompanying tables of rates and service in American cities) to 50–150 gallons (found typically in Des Moines, Iowa, with its 62 gallons and 97% of taps metered; in Winthrop, Mass., with 70 gallons and 100% metered; in Battle Creek, Mich., with 80 gallons and 100% metered; in Aurora, Ill., with 77 gallons and 100% metered; and Geneva, N. Y., with 53 gallons and 100% metered). But the reduction of consumption which may be possible to below 100 gallons per capita per day evidently does not directly result from the mere presence of meters and meter rates; for Denison, Tex., typically shows 77 gallons with 87% of taps metered; Passaic, N. J., shows 98 gallons for 50% metered; and Burlington, Iowa, shows 90 gallons for only 5% metered.

The great use of meters then remains as a means of selling water service more nearly in accordance with the cost of facilities furnished, and of eliminating extreme waste.

A large number of metered-service rates throughout the country are made in a simple stepped schedule like the following example:

```
For        0 to    2,000 cu. ft. per quarter $2.20 per 1000 cu. ft.
        2,000 to   10,000   "         "        1.40  " 1000   "
       10,000 to  100,000   "         "        0.40  " 1000   "
      100,000 to  200,000   "         "        0.20  " 1000   "
          Over  200,000     "         "        0.10  " 1000   "
```

Useful efforts have been made to make the steps smaller so as to eliminate the waste of water induced by users who naturally fall close to a dividing line and who by wasting a little can get the water at a lower rate and a lower total bill than if they used less water. Thus:

```
For        0 to    1,000 cu. ft. per quarter $2.20 per 1000 cu. ft.
 "      1,000 to    2,000   "         "        2.10  " 1000   "
 "      2,000 to    3,000   "         "        2.00  " 1000   "
 "      3,000 to    4,000   "         "        1.90  " 1000   "
 "      4,000 to    5,000   "         "        1.80  " 1000   "
 "      5,000 to    7,000   "         "        1.60  " 1000   "
 "      7,000 to   10,000   "         "        1.40  " 1000   "
 "     10,000 to   14,000   "         "        1.20  " 1000   "
 "     14,000 to   19,000   "         "        1.00  " 1000   "
 "     19,000 to   29,000   "         "        0.80  " 1000   "
 "     29,000 to   49,000   "         "        0.60  " 1000   "
 "     49,000 to   99,000   "         "        0.40  " 1000   "
 "     99,000 to  199,000   "         "        0.20  " 1000   "
          Over  199,000     "         "        0.10  " 1000   "
```

This reduces the trouble by reducing the inducement to waste. A still better plan is seen in such a schedule as follows:

```
First    1,000 cu. ft. per quarter $2.20 per 1000 cu. ft.
Second   1,000   "         "        2.10  " 1000   "
Third    1,000   "         "        2.00  " 1000   "
Fourth   1,000   "         "        1.90  " 1000   "
Fifth    1,000   "         "        1.80  " 1000   "
```

Next	2,000 cu. ft. per quarter	$1.60 per 1000 cu. ft.
"	3,000 " "	1.40 " 1000 "
"	4,000 " "	1.20 " 1000 "
"	5,000 " "	1.00 " 1000 "
"	10,000 " "	0.80 " 1000 "
"	20,000 " "	0.60 " 1000 "
"	50,000 " "	0.40 " 1000 "
"	100,000 " "	0.20 " 1000 "
"	100,000 " "	0.10 " 1000 "

The objection to such a schedule has been the extra labor and time required to compute the bill. But short cuts are open making the calculation about as easy and inexpensive as with any schedule. For instance a table can be made up in an hour or so which the billing clerks can enter at any point and complete the calculation in a moment. Such a table arranged for the schedule just given might be as follows:

For less than 1000 cu. ft. reading, multiply by $2.20.
For over 1000; multiply excess by $2.10 and add $2.20.
For over 2000; multiply excess by $2.00 and add $4.30.
For over 3000; multiply excess by $1.90 and add $6.30.
For over 4000; multiply excess by $1.80 and add $8.20.
For over 5000; multiply excess by $1.60 and add $10.00.
For over 7000; multiply excess by $1.40 and add $11.60.   Etc.

Such a rate schedule, however, is not the most logical or satisfactory that can be derived, as appears later.

Minimum Charges for Water. — Minimum or service charges have long been recognized to be as equitable in water-works practice as in other utilities. Because of custom, the minimum charge is generally found easier to impose on water customers than the service charge. There has not been as much study of classifying water customers as there has been in electricity supply so that some hardships of overwide averaging are often seen. Substantial justice can be dealt to all if only closer attention is paid to classification such as perhaps may be made by size of service pipe or size of meter. The annual service charge then is made up of about 10% of the investment in the average cost of the service connection and meter (assuming that the company or department installs them), plus the average cost of metering, bookkeeping and billing — say $1.00 to $1.50 — plus the average cost of unregistered water. The first and third items vary for each class more than the second, both the investment and the unregistered flow through the meter increasing with the size of connection. The expense of unregistered flow could be computed at the lowest figure charged for water since it is an all-day leakage and does not appreciably affect peak drafts; this may be expected to run from $2 to $200 per year per customer with water at a minimum of 10¢ per 1000 gallons. Unaccounted water has been studied by the New England Water-Works Association, through its Meter Committee. They were able to get sufficient data on 29 systems and in these it averaged 27% of the total output.

While it was not found possible to separate the unaccounted amounts into (1) leakage from mains, (2) leakage from services, (3) under-registration of meters, (4) unmetered services like street and sewer flushing, these were recognized as the causes of loss.

It was recommended that service charge for meters should be based in a general way upon their carrying capacity, (1) because of the interest on the meter and service pipe, and (2) because of the leakage past the meter. Both these expenses are always present and dependent on the size of meter. The responsibility for leakage past the meters was loaded by the New England Association Committee (Allen Hazen, chairman) upon the several sizes, as follows, after various studies of the delivering capacity and leakage of meters in service, and the possible distribution of unaccounted losses among services:

Size of Meter, Inches	Relative Capacity	Charge for Leakage
$\frac{5}{8}$	1.0	$ 2.00
$\frac{3}{4}$	1.7	3.40
1	3.0	6.00
1½	6.0	12.00
2	10.0	20.00
3	20.0	40.00
4	30.0	60.00
6	60.0	120.00

When it is advisable to use a minimum rate instead of a bald service charge, the conversion is simple. Some measurement or estimate must first be made of the average quantity most apt to be drawn by the minimum-rate customers of the given classes. The charge for that water is to be made, excluding the expense items entering the service charge, and then added to the service charge. This will fix a minimum charge below which a customer's bill should not go. It can be so stated, or it can be divided by the average draft of minimum-charge customers for a given class and that rate quoted as the first step of the schedule. The subsequent steps of the schedule will be materially less of course since they are not burdened with the service-expense items.

Proposed Standard Rate Form. — After several years of discussion and committee reports, the New England Water-Works Association in November, 1916, adopted a standard form of rate for metered service — comprising (1) a fixed charge depending on the size of the meter and (2) a varying charge proportional to the meter reading and customer's class. The committee's proposed form was essentially as follows:

For each service supplied by a ...... inch meter, there shall be a charge for the service and meter per annum (or per quarter, or per month) of $..........

In addition thereto, for all water drawn there shall be charged:

For the first 300,000 gallons of water per annum (or the first 75,000 gallons per quarter, or the first 25,000 gallons per month, or the first 10,000 cubic feet per quarter, or the first 3300 cubic feet per month) the

Domestic Rate of............ $\begin{cases} \text{cents per 1000 gallons (or} \\ \text{cents per 100 cubic feet).} \end{cases}$

For water in excess of 300,000 gallons (or the substitute figures quoted) and under 3,000,000 gallons (or under 10 times the substitute figures quoted), the *Intermediate Rate* of.......... $\begin{cases} \text{cents per 1000 gallons (or} \\ \text{cents per 100 cubic feet).} \end{cases}$

For water in excess of 3,000,000 gallons per year (or in excess of 10 times the substitute figures quoted), the

Manufacturing Rate of.............. $\begin{cases} \text{cents per 1000 gallons (or} \\ \text{cents per 100 cubic feet).} \end{cases}$

At the same time the Association accepted, with this standard, a suggestion (adopted only as such) that the fixed or service charge might be made up of three factors: (1) 10% of the cost of the meter and service pipe, where those were owned by the company; (2) $1 per year for reading, billing and collecting; and (3) from $2 to $120 per year for unregistered water leaking through the meter — depending on the size of the meter, as already noted.

Had the Association generalized this mere suggestion, it might have become an integral part of the proposed standard rate form.

A broader statement of the service charge might have been: (1) $X\%$ of the cost of meter and service pipe, (2) $Y\%$ of the cost of equipment needed to carry the peak load demand of customers, (3) $A per year for reading, billing and collecting, and (4) from $B to $C per year for water passed unregistered through the meter. The actual amounts, X, Y, A, B and C, as well as the unit price for water registered on the meter, would be determined from the accounts of the company or department. Y would be highly important only for the service type of water-works, as contrasted with the product-storing type whose peak-load equipment consists mainly of a possible addition to the diameter of mains — and even this addition may be considered as absorbed by the provisions for fire protection.

Such a rate form carried to its logical development in many cases automatically clears away much of the worry about rates to manufacturers. If one of these industrial customers arranges not to draw during peak-load hours, then the Y factor disappears and an attractive rate can be made to him that still will render a respectable profit to the water-works — or when profit is not sought, make a more continuous use of plant and increase the spread of some of the fixed charges. If a manufacturer's load cannot be secured except at a true loss, it would be better to let him develop his independent supply. The development of the two-part water rate, as outlined with X, Y, A, B and C factors, materially reduces the differences between the domestic-, intermediate- and manufacturing-quantity charges, and often even make the three distinctions useless and unnecessary.

SUMMARY OF WATER RATES AND SERVICE IN REPRESENTATIVE AMERICAN CITIES, 1914*

City	Population 1910	Municipal or Company Works	6 Room House	Bath	Closet	Stands and Tubs	Number of Taps or Customers	Number of Meters	Meter Rate, Max.-Min. Cents per 1000 Gal.	Public Hydrant, Revenue per Hydrant	Number of Hydrants	Hydrant Maintained by	Private Hydrant Rate, per Hydrant	Automatic Sprinkler Rate †	Source of Supply, Treated or Not	Gravity or Pump to Mains, Standpipe, or Reservoir	Service Line Installed by	Average Daily Consumption, 1000 Gal.
Alabama																		
Anniston	12,794	Co.	...	...	...	...	1,600	1,300	26.6-6	$45.00	130	Co.	$40.00	$ 0.10	Springs, Un.	Pump, Res.	Cons.	1,933
Mobile	51,521	Mun.	...	...	...	...	11,769	2,223	15-5	......	974	Water Dept.	12.50	0.05	Creek, Un.	Pump, Res.	Mun.	12,230
Arizona																		
Phoenix	11,134	Mun.	$12.00	$3.00	$6.00	...	4,100	300	12.5	......	280	Water Dept.	Meter	None	Wells, Un.	Pump, S. P.	Mun.	2,400
Arkansas																		
Fort Smith	23,975	Mun.	8.00	2.00	2.00	...	3,836	1,000	25-10	40-60	......	Water Dept.	45.00	0.125-0.05	Surf., Tr.	Pump, Res.	Cons.	2,361
Pine Bluffs	15,102	Co.	...	...	...	...	2,077	2,077	40-15	40-43	312	Co.	40.00	50.00	Wells, Un.	Pump, M.	Co.	......
California																		
Pomona	10,207	Co.	12.00	3.00	3.00	...	2,800	1,900	22-10	3.00	......	Water Dept.	12.00	......	Wells, Un.	Pump and Grav. Res.	Co.	2,750
Sacramento	44,696	Mun.	12.00	...	...	...	12,800	......	......	......	560	Water Dept.	......	......	River, Un.	Pump, M.	Cons.	14,187
San Francisco	416,912	Co.	4.92	3.84	2.64	0.60	61,721	17,923	33-16	2.50	4,421	Co. & Fire D.	......	......	Surf., Tr.	Pump, Grav.	Cons.	39,120
Colorado																		
Colo. Springs	29,078	Mun.	12.00	1.00	2.00	...	11,858	213	15-8	30.00	504	Water Dept.	30.00	Free	Surf., Un.	Grav.	Cons.	6,436
Connecticut																		
Bristol	13,502	Co.	6.00	3.00	3.00	...	1,848	1,351	18-5.5	13.45	130	Co.	20.00	......	Surf., Un.	Grav.	Cons.	1,000
Meriden	32,066	Mun.	5.00	2.00	3.00	...	4,500	618	15-10	......	......	Water Dept.	Free	Free	Surf., Un.	Grav. Pump, Res.	Joint.	3,122
New Haven	133,605	Co.	5.00	3.00	3.00	...	22,000	2,500	18-10	......	1,000	Water Dept.	20.00	Free	Lake, Tr.	Grav. Pump, Res.	Cons.	23,500
New London	19,659	Mun.	4.50	2.00	2.00	...	4,197	825	16.6	......	363	Water Dept.	Free	Free	Lake, Un.	Grav.	Co.	3,000
Stamford	28,836	Co.	5.00	4.00	5.00	...	3,800	2,200	20	15.40	......	City	16.00	Free	Surf., Un.	Grav.	Cons.	3,000

* Based on tabulation by F. C. Jordan and others, Journal of the American Water-Works Association, June, 1915. Some additions made. It should be noted that the rates of two cities are seldom directly comparable unless cost of fuel, labor, supplies and other items are studied at the same time; moreover loose bookkeeping in some places spoils comparisons with cities which employ good methods. A good showing is made in some cases because new construction is paid out of taxes or by abutting property owners instead of out of bonds or earnings as in other cases.

† Cents per year per sprinkler head, or dollars per installation.

SUMMARY OF WATER RATES AND SERVICE IN REPRESENTATIVE AMERICAN CITIES, 1914.—(Continued.)

City	Population 1910	Municipal or Company Works	Flat Rate Schedule: 6 Room House	Bath	Closet	Stands and Tubs	Number of Taps or Customers	Number of Meters	Meter Rate, Max.-Min. Cents per 1000 Gal.	Public Hydrant, Revenue per	Number of Hydrants	Hydrant Maintained by	Private Hydrant Rate, per Hydrant	Automatic Sprinkler Rate	Source of Supply, Treated or Not	Gravity or Pump to Mains, Standpipe or Reservoir	Service Line Installed by	Average Daily Consumption, 1000 Gal.
Delaware																		
Wilmington....	87,411	Mn.	$5.00	$3.00	$2.00	$1.00	19,331	7,574	10-5	....	935	Water Dept.	$25.00	....	Creek, Tr.	Pump, Res.	Joint.	11,231
Dist. Columbia																		
Washington....	331,069	Mun.					67,790	31,103	8-5	....	3,111	Water Dept.	....	....	River, Tr.	Pump	Cons.	62,000
Florida																		
Tampa........	37,782	Co.	8.00	5.00	4.00	..	6,495	1,383	22-12	....	603	....	None	None	Wells, Un.	Pump	....	4,250
Georgia																		
Atlanta.......	154,839	Mun.					25,434	24,670	10-7	$25.00	2,929	Water Dept.	Free	Free	River, Tr.	Pump, M.	G.	16,607
Macon........	40,655	Mun.	6.50	5.00	5.00	..	5,682	2,600	20-8	37.50	497	Co.	50.00	0.06	River, Tr.	Pump, Sp., Res.	Cons.	4,700
Illinois																		
Aurora........	29,807	Mun.	6.00	3.50	3.25	..	5,802	5,756	40.7-4	....	609	Water Dept.	Free	Free	Wells, Un.	Pump, M., S.P.	Cons.	2,313
Cairo.........	14,548	Co.	6.00	..	..	..	3,300	218	17-7	35-40	....	Co.	30.00	50.00	River, Tr.	Pump, M., S.P.	Cons.	4,000
Champaign....	20,666	Co.	6.00	..	..	..	4,120	3,700	25-6	35-40	351	Co.	40.00	100.00	Wells, Tr.	Pump, Res.	Cons.	1,500
Decatur.......	31,140	Mun.					5,300	5,492	20-5	....	614	Water Dept.	Free	Free	River, Tr.	Pump, M.	Cons.	3,650
Dixon.........	7,216	Co.	5.00	3.00	3.00	3.50	1,500	300	32-6	35.00	196	Co.	35.00	50.00	Wells, Un.	Pump, M., S.P.	Cons.	800
Lincoln.......	10,892	Co.	5.75	4.00	3.00	..	1,260	541	40-8	35.00	190	Co.	50.00	0.05	Wells, Un.	Pump, M., S.P.	G.	670
Oak Park.....	19,444	Mn.					5,043	5,043	....	20-10	790	Water Dept.	None	None	Lake, Un.	Pump, M.	Cons.	1,570
Peoria........	66,950	Co.	6.00	3.00	3.00	0.50	10,700	365	20-6	52-41-25	1,376	Co.	50.00	0.20	Wells, Un.	Pump, M., Res.	Joint.	8,400
Quincy.......	36,587	Co.	6.00	4.75	5.00	..	5,650	3,500	45-6	43-30-20	407	Co.	30.00	0.10	River, Tr.	Pump, M., Res.	Cons.	1,999
Indiana																		
Anderson.....	22,476	uM.	4.00	2.50	2.50	2.50	2,610	388	12-4.5	39.84	379	Water Dept.	50.00	50.00	River, Tr.	Pump, M.	G.	1,374
Brazil........	9,340	Mun.					850	820	26-6	....	136	Water Dept.	None	None	Wells, Un.	Pump, M.	Cons.	500
Elkhart.......	19,282	Co.	4.00	2.50	2.50	1.50	3,979	3,070	12-8	40.00	343	Co.	50.00	25.00	Wells, Un.	Pump, M.	Cons.	2,145

SUMMARY OF WATER RATES AND SERVICE IN REPRESENTATIVE AMERICAN CITIES, 1914. — (Continued.)

City	Population 1910	Municipal or Company Works	Flat Rate Schedule 6 Room House	Flat Rate Schedule Bath	Flat Rate Schedule Closet	Flat Rate Schedule Stands and Tubs	Number of Taps or Customers	Number of Meters	Meter Rate, Max.-Min. Cents per 1000 Gal.	Public Hydrant, Revenue per Hydrant	Number of Hydrants	Hydrant Maintained by	Private Hydrant Rate, per Hydrant	Automatic Sprinkler Rate	Source of Supply, Treated or Not	Gravity or Pump to Mains, Standpipe or Reservoir	Service Line Installed by	Average Daily Consumption, 1000 Gal.
Indiana (Continued)																		
Evansville	69,617	Mun.	$5.00	$2.00	$4.00	$2.00	8,600	43	20-4.5	....	734	Water Dept.	Free	Free	River, Tr.	Pump, M.	Cons.	9,359
Indianapolis	233,650	Co.	5.00	3.00	3.00	....	41,300	3,500	18-4.5	$45.00	2,971	Co.	$25.00	$0.05	River, Tr.	Pump, M.	Cons.	22,500
Kokomo	17,010	Co.	4.90	3.00	2.80	2.10	3,953	271	25-8	25.00	397	Co.	....	Free	Wells, Un.	Pump, M.	Co.	2,034
Marion	19,359	Mun.	4.44	2.22	2.78	....	3,680	784	15-6	Tax	346	Water Dept.	Free	Free	Wells, Un.	Pump, Res.	Cons.	1,705
Mishawaka	11,886	Mu.	2.00	2.00	3.00	3.00	1,500	200	12-5	Tax	176	Water Dept.	Free	Free	Wells, Un.	Pump, M.	Cons.	3,500
Richmond	22,324	G.	6.00	2.50	3.00	1.00	4,811	341	25-6	55-49	325	Co.	None	None	Surf., Un.	Pump, Grav. M., Res.	Cons.	2,681
Terre Haute	58,157	G.	5.00	3.00	3.00	....	5,960	2,093	30-8	40.00	1,078	Co.	5-20	5-20	River, Tr.	Pump, M.	Cons.	4,400
Vincennes	14,895	Co.	5.10	3.50	5.00	2.00	1,600	235	50-15	33.33	275	Co.	40 00	60.00	River, Tr.	Pump, S. P.	Co.	2,250
Iowa																		
Burlington	24,324	Co.	6.00	5.00	5.00	....	4,178	200	25-10	Tax	474	Co.	50.00	50.00	River, Tr.	Pump, M.	Cons.	2,194
Council Bluffs	29,292	Mun.	7.75	3.00	3.00	1.00	5,500	2,800	35-8	56.00	362	Co.	None	None	River, Tr.	Pump, Res.	Cons.	3,125
Davenport	43,028	Co.	6.00	3.50	4.50	....	8,800	5,800	33-10	38.00	773	Co.	40.00	Free	River, Tr.	Pump, M.	Cons.	4,000
Des Moines	86,368	Co.	4.00	3.00	3.00	....	15,004	14,553	35-10	33.50	1,665	Co.	Free	Free	Surf., Tr.	Pump, M.	Cons.	5,386
Muscatine	16,178	Mun.	4.00	3.00	4.00	2.00	2,800	250	35-6	....	357	Mun.	None	Meter	Wells, Un.	Pump, Res.	Cons.	1,500
Ottumwa	22,012	Mun.	8.00	5.00	5.00	....	1,600	850	30-10	....	282	Water Dept.	15.00	50.00	River, Tr.	Pump, Res.	Cons.	1,701
Sioux City	47,828	Mu.	....	....	....	....	6,200	6,221	25-10	....	476	Water Dept.	Free	Free	Wells, Un.	Pump, S. P., Grav., Res.	Cons.	3,095
Kansas																		
Atchison	16,429	Co.	5.60	3.50	3.70	....	2,405	340	30-10	32.00	182	Co.	Free	Free	River, Tr.	Pump, M.	Cons.	1,500
Fort Scott	10,463	Mu.	8.80	3.40	2.20	....	2,000	1,200	27.5-7	20.00	200	Water Dept.	50.00	50.00	River, Tr.	Pump, S. P., Res.	Cons.	1,250
Lawrence	12,374	Co.	6.00	2.00	2.00	2.00	2,087	1,565	25-15	31.50	171	Co.	30.00	50.00	Wells, Un.	Pump, S. P.	Cons.	....
Pittsburg	14,755	Mun.	8.00	2.00	2.00	....	3,817	962	50-11	46-45	254	Water Dept.	Meter	None	Wells, Un.	Pump, S. P.	Cons.	1,250
Kentucky																		
Henderson	11,452	Mun.	5.00	2.00	3.00	....	3,150	80	20-8	....	189	....	Free	Free	River, Un.	Pump, S. P., Res.	Cons.	....
Lexington	35,099	Co.	....	2.50	....	....	5,130	5,130	15-6	50.00	605	Co.	50.00	10.00	Surf., Tr.	Pump, M.	Cons.	2,261
Louisville	223,928	Mun.	6.00	....	3.00	1.00	33,733	3,022	....	....	1,955	Fire Dept.	25.00	25.00	River, Tr.	Pump, M.	Cons.	25,203

SUMMARY OF WATER RATES AND SERVICE IN REPRESENTATIVE AMERICAN CITIES, 1914.—(Continued.)

City	Population 1910	Municipal or Company Works	6 Room House	Bath	Closet	Stands and Tubs	Number of Taps or Customers	Number of Meters	Meter Rate, Max.-Min. Cents per 1000 Gal.	Public Hydrant, Revenue per Hydrant	Number of Hydrants	Hydrant Maintained by	Private Hydrant Rate, per Hydrant	Automatic Sprinkler Rate	Source of Supply, Treated or Not	Gravity or Pump to Mains, Standpipe or Reservoir	Service Line Installed by	Average Daily Consumption, 1000 Gal.
Louisiana																		
Alexandria	11,213	Mun.					1,200	1,200			126	Water Dept.	Free	None	Wells, Un.	Pump, S. P.	Cons.	556
Baton Rouge	14,897	Co.					2,500	1,350	35–10	$50.00		Co.	$16.00	Special	Wells, Un.	Pump, Sp. Res.	Cons.	811
New Orleans	339,075	Mun.					33,959	33,873	10–7	40.00	5,103	Water Dept.	Free		River, Tr.	Pump, M.	Mun.	16,880
Maryland																		
Cumberland	21,839	Mun.	$ 6.00	$3.00	$2.00		4,285	4				Water Dept.			River, Tr.	Grav.	Mun.	6,000
Hagerstown	16,507	Co.	10.00				4,120	625		17.26–45	104	Co.	50.00	50.00	Springs, Tr.	Grav.	Cons.	2,550
Massachusetts																		
Beverly	18,650	Mun.	5.00	2.50	2.50		4,405	726	20		469	Water Dept.	Free	Free	Lake, Un.	Pump, M.		1,876
Brockton	56,878	Mun.					8,695	8,710	22–13		1,054	Water Dept.	Free	Free	Lake, Un.	Pump, Res.	Joint.	2,943
Cambridge	104,839	Mun.	4.00	3.00	2.00	$2.00	16,194	5,045	20–10		1,125	Water Dept.		Free	Surf., Un.	Pump, Res.	Joint.	10,400
Chelsea	32,452	Mun.	7.00		5.00		4,682	4,617	16–10		311	Water Dept.	Free	Free	Surf., Un.	Grav.	Mun.	2,701
Clinton	13,075	Mun.	5.00	4.00	4.00	2.00	1,856	1,680	33–8	25.00	192	Water Dept.	Free	Free	Surf., Un.	Grav.	Joint.	633
Concord	6,421	Mun.	6.00	4.00	5.00	3.00	1,214	32	26–10	12.00	224	Water Dept.	Free	Meter	Pond, Un.	Grav.	Joint.	632
Everett	33,484	Mun.	7.00		5.00		5,660	1,900	16–10		559	Water Dept.	None	None	River	Grav., Res.	Cons.	2,451
Framingham	12,948	Mun.	10.00	3.00	3.00		2,058	2,063	33–12	27.50	239	Water Dept.	None	None	Surf., Un.	Pump, S. P. Res.	Joint.	819
Gardner	14,699	Mun.	6.00	6.00	6.00		1,863	129	30–15	32.20	183	Water Dept.		None	Lake, Un.	Pump, Res.	Joint.	757
Gloucester	24,398	Mun.	6.00	6.00	6.00	3.00	4,771	399	30–15	12.15	329	Water Dept.	25.00	50.00	Surf., Un.	Pump, Res.	Joint.	1,311
Haverhill	44,115	Mun.	4.50	3.00	4.00		7,054	1,543	21–10			Water Dept.	Free	Free	Pond, Un.	Grav., Res. Pump, Res.	Cons.	5,850
Lowell	106,294	Mun.	6.00	3.00	4.00	2.00	12,952	10,541	18–13		1,283	Water Dept.			Wells, Un.	Pump, Res. Pump	Mun.	5,369

SUMMARY OF WATER RATES AND SERVICE IN REPRESENTATIVE AMERICAN CITIES, 1914. — (Continued.)

City	Population 1910	Municipal or Company Works	Flat Rate Schedule 6 Room House	Bath	Closet	Stands and Tubs	Number of Taps or Customers	Number of Meters	Meter Rate, Max.-Min. Cents per 1000 Gal.	Public Hydrant, Revenue per Hydrant	Number of Hydrants	Hydrant Maintained by	Private Hydrant Rate, per Hydrant	Automatic Sprinkler Rate	Source of Supply, Treated or Not	Gravity or Pump to Mains, Standpipe or Reservoir	Service Line Installed by	Average Daily Consumption, 1000 Gal.
Massachusetts(Con.) New Bedford	96,652	Mun.	$2.50	$2.50	$2.50	$2.50	13,643	9,998	15-2.5	......	1200	Water Dept.	Free	Free	Lake, Un.	Pump	Mun.	8,280
Springfield	88,926	Mun.	....	....	....	....	13,407	12,800	20-6	......	1439	Water Dept.	Free	Free	River, Tr.	Grav.	Mun.	10,660
Taunton	34,259	Mun.	5.00	3.00	5.00	2.00	5,420	2,938	25-9	......	832	Water Dept.	Free	Free	Pond, Un.	Pump, M.	Cons.	2,367
Winthrop	10,132	Mun.	....	....	....	....	2,655	2,655	19	$12.45	211	Water Dept.	None	None	Surf., Un.	Grav., S. P.	Joint.	717
Michigan Adrian	10,763	Co.	5.00	3.00	4.00	1.50	1,800	500	20-10	50.00	159	Co.	$50.00	$50.00	Creek, Tr.	Pump, M.	Co.	1,464
Alpena	12,706	Mun.	4.00	2.00	2.00	....	2,711	64	10-4	40.00	241	Water Dept.	Free	......	Lake, Tr.	Pump, M.	Cons.	2,243
Ann Arbor	14,817	Co.	3.50	3.00	3.00	....	3,879	350	20-8	40-45	258	Co.	200.00	75.00	Surf., Tr.	Res.	Co.	2,238
Battle Creek	25,267	Mun.	4.00	2.00	3.00	....	5,920	5,769	13-6	......	683	Water Dept.	200.00	25.00	Lake, Un.	Pump, S. P.	Joint.	2,000
Detroit	465,766	Mun.	3.20	1.00	1.60	0.50	103,487	10,807	5-3	......	5849	Fire Dept.	Free	Free	River, Tr.	Pump, M.	Cons.	105,833
Escanaba	13,194	Co.	1.50	1.00	1.00	0.50	2,000	400	30-10	50-38	221	Co.	38.00	50.00	Lake, Tr.	Pump, M.	Cons.	1,958
Ishpeming	12,448	Mun.	4.50	1.50	1.50	....	2,018	1,577	10-4	......	139	Water Dept.	Free	......	Lake, Un.	Pump, M.	Joint.	1,216
Jackson	31,433	Mun.	....	....	....	....	6,200	6,175	......	......	694	Water Dept.	None	None	Wells, Un.	Grav., Res.	Cons.	2,853
Ludington	9,132	Mun.	6.00	2.00	3.00	1.50	1,800	1,600	10	40.00	225	Water Dept.	50.00	Free	Lake, Tr.	Pump, M.	Cons.	1,116
Marquette	11,503	Mun.	8.00	5.00	3.00	....	2,050	1,010	13-4	50.00	201	Water Dept.	None	None	Lake, Tr.	Pump, M.	Cons.	2,209
Saginaw	50,510	Mun.	6.00	2.50	3.00	0.50	7,873	340	11-4	......	947	Water Dept.	None	None	River, Un.	Pump, M.	Cons.	9,820
Minnesota Duluth	78,466	Mun.	6.50	2.00	2.00	2.00	11,558	6,552	23	50.00	959	Water Dept.	....	....	Lake, Tr.	Pump, Res.	Cons.	7,648
St. Paul	214,744	Mun.	3.80	2.00	3.00	....	33,129	19,584	8	14.00	3293	Water Dept.	18.00	25.00	Lake, Un.	Pump, Res.	Cons.	13,350
Stillwater	10,198	Mun.	7.00	3.00	4.00	....	1,000	0	......	63.18	151	Water Dept.	None	100.00	Lake, Un.	Pump, S. P.	Cons.	1,000
Virginia	10,473	Co.	16.00	total	....	....	1,800	200	46-16	60-100	110	Water Dept.	100.00	None	Wells, Un.	Pump, S. P.	Cons.	600

SUMMARY OF WATER RATES AND SERVICE IN REPRESENTATIVE AMERICAN CITIES, 1914.—(Continued.)

City	Population 1910	Municipal or Company Works	6 Room House	Bath	Closet	Stands and Tubs	Number of Customers or Taps	Number of Meters	Meter Rate, Max.-Min. Cts. per 1000 Gal.	Public Hy-drant, Revenue per Hydrant	Number of Hydrants	Hydrant Maintained by	Private Hy-drant Rate, per Hydrant	Automatic Sprinkler Rate	Source of Supply, Treated or Not	Gravity or Pump to Mains, Standpipe, or Reservoir	Service Line Installed by	Average Daily Consumption, 1000 Gal.
Mississippi																		
Jackson......	21,262	Mun.	$6.00	$6.00	$5.00	$4.50	4,100	1,600	26-8	......	510	Water Dept.	Free	Free	River, Un.	Pump, Res.	Cons.	3,250
Missouri																		
Independence	9,850	Co.	7.00	2.00	2.25	...	1,768	1,396	35-25	47-40	127	Co.	$40.00	$40.00	River, Tr.	Pump, S.P.	Cons.	830
Kansas City...	248,381	Mun.	5.50	3.50	3.50	...	53,000	25,269	25-7	......	6,000	Water Dept.	None	None	River, Tr.	Pump, Res.	Cons.	28,341
Bay.........	10,923	Mun.	6.00	4.00	3.00	...	1,295	1,170	50-20	......	93	Water Dept.	None	None	Surf, Un.	Pump, M.	Cons.	3,000
St. oseph....	77,403	Co.	4.50	3.00	3.00	...	12,648	2,187	30-6	40.00	1,081	Water Dept.	40.00	Free	River, Tr.	Pump, Res.	Cons.	9,112
St Louis.....	687,029	Mun.	4.00	2.00	3.00	...	109,624	7,366	25-8	......	11,103	Water Dept.	Free	Free	River, Tr.	Pump, Res.	Cons.	82,100
Sedalia......	17,822	Co.	6.00	5.00	5.00	3.00	1,993	705	30-10	30.00	229	Water Dept.	30.00	0.005	River, Tr.	Pump, Res.	Cons.	2,375
Springfield...	35,201	Co.	8.00	2.00	2.00	...	6,900	1,300	25-10	40.00	376	Co.	50.00	50.00	Springs,Tr.	Pump, S.P.	Cons.	4,101
Montana																		
Billings.....	10,031	Co.	10.00	4.00	4.00	3.00	2,100	360	33-13	59.55	170	......	30.00	None	River, Un.	Pump, Res.	Iot	2,500
Missoula.....	12,869	Mun.	24.00	6.00	6.00	...	2,450	150	34-14	......	......	......	60.00	None	River, Un.	Grav.	Iot	8,000
New Hampshire																		
Concord......	21,497	Mun.	5.00	3.00	3.00	1.00	3,752	2,243	20-6	......	430	Water Dept.	Free	Free	Lake, Un.	Grav.Pump,Res.	Iot	3,000
Dover	13,247	Mun.	[6.00	5.00	5.00	...	1,931	1,438	30-20	18.35	218	Water Dept.	Meter	None	Ponds, Un.	Pump, Res.	Cons.	551
Keene	10,068	Mun.	5.50	4.00	4.00	...	2,127	190	26-2	......	282	Water Dept.	Free	Free	Lake, Un.	Grav.	Cons.	......
Manchester...	70,063	Mun.	4.00	1.75	2.00	1.00	7,352	5,689	13-9	25.00	941	Water Dept.	25.00	Free	Lake, Un.	Pump, Res.	Joint	4,122
New ersey																		
...ton......	14,209	Mun.	5.00	3.00	2.00	2.00	2,983	0	15-4	......	275	Pub. Wks.	Free	5.00	Creek, Tr.	Pump, S.P.	Cons.	1,380
Camden......	94,538	Mun.	5.00	3.00	3.00	2.00	20,471	1,131	20-10	......	897	Water Dept.	Free	Meter	Wells, Un.	Pump, M.	Cons.	11,986
Garfield......	10,213	Mun.	...	5.00	...	...	1,425	1,300	40-14	25.00	160	Water Dept.	30.00	75.00	Wells, Un.	Pump, M.	Cons.	450
Newark......	347,469	Mun.	6.25	5.00	2.50	...	44,772	24,729	40-14	......	3,048	Water Dept.	15.00	15.00	River, Un.	Grav.	Cons.	42,643
Passaic......	54,773	Co.	12.00	...	3.00	...	7,207	3,782	30-10	20-53.13	642	Co.	Free	50.00	River, Tr.	Pump, Res.	Cons.	5,300
Perth Amboy..	32,121	Mun.	6.00	4.00	3.00	1.00	4,000	1,366	15-5	......	308	Water Dept.	....	Meter	Wells, Un.	Pump, S.P.	Cons.	7,100
Rahway......	9,337	Mun.	6.00	5.00	3.00	...	1,789	180	20-5	......	190	"	Free	Free	River, Tr.	Pump, S.P.	Cons.	2,012

SUMMARY OF WATER RATES AND SERVICE IN REPRESENTATIVE AMERICAN CITIES, 1914. — (Continued.)

City	Population 1910	Municipal or Company Works	6 Room House	Bath	Closet	Stands and Tubs	Number of Taps or Customers	Number of Meters	Meter Rate, Max.-Min. Cents per 1000 Gal.	Public Hydrant, Revenue per Hydrant	Number of Hydrants	Hydrant Maintained by	Private Hydrant Rate, per Hydrant	Automatic Sprinkler Rate	Source of Supply, Treated or Not	Gravity or Pump to Mains, Standpipe, or Reservoir	Service Line Installed by	Average Daily Consumption, 1000 Gal.
New Mexico																		
Albuquerque	11,020	Co.					2,478	2,478	35-20	$35-50	227	Co.	None	None	Wells, Un.	Pump, M.	Cons.	...
New York																		
Binghamton	48,443	Mun.	$3.00	$3.00	$3.00	$3.00	10,417	4,000	12-6	...	855	Water Dept.	Free	Free	River, Tr.	Pump, Res.	Cons.	7,195
Buffalo	423,715	Mun.	3.00	1.50	1.50	...	77,260	3,459	6-2	15.00	5210	Water Dept.	33.33	...	Lake, Un.	Pump, Res.	Cons.	134,927
Cortland	11,504	Mun.	6.00	3.00	4.00	4.00	2,400	1,640	40-20	33.33	218	Water Dept.	Free	...	Springs, Un.	Pump, S.P.	Cons.	1,163
Dunkirk	17,221	Mun.					3,195	3,188	7-3	...	199	Water Dept.	Free	Free	Lake, Un.	Pump, M.	Cons.	4,353
Geneva	12,446	Mun.	5.00	3.00	4.00	...	3,090	2,950	20-6	10.00	286	Pub. Wks.	None	None	Lake, Tr.	Pump, Res.	Cons.	66
Glens Falls	15,243	Mun.	4.00	4.00	3.00	1.50	3,372	39	16-3	...	332	Water Dept.	None	None	Surf, Un.	Grav.	Cons.	104
Kingston	25,908	Mun.					5,275	125	16-6	...	479	Water Dept.	25.00	25.00	Creek, Tr.	Grav.	Cons.	3,700
Mt. Vernon	30,919	Co.					6,021	5,000	40-13	30.00	708	Co.	30.00	100.00	River, Tr.	Pump, S.P.	Cons.	3,187
New Rochelle	28,867	Co.	8.00	0.50	0.50	...	6,230	6,164	30-20	30.00	874	Co.	30.00	30.00	River, Un.	Pump, S.P.	Cons.	3,170
Newburgh	27,805	Mun.					4,667	3	10-3	...	414	Water Dept.	None	Meter	Lake, Tr.	Pump, Res.	Cons.	4,455
Olean	14,743	Mun.					2,877	2,877	13-5	...	320	Fire Dept.	Reg.	...	Wells, Un.	Pump, M.	Cons.	1,625
Peekskill	15,245	Mun.					2,500	2,100	13-6	...		Water Dept.	...	...	Lakes, Tr.	Pump, Res.	Cons.	3,000
Schenectady	72,826	Mun.	4.00	1.50	1.50	...	12,000	240	16-5	...		Water Dept.	Free	Free	Wells, Un.	Pump, M.	Cons.	10,935
Troy	76,813	Mun.	6.40	2.00	3.00	...	11,462	400	5	...	1075	Co.	Free	Free	Creek, Un.	Grav.	Cons.	17,000
Utica	74,419	Co.					12,588	12,411	30-6	35.00	1181	Co.	...	18.00 0.125	River, Tr.	Pump, Res.	Cons.	7,775
Waterford	3,245	Co.					...	All	20-8	25-50	101	Co.	50.00	0.166	River, Un.	Pump, M.	Cons.	17
Watertown	26,730	Mun.	4.00	1.00	2.00	...	5,000	690	20-3	...	426	Water Dept.	Free	Free	River, Tr.	Pump, Res.	Cons.	5,083
White Plains	15,949	Mun.					3,250	3,213	31-20	...	388	Water Dept.	35.00	50.00	Surf, Un.	Pump, S.P.	Joint	1,408
Yonkers	79,803	Mun.					8,697	9,010	16-8	...		Water Dept.	Free	Free	River, Tr.	Pump, Res.	Cons.	254,016

SUMMARY OF WATER RATES AND SERVICE IN REPRESENTATIVE AMERICAN CITIES, 1914.—(Continued.)

City	Population 1910	Municipal Works or Company	Flat Rate Schedule				Number of Taps or Customers	Number of Meters	Meter Rate, Max.-Min. Cents per 1000 Gal.	Public Hydrant, Revenue per Hydrant	Number of Hydrants	Hydrant Maintained by	Private Hydrant Rate, per Hydrant	Automatic Sprinkler Rate	Source of Supply, Treated or Not	Gravity or Pump to Mains, Standpipe, or Reservoir	Service Line Installed by	Average Daily Consumption, 1000 Gal.
			6 Room House	Bath	Closet	Stands and Tubs												
North Carolina Durham.........	18,241	Co.	...	...	...	...	3,150	1,350	25-18	100 Free 40.00	215	Co.	$40.00	...	River, Tr.	Pump, Res.	Cons.	1,133
North Dakota Grand Forks...	12,578	Mun.	$2.25	...	...	...	2,250	1,760	50-12	......	252	Water Dept.	Free	Free	River, Tr.	Pump, M.	Cons.	882
Ohio Canton.........	50,217	Mun.	7.00	$2.38	$1.42	$0.86	10,997	926	7	......	560	Water Dept.	Free	None	Wells, Un.	Pump, M.	Cons.	7,000
Cincinnati.....	363,591	Mun.	4.16	...	...	...	53,560	25,489	10	......	......	Fire Dept.	Free	Free	River, Tr.	Pump, Res.	Cons.	51,440
Columbus......	181,511	Mun.	...	...	...	...	28,736	26,769	12-10	......	......	Fire Dept.	6.00	6.00	Wells, Un.	Pump, Res.	Cons.	16,456
Marion.........	18,232	Co.	...	...	...	...	2,150	2,100	25-6.5	37-30	430	Co.	8.75	8.00	Wells, Un.	Pump, Res.	Cons.	1,552
Middletown....	13,152	Mun.	4.40	2.75	...	1.10	2,720	1,450	14-8	......	287	Water Dept.	Free	Free	Wells, Un.	Pump, M.	Mun.	2,750
Newark........	25,404	Mun.	6.75	3.50	1.50	...	3,500	2,300	18-10	......	711	Pub. Saf'ty	None	None	Surf, Un.	Pump	Mun.	2,500
Piqua.........	13,388	Mun.	4.00	2.00	2.00	...	1,950	0	...	......	260	Water Dept.	Free	Free	Canal, Un.	Grav.	Cons.	2,100
Youngstown...	79,066	Mun.	5.28	2.64	2.64	...	14,500	4,161	16-8	......	1490	Water Dept.	Free	Free	River, Tr.	Pump, S. P.	Cons.	9,797
Zanesville....	28,026	Mun.	5.30	1.00	3.00	...	8,000	50	6	......	......	Water Dept.	Free	Free	River, Tr.	Pump, Res.	Cons.	6,000
Oklahoma Guthrie........	11,654	Mun.	5.00	3.00	6.00	1.00	1,300	850	50-10	......	130	Fire Dept.	None	None	River, Tr.	Pump, S. P.	Cons.	500
Okla. City....	64,205	Mun.	13.60	1.20	1.80	...	10,604	7,350	20-10	......	795	Water Dept.	None	None	River, Tr.	Pump, M.	Cons.	6,766
Oregon Portland.......	207,214	Mun.	6.00	...	...	...	54,481	13,221	22.3-13	......	4007	Fire Dept.	12.00-60.00	12.00-60.00	River, Un.	Grav.	Cons.	67,500
Pennsylvania Allentown.....	51,913	Mun.	7.50	2.50	4.00	...	13,179	11,730	53-8	None	537	Fire Dept.	None	None	Springs, Un.	Grav., S. P.	Cons.	7,844
Bradford......	14,544	Mun.	3.80	0.80	1.20	...	3,883	116	6-4	None	282	Water Dept.	None	None	Wells, Un.	Pump, Res.	Mun.	2,000

SUMMARY OF WATER RATES AND SERVICE IN REPRESENTATIVE AMERICAN CITIES, 1914. — (Continued.)

City	Population 1910	Municipal or Company Works	Flat Rate Schedule				Number of Taps or Customers	Number of Meters	Meter Rate, Max.-Min. Cents per 1000 Gal.	Public Hydrant, Revenue per Hydrant	Number of Hydrants	Hydrant Maintained by	Private Hydrant Rate, per Hydrant	Automatic Sprinkler Rate	Source of Supply, Treated or Not	Gravity or Pump to Mains, Standpipe, or Reservoir	Service Line Installed by	Average Daily Consumption, 1000 Gal.
			6 Room House	Bath	Closet	Stands and Tubs												
Pennsylvania (Con.)																		
Erie	66,525	Mun.	$4.00	$3.00	$3.00	$3.00	14,551	406	20-4	None	918	Water Dept.	Free	Free	Lake, Tr.	Pump, Res.	Mun.	15,679
Johnstown	55,482	Co.	9.75	3.00	3.00	2.00	10,250	1,511	40-5	$25.00	232	Co.	$37.50	10.00	River, Un.	Grav.	Cons.	10,280
Lebanon	19,240	Mun.	5.00	2.00	2.50	1.00	4,730	117	20-4.5	None	208	Water Dept.	Free	Free	Springs, Un.	Grav.	.....	2,280
Philadelphia	1,549,008	Mun.	5.00	3.00	1.00	2.00	360,000	4,850	4	None	16,942	Water Dept.	Free	Free	River, Tr.	Pump, Res.	Cons.	319,000
Reading	96,071	Mun.	4.50	2.50	2.00	...	22,792	4,177	40-29	None	982	Water Dept.	....	....	Surf., Tr.	Pump, Res.	Cons.	14,321
Sharon	15,270	Co.	6.00	5.00	5.00	4.00	4,037	1,354	35-10	35.00	234	Water Dept.	....	....	River, Tr.	Pump, Res.	Cons.	2,449
Williamsport	31,860	Co.	5.70	4.75	1.90	1.90	6,925	115	10	5.00	356	City	50.00	75-100	Surf., Un.	Pump, M.	Cons.	6,000
Rhode Island																		
Providence	224,326	Mun.	6.00	5.00	5.00	5.00	29,261	26,298	20-10	8.20	2,445	Water Dept.	....	....	River, Tr.	Grav., Pump, Res.	Mun.	17,488
South Carolina																		
Columbia	26,319	Mun.	...	...	...	...	3,120	3,120	15-8	None	309	Water Dept.	10.00	80.00	River, Tr.	Pump, S.P.	Mun.	4,500
Tennessee																		
Memphis	131,105	Mun.	4.50	3.75	3.75	...	22,831	12,451	24-10	None	1,522	Water &F.D.	24.00	36.00	Wells, Un.	Pump, Res.	Mun.	13,652
Nashville	110,364	Mun.	9.00	4.00	5.00	...	16,729	13,320	20-8	None	1,420	Water Dept.	Meter	8.00	River, Tr.	Grav., Res.	Cons.	12,125
Texas																		
Denison	13,632	Mun.	...	...	...	...	3,000	2,600	50-7	None	171	Water Dept.	Free	Meter	Surf., Un.	Pump, S.P.	Mun.	1,000
Galveston	36,981	Mun.	...	...	...	...	6,041	6,041	26-9	None	....	Water Dept.	....	....	Wells, Un.	Pump, Res.	Cons.	3,500
San Antonio	96,614	Co.	5.00	4.50	3.00	...	20,000	4,542	15-9	19.40	1,341	Water Dept.	25.00	25.00	Wells, Un.	Pump, M.	Cons.	13,510
Waco	26,425	Mun.	7.00	5.00	3.00	6.00	8,758	650	30-15	24.00	520	Water Dept.	Free	Free	Wells, Un.	Pump, Res.	Cons.	6,250
Utah																		
Ogden	25,580	Mun.	6.50	1.00	1.50	1.50	5,600	325	20-5	35.00	147	Water Dept.	35.00	35.00	Creek, Un.	Grav.	Cons.	6,000
Salt Lake City	92,777	Mun.	4.75	1.00	2.00	3.00	17,564	800	7-6	None	1,725	Water Dept.	Free	Free	Creek, Un.	Grav.	Cons	22,000

SUMMARY OF WATER RATES AND SERVICE IN REPRESENTATIVE AMERICAN CITIES, 1914. — (Concluded.)

City	Population 1910	Municipal or Company Works	Flat Rate Schedule — 6 Room House	Bath	Closet	Stands and Tubs	Number of Taps or Customers	Number of Meters	Meter Rate, Max.-Min. Cents per 1000 Gal.	Public Hydrant, Revenue per Hydrant	Number of Hydrants	Hydrant Maintained by	Private Hydrant Rate, per Hydrant	Automatic Sprinkler Rate	Source of Supply, Treated or Not	Gravity or Pump to Mains, Standpipe, or Reservoir	Service Line Installed by	Average Daily Consumption, 1000 Gal.
Vermont																		
Burlington......	20,468	Mun.	$6.00	$4.00	$4.00	...	4,009	3,503	20-8	$20.00	...	Water Dept.	Free	Free	Lake, Tr.	Pump, Res.	Mun.	13,812
Rutland........	13,546	Mun.	5.00	2.00	2.00	...	2,879	150	8-4	None	169	Water Dept.	None	None	Creek, Un.	Grav.	Joint	3,000
Virginia																		
Lynchburg......	29,494	Mun.	6.00	3.00	3.00	...	5,800	475	20-3	None	425	Water Dept.	None	None	River, Un.	Grav.	Mun.	......
...nd......	127,628	Mun.	4.00	3.50	3.00	...	26,000	18,739	14-5	None	1239	Water Dept.	Mer	Meter	River, Tr.	Pump, Res.	Mun.	14,638
Roanoke........	34,874	Co.	9.00	3.00	3.00	$5.00	6,898	3,483	25-15	20.00	287	Co.	...	$20.00	Springs, Un.	Pump, Res.	Co.	4,223
Washington																		
N. Yakima......	14,082	Co.	7.80	2.40	2.40	...	3,085	3,226	20-7	45.00	5108	City	None	None	River, Tr.	Grav., Pump	Co.	1,200
Seattle........	237,194	Mun.		2.40	2.40	...	41,163	31,890	6-5	12.00	...	Water Dept.	None	None	River, Un.	Grav.	Joint	28,500
Spokane........	104,402	Mun.	12.00	2.40	2.40	...	20,606	7,690	10	42.00	2142	Water Dept.	None	30.00	Wells, Un.	Pump, Res.	Cons.	32,496
Walla Walla....	19,364	Mun.	12.00	3.00	3.00	...	3,659	182	20-8	......	...	Water Dept.	Free	Free	River, Un.	Grav.	Cons.	6,000
Wisconsin																		
Ashland........	11,594	Co.	9.00	5.00	4.00	...	1,978	543	21-13	61.20	247	Co.	...	50.00	Lake, Tr.	Pump, M.	Co.	1,181
Green Bay......	25,236	Co.	5.00	2.00	3.00	2.00	3,623	3,623	20-4	57.75	416	Co.	None	75.00	Wells, Un.	Pump, M.	Co.	1,450
La Crosse......	30,417	Mun.	5.00	2.00	3.00	2.00	5,300	2,470		......	541	Water Dept.	...	None	River, Un.	Pump, M.	Cons.	2,756
Marinette......	14,610	Co.	6.00	3.00	2.50	1.00	2,798	97	30-15	30.00	...	Co.	$30.00	50.00	Lake, Tr.	Pump, M.	Cons.	1,300
Milwaukee......	373,857	Mun.	6.00	3.00	2.00	...	58,357	57,657	8-6	5.00	3340	Water Dept.	None	None	Lake, Tr.	Pump, Res.	Cons.	47,556
Superior.......	40,384	Co.	5.89	3.68	4.05	2.94	5,056	4,408	40-8.7	40.00	776	Co.	40.00	40.00	Wells, Tr.	Pump, M.	Cons.	2,010
Wyoming																		
Cheyenne.......	11,320	Mun.	6.00	5.00	5.00	...	2,000	1	6-2	None	164	Water Dept.	3-5	None	Creek, Un.	Grav.	Cons.	3,610

CHAPTER XIV

RATE PROBLEMS OF GAS UTILITIES

Development and Magnitude of Gas Industry. — While there had been some experimentation with distilling gases from coal (such as by Mincklers at Louvain in 1784, by Dundonald in England in 1785, and by Lebon in Paris in 1786) William Murdock is commonly accredited originator of the use of coal gas for illumination. He began his experiments at Redruth, Cornwall, England, in 1792. In 1797 he lighted his premises at Old Cummock, Ayrshire. About that time he became connected with the famous firm of engine builders, Boulton & Watt of Soho, Birmingham, England, and this firm built a large generator to make gas for lighting their works. There was a public display at Soho in 1802. News of the progress of Lebon's experiments at Paris stimulated the firm to push the invention. However it was due probably to the imagination and ingenuity of a contemporary, F. A. Winsor, that the distribution of illuminating gas from a central station was then started. He appears to have been the original utility promoter, the prototype of the later generation. After many rebuffs, in 1812 a gas and coke company was incorporated in London; in 1813 Westminster Bridge was gas lighted. In 1813, one Samuel Clegg of the Boulton & Watt works was engaged as engineer for the pioneer concern, the Chartered Gas-Light and Coke Co. Clegg is credited as having invented the gas meter, pressure governor, cylindrical holder, and having first commercialized city gas lighting on a large scale.

Before the second London gas company was chartered, Baltimore in 1816 granted a charter to the first American company, and here also the first American gas meters were made. Nevertheless, the real history of American gas lighting runs farther back than the Baltimore project. In 1806, one Daniel Melville, of Newport, R. I., lighted his premises with coal gas made in his own apparatus. In 1813 he secured a patent and built a plant for a cotton mill in Watertown, Mass. In 1822

277

Boston adopted the innovation; in 1823 a company was organized in New York City, and in 1825 one in Brooklyn. Gas was introduced in New Orleans in 1835, in Philadelphia and Pittsburgh 1836, Louisville 1838, Cincinnati 1841, Albany 1845, and in other cities soon after.

Gas was a great success in both house and street illumination — as it was, up to 1878, unrivalled as a means of central-station lighting. The electric arc appeared in that year, but its use was restricted and not until after 1881 was there any menace of competition; then came the Edison incandescent electric lamp. While the great advantages of the electric lamp in safety, heating effect, steadiness of illumination and easy control caused alarm among gas men, yet the history of both systems shows no permanent disaster. Gas lamps were improved and cheapened, and with reduced prices for gas came greater and greater uses for it as a special fuel, as in domestic cooking, in small industrial furnaces, etc. The natural fields in which gas and electricity showed their special advantages slowly defined themselves and all idea of one completely outrivaling the other gradually was lost by about 1900. Competition in lighting service has been less active, no doubt, as a result of the wide consolidation in the past 15 years of gas and electric concerns into single companies. Under present conditions, the major use for gas is for heating of one sort or another, with lighting and power as minor services; the major uses for electricity are light and power with heating quite minor. The two utilities fit well together and there has been apparent no serious public hardship in their consolidation.

The last government census of the American gas industry (1914) shows 1183 gas utilities compared with about the same number in 1909. The larger number (427) produced carburetted water gas — 90,017,725,000 cubic feet valued at $74,516,534. Straight coal gas was produced in 274 plants — 10,509,946,000 cubic feet valued at $10,726,514. Oil gas was made in 85 works — roughly 8,300,000,000 cubic feet worth $7,500,000; and mixed coal, water and oil gas in 156 plants — 86,281,339,000 cubic feet valued at $72,012,021. Finally 129 plants made acetylene (not including concerns distributing in containers), and 112 made gasoline gas. Of the last two, the outputs were 16,453,000 and 181,412,000 cubic feet valued at $319,316 and $254,718.

The coke and byproducts disposed of aggregated $13,378,000 in value. There was an income of $20,815,800 from resale of purchased gas, and $10,977,774 from rental and sales of lamps and heating appliances.

The coke retort ovens in 1914 made 61,364,375,000 cubic feet of gas, valued at $6,009,600 — compared with 15,791,200,000 cubic feet in 1907 worth $2,609,200. Of this 1914 product, 28,351,774,000 cubic feet was sold to gas utilities for $8,883,016.

From 1909 to 1914 the gas companies output increased by 35.1% in quantity and 26.3% in value. The quantity of coal gas decreased in this time by 47.4% and gasoline gas by 16.3%. Carburetted water gas increased 10.9% and mixed coal and water gas by 111.6%. All-oil gas increased 91.1%, due to growth of the industry on the Pacific coast.

The 1914 income of these 1183 gas utilities (United States only) as reported by the census, was about $165,330,000. An estimate of the value of property then used in their service is $1,040,000,000. Current estimates of the status of the gas industry for 1916 give 1350 plants in both United States and Canada, with an investment of $1,100,000,000, and an output of 190,000,000,000 cubic feet per year. Of all these companies only some 125 are municipal utilities, and of these three fourths are small concerns producing acetylene and gasoline vapor in places unattractive to private capital.

The gas-utility business cannot be discussed without some mention of the natural-gas output. The studies of the U. S. Geological Survey showed that for 1914 the used output of wells was 591,887,000,000 cubic feet worth $94,115,524 — 2% over the year previous. Some 34% was supplied directly to domestic consumers at an average of 28.04¢ per 1000 cubic feet; 66% went to commercial customers at 9.56¢.

Gas Works Technology. — Artificial gas fuel for domestic lighting and cooking and for industrial heating is manufactured at a central plant and distributed, at a pressure of a few ounces per square inch, in iron or steel pipes under street pavements, etc. The gas may be transmitted in long mains, or in feeders at higher pressures to reducing stations feeding the distributing mains. From the mains there branch off service lines to the private premises. A meter is interposed between the service line and the house piping. For lighting, the oldest and simplest burners were simple slot orifices supporting an open flame. These have been largely supplanted now by the more economical Welsbach-type burners — high-temperature Bunsen burners with a mantle of refractory rare oxides surrounding the flame. Gas stoves for domestic cooking are but adaptations of Bunsen-burner groups in which a complete and smokeless combustion is secured. Industrial gas-fired furnaces largely employ Bunsen burners though using large amounts of gas.

Evidence points to the facts that (1) for lighting, the old open flame burners are steadily going out of use, (2) the greater part of the gas used today in American towns and cities is for heating appliances of one sort or another. A good example of this is afforded by a careful survey made by the gas company in Middletown, N. Y.* Summed up, the results showed that of 1139 consumers, 46% used gas only for cooking or heat; 65% used all their gas in a way for which calorific value controlled — as in heating appliances and mantle burners; 6% used no lighting gas in mantles, and 5% used no gas for cooking and heating.

The majority of open-flame burners in place were for occasional use such as in cellars, spare rooms, storehouses, etc., where the greater ruggedness and readiness of the simple open flame overcomes its lack of economy and where the candle-power of the flame is a very minor matter. In a large city there are undoubtedly proportionately more open flame burners than in the smaller places but this is offset by the greater use of industrial heating appliances.

It is probably true that 90% of the gas output of the country is used in Bunsen-type burners. When this situation is universally recognized there will be a general discarding of the public requirements that the gas supply have a certain candle-power value (when burned at a specified rate in an open burner). For this will be substituted the requirement of heat units released in the combustion of a given quantity. This will relieve gas works of the uneconomical burden of enriching their output with high illuminants, and tend toward the desirable end of cheaper gas. When gas is held at high pressures or low temperatures, or when forced through long lines at moderate

* Reported by C. H. Stone, Proceedings of the American Gas Institute, 1913, p. 76.

pressures and temperatures, the changes in candle-power are much greater than in calorific value.

At the gas manufacturing plant any one or more of several processes may be found. The simplest and oldest consists in the destructive distillation of bituminous coal, making it yield up its volatile hydrocarbons as fixed gases and leaving a residue of solid carbon and ash — coke. The coal is charged into retorts, commonly large horizontal closed fireclay tubes projecting into or passing through a furnace burning coke, coal or even gas. In recent years inclined and vertical retorts have been introduced to treat the coal in larger quantities and at reduced cost of handling. The gas as generated is drawn from the retorts and passed through a closed water-loaded trough where it deposits much of its tar and oil vapor. It passes through tar extractors, vapor condensers, and a series of purifying and byproduct-recovery washers and scrubbers; finally it goes through a station meter and into the holders and mains.

Some 4 to 6 cubic feet of gas can be made from a pound of coal. It consists typically of about 30–40% methane, 5–8% heavy hydrocarbons, 40–50% hydrogen, 2–15% carbon monoxide and 1–3% nitrogen. The byproducts of value are coke, tar oils and pitches, ammonia, and cyanides; their recovery is of importance to utility customers so far as it decreases the net cost of gas. A notable advance has been the use of byproduct-recovery coke ovens in connection with the manufacture of illuminating gas. In these, coke of a superior quality is made in great quantities, and the surplus gas from the distillation is saved instead of burned in the open air as with the old beehive coke ovens. Often only gas secured in the early part of the coking period is rich enough to replace the older coal gas; gas from the last stages of the process then is of low calorific and illuminating value and it must be used solely as special fuel and not discharged into the mains. It is possible, however, to utilize all the gas from these ovens and this is done in some places.*

* Use of coke-oven gas introduces a difficult problem in gas-rate making, for the return to be allowed on an industrial and non-utility plant like coke ovens is not easily fixed. Even the actual cost of the oven gas is a matter of debate — depending on whether the gas or the other products are to be regarded as the main output and to bear the fixed charges. When oven gas is bought, any purchase price notably below the cost of making coal, water, oil or mixed gas is apt to be regarded as reasonable.

An illuminating gas is made out of coal, steam and oil.   Coal or coke is burned with a deficiency of air in a gas generator yielding carbon monoxide, which is later burned to dioxide in passages filled with refractory checkerwork — the superheater and carbureter.   When maximum temperature is reached all the air is shut off and steam is turned on under the generator grates.   The water vapor is split up and finally a mixture of hydrogen and carbon monoxide secured in the first checkerwork or carbureter.   Oil is sprayed in, to be converted to a fixed gas in the superheater.   This is carried on nearly until the temperature of fuel bed and checkerwork are too reduced in temperature to function as intended.   Then steam is turned off, air put on and the cycle repeated — giving a series of "blows" and "runs."   This gas burns with a whiter and more brilliant flame than coal gas, and the illuminants are fixed gases which do not condense out much under reduced temperature or increased pressure.   In such a gas the carbon monoxide constitutes about 31%, the unsaturated hydrocarbons 14%, the saturated hydrocarbons 16%, hydrogen 32%, the rest being mostly nitrogen and carbon dioxide.

Where coal is expensive and oil plentiful, as in California, an illuminating gas is produced with oil, air and steam alone. In the production of the all-oil water gas, the generators consist of two upright shells, one short and the other tall, both filled with fire-brick checkerwork.   The short shell serves as the generator and the long shell as the superheater.   The discharge for heating-blast gases is at the top of the second shell; the take-off for illuminating gas is at the middle of the same shell. In operation, oil and steam are blown into the top of the generator shell and air blast is admitted at the center.   After a heating period of 12 minutes the blast is turned off, additional oil and steam let in at the top of the second shell, and gas taken off to the purifiers and scrubbers.   The injection of oil is rapid at first but is diminished steadily for 8 minutes.   There is a final 2-minute period to the run when only steam is injected — to clean the shells.   This gas more nearly resembles coal than water gas.   These machines have many points of advantage affecting gas rates.   They can be made in large units so that labor costs are diminished, and no time is lost in removing ash and clinker. They can be worked continuously, and a reduction in holder capacity might be expected, though it has not been observed.

The price of gas oil, in the eastern states at least, has continually increased and so much as to cause uneasiness of operating men as to their ability to produce gas without general increases in rates that would discourage business. It seems probable therefore that less and less oil will be used especially as its benefit beyond a certain point is largely in increasing candle-power rather than calorific value.

Gas service is now universally metered, except for definite use of street lamps. There were a few early attempts to rely on flat rates but they did not long persist. Indeed one of the important inventions of the pioneer gas engineer, Samuel Clegg, was a bellows gas meter. The most common type of meter is a large tin case with two compartments separated by a tight diaphragm, each chamber having a bellows alternately connected to the service and house pipes by a slide valve and, in emptying and filling, working a train of gears which records the displacement. There are other meters, like the rotary-vane type, though in somewhat less extended use.

Uniform Rate Persists. — Long before scientific rate making was attempted, the gas utilities were engaged in stiff competition with the invader electricity, under which conditions persistence of the simple uniform rate was not unexpected. Even when it was realized that this burdened the largest customers for the benefit of the smallest, it appears to have been feared that a sliding schedule would seriously discourage the small users and interrupt the business. Some such feeling persists today but is fading — owing to experience under commission-made sliding schedules and to deeper study by the gas men themselves.

. Accurate data as to the amount of discrimination existing through single-unit prices is not at hand, but a few opinions based on experience have been published. Some report * that two-thirds of the customers carry the other third. One statement† is to the effect that one-third of the customers do not pay their expenses, one-third do not pay any profit, and one-third pay the profit for the other two-thirds plus some of the cost of one-third. But it appears that the fair increase in charges to the unprofitable two-thirds need not be large.

* A. S. Miller, Proceedings, Am. Gas Inst.; 1913, p. 197.
† A. E. Forstall, Proceedings, Am. Gas Inst.: 1913, p. 203.

The reaction in a few gas men's minds has been so great, however, that the mental pendulum has swung far in the other direction and more cost items are often advocated loaded upon the small customer and upon the customer's demand than can be supported with reason. One reason why the urged movement away from a uniform price is sometimes over-violent is probably due to the misconception which some may have that all the fixed charges are to be allocated over customers in accordance with their maximum demands — irrespective of whether a part of the investment is working steadily against storage regardless of peak loads. If a division of plant is working steadily the fixed charges, including retirance, can fairly be combined with labor, supplies, repairs, etc., and apportioned over the output of that division. Only when there is a marked peak load on a division — or would be if the no-load valleys were not filled with low-price service won by competition with other kinds of service — can it logically be regarded that apparatus is reserved to meet the customers' demand, and that the fixed charges on such equipment are to be apportioned on the basis of demand. If there is a small peak effect there can be a small apportionment of fixed charges upon demand and a large one upon output.

To illustrate: the gas manufacturing plant is commonly designed to meet the maximum daily output — about $\frac{1}{210}$ to $\frac{1}{300}$ of the aggregate annual output, instead of $\frac{1}{365}$ for no peak at all. The distributing system is designed to carry the maximum hourly draft, which is $\frac{1}{3000}$ to $\frac{1}{3500}$ of the aggregate annual output, instead of the $\frac{1}{8760}$ for no peak demand. About half the cost of the works is in the distribution system. Under these conditions it often may be sufficient to hold that all the fixed charges on the manufacturing and storage division may be lumped with operating costs and spread over the entire output; while all the fixed charges on the distribution half of the plant may be assessed on the basis of customers' demand or size of meter (increased or diminished by the ratio of peak hourly draft to aggregate maximum capacity of meters). If a closer approximation to ideal charges is attempted, it would be to apportion 31.5% of the fixed charges on the manufacturing division according to customers maximum demand, or to some equivalent (the excess capacity required for the typical peak is 31.5% of the actual capacity), and 68.5% according to output. Then 77.3% of fixed charges on the distribution division would properly be assessed on demand and 22.7% on output (since the excess capacity of mains is 77.3% of the steady-flow requirement).

Some would favor apportioning all the fixed charges on holders to the customers' demand — on the ground that if there was no peak demand at all there would need be no holder. In many cases, however, the gas holder has a storage capacity equal to the daily manufacturing capacity and in few cases probably does it fall below 85% of the latter. Therefore there is good reason for considering it a part of the manufacturing plant. If the capacity is 85% of the daily manufacturing capacity, or $\frac{1}{244}$ of the annual output, then 19.6% of the fixed charges on the holder might go to demand and 80.6% to output, instead of in proportion to the 31.5% and 68.5% holding for the rest of the manufacturing plant.

It would be fair then to charge a customer a sum more or less depending on the size of his meter, plus a sum depending on the meter reading, and plus a customer charge for meter reading, billing, etc. (about $0.50 per month is commonly found to cover these). If these fixed and customer costs be spread over only the first one, two, three or four thousand cubic feet of gas (depending on the size of the meter) there is not found such an initial price that small consumers need be scared away. An easy way to change over from the common uniform metered rate to a logical system is to establish a transition period in which there is for all a high price for the first 1000 cubic feet, then a lower charge for the next 3000 cubic feet and a still lower one for the next 6000, etc. This has been done in Wisconsin.

In an altogether new place, or in an old one after the transition period is past, the high rate may apply to the first X 1000 cubic feet — X depending on the size of the meters installed or some equivalent way of measuring maximum demand. The high rate for X 1000 cubic feet would cover the customer and demand charges and might be accompanied by a minimum charge to insure their receipt.

Variation in Gas Cost for Large Use. — How the quantity of gas used by different customers can change the true unit cost may be illustrated in a hypothetical case where the output cost was assumed to be 60¢ per 1000 cubic feet, and the customer cost was taken as follows:

3-light meter...............................	18¢ per month.
5- " "	21¢ " "
10- " "	24¢ " "
20- "	27¢ " ..
30- "	32¢ " ..
45- "	41¢ "
60- "	50¢ "

The demand costs were:

3-light meter...............................$	4.00 per year
5- " "	9.00 " "
10- " "	20.00 " "
20- "	35.00 " "
30- "	50.00 " "
45- "	90.00 " "
60- "	130.00 " "

Then the cost to customers would decrease thus:

Size of Meter	Cu. Ft. per Month per Month	Customer Cost	Demand Cost	Output Costs	Total Cost	Cost per 1000 Cu. Ft.	Published Rate	Minimum Monthly Bill
3-light.....	1,000	$0.18	$0.33	$1.20	$1.11	$1.11	$1.15	$0.60
5- "	3,000	0.21	0.75	2.70	2.76	0.92	0.95	1.15
10- "	8,000	0.24	1.66	6.00	6.70	0.84	0.85	2.30
20- "	17,500	0.27	2.90	10.50	13.67	0.78	0.78	3.75
30- "	25,000	0.32	4.15	15.00	19.47	0.78	0.78	5.50
45- "	50,000	0.41	7.50	30.00	37.91	0.76	0.76	9.90
60- "	75,000	0.50	10.80	45.00	56.30	0.75	0.74	14.30

Gas-utility Accounting. — Through the control exercised by state commissions over gas-companies, satisfactory and uniform accounts in recent years have been more employed than before. The matter has also been studied by the organizations of the industry. Possibly not as much has been done as with electric and street-railway accounts, but certainly more than in the water-works field. The adopted standard accounts will permit of the analysis of cost items as laid down in the general notes on cost of service. Little more needs to be said about building up a schedule of true costs under demand, output and customer heads beyond that just given in connection with proportioning the fixed charges for the manufacturing and distributing divisions. It may be well to recall, however, that the customer charge should include interest, depreciation and repairs on meters and service lines. Some managers would push their analysis so far as to separate from the customer charge, and place in the output group, a portion of interest, depreciation and repairs on meters and services, depending on the capacity ratio of a no-peak-load equipment to the actual. These distinctions may be justified in some places but the amounts are not large enough to cause very great differences in rates.

Some accounting difficulties are encountered when a single concern gives both gas and electric service. The majority of expense items entering into a study of the cost of service can be directly apportioned to the proper department. But there is a class of expenses, the "overhead" or "indirect" costs, which are not directly assignable on any physical evidence. It is common to apportion them between the two departments according to the ratio of the direct expenses. Such a practice is justified on the ground that each increment of direct expense leads to a proportionate increment in the overhead; in other words, the overhead expenses depend on the relative activities and magnitudes of the two branches, and these in turn are well measured by the aggregates of the direct expenses. Such practice has been permitted by the Wisconsin and other state commissions, and is very similar to the apportionment of unassignable items in railway accounts practiced by the Interstate Commerce Commission. Such a division of overhead costs between two departments is based on the assumption that the two utilities are fairly similar in their administration, financing, character of business, etc. When that is not approximately true it may be advisable to devise some modified or substitute apportionment based on the demands of local conditions.

Natural-gas Utilities. — Natural gas of high calorific value is sold, in districts within piping distance of the oil and coal regions where gas may be obtained, at rates usually beyond competition of manufactured gas. There are no raw materials to be consumed and handled, and there is no manufacturing plant to contribute fixed charges (though there are wells and collecting lines). But in spite of this, natural gas is no free gift of nature as it comes to the consumer's premises, and its use is not unchallenged. Natural gas varies in composition markedly according to the field; its value depends on its content of methane (50 to 90%) and hydrogen (5 to 35%). The Baltimore artificial-gas low-rate new-business campaign of 1916 was based on the assumption and argument that the high hydrogen content and the impurities of natural gas made it necessary to lead the burned gases off with higher temperatures and more water vapor so that the artificial gas became economical in spite of its lower heat value (600 B.t.u. per cubic foot instead of 1100).

A company supplying natural gas has no manufacturing plant or holders but its wells and distributing works, constituting about all the physical plant, have to be large enough to permit peak-load flow with good service conditions as to pressure, fluctuation, etc. The rates that can be made therefore should vary as markedly for long hours of use, small peak and off-peak drafts as does electric central-station service. The rate of return to be allowed a natural-gas utility in justice must be considerably higher than for an artificial-gas concern or an electric company, or else the earnings must be large enough to give heavy amortization of investment. This results from the inherent hazards of the natural-gas business. It is essentially a mining venture with most of the usual uncertainties. Promising ground has to be secured, and money sunk in prospecting; soon after the field lines have been laid down the supply may give out.

A good example of natural-gas rates is shown in the accompanying 1915 schedule of the Louisville (Ky.) Gas and Electric Co.*   Here an effort was made to have the rates include proper demand and customer charges, although not announced as such. The schedule was not quite ideal but was forced as a compromise measure in place of smoother scale and a service charge. It is reported that both company and consumers are satisfied.

LOUISVILLE GAS AND ELECTRIC CO.
NATURAL GAS RATES. *Effective March 4, 1915.*

The following will be the classification under which consumers will be supplied with natural gas:

SCHEDULE A.—Domestic consumers, gas engine consumers and other consumers who require continuous service.

* As described by Donald McDonald before the Natural-Gas Association, in the paper "Equitable Rates For Natural Gas"; see "Gas Age" June 15, 1915.

Rate. — For the consumption in one month of —

100 cu. ft. or less	$0.40	1,100 cu. ft	$0.83
200 cu. ft	0.47	1,200 cu. ft	0.83
300 cu. ft	0.62	1,300 cu. ft	0.94
400 cu. ft	0.62	1,400 cu. ft	0.94
500 cu. ft	0.62	1,500 cu. ft	1.02
600 cu. ft	0.62	1,600 cu. ft	1.08
700 cu. ft	0.72	1,700 cu. ft	1.16
800 cu. ft	0.72	1,800 cu. ft	1.21
900 cu. ft	0.72	1,900 cu. ft	1.33
1,000 cu. ft	0.72	2,000 cu. ft	1.33

All additional gas over the first 2,000 cu. ft. per month at the rate of 38.88 cents per 1,000 cu. ft.

Cash Discount. — A discount of 10 per cent will be allowed for payment of bills within ten days from their date.

SCHEDULE B. — Commercial consumers who do not require continuous service, who are prepared and willing to substitute other fuel on short notice, and who agree to have their supply of gas shut off either temporarily or permanently for the purpose of giving Schedule A consumers sufficient supply of gas.

Rate. — Based on monthly consumption —
· First 200,000 cu. ft. at 38.88 cents per 1,000 cu. ft.
Next 200,000 cu. ft. at 33.33 cents per 1,000 cu. ft.
Next 200,000 cu. ft. at 22.22 cents per 1,000 cu. ft.
All over 600,000 cu. ft. at 13.33 cents per 1,000 cu. ft.

Cash Discount. — A discount of 10 per cent will be allowed for payment of bills within ten days from their date.

NOTE. — Consumers served at Schedule B rate whose consumption is less than 100,000 cu. ft. shall revert to Schedule A rate.

SCHEDULE C. — Industrial consumers whose monthly consumption is not less than 200,000 cu. ft. who do not require continuous service and who are prepared and willing to substitute fuel on short notice and who agree to have their supply of gas shut off either temporarily or permanently for the the purpose of giving Schedule A and Schedule B consumers sufficient supply of gas.

Rate. — Based on monthly consumption —
First 100,000 cu. ft. at 38.88 cents per 1,000 cu. ft.
Next 100,000 cu. ft. at 22.22 cents per 1,000 cu. ft.
All over 200,000 cu. ft. at 13.33 cents per 1,000 cu. ft.

Cash Discount. — A discount of 10 per cent will be allowed for payment of bills within ten days from their date.

NOTE. — Consumers in Schedule C whose consumption is less then 200,000 cu. ft. shall revert to Schedule B. In the event it becomes necessary for the company to cut off the supply of gas to consumers in Schedule C, the largest consumers will be cut off first. The same will apply should it be necessary to cut off consumers in Schedule B.

In consideration of the rates named in Schedules B and C and having regard for the obligations of its franchise, the company reserves the right to discontinue service without notice to customers using gas under these schedules, provided it should become necessary to do this in order to maintain a proper supply of gas in any district to Schedule A consumers.

In the event it becomes necessary to shut off the supply of gas to consumers using gas under Schedules B and C, those using gas under Schedule C will be shut off first and those under Schedule B next, and as between individual consumers the company will select those, the shutting off of which will do the most to improve the service to its domestic or Schedule A consumers.

The rates named in Schedules B and C are quoted solely for the purpose of disposing of surplus gas. No extension or enlargement of mains will be made to serve customers under these schedules. The consumer expressly waives any claim for loss or damage on account of discontinuance or interruption of service and waives any claim for priority of service over any other consumer.

New Baltimore Schedules. — The greatest departure in gas-utility practice of recent years undoubtedly is the gas-rate system placed in effect February 1916 by the Consolidated Gas Electric Light and Power Co., Baltimore, Md. To encourage the use of gas as domestic fuel *a net rate of 35¢ per 1000 cu. ft.* was made for consumption over the old normal — a lower price than for what manufactured gas had ever been known to be sold. For these consumers, the primary rate was 75¢ net — for up to 1000 cu. ft. per month per room for domestic use (counting all the main rooms in a house less two, and with a minimum primary amount of 4000 cu. ft.) and for up to 150 hours use of maximum rate of consumption in commercial service. To make the scheme applicable without the delay incident to examining and rating each domestic-customer's premises, the customer's maximum monthly draft during 1915, provided it exceeded 4000 cu. ft., was taken as the primary amount. The gas schedules of the Baltimore company can be set forth in general as in the following four paragraphs. The particularly interesting schedules, "C" and "D" are also presented in their official form. Schedule "K," covering industrial service is notable as showing a concrete case of a demand (and customer) plus an output factor.

SCHEDULE C — YEARLY CONTRACT GENERAL GAS RATES.

For convenience, called the Commercial Schedule. 75 cents net per 1,000 cubic feet, with an excess rate of 35 cents net for over 150 hours' use of the demand per month. Primary Rating reduced one-half for bakers, using gas chiefly between the hours of 8 P.M. and 6 A.M. Minimum Primary Rating 4,000 cubic feet per month.

SCHEDULE D — RATES FOR DOMESTIC SERVICE.

75 cents net per 1,000 cubic feet, with an excess rate of 35 cents net for consumption (a) over last year's maximum month for present customers, or (b) over a scheduled room basis for new customers; with the right of the (a) customers to apply the (b) basis upon request. Minimum Primary Rating 4,000 cubic feet per month.

SCHEDULE E — NON-CONTRACT GENERAL GAS RATES.

75 cents net per 1,000 cubic feet per month; for 50,000 cubic feet per month or over, 70 cents; for 100,000 cubic feet or over per month, 65 cents.

SCHEDULE K — INDUSTRIAL GAS RATES, GENERAL SERVICE.

Three-year contract; Fixed Costs $204.00 per year for 300 cubic feet of demand, $48.00 per 100 cubic feet for excess demand; Running Costs, 35 cents net per 1,000 cubic feet up to 1,000,000 cubic feet per month, 30 cents for excess.

SCHEDULE C — YEARLY CONTRACT GENERAL GAS RATES.

— Gas for any purpose will be sold under this Schedule, upon application, to any Customer who has signed an agreement for yearly gas service, embodying the usual terms and conditions of the Company now or hereafter in force.

PRIMARY RATE: Eighty-five cents gross per thousand cubic feet, seventy-five cents net when bills are paid on or before the last discount day.

SECONDARY RATE: Forty-five cents gross per thousand cubic feet, thirty-five cents net when bills are paid on or before the last discount day.

This rate will apply to all gas used per month in excess of the amount hereinafter specified as the Primary Rating, and only to such excess. The Primary Rating is the number of cubic feet per month which must be used at the Primary Rate before the Secondary Rate applies.

The Primary Rating under this Schedule will be placed at the number of thousands of cubic feet corresponding most nearly to one hundred and fifty times the Customer's Demand, the Demand being defined as the maximum hourly rate of consumption in cubic feet. This is equivalent to one hundred and fifty hours' use of the Demand per month, figured to the nearest number of even thousands of cubic feet. The Primary Rating shall remain fixed, and a fixed element in billing, so long as the Customer's conditions of maximum rate of use do not increase, but shall in no event be taken at less than 4,000 cubic feet per month (Three Dollars net).

DEMAND: The demand is the maximum rate of use by the Customer and is defined as the greatest number of cubic feet used in any one hour. It may be specified in the contract and estimated by the Company from the burner rating or otherwise, and may be redetermined from time to time according to the Customer's normal use of gas. The Demand shall not be substantially decreased during any twelve-month term of the contract, but shall be increased in accordance with and for all billing after any increase in maximum use which may from time to time occur. The Primary Rating will be changed accordingly. Upon extraordinary occasions for a certain limited period the

Company may, at its option, give permission to exceed the determined maximum rate of use by a stated amount without increasing the estimated Demand upon which the Primary Rating is based.

METERS: Not over two meters will be furnished by the Company at its expense at any one contract location under this schedule, unless installed for the Company's convenience. Additional meters will be furnished at a rental of $2.50 per month each, for meters on which demands are determined, and at a rental of $1.00 per month each for sub-meters. Where more than one meter is installed for the convenience of the Customer, the consumption shall be billed separately for each meter and the Demand and the Primary Rating determined separately for each meter.

SCHEDULE "C" NIGHT SERVICE: For installations in which gas is chiefly used for such processes as require its consumption between the hours of 8 P.M. and 6 A.M., such as the processes used by bakers, the specified Demand, or the Demand upon which the Primary Rating is based, may be taken as one-half of the maximum demand occurring between above said hours, provided that the demand upon which the Primary Rating is based shall not be less than the maximum demand during any other hour and that the Primary Rating shall not be reduced below 4000 cubic feet per month.

COMBINATION DOMESTIC AND GENERAL SERVICE: For a Customer using domestic service on the same meter with service for other uses than are provided for under the Domestic Schedule D, the Primary Rating will be taken as the sum of the Domestic Primary Rating under Schedule D and of the Primary Rating under this Schedule C.

TERMINATION: When the Customer has used the Company's service at the contract premises for over one year, the contract may be terminated at any time after ten days' written notice from either party to the other. Upon proper notice of removal, the contract will be terminated.

SCHEDULE D — RATES FOR DOMESTIC SERVICE. — Gas for domestic use will be sold under this Schedule to any Domestic Customer of this Company who has signed an agreement for the service under the usual terms and conditions now or hereafter in force. This Schedule will become effective on all consumption after the regular meter readings taken in February, 1916.

PRIMARY RATE: 85 cents gross per 1000 cubic feet, 75 cents net when bills are paid on or before the last discount day.

SECONDARY RATE: When the Customer's use of gas is in excess of the amount hereinafter specified under Primary Rating, the additional consumption so used will be at the rate of 45 cents gross per 1000 cubic feet, 35 cents net when bills are paid on or before the last discount day. This Secondary Rate will be applied only where the said additional service is supplied through the regular house meter furnished for all consumption, and only to the consumption in excess of the estimated ordinary use by the Customer, which ordinary use will be designated the Primary Rating.

PRIMARY RATING: The Primary Rating for new Customers and for present Customers at new locations will be determined as follows, it being understood that all ordinary rooms, such as living rooms, dining-rooms, kitchens, bedrooms, servants' quarters, bathrooms and laundries will be included in the list of rooms, but that cellars, closets, pantries and storerooms will not be included:

PRIVATE HOUSES

of 6 rooms or less 4,000 cubic feet per month.
of 7   "   5,000   "   "
of 8   "   6,000   "   "
of 9   '   7,000
of 10   8,000
of 11   '   9,000
of 12   "   10,000   "   ..

with an excess of 1000 cubic feet per room for each room over 12.

Individual apartments will be rated on the same basis as private houses. Boarding houses and rooming houses shall be taken at 1000 cubic feet per room per month.

In putting this Schedule into general effect for all Domestic Customers on the lines of the Company at the time of the said February meter readings, the Primary Rating will be taken in each case as the number of thousands of cubic feet per month that is nearest to the maximum consumption by the Customer in any month during the preceding twelve months at the same premises, and such maximum consumption will control the determination of the Primary Rating for all such Customers so long as they may continue at their present premises. Where the Customer has occupied premises for less than eight months, the Company shall have the right to determine the Primary Rating in accordance with the Schedule herein. The Primary Rating shall in no event be taken at less than 4000 cubic feet per month for any of the classes of Customers specified herein, and where the Customer's maximum consumption has been less than 4000 cubic feet per month, his Primary Rating shall be taken at 4000 cubic feet and the Secondary Rate shall apply for all consumption in excess thereof.

How Baltimore Schedules were Made. — The new schedules were the result of two years study of the possibilities in competing with other fuels, particularly where large quantities were used. A study of operating characteristics for years back showed prior to 1908 a load factor of 23 to 29% and since then improvement to 37% (peak-hour day, 1914) and 48% (maximum-output day, 1914). A typical daily load curve (1910–1914) showed a consumption rate of some 500,000 cubic feet per day from 6 A.M. to 3 P.M., a sharp peak rise to 1,500,000 cubic feet per day at 6 P.M. and a steady decline to 150,000 cubic feet per day at 12 A.M. and a gradual recovery.

All customers using over 50,000 cubic feet per month were classified according to use — apartment houses, boarding-houses, churches, bowling alleys, bakeries, meat shops, and their demand estimated by hourly readings during heavy-load periods in test cases. Recording devices were attached to meter dials and gearing to give a graphic record. The individual load factors varied from 6 to 100%. The average for the classes varied from 9% (shoe manufacturers and office buildings) to 39% (newspapers). Lunch rooms showed the best combination of high load factor (29%) and large number of customers.

The various expenses were grouped into customer, demand and output classes. Prior to making tentative schedules, the total customer cost was divided by the number of customers to give the unit cost per customer per year; the total demand costs divided by the aggregate customers' demands gave the unit cost per thousand cubic feet per hour demand; the output costs were divided by the sales. Several special modifications were made: (1) An allowance was added to the customer unit cost to cover cost of finding demand and applying this to rates; the customer and demand charge were merged for simplicity; (2) the output charge contained a sum for covering fixed operating cost of some special customers — including meter reading and billing; (3) ample margin was left to cover contingencies and to avoid embarrassment; (4) large spread was left between the rate curves for large and small customers to induce larger use; it was aimed to have the slope of each rate curve steep enough so that individual customers could see the advantages of improving their load.

Results in Baltimore. — During the first month after the 35¢ secondary rate went into effect, it benefited about 6000 domestic customers, out of a total of some 130,000 consumers of all sorts. In practically all cases there was no installation of new consuming equipment at this early period, but the installations rose very rapidly toward summer.

The gas distributed by the Baltimore Company is a mixed coke-oven and carburetted-water gas. The coke-oven gas is purchased from the Maryland Steel Co., at Sparrows Point, Md., and is piped $12\frac{1}{2}$ miles. The quantity available varied in 1914 from zero to 4,800,000 cubic feet. The carburetted water gas is added to make up the daily demand and the quality is adjusted so as to keep the final distributed product of 20 c.p. The coke-oven gas has varied from 7 to 14 c.p. value and from 517 to 606 B.t.u. thermal value. It is purchased on a candle-power basis and in 1914 cost per candle-power the same as carburetted water gas. The last had a thermal value of 570 B.t.u. per cubic foot. The average thermal value of the mixed gas distributed was reported in 1916 as 591.2 B.t.u.

The average net holder cost of the gas made by this company in 1913–1914 — gross cost for labor and materials — was 27¢ per 1000 cubic feet, not including interest, depreciation and other fixed charges. After the addition of charges to cover distribution, metering, new business, general expense, taxes, etc., the average cost was 52¢ at the burner.

Gas Rates in American Cities. — The gas rates in certain American cities are assembled with other pertinent data in appended tables (taken from published compilations made by J. C. Dickerman for the Utilities Bureau). · All such tables show inherent limitations of usefulness, in spite of their interesting nature. No matter how careful the citation of variable affecting conditions, the ability to transfer information from one situation to another is extremely restricted, and possible general deductions are few. For example, in the following table, Boston is shown as having 80¢ gas, while it is generally reported that the price was put down (under a dividing scale) below cost so that the holding concern might distribute some·real-estate profits used to swell the surplus fund.

These tables lead one to the view that the differences in cost of gas diminish with increased sales, being more pronounced among concerns with sales of less than 30,000,000 cubic feet per year. Differences in manufacturing cost due to different costs of fuel are evident but apparently are not of first importance. Taxes are a heavier burden on the smaller companies than the larger ones. The operating costs seem to have held up above $1 per 1000 cubic feet where less than 20,000,000 cubic feet per year was made by a works; these costs seemed to have dropped down to 80¢ for works producing about 50,000,000 cubic feet, to 70¢ for 100,000,000 cubic feet and to 50¢ for 500,000,000 cubic feet.

Cost of Artificial Illuminating Gas in American Cities

Compiled by J. C. Dickerman from published reports and printed in
" Utilities Magazine " (Utilities Bureau, Philadelphia),
July and November, 1915.

For Nineteen Larger Cities

City	Years (Inclusive)	Operating Cost per Thousand Sold §§	Taxes per Thousand Sold	Net Selling Price ‡‡	Annual Sales Approximate Total (1000 Cu. Ft.)	Gas per Meter or Consumer (Cu. Ft.)	Kind and Quality ††	
Milwaukee, Wis.*	1909–1913	$0.3184	$0.0658	$0.75–0.50 s.s.	2,820,000	36,000	98% coal	630 B.t.u.
Boston, Mass.†	1910–1914	0.4074	0.0727	0.80	5,600,000	32,600	Mixed, 51% water	650 B.t.u.
Baltimore, Md.‡	1911–1914	0.4225	.0655	0.90–0.80	3,540,000	32,000	Mixed, 25% coal	20 c.p.
New York, N. Y.	1909–1912	0.4227	0.0576	0.80	26,040,000	32,000	Mixed, mostly water	23 c p.
Racine, Wis.§	1909–1913	0.4322	0.0603	1.00–0.60 s.s.	238,000	22,000	Coal	612 B.t.u.'
Lynn, Mass.	1910–1914	0.4464	0.0595	0.75–0.50 s.s.	745,000	26,700	Mixed, 55% water	Over 16 c.p.
Minneapolis, Minn.	1911–1914	0.4480	0.0508	0.85–0.80	2,213,000	33,650	Mixed, 65% water	18 c.p.
Philadelphia, Pa.‖	1910–1914	0.4500	0.0025	1.00	180,000	27,000	Coal	15 c.p.
Hartford, Conn.	1912–1914	0.4511	0.0294	0.90–0.75	657,000	26,700	Mostly water	19 c.p.
Brooklyn, N. Y.	1909–1912	0.4516	0.0449	0.80	11,930,000	29,800	Water	23 c.p.
New Bedford, Mass.	1910–1914	0.4558	0.0804	0.80	480,000	25,500	60% water	18 c.p.
Washington, D. C.	1911–1914	0.4560	0.0635	0.85	2,500,000	42,100	Mixed 95% water	23 c.p.
Rochester, N. Y.	1909–1913	0.4683	0.0648	0.95	1,300,000	24,000	80% water	20 c.p.
New Haven, Conn.	1912–1914	0.4790	0.0601	0.90	1,230,000	26,400	Mixed, 60% water	19 c.p.
Worcester, Mass.	1910–1914	0.4902	0.0664	0.75	780,000	30,500	Mixed, 40% water	18.2 c.p.
Fall River, Mass.	1910–1914	0.4913	0.0720	0.80	560,000	24,200	Water	20 c.p.
Bridgeport, Conn.	1912–1914	0.5009	0.0605	$1.00	545,000	22,500	Water	20 c.p.
Syracuse, N. Y.	1909–1913	0.5508	0.0738	0.95–0.63 s.s.	650,000	21,500	Mixed	18 c.p.
Westchester and suburbs of New York City**	1909–1913	0.6215	0.0626	1 50–1.00	1,480,000	25,700	Water	23 c.p.

* This company purchases very large portions of its gas from by-product coke ovens and sells coke at high price.
† This company purchases about 50% of its supply from coke ovens, and sells about 14% to other companies.
‡ Purchases coke-oven gas and manufactures water-gas.
§ Coke sold to more than pay for all gas coal used.
‖ This is not the big city plant, but a small independent company operating with vertical retorts. The cost given is a maximum. Taxes estimated indirectly, but are practically nothing for city and state purposes.
** This company operates in 23 towns and villages under suburban conditions near New York City.
†† Calorific or candle-power values used.
‡‡ S.S. = Sliding Scale. [Not the British dividing scale.]
§§ Exclusive of taxes and depreciation.

FOR 74 SMALLER CITIES

COST OF ARTIFICIAL ILLUMINATING GAS IN AMERICAN CITIES

City	Years (Inclusive)	Population of District	Operating Cost per 1000 Cu. Ft. Sold*	Taxes per 1000 Sold	Net Selling Price†	Annual Sales Approximate Total (1000 Cu. Ft.)	Annual Sales Per Consumer or Meter (Cu. Ft.)	Per Cent Made, Lost, or Unaccounted for	Kind of Gas	Cost of Fuel and Oil — Coal, per Ton	Coke, per Ton	Oil, Cents per Gal.
Chippewa Falls, Wis.	1911–1913	9,000	$0.051	$1.125	$1.50	7,200	14,500	11	Water	....	$7.10	4.48
Baraboo, Wis.	1911–1913	6,500	1.140	0.070	1.25	9,000	17,000	16	Coal	$4.65	....	....
Putnam, Conn.	1912–1914	6,600	1.160	0.035	1.70–1.25	10,500	10,500	17.5	Water	6.40	....	3.00
Beaver Dam, Wis.	1912–1913	7,000	0.822	0.026	1.30	11,900	17,000	3.0	Water	....	5.25	2.90
Gardner, Mass.	1911–1914	15,000	1.277	0.072	1.90	12,100	13,000	8.0	Water	3.50	....	5.40
Marinette, Wis.	1911–1913	14,600	0.686	0.095	1.50	12,500	22,000	13.5	Coal	....	....	....
Stoughton, Wis.	1910–11 & 1913	5,000	0.691	0.050	1.25	13,000	18,500	?	Water	5.85	....	3.89
Ashland, Wis.	1911–1913	11,500	1.061	0.061	1.50–1.25	13,900	15,000	17.7	Water	7.00	....	4.03
Claremont, N. H.	1912–1913	7,000	0.718	0.040	1.60	14,500	18,000	15.5	Water	....	....	....
Amesbury, Mass.	1911–1914	12,000	1.178	0.089	2.00L–1.50 F	15,200	12,100	16.7	Water	....	....	....
Norwood, Mass.	1911–1914	8,000	1.183	0.049	1.70	16,700	14,500	14.2	Water	....	....	....
Woburn, Mass.	1911–1914	16,000	1.033	0.102	1.25	16,900	19,500	8.5	Coal	5.05	....	....
Rockville, Conn.	1912–1914	7,500	1.054	0.048	1.50–1.30	17,200	14,300	10.4	Coal	6.30	....	5.87
Port Jervis, N. Y.	1911–1913	9,500	1.003	0.085	2.00L–1.50 F	18,100	18,000	20.0	Water	....	....	....
Norwich, N. Y.	1912–1914	8,500	0.838	0.051	1.40	19,300	13,800	13.9	Water	....	....	....
Willimantic, Conn.	1911–1914	11,200	1.065	0.059	1.50	19,900	12,800	7.5	Water	....	....	3.70
Clinton, Mass.	1911–1914	13,000	1.002	0.082	1.70–1.40 s.s.	20,800	19,000	9.0	Coal	4.50	....	....
Milford, Mass.	1911–1914	15,000	1.062	0.124	1.50	20,900	19,000	8.5	Water	6.30	....	....
Hyattsville, Md.	1912–1914	7,000	0.866	0.078	1.50–0.90	21,350	17,400	6.5	Coal	5.01	....	....
Portage, Wis.	1911–1913	5,400	0.701	0.027	1.30	21,400	18,100	2.0	Coal	3.50	....	....
Salisbury, Md.	1912–1914	8,500	0.966	0.049	1.25	21,400	14,000	4.5	Water	5.25	....	4.77
Wallingford, Ct.	1912–1914	10,000	0.695	0.037	1.25	24,000	13,700	5.7	Water	6.55	....	5.00
Winsted, Conn.	1912–1914	7,000	0.846	0.043	1.50	24,200	14,200	5.4	Water	6.75	....	....
Greenfield, Mass.	1911–1914	16,000	0.968	0.125	1.50	24,700	14,100	8.0	Water	6.75	....	3.10
Nyack, N. Y.	1911–1913	12,000	1.254	0.090	1.50	24,900	20,300	16.0	Water	....	....	....
Wausaw, Wis.	1911–1913	16,500	0.848	0.093	1.25	25,000	15,800	11.0	Coal	4.50	....	....
Watertown, Wis.	1911–1913	9,000	0.837	0.066	1 60L–1.25 F	27,300	17,000	13.0	Coal	4.20	....	....

* Exclusive of taxes, depreciation and street lights. † From Brown's Directory; s.s. = sliding scale, L = light, F = fuel.

Cost of Artificial Illuminating Gas in American Cities. — (Continued.)

For 74 Smaller Cities

City	Years (Inclusive)	Population of District	Operating Cost per 1000 Cu. Ft. Sold*	Taxes per 1000 Sold	Net Selling Price†	Annual Sales		Per Cent Made, Lost, or Unaccounted for	Kind of Gas	Cost of Fuel and Oil		
						Approximate Total (1000 Cu. Ft.)	Per Consumer or Meter (Cu. Ft.)			Coal, per Ton	Coke, per Ton	Oil, Cents per Gal.
Hudson, Rensselaer, N.Y.	1911–1913	......	$1.215	$0.014	$1.35	28,400	12,000	19.3	Mixed	$3.92	...	5.07
Portsmouth, N.H.	1912–1913	11,000	0.678	0.056	1.35	28,800	17,200	9.2	Coal	4.10	...	...
Plattsburg, N.Y.	1911–1913	15,000	0.803	0.037	1.00	29,000	28,000	7.9	Water	6.25	...	5.75
Bristol, Conn.	1912–1914	17,000	0.799	0.031	1.25–1.00 s.s.	33,900	15,100	17.0	Water	5.85	...	3.4
Leominster, Mass.	1911–1914	17,500	0.952	0.106	1.40–1.25	34,100	15,500	6.7	Water	6.66	...	...
Newburyport, Mass.	1911–1914	16,400	0.876	0.140	1.35	35,100	16,000	6.0	Coal	4.41	...	...
Waukesha, Wis.	1911–1913	8,800	0.695	0.036	1.20	36,400	20,400	11.0	Coal	...	...	...
Webster, Mass.	1911–1914	28,000	0.804	0.041	1.25	38,300	12,000	6.5	Water	6.25	...	...
North Attleboro, Mass.	1911–1914	10,000	0.788	0.075	1.20–1.15	38,800	25,400	5.5	Coal	...	...	...
Eau Claire, Wis.	1911–1913	18,300	0.578	0.113	1.30–0.90 s.s.	40,600	14,500	6.6	Coal	4.50	...	...
Torrington, Conn.	1912–1914	14,500	0.907	0.070	1.50–0.90 s.s.	40,800	16,000	3.6	Water	6.75	...	...
Manitowoc, Wis.	1911–1913	13,000	0.523	0.070	1.00	41,500	19,700	10.3	Coal	3.65	...	4.91
Sheboygan, Wis.	1911–1913	26,000	0.691	0.071	1.35–1.25	44,800	14,000	8.1	Mixed	3.50	...	4.00
Hagerstown, Md.	1912–1914	25,000	0.765	0.033	1.00	51,800	15,000	9.7	Water	5.10	...	5.00
Middletown, Conn.	1912–1914	20,000	0.725	0.038	1.10	53,000	19,000	12.7	Water	6.10	...	...
Green Bay, Wis.	1911–1913	25,000	0.738	0.063	1.30L–1.00 F	53,900	15,500	20.0	Coal	...	...	5.14
Fond du Lac, Wis.	1911–1913	18,800	0.713	0.052	1.35L, 1.12½–85.5 F	54,700	18,800	10.7	Mixed	4.10	...	...
Beloit, Wis.	1911–1913	15,000	0.681	0.066	1.25	55,000	24,600	13.0	Mixed	4.25	...	3.00
Ithaca, N.Y.	1911–1913	18,800	0.736	0.097	1.25–1.00 s.s.	57,700	22,600	8.6	Mixed	3.45	...	3.87
Arlington, Mass.	1911–1914	26,000	0.907	0.044	1.25	60,000	17,000	3.7	Mixed	6.62	...	3.50
Janesville, Wis.	1911–1913	13,800	0.785	0.049	1.30–1.00 s.s.	60,600	21,600	3.4	Water	...	...	...
Attleboro, Mass.	1911–1914	16,000	0.790	0.061	1.10	61,300	21,400	5.1	Coal	5.05	$5.00	...
New London, Conn.	1912–1914	20,000	0.861	0.033	1.20–1.05	64,700	22,700	12.7	Water	5.05	4.64	...
Northampton, Mass.	1911–1914	19,000	0.847	0.081	1.10	65,300	21,500	8.9	Mixed	5.01	...	3.40

* Exclusive of taxes, depreciation and street lights.　　† From Brown's Directory.　　s.s. = sliding scale, L = light, F = fuel.

For 74 Smaller Cities   Cost of Artificial Illuminating Gas in American Cities. — (*Concluded.*)

City	Years (Inclusive)	Population of District	Operating Cost per 1000 Cu. Ft. Sold*	Taxes per 1000 Sold	Net Selling Price†	Annual Sales — Approximate Total (1000 Cu. Ft.)	Per Consumer or Meter (Cu. Ft.)	Per Cent Made, Lost, or Unaccounted for	Kind of Gas	Coal, per Ton	Coke, per Ton	Oil, Cents per Gal.
Beverly, Mass.	1911–1914	32,000	$0.759	$0.070	$1.10	70,800	15,800	9.2	Mixed	$3.85	....	....
Concord, N. H.	1912–1913	21,500	0.740	0.070	1.20–1.10	71,800	17,000	8.5	Water	....	....	3.2
Gloucester, Mass.	1911–1914	23,500	0.715	0.093	1.10	73,400	23,500	6.2	Mixed	5.40	....	3.2
Appleton, Wis.	1911–1913	28,600	0.591	0.067	1.125–0.65 s.s.	73,600	16,000	11.5	Mixed	4.15	....	5.14
La Crosse, Wis.	1911–1913	30,400	0.636	0.073	1.00	78,900	21,500	15.0	Coal	4.60	....	....
Danbury & Bethel, Conn.	1912–1914	20,000	0.760	0.049	1.25	79,000	15,000	10.3	Water	4.25	....	....
Oshkosh, Wis.	1911–1913	33,000	0.610	0.058	1.00	91,700	21,800	6.3	Coal	3.85	....	....
North Adams, Mass.	1911–1914	23,000	0.697	0.043	1.00	96,200	19,500	8.7	Mixed	5.44	....	3.5
Fitchburg, Mass.	1911–1914	38,000	0.772	0.088	1.15–0.70 s.s.	110,600	17,700	7.6	Mixed	4.55	....	....
Stamford, Conn.	1912–1914	29,000	0.711	0.044	1.10	130,000	29,000	8.9	Water	....	....	....
Taunton, Mass.	1911–1914	36,000	0.609	0.059	1.00–0.90	131,600	23,500	11.9	Coal	3.80	....	4.5
Georgetown, D. C.	1912–1914	28,000	0.612	0.076	1.00	154,000	43,000	19.2	Mixed	....	....	....
Madison, Wis.	1911–1913	25,000	0.660	0.041	1.15–0.90 s.s.	163,600	29,700	11.6	Water	....	....	....
Pittsfield, Mass.	1911–1914	32,000	0.701	0.064	1.08	164,700	21,200	2.75	Mixed	4.50	....	3.0
Meriden, Conn.	1912–1914	38,000	0.603	0.052	1.10 L / 1.00 F	171,700	20,000	4.8	Mixed	....	....	....
Derby, Conn.	1912–1914	30,000	0.595	0.034	1.05	176,000	24,400	5.7	Mixed	....	....	....
Philadelphia, Northern Liberties District	1910–1914	45,000	0.450	0.002	1.00	180,000	27,000	....	Coal	....	....	....
New Britain, Conn.	1912–1914	47,000	0.555	0.032	1.15–0.90 s.s.	187,000	20,800	4.4	Mixed	4.65	....	6.0
Binghamton, N. Y.	1911–1913	47,500	0.507	0.081	1.10	197,000	19,500	4.0	Water	....	....	....
Manchester, N. H.	1911–1913	71,500	0.657	0.066	1.10	215,000	19,100	7.0	Mixed	....	....	....
Haverhill, Mass.	1911–1914	42,000	0.574	0.062	0.90–0.85	248,000	25,700	4.7	Water	....	....	....
Racine, Wis.	1911–1913	40,000	0.424	0.060	1.00–0.60 s.s.	264,000	30,000	6.3	Coal	3.0	....	....
Schenectady, N. Y.	1911–1913	80,000	0.587	0.050	1.00–0.70	264,000	22,000	6.5	Water	4.80	....	3.5

* Exclusive of taxes, depreciation and street lights.

† From Brown's Directory; s.s. = sliding scale, L = light, F = fuel.

CHAPTER XV

RATE PROBLEMS OF ELECTRICITY SUPPLY WORKS

Nearly all Utility Problems Encountered. — The most inclusive generalized discussions of rate-making problems — particularly as regards most such matters as bearing of cost of service, peak loads, non-peak business, reserved equipment for maximum demand, classified customers, diversity factors, effect of apportioning retirances and other true expense items, minimum charges, lack of investment records and need of appraisals, franchise questions, land and water rights, discarded equipment, reasonable return, promoting initiative, discrimination, etc., — seem to apply more completely and with fewer special exceptions to electric-supply undertakings than to the other utilities like water-works and gas supplies, or railroads and electric railways. Illustrations and applications of general principles therefore have been more frequently taken from electric utilities than the others throughout this whole work. This has rendered unnecessary a lengthy presentation of electric rate-making problems. To preserve the balance of treatment and for ready information, brief review has been made in the following paragraphs of the history, growth and technology of the industry, and a few special problems have been mentioned.

History of the Electric Central Station. — The very early history of electricity supply is of course the history of the development of magneto-electric machinery, for there was no prospect of commercial service before the conversion of mechanical energy into electrical became practical and cheap. The first step was the discovery of magneto-electric induction, by Henry in 1831 and independently by Faraday about the same time. Primitive generators were made shortly thereafter but the modern machine was not possible until the principle was established of using self-supplied electro-magnets in place of weak permanent magnets to produce the necessary magnetic fields in which wire coils were to be rotated. This development was independently given by Siemens and Wheatstone in 1867. A good armature had been produced in 1860 by Pacinotti but it was more of a laboratory device than an engineering machine, and it was reinvented on the latter plane by Gramme in 1870. The Siemens I-shuttle and Gramme ring armature were combined into the drum armature in 1873 by Hefner-Alteneck.

Probably because of the lack of a cheap and convenient source of electric current, the development of a practical electric lamp had lagged. Crude low-resistance incandescent electric lamps had been made, for instance by Starr and King in 1845; and arc lamps had been built by Davy in 1812, Jablochkoff in 1876, and Serrin in 1857. But there had been no attempt at a whole system of lighting — prime movers, generators, distribution lines, and lamps — until 1878. Indeed it is probable that general mechanical and electrical engineering progress up to then had not been great enough to permit it. Finally at about the same time three systems were brought out: (1) that of Jablochkoff in France, using alternating current and arc " candles," or two thin vertical carbon pencils separated by a strip of clay; (2) that of Brush using a special direct constant-current generator and automatic arc lamps connected in series, (3) that of Edison using an improved constant-potential direct-current generator supplying high-resistance carbon-filament vacuum-bulb lamps connected in parallel.

Secrets of Early Success. — Probably the secrets of Edison's success lay in the use of a high-resistance (about 100 ohms) carbon filament where others had always attempted to use low resistances (say 10 ohms). This gave him a system of lamps connected in parallel instead of the old constant-current series-circuit idea to which others clung. He secured at once the great advantages of subdivision of light units and non-interfering control of each lamp.

The economy of distribution secured by Edison with his arrangement of a supply network connected to the generating station by feeders was also novel — others having proceeded from pipe-line experiences to develop only mains and branches, all increasing in size from the customer to the station. In further search for economy he developed the three-wire double-voltage distribution, but this was independently conceived by Hopkinson in England and Siemens in Germany. Some 60 to 70%

of the cost of copper was saved. The Edison system aroused a veritable furor of discussion both favorable and adverse. Gas company stocks dropped, and the newspapers and magazines were full of arguments, pro and con.

The Brush system achieved immediate success for street lighting, though it was of very limited use for interior illumination. The generator, regulator and lamps were each good and serviceable, and were well combined. The Brush system soon had a strong competitor in the Thomson and Houston arc system which was marked by a somewhat better generator and regulator. The Edison system was a good complement to the Brush and Thomson-Houston; it was, if anything, even better commercialized. The Edison distribution system soon had to meet competition with the Stanley-Westinghouse development of the Goulard-Gibbs alternating-current transformer; and the Sawyer-Mann, Swan and Fox incandescent lamps came on the market.

In all these developments, plus the high-speed steam engine, the multipole generator, the steam turbine and the so-called Francis hydraulic turbine, rests the technology of the modern central-station industry. The direct-current generating and distributing system of Edison have been restricted to short distances and congested districts but so well conceived were the details of his system that many persist today unchanged, although the lamps may be supplied with alternating-current. The Brush and Thomson-Houston generators and arc lamps have about completely disappeared but they paved the way for the later enclosed and luminous arcs on existing series street circuits.

First Central Station. — As a result of Edison's experimental work in the development of the multiple lamp, underground network and feeders, and three-wire system, plans were made for a station in lower Manhattan, New York City. A territory 2000 feet square was canvassed to find the number of lamps, and the number and size of motors probably required. The plant had a capacity of 2000 horsepower, using water-tube boilers, direct-connected high-speed (350 r.p.m.) generators, and a steel skeleton-frame support. Edison and his assistants, after designing the station and system down to ultimate details, had to organize and manage shops for the manufacture of the equipment. But capitalists hesitated to embark, though the new station paid financially before its technical success was admitted. Construction had to be cheapened and adapted to smaller municipalities — and in that form stations were soon built in Massachusetts, Pennsylvania, and Ohio. The Pearl Street Station, New York City, started Sept. 5, 1882, with 5500 lamps. In 14 months it had 12,732 lamps. Soon a station was built at 26th St. and another at 39th St. Then one rose in Boston and one in Brooklyn. In 1887 the first Chicago Station was started. An important technical contribution was made by the Berlin (Germany) Electricity Works about 1889 when it used vertical marine engines and multipolar generators.

There were, in 1886, 47 Edison illuminating companies, capitalized at $5,000,000; 47 stations were in operation and 10 in construction. The 57 stations supplied 160,000 lamps. Series street-lighting systems were devised for incandescent lamps and installed in Lockport, N. Y., Portland, Me., Lawrence, Mass., Jacksonville, Fla., Brookline, Mass., Denver, Col., and Lachine Canal, P. Q. Stationary power service was supplied. By 1890, 60 cities had stations. The growth of the central-station industry in recent years is shown by the accompanying table prepared by the United States Census Bureau.

The early rates (1890) were from $150 to $75 per horsepower-year, for 24-hour power; the average cost then to Edison stations was from $25 to $40 (not including fixed charges and profit). An ampere-hour electrolytic meter was early developed, but flat rates were common. For example in Hazelton, Pa., $1\frac{1}{4}$¢ per hour per 10-candle-power lamp was charged; in Tamaqua, 75¢ down to 10¢ per 10-candle-power lamp per month was fixed depending on the number of lamps. The early stations were calculated to yield 10 to 20% on the investment. This return included the then unstudied item of depreciation, simple interest, and all the rewards for capital.

Uses for Electricity. — The main uses for electric energy are: (1) general distribution for light, power, and heat, (2) electric railways, (3) electrochemistry. The first of these services was the original field of the central-station industry but railway supply has been found an attractive load for the electric companies because it adds diversity. Electrochemistry offers remarkable possibilities for non-peak and off-peak service, but comparatively little benefit has been secured by the great number of central stations. The ability of a central station to ac-

GROWTH OF COMMERCIAL AND MUNICIPAL CENTRAL ELECTRIC STATIONS *

	1912	1907	1902	Per Cent Increase 1902-1912
Number of stations †	5,221	4,714	3,620	44.2
Commercial	3,659	3,462	2,805	30.4
Municipal	1,562	1,252	815	91.7
Total income ‡	$302,115,599	$175,642,338	$85,700,605	252.5
Light, heat, and power, including free service	$286,980,858	$169,614,691	$84,186,605	240.9
All other sources	$15,134,741	$6,027,647	$1,514,000	899.7
Total expenses, including salaries and wages §	$234,419,478	$134,196,911	$68,081,375	244.3
Total number of persons employed	79,335	47,632	30,326	161.6
Total horsepower	7,528,648	4,098,188	1,845,048	308.0
Steam engines and steam turbines: ‖				
Number	7,844	8,054	6,295	24.6
Horsepower	4,946,532	2,693,273	1,394,395	254.7
Water wheels:				
Number	2,933	2,481	1,390	111.0
Horsepower	2,471,081	1,349,087	438,472	463.6
Gas and oil engines:				
Number	1,116	463	165	576.4
Horsepower	111,035	55,828	12,181	811.5
Kilowatt capacity of dynamos	5,134,689	2,709,225	1,212,235	323.6
Output of stations in kilowatt hours	11,532,963,006	5,862,276,737	2,507,051,115	360.0
Estimated No. of lamps wired for service:				
Arc	505,395	¶ 562,795	385,698	31.0
Incandescent and other varieties	76,507,142	¶ 41,876,332	18,194,044	320.5
Stationary motors served:				
Number	435,473	167,184	101,064	330.9
Horsepower capacity	4,130,619	1,649,026	438,005	843.1

* From Bulletin 124, U. S. Bureau of the Census.

† The term " station," as here used, may represent a single electric station or a number of stations operated under the same ownership.

‡ Exclusive of $36,500,030 in 1912, $20,093,302 in 1907, and $7,703,574 in 1902 reported by street- and electric-railway companies as income from sale of electric current for light or power, or from sale of current to other public-service corporations.

§ In addition to salaries and wages, includes the cost of supplies and materials used for ordinary repairs and replacement, advertising, fuel, mechanical power, electrical energy purchased, taxes, and all other expenses incident to operation and maintenance, and for 1912 charges for depreciation and charges for sinking fund.

‖ Includes auxiliary engines.

¶ Includes for purposes of comparisons 7082 arc and 267,997 incandescent lamps reported by the electric companies to light their own properties. Lamps used for such service were included in the total number reported in 1912.

quire a railway and electrochemical load depends on its ability to make a low price for energy, and this means that such customers will carry comparatively little of the fixed charge, compared with some other classes of customers.

The proportion between power and lighting loads depends on the town served; it varies all the way from that of small cities where practically all current is used for street and house lighting, to the large industrial district where most of the power is supplied to mills and factories, and only a small domestic- and street-lighting load is carried in the evening.

The requirements on different parts of a central-station system are somewhat conflicting. Power can be used in the great majority of cases only at low potentials — say up to 600 volts. Economical transmission requires high potential. For electrolytic processes direct-current is imperative; and it is desirable for street railways. For furnaces alternating current is preferable.

Technology of Supply. — The fundamental feature of a modern electricity-supply system is of course the generating plant. This is commonly a steam power station located as close to the load center of the area served as is compatible with a cheap supply of coal and water. In it then are the familiar boilers, engines or turbines, generators, switchboards, transformers, etc. In a few cases the stations have been located in coal fields close to the cheapest fuel supplies and transmitting energy over considerable distances to markets. In a number of instances, while coal remains the fuel, gas producers have been substituted for the boilers, and internal-combustion motors for the steam engines or turbines. The possibility of converting the energy of falling water to electricity has brought the hydro-electric station into importance, wherever the economy of having to purchase no fuel is not offset by the increased interest charges on extra investment and the added losses from long-distance transmission.

The smaller central stations may generate direct-current to be distributed over a restricted area. The larger plants have to employ alternating current on account of the ease of utilizing high voltages which enable economical transmission. Where a district to be served is considerable in extent, a number of substations are used, each situated near some important sub-center of the load. Generally the high voltage is stepped down in a substation to one which is safer for the local distribution on radiating lines. For special services, where the frequency of the alternating current or the current itself is unsuitable, the substation may house rotating machinery for producing a different frequency or for direct current.

At the larger customers' premises, or in the vicinity of a group of smaller customers, the current — if it be alternating — is again reduced to about 110 or 220 volts, at which potential it enters the customers' wires. In America 110 volts at the lamp is standard practice, and abroad 220. There is a saving in cost of wires and in line-voltage drop by using 220 volts, but it is more than overcome for lighting installations by the 10–15% inherently lower efficiency of 220- over 110-volt lamps. In specific cities the voltage runs from 100 to 130; this was early brought about by the impossibility of making each vacuum-tube carbon-filament lamp of a certain rigidly fixed voltage for economical service.

In large cities with underground distribution, the alternating current is at a disadvantage compared with direct, for the inductive voltage drop of the former is additive to the resistance loss with direct current, and since a multiplicity of comparatively small conductors becomes better than one or a few very large ones.

In the early days of alternating-current distribution, a small transformer was placed for each customer. It was soon realized that this was undesirable for each transformer had to be able to carry the occasional maximum so the devices were lightly loaded most of the time. But the full magnetic losses continued all day, and commonly the power drawn and paid for by the customer was only 35% of that furnished in a day's time to the transformer. By having one transformer serving a group of customers, a more efficient loading was secured, making use of the diversity of customers' demand so that the revenue power jumped to 70% of the total furnished.

Besides the transformer losses there are also line loss and leakage, meter loss and error, and possible unaccounted losses. At full load all these may be 15 to 18% of the full-load capacity, resulting in a maximum-hour capacity of 82 to 85%. The all-day losses, however, may easily be 33% of the total supply, resulting in a system efficiency of only 66%.

Development of Lighting. — Incandescent-filament lamps can be made to run on either constant-voltage or constant-current circuits, but the electric arc is essentially unstable without a constant-current supply, for the voltage drop decreases as the current increases and *vice versa*. Arc lamps are commonly designed for constant-current circuits, though by placing a steadying resistance in series with the arc it can be run on a constant-voltage circuit — at reduced efficiency. The arc-light generator was necessarily a small machine, since 100 to 150 lamps in series gave as high potential as safe to use on such circuits — 4000 to 10,000 volts. It has been made obsolete by the development of the movable-secondary constant-current, or "tub," transformer — used alone for alternating-current arcs or with mercury-arc rectifiers for direct-current lamps. This of course is supplied from constant-potential alternating-current generators of ordinary types.

In the old simple carbon-arc lamp practically all the light came from the incandescent tips of the pencils. A modern development is to incorporate in the carbon electrodes materials which are luminous in the arc stream, such as calcium and titanium. This gives increased efficiency of light production. A mercury electrode is used with the arc in a vacuum tube. An earlier improvement of the open arc consisted of using a loose enclosing globe which retarded the consumption of carbon and increased the hours of burning. The latest form of direct-current arc substitutes an electrode of iron and titanium oxides, resulting in a highly efficient, brilliant arc stream and long hours of burning. A luminous arc for alternating currents has been developed using titanium-carbide electrodes.

Edison in developing his incandescent-filament lamps early discarded metals, but later scientific researches (1905) and general advance in metallurgy made possible the tungsten filaments which have all but driven the carbon type out of the market. These have a specific consumption of 0.5 to 1.5 watts per candle compared with 3.1 to 3.5 for carbon.

While miscellaneous uses for central-station electricity supply have been developed yet practically every central station has to supply lighting current so that the great majority of generators are built for the close regulation — slight voltage fluctuation — required for such service.

Difficulties of Continuous Service. — Continuity of current supply is one matter of great importance in the real success of an electric utility and the satisfaction of customers; yet it has been painfully accomplished by the application of great amount of engineering study and no small expenditure of money. The lack of easy storage for the electric current, the dependence on rotating machinery, the delay incident to pressing idle generators into service, the local destruction wrought by the concentration of energy at a fault, etc., have conspired to make this problem of first magnitude. One important provision is ample spare capacity in generators, feeder-lines, etc., and the distribution of the fixed charges on these should be carefully studied. In many cases it will be found inequitable to include these wholly with other charges allocated upon peak-customers' demand; it may be fair to charge them in part on output — on the grounds of an expense of general maintenance of business.

Importance of the Meter. — The customer's meter constitutes one of the most important and highly developed parts of an electric-supply system. Meters are almost universally owned, maintained, and read by the utility company. They are virtually light and delicate direct- or alternating-current motors with jewel bearings; one winding takes current proportional to the line voltage and another winding to the customer's current. They are loaded with a copper disk rotating in a magnetic field so that the speed is always proportional to the energy drawn in the circuit of which they are a part. Great advance has been made in producing a low-priced but reliable and accurate watt-hour meter. Yet no meter retains its accuracy indefinitely, and occasional inspection and re-test is advisable both for the company's and the customer's interest. The required accuracy of electricity meters is commonly placed at 3, 4, or 5% fast or slow as tested. The lower limit is fair for most alternating-current meters but the higher may have to be allowed for direct-current meters. Under some rules when a meter is over-fast a rebate is ordered for the known fast period, and the company is allowed to collect an added sum from the consumer when the meter is slower than prescribed.

The meter investment remains so large and the annual cost of maintenance, reading, book-keeping, etc., commonly aggregate so much in excess of $6 per year that the unit cost of service to very small consumers is prohibitive.   A meter also absorbs 12 to 20 kw.-hr. per year, non-revenue energy. ᐧ The small customer has been successfully cultivated abroad on unmetered service with flat rates, and is longingly regarded in America as an aid to diversified use.   A barrier to use by small consumers has been the cost of interior wiring (from $1 to $6 per outlet, depending on the building ᐧand whether wires are exposed or concealed).   An inexpensive simplified system of exposed wiring (the "Concentric") has recently been introduced in America to reduce cost of such work.

Maximum Demands of Electric Customers. — Much study has been made of the probable maximum demands of various

PER CENT OF CONNECTED CAPACITY THAT IS ACTIVE LOAD

Class	Ripon *	Madison †	Wisconsin Companies Using Demand Indicator †	Chi- cago ‡
Residences, flats and rooming houses..	40	....	....	60
0.3 kilowatt connected capacity.....	....	60	....	90
0.5 " " "	....	60	....	64
1.0 " " "	....	60 and 33	....	48
2.0 " "	....	60 and 33	....	46
Public buildings......................	40	55	33	....
Churches.............................	55	55	56–85	....
Schools..............................	55	55	37–52	....
Stores, retail........................	75	70	40–100	66
Stores, wholesale.....................	....	....		70
Offices, banks........................	75	70	57–87	72
Theatres.............................	75	70	49–89	....
Depots...............................	75	70	75–95	....
Hotels...............................	60	55	28	29
Libraries.............................	60	55		
Stables..............................	60	55	52–58	60
Factories............................	55	55	53–56	....
Saloons..............................	75	70	62–92	....
Clubs................................	75	55	28	29
Electric signs........................	100	100	....	86
Street lamps.........................	100	....	....	....
Motor installations:				
single, under 10 h.p.................	....	90	....	....
several, aggregating 10 h.p..........	....	80	....	....
10–20 h.p............................	....	70	....	....
20–50 h.p............................	....	60	....	....
50–100 h.p...........................	....	55	....	....
over 100 h.p.........................	....	50	....	....
Shops................................	....	....	55	58
Machine shops........................	....	....	37–54	....
Blacksmith shops.....................	....	....	66	....

* *Ripon v. Ripon Light and Water Co.*, 1910; 5 Wis. R. R. Comm. 1.

† *Re Madison Gas and Electric Co.*, 1911; 7 Wis. R. R. Comm. 152, 167.

‡ E. W. Lloyd, "Load Factors," Nat. El. Light Assoc., 1909; G. A. McKenzie and B. F. McGuire, "Significance of Statistics," Nat. El. Light Assoc., 1910.

electricity consumers, for the need of properly distributing the heavy fixed charges, locked up in plant reserved for maximum demand, has been felt more in this utility field than in others. It is desired to find probable maximum demand without expense and complication of a demand meter in regular use. The work of the Wisconsin Commission is notable in this field. The preceding table gives some of this body's data, and a few from Chicago studies.

Diversity of Central Station Loads. — An electric plant is a true service-type of utility (as defined on page 15); there is required generating and distributing capacity sufficient to satisfy the maximum demand of the year, and this is in some part idle all during the rest of the year. In winter the load curve of a typical winter day for a small utility rises slowly from 10% output at 2 A.M. to 25% at 2 P.M., then more sharply to 100% at 5 or 6 P.M. and then steadily drops off to 10% at 2 A.M. again. For a summer day the first rise is from 10% at 2 A.M. to 25% at 7 P.M., and an 80% peak comes at 8 to 9. On a large system, say of 100,000 kilowatts capacity, supplying light, stationary and traction power, there is typically a low 15% period from 2 to 5 A.M., a rise to 75% output at 9 A.M., a 65% period from 10 A.M. to 4 P.M., a 100% peak at 6 P.M., and a steady decline thereafter.

The general phenomena of time-diversity of utility demand and its effect on investment has already been discussed (page 32) and illustrated by reference to electricity-supply works. It is necessary only to append here for illustration some experience data * on "diversity factors" (ratio of sum of maximum demands of subdivisions to actual experienced maximum demand on the system or main division thereof). The following applies to Chicago, but is undoubtedly typical of the larger American cities.

CHICAGO LIGHTING SYSTEM, DIVERSITY FACTORS

	Residence Lighting	Commercial Lighting	Retail Power	Large Users
Meter to transformer............	3.35	1.46	1.44	1.0
Transformer to feeder..........	1.3	1.3	1.35	1.15
Feeders to substation..........	1.15	1.15	1.15	1.15
Substation to generating station	1.1	1.1	1.1	1.1
Meter to generating station.....	5.5	2.4	2.46	1.45

* From "Application of Diversity Factor," by H. B. Gear; Proceedings, National Electric Light Assoc., June 1915.

Residence Tariffs. — The problem of securing a good rate schedule for residence-supply customers is particularly difficult, compared with industrial-supply customers. The latter are more apt to have enough technical knowledge to understand a two- or three-part charge and their long hours of use generally result in satisfactory low cost of energy. The former require a very simple tariff for them to understand, while their service is in peak-load hours and of short duration so that their cost of energy is apt to be comparatively high — although they cannot readily see how. It is universally desirable that the residence consumer should be well satisfied and that the tariff should be so framed as to stimulate longer hours of use. A simple classification into size classes, with various unit prices for each, ordinarily is not sufficient to attain all the desired ends. Some of the simpler differential schemes that have been employed to make the charges approximate true costs are noted below.

"Norwich" Tariff. — The two- or three-part rate with a Wright (or substitute) maximum-demand indicator has not been well received by the ordinary residence consumer and where tried has added to the investment, accounting and adjustment expenses of lighting service. One of the attempts to sugar-coat the pill, named after Norwich, England, where it was early tried, was to charge the consumer a fixed sum equal to such a percentage of his tax " rateable valuation " as would return on the average, his probable demand and customer cost, the plausible argument being used that the peak demand for current depended on the size of and investment in the dwelling. This has been found to work fairly well in a community where all the residences are rated on the same basis. But, in most cases, position in the town and in the block affect the renting value of the dwelling house, and so does the extensiveness of the grounds, while neither condition appreciably affects lighting. There is apt to be, for America, undue discrimination. The percentage figure used has commonly been of the order of 10 to 15% of the "rateable values." To it of course has been added an energy charge, say 1 to 3¢ per kilowatt-hour, for whatever quantity the watt-hour meter recorded. The British " Point Five Association " has successfully exploited this scheme with a 1¢ (0.5d) energy charge.

"Telephone" Tariff. — The obvious shortcomings of the "Norwich" tariff have led to other schemes, prominent among which is one called in England the "Telephone" tariff because of its similarity to systems of charging for telephone service. The customers were assessed an advance charge intended to cover the demand and customer costs, plus a per-unit energy charge in accordance with the watt-hour meter reading.

The best example of this probably was at St. Marylebone, England,* where 70% of the capacity of the lamps (not counting mere "convenience" lamps in storerooms, cellars, etc., or decorative sockets) was charged at about $70 per kilowatt per year as the primary factor. The secondary charge was 2¢ per kilowatt-hour.

In connection with such a tariff, the customer contracted to use only electricity for lighting, and the low secondary unit charge stimulated miscellaneous services and longer hours of lighting. Maximum-demand indicators were used for accumulating experience about the demand factors of residence installations. These showed that the small dwellings had a demand equal to about 80% of the total installed lamps while the largest residences showed only 33%; the elimination of decorative and convenience lamps made 70% fair for all. It was necessary, however, in considering decorative lighting to rule that there should be a service lighting of 1 watt per square foot of floor area.

Wisconsin System. — The earlier Wisconsin studies † of the various classes of customers showed notable uniformity in the use of their installed capacity, the proportion of "active" to "connected" load running from 40 to 50% for residences, 50 to 80% for stores, etc., as has already been stated in detail. It has been considered that 60% of the first 500 watts connected capacity in a residence should be considered as active and 33% of all over that. A typical schedule called for 12¢ per kilowatt-hour for the first 30 hours' use of each kilowatt of active load, 6¢ per kilowatt-hour for the next 60 hours use, and 2¢ per kilowatt-hour for all hours use beyond that. Making up a customer's bill may be shown by an illustration:

* See the paper "Residence Tariffs," by A. H. Seabrook, before the British Institution of Electrical Engineers, Dec. 14, 1911.

† "Rates For Electric Plants," by Halford Erickson, Ohio Electrical Assoc., July 1914.

Monthly meter reading.......... 100 kilowatt-hours
Connected load.................. 1100 watts
Rated active load............... 700 watts
   30 hr. use of active load,
     21 kilowatt-hour @ 12¢.... $2.52
   60 hr. use,
     42 kilowatt-hour @ 6¢.... $2.52
   Balance of use,
     37 kilowatt-hour @ 2¢.... $0.74
   Total......................... $5.78

The Wisconsin scheme, it is seen, modifies the strictly logical use-of-demand plan (which would make the secondary charges proportional to only operating expenses — the fixed and customer charge being paid by the first period of use of the customers' lamps). The break is eased more gradually, apparently for commercial reasons.

The Detroit System. — A scheme was worked out about 1908 by the Detroit Edison Co., based on the number of rooms in the residence. A net charge of 12.6¢ per kilowatt-hour is imposed for up to 2 kilowatt-hours per month for the principal rooms; only 3.6¢ per kilowatt-hour is charged for all in excess. Lavatories, baths, kitchens, storerooms, closets, stairways and halls, pantries, porches, vestibules, servants' rooms and bedrooms up to three are not counted. Once the number of units to be charged at the primary rates is fixed, it is subject to change only by structural alteration of the house. Unless a house has altogether less than three rooms, the net minimum charge is $0.76 — six units at the primary rate. In the experience of the Detroit company, the residence rate in 1916 averaged about 5.8¢ per kilowatt-hour and tended to fall.

For commercial lighting installations this company uses the maximum-demand indicator in connection with the watt-hour meter. The gross charge is 10¢ per kilowatt-hour for the first 30 hours' use per month of the maximum demand, plus 4¢ per kilowatt-hour for the next 120 hours use, and plus 2¢ per kilowatt-hour for the remainder. There is a discount of 10% for prompt payment on bills of less than $50 per month, 15% on $50 to $100, 20% on $100 to $200, and 25% on $200 and over. Lighting rates include free renewals of tungsten lamps in 40-, 60- and 100-watt sizes, and reduced prices on larger lamps.

Alternating-current power is sold in Detroit on a two-part rate — $4.50 gross per month per kilowatt of demand up to 20 kilowatts, and $3 for over that figure, plus 1¢ per kilowatt-hour for all current. Direct-current power is sold at $4.50 per kilowatt of demand for up to 100 kilowatts and $3 for the excess, plus 1¢ per kilowatt-hour for the first 250 hours use of maximum demand per month and 0.6¢ per unit for the excess. Power is also sold at 4¢ per kilowatt-hour for those who require short-term contracts. Where such power is incidental to lighting, as in department stores, it may be recorded on the lighting meter (but then is not shown on the demand indicator) and all current in excess of the first 30 hours use of the lighting demand is charged at 4¢ per kilowatt-hour. Both customer and company benefit by this last arrangement; the customer reduces his lighting bill and the company saves the cost of a separate meter and separate account.

Canadian Cities System. — Several Canadian cities and towns taking current from the Ontario Hydro-Electric Commission have adopted two-part rate schemes recommended by the Commission. The residence lighting schedule resembles that in use in Detroit, substituting square feet of floor area for number of rooms. There is typically (City of London in 1915) a primary charge (neglecting 10% prompt-payment discount) of 3¢ per 100 square feet of floor space plus 2¢ per kilowatt-hour for all consumption up to 4 kilowatt-hours per month per 1000 square feet of floor area for the first 1000 square feet, and up to 3 kilowatt-hours per month for each 1000 square feet additional; plus 1¢ per kilowatt-hour for all additional. The floor area is taken as the product of outside dimensions, excluding bay windows, porches, etc., multiplied by the number of floors. Thus basements, verandas, unfinished attics, etc., are not included.

The foregoing is for domestic service; for commercial lighting, the charge is 5¢ per kilowatt-hour for the first 30 hours use of load, plus 2¢ per kilowatt-hour for the next 70 hours use, plus 0.5¢ per kilowatt-hour for all additional consumption. For 24-hour unrestricted power there is a service charge of $1 per horsepower per month, plus 2½¢ per kilowatt-hour for the first

50 hours use of load, plus 1.7¢ per kilowatt-hour for the next 50 hours use and 0.2¢ per kilowatt-hour for all additional energy.   Over this is 10% off for prompt payment.

The Kapp Rate System. — Any review of electric rates would be incomplete without at least passing mention of the Kapp or two-rate system of metering.   As first planned, it was decided what weight off-peak energy should have compared with peak, and then the meter was rigged to record full quantities at peak hours and some fraction of actual delivery at off-peak hours. The meter reading, of course, was multiplied by some price for peak-load current.   The name is now often stretched somewhat to cover separate metering of peak and off-peak consumption, there being different prices for the two.

Comparison of Rates in American Cities. — There is a marked lack of published tabulations of American electricity rates, in contrast with the tables cited herein for gas and water utilities.   The U. S. Census reports, the central-station directories and even the various state-commission utility-statistics reports show this lack. This seems to be because no tabulation fairly discloses operations and rates without special study of each concern and conversion to some common basis of comparison — which conversion itself, however, prevents seeing the form in which rates are promulgated. This need of conversion in turn arises from the many classes and qualities of service given, the spread of supply systems to several unlike communities, etc.   Therefore attempts to tabulate rates for typical cities have been abandoned here and in place of such figures the preceding notes on important types of schedules have been substituted.

Isolated Plants and Breakdown Service. — The thorn in the flesh of central-station sales stimulators and contract agents is the so-called "isolated plant" in the larger cities.   There are those who claim, on the one hand, that in the majority of cases a large building will save money to generate its own current for lighting, elevators and tenants' power — especially if exhaust steam can be used for winter heating.   There are, on the other hand, those who claim that if all the true costs, rental, losses, etc., are included in the accounts, the isolated-plant expenses will mount up so rapidly that central-station service must be cheaper.   The truth, as common in controversies, probably lies between the two extremes.   Surely there are cases where the private interior plant can be so favored as to conspire with the handicap of expensive transmission and distribution from the outside plant to make self-service the more economical. Obviously there are plants where insufficient economies are possible to come down to the cost of outside current. Into which class a given project might fall cannot be settled off-hand; the determination requires careful engineering study and use of good judgment.

Any isolated plant is of course less certain as to continuity of supply than a large system with perhaps several prime sources of energy. On this account so-called breakdown service has been furnished at times and indeed can be required on payment of proper costs. Such service means peak-load capacity set aside more or less in proportion to the possible demand of all such customers; little or no current is drawn. The rate which is fair gives the central station a return on the capacity held in reserve and a little for special inspection, regular customer charges, and, at a low rate, for what current had been used.

Charges for Street Lighting. — Rates for street and park lighting are commonly on a flat or a lump-sum basis, and this is logical as the number of lamps, power requirement and hours of use can be accurately ascertained in advance. Street lighting results in long hours use of the special generating machinery and distributing lines so that the unit price for energy is fairly low; however it is a peak-load service and the unit price in a given locality cannot ordinarily come down as low as for some industrial-power services. The cost of maintenance of arc-lamp systems is high on account of the necessity of continual cleaning and trimming. The introduction of high-candle-power tungsten-filament incandescent lamps, having a specific consumption (0.5 watt per candle) about as low as the arc, has eliminated most of the inspection and trimming expense. For example in New York City between Nov. 1, 1914, and Jan. 1, 1916, 15,000 of the 300- and 400-watt tungsten lamps were substituted for arcs, and 50,000 of the 200-watt tungstens for various electric, gas and naphtha lamps.

A novel indeterminate-term contract for street lighting was made possible for the smaller cities of Wisconsin by an act of the state legislature in 1915. Under this plan the lighting rate would depend upon the fixed charges on equipment, both special and joint, and upon the direct and joint operating expenses. Should the contract be terminated, the municipality would take over the special lighting equipment at the difference between cost (less scrap value) and the aggregate repaid retirance.*

Charges for Ornamental Street Lighting. — One of the most conspicuous of recent movements in municipal street lighting has been the development of large-powered ornamental systems for the business districts, making what have been popularly termed "white ways." Such street lighting was first exploited by associated retail merchants to make the local business streets more attractive after working hours of prospective customers. But the effect was so popularly appreciated that it came to be regarded by municipal authorities as a civic improvement.

Installations of such systems have been financed in various ways, and the annual expenses have been covered as variously. In the older cases, some local organization, like a Chamber of Commerce, has raised a special fund to pay for the initial installation and has provided the annual revenue required for electric current and maintenance. Contracts for the standards, globes, lamps and circuits (generally underground) in some cases have been let to the local central station, as well as (separately) for the maintenance and current. Sometimes the central station has made an annual figure per lamp for energy and care, and in other cases the total annual expense has been subdivided on a frontage basis, the electric company collecting. A logical development has been to have the municipality assume the annual burden.

In a few cases the central-station companies themselves own the complete installation, the city, or some local association, paying a lump sum, or a lamp rate, that covers interest, retirance, care and current. In other cases popular clamor (stimulated a little perhaps) has led the city to pay both first and annual cost.

Whatever basis of financing is adopted, plans seem to be growing in favor by which the central-station company makes a two-part lamp rate, one part covering interest on investment, retirance (if fixtures are company owned), and maintenance, and the other part covering energy supplied. This plan facilitates various adjustments of hours of burning, etc.

* Details of such a contract were described by G. W. Vanderzee, before the Wisconsin Electrical Association, March 17, 1916.

CHAPTER XVI

PROBLEMS OF TELEPHONE RATE-MAKING

Some Telephone History. — The history of the development of electric speech transmission as a public service is perhaps the most interesting story in utility fields. The struggles of the inventor of the telephone, the early indifference of capitalists and their later scrambles to get inside the industry, the assaults of the organized telegraph industry, the victory of a few unrecognized men of limited means over the many of prestige and backing, the rapid multiplication of subscribers, the spread of long-distance lines — all these topics combine into a tale of absorbing interest. The very good showing of the telephone monopoly, conducted first as a private enterprise, when later subjected to the searching scrutiny of public regulation, has taught utility officials everywhere the value of conservative capitalization combined with liberal provision for maintenance, development, and retirance.

The electric telephone was invented by Alexander Graham Bell in the period of 1874–1876. The date of his fundamental patent was March 7, 1876, but the various ideas involved gradually took shape in the previous years while the inventor was working on a harmonic telegraph. Indeed Bell's conception laid a broad basis for the whole modern development of telephony for he realized that a ." talking telegraph " must be forced to respond to the resultant of complex air impulses — sound waves — and must transmit these from place to place as undulating or oscillatory currents of high frequency.

Bell's telephone was but the prototype of what is today the ear receiver, the sound reproducer of the spoken message. The earliest telephone outfit was merely a pair of similar simple instruments — in each an iron disk vibrating before a polarized electromagnet — connected by a simple circuit. Each machine could be worked as the transmitter or the receiver as desired. But as the possibilities of a telephone system, providing immediate local intercommunication, became more and more obvious, the simple early apparatus showed limitations due to the small amounts of energy in the telephonic currents. Indeed in the earliest days Bell had recognized the feeble nature of these induced currents and only by chance found that unreinforced they were sufficient for practical operation.

The first change was when the battery-operated transmitter was employed to send stronger impulses out on the line. The open road was to cause changes in liquid or solid resistance by the movement of a transmitter diaphragm, and thus to set up stronger undulatory currents. Bell had made this scheme one of the claims in his patent of March 7, 1876, but it was the versatile T. A. Edison who constructed the first practical transmitter of this sort. He had been retained by the Western Union Telegraph Co., in its endeavor to wrest the telephone business from Bell and his associates. Edison's patent specifications, however, did not disclose the true nature of the actions involved so that it was possible for Emile Berliner, 1877, David Hughes, 1878, and Francis Blake, 1878, to employ the true principle and reach the same goal. Berliner and Blake were employed by the Bell company and gave the pioneer system a device superior to that of their great competitor. The Supreme Court also gave Berliner priority over Edison. To the latter, however, belongs credit for the use at that time of an induction coil to step up the potential of the transmitter's undulatory battery currents for sending out on the lines and through the receivers.

The first telephones were intended for connecting always the same two places — like the customer's residence and factory — although an undeveloped idea of widespread flexible popular intercommunication by word of mouth was disclosed by Bell in 1877. This idea of a possible telephone central station no doubt was inspired by the telegraph intercommunicating systems already in use in England (1865), Philadelphia (1867), and New York (1869). The American District Telegraph Co. early used telephones as adjuncts of their messenger call lines; they were introduced also by the New York Law Telegraph system and the Holmes Boston Burglar Alarm service. But the first true commercial telephone exchange is commonly accounted as the Bell plant established in New Haven, in January, 1878, though it was quickly followed by similar ones in Bridgeport, Meriden, New York, Philadelphia, and Chicago.

The switchboard adopted by the Bell licencees was an adaptation of the telegraph board with its multiplicity of cross strips and connecting pegs. The modern type of switchboard, which even in its crudest forms was a radical departure from old telegraph ideas, strangely enough was developed by the Western Electric Co., then the manufacturing associate of the Bell rival — the Western Union Telegraph Co.

Development of the Business. — The business development of the telephone industry is as interesting to utility students as the technical history — and even more significant. The Bell system, while a natural monopoly, is unique among utilities, in that the early conceptions of the organizers of the business seem to have been broad enough so that the same concern, or group of concerns, has accommodated the growth of succeeding years while keeping their procedures always economically sound enough to weather strange and unforeseen business conditions. The Bell corporation is unique too in that the present head (1916) is the same mind that gave the industry its first adequate organization. The whole development of this utility seems to have been toward the goal of universal service — practically accomplished by 1915 with generally satisfied patrons in all the years, with constantly improved and extended lines, with increasing convenience and simplicity for the users, with all the tremendous costs of development constantly amortized, with the value of final physical plant greater than the issued stocks and bonds, with rates widely acceptable, and with usually pleasant public relations in spite of a nation-wide aversion to great monopolies and aggregations of capital.

In August, 1877, a "Bell Telephone Association" was formed by Bell, Gardner G. Hubbard and Thomas Sanders, who had financed the early experiments, and Thomas A. Watson, Bell's technical assistant. In 1878 the New England Telephone Co., and the Bell Telephone Co., were formed to use, licence and manufacture telephones; they were consolidated in 1879. Theodore N. Vail, the present head of the Bell system (1916), then the head of the Federal Mail Service and an intimate of Hubbard, was secured as general manager of the parent company. His first task was stiffening up the defense of the

• little company against its formidable opponent, the Western Union. The assault of the telegraph company on the Bell patents was unsuccessful and the Western Union abandoned the field, the telephone company agreeing not to enter the telegraph industry. Vail formulated a consistent business policy and practice in the matter of licences and contracts, confining agents to cities and reserving all the toll lines and an interest in local concerns to the parent concern. He started out for standardization of equipment. Apparently all his acts were guided by the great motive of this organization — a single universal country-wide system.

The financial means and resources of Bell, Hubbard and Sanders were early overtaxed. Vail himself secured a few small stockholders in his venture. Finally Boston capitalists were interested and W. H. Forbes a man of much local influence became President of the company. After the Western Union agreement was made, in 1880, the business was reorganized as the American Bell Telephone Co., with $6,000,000 capital. About this time Bell, Sanders, Hubbard, and Watson retired from active participation in the company's affairs — apparently wealthy and not attracted by the prospective magnitude of the concern. On March 1, 1880, there were 138 exchanges with about 30,400 stations (complete sets of talking instruments). On March 1, 1881, there were 408 exchanges with some 66,300 stations, including 10,440 taken over from the Western Union. By 1889 there were 743 main exchanges in this country with 158,700 stations or subscribers. The status of company then is shown by a few figures: 127,902 miles of wire on poles, 9458 miles of wire on buildings, 8009 miles under water; 6182 employes, and 369,203,705 connections, or conversations, completed in a year.*

Long-distance Service. — In the first few years, long-distance conversation was only on an experimental scale — owing to the more pressing matters of local exchanges and patent litigation. But the commercial possibilities were not lost sight of, and only the local rights were contracted out.

The first commercial attempt at long-distance conversation seems to have been between Boston and Lowell in 1879 (ex-

* From a summary of figures in American Bell Telephone Co. reports, by J. E. Kingsbury in "The Telephone and Telegraph Exchanges," 1915.

cluding the Boston-Cambridge and Boston-Somerville private ·
lines of 1877). The next jump was across the 45 miles from
Boston to Providence. This was successful after the circuit was
made all metallic — the earth return abandoned. In 1884
Boston was connected with New York. In 1885, after the
Massachusetts legislature refused to allow a larger capitalization for the American Bell Telephone Co., the American Telephone and Telegraph Co. was formed under the New York
laws to carry on the long-distance work. The lines spread
rapidly from place to place after 1885 so that when Chicago and
New York were connected (1892) the company had some 140,000
miles of wire strung — compared with the 13,600 miles in use
at the time just before Boston could talk to New York. In
1899 this new company, by reason of its broader powers, absorbed the Bell Company, assuming an interest in all the local
operating companies, owning the talking instruments, handling
all inventions, developments, patents, legal troubles, and financing. In 1911, when New York and Denver were connected, the
company's "long-distance" wires totaled 1,805,000 miles. By
1913, the service was pushed to Salt Lake City and by 1915 to
San Francisco. This distance is 3400 miles. The talking distance a little later was increased by connecting Florida with California — 4300 miles of line. At that time there were 2,438,000
miles of wire in toll service.

By the beginning of 1916, it was possible to talk from some
point, at least, in each state of the Union to some point in every
other state. It was possible to talk between all the more important centers in the great majority of the states. The Bell
system connects almost every city, town and village in the
country — though a great many of the small places are reached
by independent companies having only connection privileges.
In 1912 * the Bell system operated 74.6 per cent of the total
mileage of wire, 58.3 per cent of total number of telephones in
the country, and 51.0 per cent of the exchanges. Of the 1916
more important systems (with annual incomes of $5000 or more)
the Bell interests controlled only 9.2 per cent (or 176), but this
smaller number handled 65.5 per cent of the traffic, produced
80.8 per cent of the income, possessed 72 per cent of the assets,

* See "Report of U. S. Census Bureau on Telephones and Telegraphs
in 1912," published in 1915.

and employed 77.4 per cent of the persons engaged. Bell companies operated then in every state of the Union, and the independents in all but Rhode Island and the District of Columbia. The independent companies were strongest in South Dakota with 88.1 per cent of the telephones. The Bell companies were strongest in New England where they controlled 92.7 per cent of the telephones.

At the beginning of the year 1916, the Bell system proper comprised 5300 exchanges, 16,050,000 miles of wire in exchange lines, 2,450,000 miles of wire in toll lines, 6,155,900 subscribers' stations. There were in addition 2,995,321 stations of 28,306 connecting systems. The daily average of completed local exchange connections was about 25,184,000 and of toll-line connections 819,000. The per cent of telephones in the country connecting with the Bell system had risen to some 65.

The present condition and operations of the Bell system are of interest, and the following comparative figures are appended from the annual reports for 1915.

REVENUE AND EXPENSES OF BELL SYSTEM, 1915

EXCLUDING DUPLICATIONS AND PAYMENTS BY ASSOCIATED COMPANIES

Stocks, bonds and notes outstanding in hands of public		$796,352,584
Book value plant, tools and supplies..............		896,021,102
Appraisal value, tools and supplies...............		957,021,102
Gross revenue...................................		239,909,649
Expenses:		
Operation.....................	$84,550,665	
Maintenance...................	31,171,272	
Depreciation..................	44,888,702	
Taxes........................	13,117,253	
Total.....................................		$173,727,892
Net revenue....................................		48,086,114
Deduct dividends paid..........................		32,897,065
Deduct interest................................		18,095,643
Balance for surplus............................		$ 15,189,049

AVERAGE OPERATING UNITS OF ASSOCIATED BELL OPERATING COMPANIES,
1895 TO 1915

COVERING ALL THE EXCHANGES AND TOLL LINES OF THE BELL TELEPHONE
SYSTEM EXCEPT THE LONG-DISTANCE LINES OF AMERICAN TELEPHONE
AND TELEGRAPH CO.

Average per Exchange Station	1895	1900	1910	1914	1915
Annual earnings:					
Exchange service...............	$ 69.75	$ 44.68	$ 31.28	$ 29.81	$ 29.80
Toll service....................	11.35	12.60	9.47	8.60	8.65
Total......................	$ 81.10	$ 57.28	$ 40.75	$ 38.41	$ 38.45
Expenses:					
Operation.....................	$ 29.15	$ 21.63	$ 15.14	$ 15.88	$ 15.61
Taxes.........................	2.23	2.37	2.00	2.00	2.02
Total......................	$ 31.38	$ 24.00	$ 17.14	$ 17.88	$ 17.63
Balance......................	49.72	33.28	23.61	20.53	20.82
Maintenance and depreciation..	26.20	17.68	13.46	12.62	12.38
Net earnings.................	23.52	15.60	10.15	7.91	8.44
Per cent operation expense to telephone earnings.............	35.9	37.8	37.2	41.4	40.6
Per cent telephone expense to telephone earnings.............	71.0	72.8	75.1	79.4	78.1
Per cent maintenance and depreciation to average plant, supplies, etc......................	9.1	8.4	9.5	8.9	8.8
Per cent increase exchange stations *.........................	15.7	26.5	11.8	6.4	6.9
Per cent increase miles exchange wire *........................	15.9	33.2	12.0	9.2	6.8
Per cent increase miles toll wire * (excluding long-distance lines)	21.3	25.2	11.5	5.5	0.9†
Average plant cost per exchange station (exchange and toll construction, excluding long-distance lines)...................	$260	$199	$142	$141	$138
Average cost per mile of toll wire (including poles and conduits, excluding long-distance lines)..	$ 81	$ 71	$ 66	$ 69	$ 70
Per cent gross telephone earnings to average plant...............	29.7	28.4	28.8	27.6	27.7
Per cent total net earnings to average capital obligations.....	9.76	8.85	7.52	6.66	7.20
Per cent total net earnings to plant and other assets‡.........	9.36	7.96	6.65	5.51	5.84
Per cent paid out on an average capital obligations.............	5.13	6.10	6.01	5.88	5.88
Per cent paid out on plant and other assets ‡.................	5.09	5.57	5.31	4.87	4.76

* Increase during year shown, over previous year.
† Small increase mainly due to increase in radius covered by exchange rates.
‡ Book value of plant taken which was less than reproduction value.

Telephone Technology. — For communication between a couple of relatively near points, only simple equipment is necessary — a couple of telephone sets (transmitter, battery, receiver and call bell) and a line wire. When telephones are idle, call circuits are ready for use. When more than two points are to be intercommunicating, a wire, or a pair of wires, may enter each set from all the others and run to the same number of selector switches. For the more complicated exchange systems in a town, all the subscribers are connected by separate circuits which enter a central switching office and go to an indicator and "jack" or set of spring contacts. In a small place the jacks are disposed in numbered rows and two subscribers are placed in communication by flexible conductors between jacks. But this simple switchboard serves for only a few hundred subscribers at most and it is necessary after that to go to the "multiple board."

A "multiple board" is, in its ordinary form, a switchboard on which the subscribers' line jacks are duplicated on each section, or at each third operator's position, so that each operator usually has within reach a line jack for each subscriber in that exchange.

Subscribers then are divided into groups of about 300 and calling jacks and indicators for each group are placed before a group of operators. Within reach of each group of operators are line jacks for the entire number of subscribers, so that any one in these operators' groups can be immediately connected to any other subscriber in the exchange. This requires a great duplication of jacks, and arrangements are necessary for showing when a desired subscriber's line is busy and when a conversation between two subscribers has ended.

If an exchange provides for 4900 subscribers (the usual limit of an ordinary multiple board, after which a second exchange is established and connected by trunk lines), the switchboard commonly shows 16 sections with three operators at each section. Each section usually has seven panels on each of which 700 lines would terminate on jacks — making 78,400 jacks on the complete board. But only 307 of the lines coming to a section are connected to indicators and answering jacks. Each operator's manipulation of panels overlaps her neighbor's in that section, which helps one from becoming overtaxed and another idle. A few standard boards have been made for 9600 subscribers — there being then 40 sections of eight panels each, 240 indicators and answering jacks for the three operators of each section, and 1200 multiple jacks per panel or 384,000 for the exchange. These figures really apply to boards for average conditions only. The actual number of sections and panels depends on the rate at which subscribers call. Special requirements arise also to cause various departures from ordinary arrangements of a board.

It should be noted that, for a little less than double capacity rise between the 4900 and 9600 subscriber exchanges, the number of jacks and line extensions has had to be increased nearly five times; this is one of the elements entering into the added expense of service in large exchanges. If it were attempted to serve 24,000 subscribers from one exchange there would be required an impossible board of 100 sections, 2000 panels, 2,400,000 multiple jacks, and 300 to 700 operators. The multiple would be out of the operator's reach entirely. This shows why it is necessary to limit a city exchange to a certain district and connect the exchanges by special lines. When there is more than one exchange in a city, two separate boards are provided — commonly designated as the "A" and "B" boards. The "A" board is a regular multiple board as noted. The "B" board usually is a full multiple; each subscriber's line has a line jack within reach of each "B" operator. From trunk jacks on each "A" board, lines run to plugs on the "B" boards in every other exchange in the city (as many lines as experience shows necessary to handle the traffic). Similarly, auxiliary "order" circuits run from the "A" to the "B" operators. Then if a subscriber calls some one outside. his own exchange district, his "A" operator informs the proper distant "B" operator who connects to the desired subscriber's jack one of "A's" trunk plugs and the "A" operator uses the corresponding trunk jack as though it were a subscriber's line jack on her own board.

In most cities the "common-battery" system is used in which a single battery at the central office operates all the transmitters and a single generator rings all the bells. The voltage of the common battery is higher than was that of the local batteries used at each subscriber's instrument. This introduces many important changes in the equipments. The central operator is called by switchboard lamps operated on central-battery current controlled by the subscriber.

The common-battery system was preceded by the magneto system which is still largely used in the smaller places. Each subscriber's set had a hand generator, or "magneto," for calling central, and a battery for working the transmitter.

Most business offices having several telephone lines have a "private-branch exchange" or a small board tended by private employees. With these, internal communication is made easy and much fewer lines to the city exchanges are required. The "P. B. X." boards of some concerns have upward of 15 operators.

In rural districts where the expense of long single- or few-party lines is prohibitive, a large number are placed on one line and code ringing resorted to. As many as 20 subscribers may be on one such circuit, compared with two or four on town lines; the service, of course, is inferior as the number of parties rises.

Automatic Telephone Systems. — To avoid the large number of operators required in an exchange, several automatic systems have been devised substituting mechanism controlled directly by the subscribers. In general, the subscriber moves a dial on his telephone, or works some similar contrivance, to send various groups of electrical impulses to the exchange where relays step up contact bars accordingly, to connect with the desired lines and ring.

The argument against automatic systems is that the subscriber really does the switching which an operator does for him in the manual system; the subscriber being less expert is apt to be slow and to multiply mistakes. The delicate apparatus requires very expert supervision and maintenance to preserve good service.

Several semi-automatic systems have been brought out, one by the Bell interests. This one replaces the "B" operator in a city exchange (whose duties are largely mechanical) with a selective mechanism.

Telephone Service Compared with Transportation. — Telephone utilities are most decidedly of the service type (as defined on page 5); they cannot acquire or store a product against the hours of maximum demand, and their plant investment is greatly increased by effect of peak loads. The service is a peculiarly personal one — that of bridging distance and time, and placing in communication, in contact, the minds of two persons.

It is even more personal a service than railway passenger transportation. Telephone service resembles railway freight transportation in that usually a great variety of service is furnished by each important company and that distributed over a great geographical area.

The large number of different services, or classes of service or diverse uses of service, and the distribution of activities over many different communities and states, impose somewhat the same difficulties to the accurate apportionment of expenses, to the definite location of cost of an individual service, and to the use of a cost-of-service rate basis, that are encountered in railway work. Anyone who takes up in detail the study of telephone service costs and rates immediately realizes the complexity introduced by serving separated communities in different ways, compared with the simple cases of water, gas and electric companies operating within the confines of a single district and giving one or a few classes of impersonal service. In the case of the simpler utilities, cost-of-service becomes the logical basis of scrutinizing indiv dual rates. As an utility's activities spread greatly and become diversified, then value-of-service looms up of greater and greater importance in the practical adjustment of charges.

Importance of Adequate Telephone Service. — Earlier in these discussions it has been stated that adequate utility service generally is placed ahead of low rates, and that, in any scrutiny of rates, a question as to adequacy of service is necessarily involved. A query then must arise about what constitutes adequate telephone service. Is it merely furnishing facilities in each of the communities served by a company in accordance with the prices which the inhabitants are willing to support, or is it something more comprehensive? Asked another way: Does "adequate service" necessitate considering the interrelations of the various communities — hamlets, villages, towns, suburban districts, cities, manufacturing centers, residential districts, agricultural areas? In considering each question it becomes obvious that the peculiar personal character of telephone service, as well as the multiplication of classes of subscribers and the geographical stretch of required communication, make standards of adequate service different from those applicable to a water, gas, or electric company operating within the confines of a single district and having any one customer little aware of the existence or absence of all other customers.

In the United States the spread and development of telephone service is very much greater than in any other nation, and to a very great measure this has been accomplished without the present public regulation and under the Bell organization's idea that adequate service meant an universal system with individual rates adjusted one to another more in proportion to ratios of their respective values to subscribers than their respective "costs" — "costs" being here considered for the moment as the annual expense of giving a subscriber the means of originating traffic, not distributed at all on subscribers called. (There is some evidence that the future will see a different definition of cost — one that (1) will place on some subscribers some of the expense of extending into unremunerative districts and that (2) will apportion between both parties to a telephone conversation the expense of the connection. Such a definition it must be emphasized still will be one of costs and not of rates, though there may be a closer relation between costs, so defined, and rates.)

Peculiarities of Telephone Investments. — The phenomenon of jumps in required investment, with steadily growing service, is, perhaps, more pronounced in a telephone utility than in most others. Whenever demands catch up with facilities, the additions then made must be in part more than sufficient for many years, according to the dictates of ordinary foresight in preventing too much costly piecemeal construction. In the telephone field one such step may mean the erection of a new building, the establishment of a new exchange, the installation of a new switchboard, and the construction of an underground conduit system. The interest charges on such plant must be allowed to enter the cost computations — even though the plant be partly idle, if only prudently extended. Such effects may entirely vitiate cost comparisons for two communities served by the same concern, or for the same community at different dates.

The brief notes already given on telephone technology have been sufficient to show that a large part of the investment in a central exchange is due to the duplication of subscribers' switchboard equipment and terminal lines, and multiplication of operators' positions in order to handle the calls that are made in peak-load hours. The shorter the hours of local office and mercantile activity, the sharper are the telephone-service peaks and the greater are the effects in increasing investment — a phenomenon which is more pronounced in larger cities.

There are other effects (already noted under the review of telephone technology) that tend to make unit telephone investment rise with the size of the exchange and of the community. The cost in the largest cities is unhanced by expensive types of construction required and multiplication of exchanges. There are still other effects, however, that tend to decrease the cost under such growth — the reduction in average length of line, the economy from large-scale operation, etc.

Development of Rate System. — The early exploiters of Bell's invention proceeded as is common with patented devices — they merely rented the instruments with a licence for use, retaining title to all the important equipment and supervising up-keep. This is a plan that has been preserved even though the fundamental patents have long since expired. The first charges of the Bell promoters were $20 a year for telephones for "social service" and $40 for business use. When exchange service started, the rates had to be made without experience as to the costs involved; even then the competition of the Western Union company caused the first desired rate in some cases to be cut in two. However, in such cases there was a later rise for which the transmitters were put in, or metallic circuits and single-party lines used

The early rates for telephone service were flat annual sums; but the charges were not the same to all in the same locality. Customers were classified by the service they took, and different annual charges made for business and residence use, for one-party or multi-party subscribers. But there was for years generally no change in the basis of the annual charge so that it was not in any way dependent on the extent to which the telephone was used, except in a few towns and cities where the quantity of service was considered. Buffalo and San Francisco (1881) were pioneer cities in adhering to a measured basis. Several other places used this basis for a little while but slipped back. In the early '80's the flat rates ran from $25 to $100 or over, $48 being the popular price most often found. Up to 1895 these flat rates for unlimited service to all users continued to be employed but this was seen then to be a great handicap. The development of a practical scheme of price differentiation according to the business needs of the patron and the number of connections is credited to E. J. Hall, of Buffalo, and U. N. Bethell, of New York. Once widely introduced, it seemed to unlock the business — from 1895 to 1900 the subscribers more than tripled, by 1905 increased to 11½ times, by 1910 multiplied to 17 times, and by 1915 had risen to 37 times the earlier figure.

The measured-rate plan was applied in New York City in 1894; it appeared elsewhere quickly after that. A part of the New York 1894 schedule was as follows:

ON ONE-PARTY LINES

Initial annual charge, $150 allowing 1000 calls, extra calls $12 per 100
"   "   "   172 "   1300 "   "   "   10 "
"   "   "   225 "   2100 "   "   "   7 "

ON TWO-PARTY LINES

Initial annual charge, $100 allowing 700 calls, extra calls $15 per 100
"   "   "   110 "   800 "   "   "   12 "

Under the one-party schedule the common 1894 charge per single call varied from 8 to 12¢, depending on the number made. This cost has steadily dropped until in 1915 it ranged from 3 to 5¢.

Value of Service Used in the Past. — The best defense of the industry's use of a basis approaching value of service, rather than cost, in adjusting rates is what has been accomplished broadly in the development of telephone utilities in America in the past. There is practically no hamlet now but what is connected to the outside world by telephone wires. All the outlying rural districts are connected to their trading and social centers. All of these outposts contribute to the value of the service everywhere throughout a company's system; for, while some of the subscribers in the smaller exchanges probably never call beyond their local office and seldom ask for more than 25 different parties therein, yet in the smallest exchanges there is found to be a constant and surprising amount of toll business.

" Value-of-service," as employed by the Bell companies, does not mean " all the traffic will bear "; it means rather total expense of a company apportioned over towns, cities and classes of subscribers in proportion to the *relative* worths of the services and the *relative* abilities to pay.

The widest development of telephone service that can be reasonably stimulated adds to the benefits of all connected, and change to any operating or administrative policy which would hinder present development or cause retrogression in the end would be widely regretted by the public. Therefore, the substitution of cost-of-service in place of value-of-service as. the universal criterion of rates must be carefully approached in the public interest. It is practically certain that if the small exchange stood unsupported — had to meet all. its expenses by its own revenues — the rates would have to be so high as to cause many of the subscribers to drop away. Similarly within more prosperous areas, if the full fixed and operating charges on the outlying residential lines were carried by those customers alone, there would be few of them.

The more the whole telephone situation is studied the more it is realized that the development of the service is still incomplete, still removed from saturation or equilibrium. Utterly to disregard the ways in which the present growth has been attained would be expected to check further extension. It seems to have demonstrated in all these years that the persons who most want telephone service are willing, and can afford, to pay whatever is necessary over and above the bare cost of their own facilities in order to permit securing the maximum number of subscribers who may have serious use for a telephone.

All of this, of course, does not mean that all the old rate schedules have been, or the existing ones are, completely fair in all their tariffs, as built up on judgment sometimes incompletely fortified by a knowledge of probable costs of service. Such weaknesses as exist, however, may be regarded as side effects of a very rapid technical and commercial development — unrelated errors which have not yet been eliminated.

Commission Regulation of Telephone Rates. — From the preceding discussions of the important part that " value-of-service " has played in making existing telephone rates, and still must play in the future development of the service, it is obvious that an intimate knowledge of municipal development, experience in telephone operation, and general good judgment are required for the greatest success in telephone rate-making. The handicap which most regulating commissions experience is in having a large enough staff of men with sufficient knowledge of telephone-system operation.

It is undeniable that great good to telephone subscribers and companies alike has come from the stricter accounting to which the operating companies have been called in recent years. Telephone companies have come through with less criticism than have other types of utilities subjected to public regulation for the first time — a fact that speaks well for the aims and efforts of the telephone officials. The reverse of over-capitalization has been demonstrated; but it has been seen that ten years ago the telephone companies themselves had a very scant knowledge of the true value of their plants or recognized possibilities of distribution of annual costs beyond the common operating items.

The standards of judging telephone rates held by the companies and by the commissions are likely not to coincide for years to come, if ever. The operating experience of a company's commercial engineers naturally impresses on them the importance of value of service and the debatable features of every basis of apportioning expense items.

Commission telephone rate-making has one peculiar difficulty. Here perhaps more than in any other utility service, except possibly in railway work, the claims of the operating company are to be given great weight when the commission can be assured that the officials are honest and earnest in promoting the subscribers' welfare. But proper attention to a company's claims is very apt to be misconstrued in the popular mind as one of those surrenders to capital which politicians have been wont to picture. While recognizing the value of the telephone officials' experience, the Commissions cannot rely solely on such partisan statements and still hold public confidence; they are forced to find some basis of independent judgment and they naturally tend to take up the cost criterion which is so applicable in restricted local-utility service.

Commission Study of Value of Service. — It is true that a commission usually must present a good exposition of its studies in order to justify its pronouncements before a critical public, and this naturally leads them almost invariably to attempt to investigate the cost of a given service. But the independent determination of value of service is equally open. It is only essential that a commission should proceed in a scientific manner with considerable scope of plan, compensating thus for their lack of that accumulated operating experience and long-trained judgment which the telephone companies' officials may possess.

If it be accepted in a given case that the rates and service for a single community are not to be scrutinized isolated from those for all other communities, then the starting point for a value study is the total area served by a company — the field of an operating entity distinguished from a group of merely affiliated interests. A first step is to list the several communities within the given area and to apply to them rating coefficients which shall express the relative differences to be expected in value of telephone service therein — differences depending on such industrial and social factors as total population, percentage of population served, proportion of foreign-born and illiterate persons, average income, character of industries, real-estate development, etc. Such a rating index of cities and towns then may be the basis of informally varying the price of a given service among the different places, proceeding in a cut-and-try fashion until a schedule is whittled out that yields the gross income considered necessary.

But it would seem logical and desirable very often, for a commission to push this sort of value study to a natural conclusion instead of resting content with the partial results commonly accepted as sufficient. To start with, it may be advisable to preserve intact at first the several ratings of the community in regard to size and character of population, character of industrial and real-estate development, average income of citizens, etc. Then it may be necessary to list alongside of these the several classes of service within the municipalities indexed, and to combine the various ratings into a rating coefficient for each class as it exists in several places, and as one or more of the community characteristics affect its worth from town to town.

In this way definite numerical comparative ratings may be recorded for the value of all classes of service. Multiply the number of subscribers in each class of each town by the proper combined-rating coefficient, add the products and there results a number which may be called the " expense (or revenue) distributor " of the system. Dividing the total annual expense of the company — including fair return on fair value — or the total required revenue, by this expense distributor, gives a " carrier " which may be multiplied by the rating for any class of any town to show a sort of average flat rate that would be indicated as fair for that town and class of customer. Multiplying the carrier by both class rating and number of telephones in a community of that class yields the total return that should come from that class as a whole. Summing such expected class returns gives the income for the local company. How such a

STATE TELEPHONE CO. VALUE-OF-SERVICE STUDY. ANNUAL EXPENSES
(LESS COST OF TOLL SERVICE) $1,262,905

	Population Rating	Industrial and Real-Estate Rating	Subscribers Income Rating	Service Class Rating	Number of Telephones	Class Product	Annual Value Rate
City A: Subscribers,							
Class 1.......		100	100	100	3,000	300,000	$125.00
Class 2.......	100	90	80	85	1,000	85,000	106.25
Class 3.......		80	70	75	2,000	150,000	93.75
Class 4.......		40	20	25	4,000	100,000	31.20
City B: Subscribers:							
Class 5......		100	100	95	1,500	142,500	100.00
Class 6......	50	90	90	80	500	40,000	100.00
Class 7......		80	80	70	1,000	70,000	87.50
Class 8......		40	30	20	2,000	40,000	25.00
City C:							
Class 9......		100	90	90	300	27,000	75.00
Class 10.....	10	90	80	75	100	7,500	94.00
Class 11.....		85	70	65	200	13,000	81.50
Class 12.....		50	30	20	400	8,000	25.00
Town E:							
Class 13.....		85	70	50	100	5,000	62.50
Class 14.....	5	75	60	40	100	4,000	50.00
Class 15.....		50	30	20	300	6,000	25.00
Town F:							
Class 16.....		80	65	45	50	2,250	56.50
Class 17.....	2.5	75	50	35	50	1,750	43.75
Class 18.....		50	30	20	200	4,000	25.00
Village G:							
Class 19......	1	75	50	35	25	875	43.75
Class 20......		40	25	15	125	1,800	18.75
Village H:							
Class 21.....	0.4	65	40	25	15	375	31.25
Class 22.....		35	25	15	85	1,275	18.75
						1,010,325	

$$\frac{\$1,262,905}{1,010,325} = \$1.25; \text{ for Class 2, } 85 \times \$1.25 = \$106.25, \text{ etc.}$$

study is pursued is partially indicated in the accompanying table made up for a hypothetical concern for purely illustrative purposes. There would be, in any actual application of the idea, several columns in place of the two columns here given up to " industrial and real-estate rating " and " subscribers-income rating." If such a table indicated that some changes in rates appeared advisable, study of the effect of the changes on the number of subscribers in each class ought to be made and a new table prepared embodying conditions as they might be with the different number of subscribers.

Telephone Cost Analysis. — The general tendency has been mentioned of utility commissions attempting to deduce probable figures for the cost of telephone service rendered to various classes of subscribers. Therefore, it is of interest to append a few notes on how attempts have been made to compute the things called " cost." It will be seen that this " cost " is to a large extent a matter of definition, and cannot be as reliable for a basis of rates as the service costs which may be deduced for water, gas and electric utilities. Detailed telephone-cost figures are of interest and significance in connection with value-of-service studies since they represent expense distribution on another basis.

The expenses of a telephone exchange and connected plant can be directly allocated or apportioned on the several classes of customers less than can be done in the case of most other non-transportation utilities. While the number of subscribers measures, in a way, the size of a telephone system, yet the investment per subscriber is not parallel to the cost per kilowatt of capacity of an electricity-supply works or per million gallons possible daily output from a water-works. Some of the exchange equipment installed to secure good peak-hour service is a duplication — an excess — of equipment that would be sufficient for the same subscribers with uniform time distribution of their calls. All this extra equipment is reserved for these particular peoples' use; it cannot be diverted to the use of other persons or classes in off-peak hours, so that there can be no economies secured by building up non-peak business to use it while it would be otherwise idle.

The annual costs of telephone service, as a whole in a given place, can be variously split into several factors, for instance: (1)

interest, retirance and maintenance on that service-plant investment which is independent of peak service or number of calls (subscribers' lines and instruments, a part of switchboards, of buildings, and of real estate); (2) interest, retirance and maintenance on investment which depends on peak load — on the number of calls made when most subscribers are calling simultaneously — (part of switchboards, auxiliary equipment, buildings, land, and of duplication of subscribers'-line terminals and exchange-connecting trunk lines); (3) those operating costs which depend on the mere existence of a subscriber whether calling or idle (including most of the billing and collecting expense, some of the operators' wages and overhead burden for supervision, management, etc.); (4) operating costs dependent on total calls made or received (the larger part of switchboard operators' wages and related overhead items, part of the accounting expense in the case of measured-local and toll-line service, etc.).

Even such a broad division of expense cannot be made wholly by direct assignment. Many items require somewhat arbitrary apportionment over more than one group. The resulting figures, moreover, are of little value unless the assumptions are plainly stated under which apportionments are planned; and when the assignment and apportionment are carried further, to groups of customers say, then the number of assumptions grows surprisingly and their validity becomes more and more debatable — no matter whether company or commission stands sponsor for them.

Chicago Telephone Studies. — About the first important telephone rate case was the Chicago 1907 survey by a special engineering commission. Here for the first time there was an adequate exposition of the complexities of the commercial side of telephony, and the discovery that the expedients which dictated rates were not based on detailed data of the operating conduct of the business. Greater use of a measured service was recommended to enable imposing the heaviest charges on the heaviest users.

Massachusetts Commission Cases. — In 1906 the Massachusetts Highway Commission, which was charged with the oversight of telephone utilities, began hearings on numerous complaints of service, overcapitalization and discrimination on the part of the Bell company (New England Telephone & Telegraph Co.) in the Boston Metropolitan district. Preliminary accounting and engineering examinations in 1907 and 1908 led to an appraisal of the entire company's plant, and to acceptance of accounting practice better able to show traffic distribution, costs of operation and maintenance, and sources of revenue.

In the first place it was shown that the plant was worth 20% in excess of the stock, bond and note obligations. The gross collections were 3.46¢ per completed call, while the large users having unlimited flat-rate service paid only ½ to 2¢ per call — and the smaller users paid from 6 to 10¢. The result was a smaller development of the small users than possible and desirable.

A zone system of rates was made by which a given subscriber's tariff applied within the territory commonly used by the majority of local subscribers with toll charges for calls between more distant zones. The individual rates were adjusted to furnish service to the small user on the lowest yearly charge that appeared fair, adjusting the other prices in accordance — also bearing in mind that the metropolitan-district was fairly to bear some of the expense of superior service imposed on the state as a whole.

Wisconsin Commission Cases. — Beginning with 1907 the Wisconsin Railroad Commission has exercised as complete jurisdiction over telephone systems as over other utilities. However, it has proceeded slowly and carefully. One of the first things changed was discrimination by free and reduced-rate service for quasi-public locations. Rules for standard quality of service were next adopted. A statute of 1911 obliged physical connections between different systems at proper compensation, and a large number of cases of that sort have been settled.* ,

The Wisconsin commission in its rate cases has proceeded slowly with the use of a cost-of-service basis of scrutiny. But it has finally gone the farthest of any commission in the development of a cost analysis for telephone services. Late in 1915 it presented a carefully arranged outline of a complete and fairly logical cost analysis applied to a small exchange (see *Re St. Croix*

* See typically *F. Winter v. La Crosse Tel. Co.*, 1913; 11 Wis. R. R. Comm. Rep. 748; 1914, 15 Wis. R. R. Comm. Rep. 36; *A. E. Monroe v. Clinton Tel. Co.*, 1912; 10 Wis. R. R. Comm. Rep. 598; *E. D. McGowan v. Rock County Tel. Co.*, 1914; 14 Wis. R. R. Comm. Rep. 529.

Telephone Co., Dec. 12, 1915; P. U. R. 1916 A 552). The most notable idea embodied there was the development of expense apportionment on the basis of calls terminating as well as originating with a given class of subscriber. In a later case (*P. B. Bogart v. Wis. Tel. Co.*, April 18, 1916; P. U. R. 1916 C 1020) a large city service was studied in the same way and some account taken of extra investment caused by peak-load service.

Classification of Subscribers.—Separation of costs into such factors as (1) those dependent on number of calls, (2) those dependent on peak loads, (3) those dependent on mere existence of subscribers, and (4) those dependent on number of calls made, does not directly lead to a figure for cost of carrying the particular classes. Such an analysis may be a preliminary to some other apportionment.

It is necessary in approaching the problems of telephone cost analysis, as in the case of other utilities, to start a detailed study by making some classification of customers, the members of the groups having similar needs, and asserting that it is reasonably just to denote the cost of serving one customer as the average for his class. The number of classes may run up toward 40 in some places, but for all practical purposes many of these classes are so unimportant, or are sufficiently similar that they may be consolidated into the more important ones. A classification may be, for instance, into (1) large or high-value business users, (2) small or low-value business subscribers, (3) large or high-value residence users, (4) small or low-value residences, (5) rural lines, (6) toll calls. Such a classification would vary greatly in various communities and as here given should not be taken as fixed, or inflexible, or indeed as more than imperfectly illustrative. In some medium-sized places it might possibly turn into: (1) direct-line or single-party measured-service business subscribers, (2) multi-party flat-rate business lines, (3) direct-line flat-rate residential subscribers, (4) two-party measured-service residential subscribers, (5) four-party flat-rate residence lines, (6) coin-box lines, (7) multi-party flat-rate rural lines, (8) toll service. In smaller places it might be simply: (1) business subscribers, (2) residential subscribers, (3) rural lines, (4) unowned connecting, or " foreign rural " lines, (5) toll service. The need of including toll service as a separate class of customers is obvious. Toll calls are distinct from all calls within

an exchange area, are separately accounted for and are billed at
definite rates.

Bases for Apportioning Expense. — An attempted apportionment of annual cost of service upon the several classes of customers cannot be made on the same basis for all items of expense
involved. Here again local conditions intervene and prevent
any closely fixed scheme from being broadly or universally
applicable. But a system of apportionment found logical and
acceptable in one case is generally illustrative and usually suggestive of proper procedure in other cases; the changes which
should be made in the basis of apportioning this or that item, or
group of items, usually can be seen without great difficulty.

Sometimes items have been apportioned in proportion to number of telephones — " substations " in telephone parlance.
Others have been apportioned in proportion to the number of
lines, irrespective of substations thereon. Some have been
allocated according to the number of miles of wire; some in proportion to the number of calls originated; and some according
to the number of calls originated, the time of day and the relative
time consumed for each class of customer. Items of expense
which are so general that no special basis of apportionment
is evident have been split up in proportion to the several
aggregates of apportionment upon the various classes of customers.

Adjusting for Interdependence. — Such apportionments of a
local system's expense, upon its several classes of customers as
outlined, usually have been based on an independence of the
service rendered to the several classes which did not exist.
When a business customer, for instance, calls a residence customer, each one really uses the other's line and telephone as
well as his own. When a residential subscriber calls some other
residence, each uses two residential lines and substations. That
in general describes the inter-class participation in use of equipment and gives a plausible (but not unassailable) excuse for
demanding that a good cost allocation should equitably redis-
tribute over all the classes, the expenses for which otherwise the
respective groups would be liable independently.

The Wisconsin state commission has probably gone the farthest
of all public bodies in developing such a cost analysis and late in
1915 it began to apply a scheme for redistributing certain ex-

penses on the basis of calls received as well as calls made. (See
Re St. Croix Telephone Co., Dec. 12, 1915; P. U. R. 1916 A 552.)

Wisconsin Cost Analysis. — It is not necessary here to discuss at length the recent Wisconsin telephone cases; but it is
useful to point out some of the more significant and suggestive
features of the cost analysis. The St. Croix case, already mentioned, related to a small local system showing about $28,000
cost new and $19,500 present worth of physical property. The
village served (Richmond) had only 2000 population, but there
were 377 subscribers within it and 501 outside. The maximum
rates were only $30 per year.

The principal expense items for such a small system, according
to the Wisconsin scheme of accounts, were:

1. Exchange operators' salaries,
2. Exchange expenses,
    2a. Directory and stationery,
    2b. Fuel, water, light and building maintenance,
    2c. Power and freight (largely on storage batteries),
    2d. Miscellaneous,
3. Exchange maintenance,
4. Wire-plant maintenance and operation,
5. Substation maintenance and operation,
6. Commercial expense,
7. General and undistributed expense,
8. Interest and depreciation.

In the first distribution, "1 — Operators' salaries" was
divided between "local" and "toll" service in proportion to
the actual time spent on the local and toll boards. The item,
"2a — Directory and stationery," was divided among the
classes in proportion to the number of subscribers in each. The
item, "2b — Fuel, water, light and building maintenance," was
allocated on toll and local business in accordance with space
requirements; the local fraction was split among subscribers'
classes, half in proportion to number of stations and half in proportion to number of lines. The item, "2c — Power and
freight," was apportioned according to the terminating calls —
weighted to correct for code ringing on rural lines. The item,
"2d — Miscellaneous," was divided as an overhead on the preceding three items. The account, "3 — Exchange mainte-

nance," was split up half in proportion to the number of lines per class and half according to originating calls; " 4 — Wire-plant maintenance and operation " was distributed in proportion to the wire-miles per class; " 5 — Substation maintenance and operation " was allocated according to the number of instruments. The item, " 6 — Commercial expense," was split between toll and local business after a scrutiny of the uses for sub-items; then the local fraction was distributed in proportion to the number of billings made per class. Item " 7 — General and undistributed expense " was not touched until later. Finally for " 8 — Interest and depreciation " an appraisal was made to show the kind, investment and life of equipment directly serving each class of service; for equipment not definitely assignable to classes the retirance was neglected until a little later. Interest was handled similarly. This ended the first assignment, which it is seen was not a complete one.

The second assignment was then started — reapportioning the costs as assessed on the several classes in proportion to their activity in originating and terminating calls. A traffic study was necessary to measure this inter-class activity — to find the calls residence-to-residence, residence-to-business, business-to-business, residence-to-rural, etc. The residence-residence calls were multiplied by two (since they were recorded as originating calls only) and charged all to the residence class. The business-business calls were similarly handled. The residence-business terminating and originating calls were added and charged half against the business class and half against residence; and so on through all the possible combinations.

The reapportionment of expenses already tentatively assigned to classes was then taken up class by class. For instance, the first tentative amount of residence-class expense was redivided among all the classes in proportion to the number of residence conversations they were concerned with. Thus the residence class would get finally a portion of the first residence costs, a portion of the first business-class costs, a portion of the rural-line costs and so on, each of these portions being in part proportional to the number of conversations which residential subscribers had with the several classes enumerated. Finally the items of " General and undistributed expense " and " Interest and retirance on unassignable equipment " (which had been left suspended) were apportioned in proportion to the final expense sums levied on the various classes.

This would have completed the finding of class costs in the St. Croix case, except that the " foreign-rural " group had been assessed a portion of the St. Croix exchange costs, while the St. Croix subscribers using the unowned foreign lines paid none of the costs of these lines. To remedy this the expenses of the privately owned foreign lines were distributed over all classes just as were the company exchange costs. This gave an addition to each St. Croix class and a residue for the privately owned foreign lines. The sum of these class additions deducted from the aggregate apportionment of company-system costs on the foreign-rural group gave the uncompensated part of the cost of switching the foreign lines.

This yielded a " cost " of serving each class of customer. Dividing that figure by the number of subscribers in the class showed an average cost of serving one of them, and afforded a figure which was compared with the prevailing flat rate.

Cost Analysis in Milwaukee Case. — About four months after the St. Croix case, the Wisconsin Commission applied and extended the scheme of costs analysis there laid down to the large telephone system of Milwaukee, which had been complained of as having unreasonable rates. This company's property was valued at $5,269,000, compared with a book cost of $5,001,000. There was no switching service for foreign-rural lines, but there were 40 classes of customers, including such as private-branch exchanges, nickel-slot stations, one-, two-, and four-party lines, and both flat-rate and measured services. Large commercial department expenses were involved.

The system of accounts kept by the Wisconsin Telephone Co., as studied in the Milwaukee case, were arranged as follows:

1. General expense,
2. Commercial expense,
3. Traffic expense,
4. Repair expense,
5. Substation removals and changes,
6. Depreciation [retirance] on plant,
7. Rights, privileges, and use of property,
8. Insurance,
9. Taxes,
10. Interest.

While the cost apportionment in this case followed the principles laid down in the St. Croix case, it required the extension of those ideas since the trunking system was employed in Milwaukee between exchanges with heavy multiple equipment, and because the effect of peak-loads in increasing investment was considerable. How some of these new matters were handled will be shown briefly.

Interest and retirance on trunking central-office equipment (9 per cent of total central-office investment) were apportioned one-third on the basis of originating and terminating trunked calls for each class at the time of city peak load (7 A.M. to 8 P.M.) and two-thirds on the basis of total originating and terminating calls. No reapportionment of this was made on the basis of interclass participation.

The line-terminal interest and retirance (32 per cent of the central-office investment) was apportioned directly to the classes for which the investment was made, and later reapportioned with other class costs in accordance with the interclass participation.

The interest and retirance on much of the remaining central office equipment (keyboard, 10 per cent of total; power plant, 8 per cent; desk and testing apparatus, 3 per cent) were apportioned among the various classes of subscribers — two-thirds according to the day's (24 hours') total originating and terminating calls and one-third according to percentage of total peak-load calls caused by each class. No reapportionment was made.

In considering the interest and depreciation on multiple equipment (38 per cent of total central-office investment) part was allocated over the classes in proportion to the number of lines (two-party lines being given a weighting of two) and part in proportion to the ration of average to peak-load total traffic. The first fraction was later reapportioned but the second was not.

The expense of supervising the commercial department was split into two parts for apportionment. One part was proportioned to the aggregate of " advertising," " canvassing," " uncollectable accounts," and thrown in with the general overhead expenses to be later distributed according to amounts of direct apportionments on the several classes. The other part was distributed as an overhead on several accounts: (1) " directory," which was divided half in proportion to number of insertions to which the classes were entitled and half in proportion to number of directories supplied; (2) " revenue accounting," and (3) " revenue collecting," both of which were split up after inspection of employees' duties and were not reapportioned.

" Pay-station commissions " were divided among pay-station classes on the basis of number of origination calls. These apportionments were later reapportioned. " Traffic supervision " was apportioned over various underlying accounts as an overhead. Those fractions laid on " operators' wages," " rest and lunch rooms," " operators' schooling," " miscellaneous operating expense," " pay-station salaries," were considered to be final apportionments, as the apportionment of these sub-accounts took into consideration both originating and terminating traffic.

The items " central-office rent," " real-estate repairs," " real-estate interest and depreciation," other than real-estate expense for Grand Building, stables, garages, etc., were consolidated for apportionment; the division was made similarly to main real-estate expense — on " canvassing," " revenue collecting," " service inspection," " rest and lunch rooms," " operators' schooling," " central-office rent," " pay-station expense," " wire-chief expense," and " supply expense."

" Pay-station expense ' was split into two parts and one apportioned over the attended pay-stations — half in proportion to substations (later reapportioned) and half in proportion to total traffic (not reapportioned); the other part was apportioned over non-attended pay-stations in proportion to number of substations and was later reapportioned.

The item " repairs supervision " was prorated over, or added to, subsidiary accounts (" wire-plant repairs," " central-office equipment repairs," and " substations repairs ") and apportioned with these. The handling of private-branch-exchange expenses is of interest; charges for maintenance, removal and change, and supervision of repairs were divided among the P. B. X. classes on the basis of number of lines connected. On account of intra-office use of the P. B. X. equipment (for intercommunicating service), half of these P. B. X. expense items named were considered as finally allocated when placed in accordance with number of lines, and half were considered reapportionable.

So far after the first attempt to apportion expense, it is seen that there were three groups of items: (1) finally placed items, (2) reapportionable items, and (3) unassigned items. The sum of reapportionable items for each class was redivided among all the classes in proportion to the proportions each showed of total originating and terminating calls, as already worked out in the St. Croix case. The sums thus reassigned to the several classes gave a new partial total for each class, to which were added the final distributions made at the start. Upon these sums the undistributed expenses were laid as an overhead charge.

The 4½ Per Cent Payments to Parent Bell Company. — One of the most misunderstood items of expense which have figured in telephone-rate cases is that of payments of 4½ per cent of gross earnings by the Bell operating companies to the central concern, the American Telephone and Telegraph Co. This fee has been approved in Wisconsin* and Maryland.†

The Wisconsin Commission reported that it would deem reasonable an agreement with an unrelated company giving the same service at the same cost; that the Wisconsin company could not supply the equivalent service at less cost; that the need of uniformity and standardization were great and securable only through a central company; that the service consisted of two parts, one relating to furnishing and repairing the subscribers' talking instruments and the other to engineering, accounting, legal, traffic and other special services. The annual cost of this 4½ per cent payment was $1.45 per telephone — 60c. properly going to use and repair of instruments, 22.2c. for construction expense and 56.8c. for operation and plant maintenance.

The Maryland Commission laid great stress on the promotion and financing secured by the subsidiary in exchange.

American Telephone-Rate Examples. — The classes of subscribers are so numerous and the conditions of service so variable that it is practically impossible to present an illustrative tabulation of rates. The Census Bureau studied the possibility of making such a table and finally selected and reprinted the schedules of 252 cities — occupying 106 pages in the "Report of Census on Telegraphs and Telephones for 1912," published in 1915.

* *Bogart v. Wisconsin Tel. Co.*, April, 1916, P. U. R. 1916 C 104.

† Re *Chesapeake & Potomac Tel. Co.*, Case 690, March 8, 1916, P. U. R. 1916 C 929.

APPENDIX A

PROBABLE APPROXIMATE COST OF BRICK BUILDINGS

The appended diagrams and tables were first prepared by Charles T. Main, Consulting Engineer, of Boston, for appraising brick manufacturing buildings and estimating on proposed structures. They were revised in 1910 and printed in Engineering News, Jan. 27, 1910. The figures employed represent an average cost of material and labor; additions and deductions are required to meet special conditions and changes in prices.

The height of stories is assumed to be 13 feet for 25 feet width, 14 feet for 50 feet width, 15 feet for 75, and 16 for 100 or over. The construction involved is the so-called "slow-burning" mill type—brick walls with heavy timber floors and columns. The cost of brick walls (see table) is based on 22 bricks per cubic foot costing $18 per M laid. Foundations (see table) comprise from 5 per cent (for large buildings) to 15 per cent (for small buildings) of the total cost. At wall openings, 40¢ per square foot was allowed for windows, doors and sills. Mill floors have been taken at 32¢ per square foot, which figure is based on $40 per M feet B. M. for southern-pine timbers and $30 for spruce planking. Cost of ordinary mill roofs, with tar and gravel cover, has been used at 25¢ per square foot. Columns added 6¢ per square foot of floor area, for columns at $15 each, including castings and piers.

DATA FOR ESTIMATING COST OF BUILDINGS

	Foundations Including Excavations, Cost per Lin. Ft.		Brick Walls, Cost per Sq. Ft. of Surface		Columns Including Piers and Castings
	For Outside Walls	For Inside Walls	Outside Walls	Inside Walls	Cost of One
One-story building	$2.00	$1.75	$0.40	$0.40	$15.00
Two " "	2.90	2.25	0.44	0.40	15.00
Three " "	3.80	2.80	0.47	0.40	15.00
Four " "	4.70	3.40	0.50	0.43	15.00
Five " "	5.60	3.90	0.53	0.45	15.00
Six " "	6.50	4.50	0.57	0.47	15.00

Ordinary plumbing is included in the costs (two fixtures at $75 each, for each floor up to 5000 square feet, and one fixture for each additional 5000 square feet or fraction). Cost of two stairways is to be added at $100 per flight, and one elevator tower for buildings up to 150 feet long; two stairways and two towers for buildings 150 to 300 feet long. For incidentals a final 10 per cent is to be added.

The following modifications were recommended by Mr. Main in 1910.

(a) If the soil is poor or the conditions of the site are such as to require more than the ordinary amount of foundations, the cost will be increased.

(b) If the end or a side of the building is formed by another building, the cost of one or the other will be reduced slightly.

(c) If the building is to be used for ordinary storage purposes with low stories and no top floors, the cost will be decreased from about 10% for large low buildings, to 25% for small high ones, about 20% usually being a fair allowance.

(d) If the buildings are to be used for manufacturing purposes and are to be substantially built of wood, the cost will be decreased from about 6% for large one-story buildings, to 33% for high small buildings; 15% would usually be a fair allowance.

(e) If the buildings are to be used for storage with low stories and built substantially of wood, the cost will be decreased from 13% for large one-story buildings, to 50% for small high buildings; 30% would usually be a fair allowance. The cost of very light wooden structures is much less than the above figures would give.

(f) If the total floor loads are more than 75 pounds per square foot the cost is increased.

(g) For office buildings, the cost must be increased to cover architectural features on the outside and interior finish.

RATIO OF COST OF VARIOUS BUILDINGS TO THAT OF BRICK MILLS, STANDARD CONSTRUCTION

Superficial Feet of Floor in One Story	Frame Mills						Brick Store House						Frame Store House					
	1 Sto.	2 Sto.	3 Sto.	4 Sto.	5 Sto.	6 Sto.	1 Sto.	2 Sto.	3 Sto.	4 Sto.	5 Sto.	6 Sto.	1 Sto.	2 Sto.	3 Sto.	4 Sto.	5 Sto.	6 Sto.
1,250	$0.86	$0.67					$0.80	$0.73					$0.70	$0.51				
2,500	0.86	0.73					0.85	0.73					0.75	0.58				
5,000	0.89	0.78	0.75	0.73	0.70	0.67	0.83	0.80	0.78			0.75	0.74	0.60	0.56	0.53	0.51	0.48
7,500	0.90	0.79	0.77	0.74	0.71	0.69	0.85	0.81	0.78	0.76	0.76	0.76	0.77	0.63	0.58	0.55	0.53	0.51
10,000	0.90	0.80	0.78	0.75	0.73	0.70	0.87	0.81	0.79	0.77	0.76	0.76	0.78	0.65	0.60	0.57	0.55	0.53
15,000	0.91	0.82	0.79	0.77	0.75	0.72	0.89	0.83	0.81	0.78	0.77	0.78	0.81	0.67	0.64	0.61	0.59	0.56
20,000	0.92	0.83	0.81	0.79	0.77	0.74	0.90	0.84	0.82	0.79	0.78	0.79	0.82	0.70	0.67	0.64	0.61	0.59
25,000	0.92	0.85	0.82	0.80	0.78	0.76	0.91	0.85	0.83	0.80	0.80	0.80	0.83	0.72	0.69	0.66	0.63	0.61
30,000	0.93	0.86	0.84	0.81	0.80	0.77	0.91	0.86	0.84	0.82	0.81	0.81	0.84	0.73	0.70	0.67	0.65	0.62
35,000	0.93	0.87	0.84	0.82	0.80	0.78	0.92	0.86	0.84	0.83	0.82	0.81	0.85	0.74	0.71	0.68	0.66	0.63
40,000	0.93	0.87	0.85	0.83	0.81	0.79	0.92	0.87	0.85	0.84	0.83	0.82	0.86	0.75	0.72	0.69	0.67	0.64
45,000	0.94	0.87	0.85	0.83	0.82	0.79	0.92	0.87	0.85	0.84	0.83	0.82	0.86	0.76	0.72	0.70	0.67	0.65
50,000	0.94	0.88	0.86	0.84	0.82	0.80	0.92	0.88	0.86	0.84	0.83	0.83	0.87	0.77	0.73	0.71	0.69	0.66

The diagrams, of course, do not apply to the abnormally high prices prevailing from 1915 to 1917, but their use is probably justified for work where the value sought is for recent normal prices.

The various prices on which such curves may be based are stated by Mr. Main as follows:

	1903	1907	1916
Excavation (including backfill), per cu. yd.	....	....	0.50
Concrete (including forms), per cu. yd....	....	....	7.00
Brickwork in walls, per M...............	15.00	18.00	22.00
Floors, per sq. ft.......................	0.25	0.32	0.35
Roofs, per sq. ft........................	0.20	0.25	0.30
Window openings, wood sash, per sq. ft....	0.33	0.40	0.67
Stairs, including partitions, each........	100.00	100.00	150.00
Plumbing sets; fixtures, piping and partitions, each.........................	75.00	75.00	100.00
Columns; southern pine, incl. piers, etc., each...............................	12.00	15.00	18.00

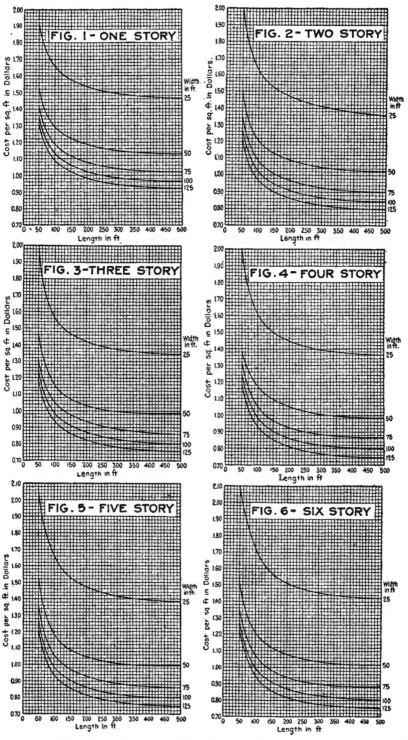

SIZE COST DIAGRAMS FOR BRICK MILL BUILDINGS (351)

APPENDIX B

TABLES FOR SINKING-FUND AND PRESENT-VALUE COMPUTATIONS

For Annually Compounded Interest. — The first two appended tables (reprinted from Engineering News, Jan. 25, 1894) were prepared by John W. Hill, of Cincinnati, for his consulting practice. They have since been found of great use to engineers, being more convenient than some available actuarial tables. The first table is of use in compound-interest (sinking-fund) computations for depreciation and retirance. The second table is for present worths of annual charges. The third table shows the growth of depreciation when a definite life is assumed and the effect of interest is not neglected.

ANNUITY REQUIRED TO REDEEM 1000 DOLLARS IN FROM 1 TO 50 YEARS

Rate of Interest, Per Cent

Years to Run	2	2¼	2½	2¾	3	3¼	3½	3¾	4	4¼	4½	4¾	5	5¼	5½	5¾	6
2	495.05	494.50	493.78	493.23	492.69	492.05	491.42	490.81	490.20	489.60	489.00	488.40	487.80	487.21	486.62	486.02	485.43
3	326.72	325.94	325.14	324.35	323.56	322.75	321.94	321.13	320.36	319.57	318.77	317.99	317.22	316.42	315.63	314.87	314.10
4	242.63	241.74	240.84	239.93	239.02	238.14	237.26	236.38	235.50	234.72	233.74	232.84	231.95	231.12	230.29	229.45	228.60
5	192.16	191.18	190.24	189.30	188.35	187.42	186.49	185.56	184.63	183.71	182.79	181.88	180.98	180.05	179.13	178.26	177.39
6	158.53	157.53	156.56	155.58	154.61	153.64	152.67	151.73	150.79	149.83	148.88	147.95	147.02	146.10	145.18	144.27	143.36
7	134.52	133.51	132.49	131.50	130.51	129.54	128.57	127.59	126.61	125.64	124.67	123.74	122.82	121.89	120.96	120.04	119.13
8	116.51	115.48	114.47	113.46	112.46	111.47	110.48	109.50	108.53	107.56	106.60	105.66	104.72	103.79	102.86	101.94	101.03
9	102.52	101.48	100.46	99.45	98.44	97.44	96.44	95.46	94.49	93.53	92.57	91.63	90.69	89.76	88.83	87.92	87.02
10	91.33	90.29	89.25	88.24	87.24	86.24	85.24	84.26	83.29	82.33	81.38	80.44	79.50	78.58	77.67	76.77	75.87
11	82.18	81.14	80.11	79.09	78.07	77.08	76.09	75.12	74.15	73.20	72.25	71.32	70.39	69.48	68.57	67.68	66.79
12	74.56	73.52	72.49	71.47	70.46	69.47	68.48	67.51	66.55	65.61	64.67	63.75	62.83	61.93	61.03	60.15	59.28
13	68.12	67.08	66.05	65.04	64.03	63.05	62.06	61.10	60.14	59.20	58.27	57.36	56.45	55.56	54.68	53.82	52.96
14	62.60	61.56	60.54	59.53	58.53	57.55	56.57	55.62	54.67	53.74	52.82	51.92	51.02	50.15	49.28	48.43	47.58
15	57.83	56.79	55.77	54.77	53.77	52.79	51.82	50.88	49.94	49.02	48.11	47.22	46.34	45.48	44.62	43.79	42.96
16	53.65	52.62	51.60	50.60	49.61	48.64	47.68	46.70	45.82	44.91	44.01	43.14	42.27	41.42	40.58	39.13	38.95
17	49.97	48.94	47.93	46.94	45.95	44.99	44.04	43.12	42.20	41.31	40.42	39.56	38.70	37.87	37.04	36.24	35.44
18	46.70	45.67	44.67	43.69	42.71	41.76	40.82	39.90	38.99	38.11	37.24	36.39	35.54	34.73	33.92	33.15	32.36
19	43.78	42.76	41.76	40.78	39.81	38.87	37.94	37.04	36.14	35.27	34.40	33.57	32.75	31.95	31.15	30.85	29.62
20	41.15	40.14	39.14	38.18	37.22	36.29	35.36	34.47	33.58	32.72	31.87	31.06	30.24	29.46	28.68	27.93	27.18
25	31.22	30.24	29.27	28.35	27.43	26.55	25.67	24.84	24.01	23.22	22.44	21.69	20.95	20.25	19.55	18.89	18.23
30	24.65	23.70	22.78	21.90	21.02	20.19	19.37	18.60	17.83	17.11	16.39	15.72	15.05	14.42	13.80	13.22	12.65
35	20.00	19.09	18.20	17.37	16.54	15.77	15.00	14.29	13.58	12.92	12.27	11.67	11.07	10.92	9.97	9.47	8.97
40	16.55	15.68	14.84	14.05	13.26	12.54	11.83	11.17	10.52	9.93	9.34	8.81	8.28	7.80	7.32	6.89	6.46
45	13.91	13.07	12.27	11.52	10.78	10.12	9.45	8.85	8.26	7.73	7.20	6.73	6.26	5.85	5.43	5.06	4.70
50	11.82	11.02	10.26	9.56	8.87	8.25	7.63	7.09	6.55	6.07	5.60	5.19	4.78	4.42	4.06	3.75	3.44

CAPITALIZATION OF ANNUITY OF $1000 FOR FROM 5 TO 100 YEARS

Years	Rate of Interest, Per Cent							
	2¼	3	3½	4	4½	5	5½	6
5	4,645.88	4,579.60	4,514.92	4,451.68	4,389.91	4,329.41	4,268.09	4,212.40
10	8,752.17	8,530.13	8,316.45	8,110.74	7,912.67	7,721.69	7,537.54	7,360.19
15	12,381.41	11,937.80	11,517.23	11,118.06	10,739.42	10,379.53	10,037.48	9,712.30
20	15,589.215	14,877.27	14,212.12	13,590.21	13,007.88	12,462.13	11,950.26	11,469.96
25	18,424.67	17,413.01	16,481.28	15,621.93	14,828.12	14,093.86	13,413.82	12,783.38
30	20,930.59	19,600.21	18,391.85	17,291.86	16,288.77	15,372.36	14,533.63	13,764.85
35	23,145.31	21,487.04	20,000.43	18,664.37	17,460.89	16,374.36	15,390.48	14,488.65
40	25,103.53	23,114.36	21,354.83	19,792.65	18,401.49	17,159.01	16,044.92	15,046.31
45	26,833.15	24,518.49	22,495.23	20,719.89	19,156.24	17,773.99	16,547.65	15,455.85
50	28,362.48	25,729.58	23,455.21	21,482.08	19,761.93	18,255.86	16,931.97	15,761.87
100	36,614.21	31,598.81	27,655.36	24,504.96	21,949.21	19,847.90	18,095.83	16,612.64

Economic Depreciation and Earning Condition of Utility Physical-Property Items of Definite Life and Interest Rate *

Arranged for lives of from 5 to 50 years and for interest at from 4 to 7 per cent. Interest annually compounded. "Depreciation" is that during the year named; "Value" is that at the end of the year.

5-YEAR LIFE.

Age, in years.	Interest Rate. 4%		Interest Rate. 5%		Interest Rate. 6%		Interest Rate. 7%	
	Value.	Dep.	Value.	Dep.	Value.	Dep.	Value.	Dep.
0	100.0000		100.0000		100.0000		100.0000	
		18.4627		18.0975		17.7396		17.3891
1	81.5373		81.9025		82.2604		82.6109	
		19.2012		19.0023		18.8041		18.6063
2	62.3361		62.9002		63.4563		64.0046	
		19.9693		19.9525		19.9822		19.9087
3	42.3668		42.9477		43.5241		44.0959	
		20.7680		20.9501		21.1282		21.3024
4	21.5988		21.9976		22.3959		22.7935	
		21.5988		21.9976		22.3959		22.7935
5	0.0000		0.0000		0.0000		0.0000	
		100.0000		100.0000		100.0000		100.0000

10-YEAR LIFE.

Age, in years.	Value.	Dep.	Value.	Dep.	Value.	Dep.	Value.	Dep.
0	100.0000		100.0000		100.0000		100.0000	
		8.3291		7.9505		7.5868		7.2377
1	91.6709		92.0495		92.4132		92.7623	
		8.6623		8.3480		8.0420		7.7444
2	83.0086		83.7015		84.3712		85.0179	
		9.0088		8.7654		8.5245		8.2865
3	73.9998		74.9361		75.8467		76.7314	
		9.3690		9.2037		9.0360		8.8666
4	64.6308		65.7324		66.8107		67.8648	
		9.7439		9.6638		9.5782		9.4872
5	54.8869		56.0686		57.2325		58.3776	
		10.1336		10.1470		10.1528		10.1513
6	44.7533		45.9216		47.0797		48.2263	
		10.5389		10.6544		10.7620		10.8619
7	34.2144		35.2672		36.3177		37.3644	
		10.9606		11.1871		11.4078		11.6223
8	23.2538		24.0801		24.9099		25.7421	
		11.3989		11.7464		12.0922		12.4358
9	11.8549		12.3337		12.8177		13.3063	
		11.8549		12.3337		12.8177		13.3063
10	0.0000		0.0000		0.0000		0.0000	
		100.0000		100.0000		100.0000		100.0000

15-YEAR LIFE.

Age, in years.	Value.	Dep.	Value.	Dep.	Value.	Dep.	Value.	Dep.
0	100.0000		100.0000		100.0000		100.0000	
		4.9941		4.6342		4.2963		3.9795
1	95.0059		95.3658		95.7037		96.0205	
		5.1939		4.8660		4.5540		4.2580
2	89.8120		90.4998		91.1497		91.7625	
		5.4016		5.1092		4.8273		4.5561
3	84.4104		85.3906		86.3224		87.2064	
		5.6177		5.3646		5.1170		4.8750
4	78.7927		80.0260		81.2054		82.3314	
		5.8424		5.6330		5.4239		5.2162
5	72.9503		74.3930		75.7815		77.1152	
		6.0760		5.9146		5.7493		5.5814
6	66.8743		68.4784		70.0322		71.5338	
		6.3192		6.2103		6.0944		5.9722

* Embodying the compound-interest depreciation tables of the Valuation Committee of the American Society of Civil Engineers, accompanying its 1914 (progress) and 1916 (final) reports. See the Proceedings of the American Society of Civil Engineers, December 1916, p. 1937. The committee's tables go to 100 years life.

15-YEAR LIFE.—(*Continued.*)

Age, in years.	Interest Rate. 4% Value.	Dep.	Interest Rate. 5% Value.	Dep.	Interest Rate. 6% Value.	Dep.	Interest Rate. 7% Value.	Dep.
7	60.5551		62.2681		63.9378		65.5616	
		6.5719		6.5209		6.4601		6.3901
8	53.9832		55.7472		57.4777		59.1715	
		6.8348		6.8468		6.8476		6.8375
9	47.1484		48.9004		50.6301		52.3340	
		7.1081		7.1892		7.2584		7.3160
10	40.0403		41.7112		43.3717		45.0180	
		7.3925		7.5487		7.6941		7.8282
11	32.6478		34.1625		35.6776		37.1898	
		7.6882		7.9261		8.1555		8.3762
12	24.9596		26.2364		27.5221		28.8136	
		7.9957		8.3224		8.6450		8.9625
13	16.9639		17.9140		18.8771		19.8511	
		8.3156		8.7385		9.1636		9.5899
14	8.6483		9.1755		9.7135		10.2612	
		8.6483		9.1755		9.7135		10.2612
15	0.0000		0.0000		0.0000		0.0000	
		100.0000		100.0000		100.0000		100.0000

20-YEAR LIFE.

Age, in years.	Value.	Dep.	Value.	Dep.	Value.	Dep.	Value.	Dep.
0	100.0000		100.0000		100.0000		100.0000	
		3.3582		3.0243		2.7185		2.4393
1	96.6418		96.9757		97.2815		97.5607	
		3.4925		3.1755		2.8815		2.6100
2	93.1493		93.8002		94.4000		94.9507	
		3.6322		3.3342		3.0545		2.7928
3	89.5171		90.4660		91.3455		92.1579	
		3.7775		3.5010		3.2377		2.9882
4	85.7396		86.9650		88.1078		89.1697	
		3.9286		3.6760		3.4320		3.1974
5	81.8110		83.2890		84.6758		85.9723	
		4.0857		3.8598		3.6379		3.4213
6	77.7253		79.4292		81.0379		82.5510	
		4.2492		4.0528		3.8561		3.6607
7	73.4761		75.3764		77.1818		78.8903	
		4.4191		4.2554		4.0876		3.9169
8	69.0570		71.1210		73.0942		74.9734	
		4.5959		4.4682		4.3328		4.1912
9	64.4611		66.6528		68.7614		70.7822	
		4.7797		4.6916		4.5928		4.4845
10	59.6814		61.9612		64.1686		66.2977	
		4.9709		4.9262		4.8684		4.7985
11	54.7105		57.0350		59.3002		61.4992	
		5.1698		5.1725		5.1604		5.1343
12	49.5407		51.8625		54.1398		56.3649	
		5.3766		5.4311		5.4701		5.4938
13	44.1641		46.4314		48.6697		50.8711	
		5.5916		5.7027		5.7982		5.8783
14	38.5725		40.7287		42.8715		44.9928	
		5.8152		5.9878		6.1462		6.2898
15	32.7573		34.7409		36.7253		38.7030	
		6.0479		6.2872		6.5149		6.7301
16	26.7094		28.4537		30.2104		31.9729	
		6.2898		6.6016		6.9059		7.2012
17	20.4196		21.8521		23.3045		24.7717	
		6.5414		6.9317		7.3202		7.7052
18	13.8782		14.9204		15.9843		17.0665	
		6.8031		7.2783		7.7593		8.2446
19	7.0751		7.6421		8.2250		8.8219	
		7.0741		7.6421		8.2250		8.8219
20	0.0000		0.0000		0.0000		0.0000	
		100.0000		100.0000		100.0000		100.0000

25-YEAR LIFE.

Age, in years.	Interest Rate. 4%		Interest Rate. 5%		Interest Rate. 6%		Interest Rate. 7%	
	Value.	Dep.	Value.	Dep.	Value.	Dep.	Value.	Dep.
0	100.0000		100.0000		100.0000		100.0000	
		2.4012		2.0952		1.8227		1.5811
1	97.5988		97.9048		98.1773		98.4189	
		2.4972		2.2001		1.9320		1.6917
2	95.1016		95.7047		96.2453		96.7272	
		2.5972		2.3100		2.0480		1.8101
3	92.5044		93.3947		94.1973		94.9171	
		2.7010		2.4254		2.1708		1.9369
4	89.8034		90.9693		92.0265		92.9802	
		2.8091		2.5468		2.3011		2.0724
5	86.9943		88.4225		89.7254		90.9078	
		2.9214		2.6742		2.4891		2.2175
6	84.0729		85.7483		87.2863		88.6903	
		3.0383		2.8078		2.5855		2.3728
7	81.0346		82.9405		84.7008		86.3175	
		3.1598		2.9482		2.7406		2.5388
8	77.8748		79.9923		81.9602		83.7787	
		3.2862		3.0957		2.9051		2.7165
9	74.5886		76.8966		79.0551		81.0622	
		3.4176		3.2504		3.0794		2.9067
10	71.1710		73.6462		75.9757		78.1555	
		3.5544		3.4129		3.2641		3.1102
11	67.6166		70.2333		72.7116		75.0453	
		3.6965		3.5836		3.4600		3.3279
12	63.9201		66.6497		69.2516		71.7174	
		3.8444		3.7627		3.6675		3.5608
13	60.0757		62.8870		65.5841		68.1566	
		3.9982		3.9509		3.8877		3.8101
14	56.0775		58.9361		61.6964		64.3465	
		4.1581		4.1485		4.1208		4.0768
15	51.9194		54.7876		57.5756		60.2697	
		4.3244		4.3559		4.3682		4.3622
16	47.5950		50.4317		53.2074		55.9075	
		4.4974		4.5736		4.6302		4.6675
17	43.0976		45.8581		48.5772		51.2400	
		4.6773		4.8024		4.9081		4.9942
18	38.4203		41.0557		43.6691		46.2458	
		4.8643		5.0424		5.2025		5.3439
19	33.5560		36.0133		38.4666		40.9019	
		5.0590		5.2946		5.5147		5.7179
20	28.4970		30.7187		32.9519		35.1840	
		5.2613		5.5593		5.8455		6.1181
21	23.2357		25.1594		27.1064		29.0659	
		5.4718		5.8373		6.1963		6.5465
22	17.7639		19.3221		20.9101		22.5194	
		5.6906		6.1291		6.5681		7.0047
23	12.0733		13.1930		14.3420		15.5147	
		5.9183		6.4356		6.9621		7.4950
24	6.1550		6.7574		7.3799		8.0197	
		6.1550		6.7574		7.3799		8.0197
25	0.0000		0.0000		0.0000		0.0000	
		100.0000		100.0000		100.0000		100.0000

30-YEAR LIFE.

0	100.0000		100.0000		100.0000		100.0000	
		1.7830		1.5051		1.2649		1.0586
1	98.2170		98.4949		98.7351		98.9414	
		1.8543		1.5804		1.3408		1.1328
2	96.3627		96.9145		97.3943		97.8086	
		1.9285		1.6595		1.4212		1.2120
3	94.4342		95.2550		95.9731		96.5966	
		2.0057		1.7423		1.5065		1.2969

30-YEAR LIFE.—(*Continued.*)

Age, in years.	Interest Rate. 4%		Interest Rate. 5%		Interest Rate. 6%		Interest Rate. 7%	
	Value.	Dep.	Value.	Dep.	Value.	Dep.	Value.	Dep.
4	92.4285		93.5127		94.4666		95.2997	
		2.0859		1.8296		1.5969		1.3877
5	90.3426		91.6831		92.8697		93.9120	
		2.1693		1.9209		1.6927		1.4848
6	88.1733		89.7622		91.1770		92.4272	
		2.2560		2.0171		1.7943		1.5887
7	85.9173		87.7451		89.3827		90.8385	
		2.3463		2.1179		1.9019		1.6999
8	83.5710		85.6272		87.4808		89.1386	
		2.4402		2.2238		2.0161		1.8190
9	81.1308		83.4034		85.4647		87.3196	
		2.5378		2.3349		2.1370		1.9462
10	78.5930		81.0685		83.3277		85.3734	
		2.6393		2.4518		2.2652		2.0825
11	75.9537		78.6167		81.0625		83.2909	
		2.7449		2.5743		2.4011		2.2283
12	73.2088		76.0424		78.6614		81.0626	
		2.8545		2.7030		2.5452		2.3843
13	70.3543		73.3394		76.1162		78.6783	
		2.9689		2.8382		2.6980		2.5511
14	67.3854		70.5012		73.4182		76.1272	
		3.0877		2.9800		2.8597		2.7297
15	64.2977		67.5212		70.5585		73.3975	
		3.2111		3.1291		3.0314		2.9209
16	61.0866		64.3921		67.5271		70.4766	
		3.3395		3.2856		3.2133		3.1254
17	57.7471		61.1065		64.3138		67.3512	
		3.4731		3.4498		3.4061		3.3439
18	54.2740		57.6567		60.9077		64.0073	
		3.6121		3.6223		3.6104		3.5782
19	50.6619		54.0344		57.2973		60.4291	
		3.7565		3.8034		3.8271		3.8286
20	46.9054		50.2310		53.4702		56.6005	
		3.9068		3.9936		4.0566		4.0966
21	42.9986		46.2374		49.4136		52.5039	
		4.0631		4.1983		4.3001		4.3833
22	38.9355		42.0441		45.1135		48.1206	
		4.2256		4.4029		4.5581		4.6902
23	34.7099		37.6412		40.5554		43.4304	
		4.3946		4.6231		4.8316		5.0186
24	30.3153		33.0181		35.7238		38.4118	
		4.5704		4.8543		5.1214		5.3698
25	25.7449		28.1638		30.6024		33.0420	
		4.7532		5.0968		5.4288		5.7457
26	20.9917		23.0670		25.1736		27.2963	
		4.9433		5.3519		5.7544		6.1479
27	16.0484		17.7151		19.4192		21.1484	
		5.1411		5.6194		6.0998		6.5782
28	10.9073		12.0957		13.3194		14.5702	
		5.3467		5.9005		6.4657		7.0387
29	5.5606		6.1952		6.8537		7.5315	
		5.5606		6.1952		6.8537		7.5315
30	0.0000		0.0000		0.0000		0.0000	
		100.0000		100.0000		100.0000		100.0000

35-YEAR LIFE.

Age, in years.	Value.	Dep.	Value.	Dep.	Value.	Dep.	Value.	Dep.
0	100.0000		100.0000		100.0000		100.0000	
		1.3577		1.1072		0.8974		0.7234
1	98.6423		98.8928		99.1026		99.2766	
		1.4121		1.1625		0.9512		0.7740
2	97.2302		97.7303		98.1514		98.5026	
		1.4685		1.2207		1.0083		0.8282
3	95.7617		96.5096		97.1431		97.6744	
		1.5273		1.2816		1.0688		0.8862

35-YEAR LIFE.—(*Continued.*)

Age, in years.	Interest Rate. 4%		Interest Rate. 5%		Interest Rate. 6%		Interest Rate. 7%	
	Value.	Dep.	Value.	Dep.	Value.	Dep.	Value.	Dep.
4	94.2344		95.2280		96.0743		96.7882	
		1.5884		1.3458		1.1329		0.9488
5	92.6460		93.8822		94.9414		95.8399	
		1.6519		1.4131		1.2010		1.0146
6	90.9941		92.4691		93.7404		94.8253	
		1.7179		1.4837		1.2729		1.0856
7	89.2762		90.9854		92.4675		93.7397	
		1.7867		1.5579		1.3493		1.1616
8	87.4895		89.4275		91.1182		92.5781	
		1.8581		1.6358		1.4303		1.2429
9	85.6314		87.7917		89.6879		91.3352	
		1.9325		1.7176		1.5162		1.3300
10	83.6989		86.0741		88.1717		90.0052	
		2.0098		1.8035		1.6071		1.4230
11	81.6891		84.2706		86.5646		88.5822	
		2.0902		1.8936		1.7034		1.5226
12	79.5989		82.3770		84.8612		87.0596	
		2.1787		1.9883		1.8058		1.6293
13	77.4252		80.3887		83.0554		85.4303	
		2.2607		2.0877		1.9140		1.7432
14	75.1645		78.3010		81.1414		83.6871	
		2.3512		2.1922		2.0289		1.8653
15	72.8133		76.1088		79.1125		81.8218	
		2.4452		2.3017		2.1506		1.9959
16	70.3681		73.8071		76.9619		79.8259	
		2.5430		2.4168		2.2797		2.1356
17	67.8251		71.3903		74.6822		77.6903	
		2.6447		2.5377		2.4165		2.2851
18	65.1804		68.8526		72.2657		75.4052	
		2.7505		2.6645		2.5614		2.4450
19	62.4299		66.1881		69.7043		72.9602	
		2.8605		2.7978		2.7152		2.6162
20	59.5694		63.3903		66.9891		70.3440	
		2.9750		2.9376		2.8780		2.7993
21	56.5944		60.4527		64.1111		67.5447	
		3.0939		3.0845		3.0507		2.9953
22	53.5005		57.3682		61.0604		64.5494	
		3.2178		3.2388		3.2338		3.2049
23	50.2827		54.1294		57.8266		61.3445	
		3.3464		3.4007		3.4278		3.4298
24	46.9363		50.7287		54.3988		57.9152	
		3.4803		3.5708		3.6334		3.6693
25	43.4560		47.1579		50.7654		54.2459	
		3.6195		3.7492		3.8515		3.9262
26	39.8365		43.4087		46.9139		50.3197	
		3.7642		3.9367		4.0826		4.2010
27	36.0723		39.4720		42.8313		46.1197	
		3.9149		4.1337		4.3275		4.4951
28	32.1574		35.3383		38.5038		41.6236	
		4.0714		4.3403		4.5871		4.8097
29	28.0860		30.9980		33.9167		36.8139	
		4.2343		4.5572		4.8624		5.1464
30	23.8517		26.4418		29.0543		31.6675	
		4.4037		4.7851		5.1541		5.5067
31	19.4480		21.6557		23.9002		26.1608	
		4.5798		5.0244		5.4634		5.8922
32	14.8682		16.6313		18.4368		20.2686	
		4.7630		5.2756		5.7911		6.3046
33	10.1052		11.3557		12.6457		13.9640	
		4.9535		5.5394		6.1387		6.7459
34	5.1517		5.8163		6.5070		7.2181	
		5.1517		5.8163		6.5070		7.2181
35	0.0000		0.0000		0.0000		0.0000	
		100.0000		100.0000		100.0000		100.0000

40-YEAR LIFE.

Age, in years.	Interest Rate. 4%		Interest Rate. 5%		Interest Rate. 6%		Interest Rate. 7%	
	Value.	Dep.	Value.	Dep.	Value.	Dep.	Value.	Dep.
0	100.0000		100.0000		100.0000		100.0000	
		1.0524		0.8278		0.6462		0.5009
1	98.9476		99.1722		99.3538		99.4991	
		1.0944		0.8692		0.6849		0.5360
2	97.8532		98.3030		98.6689		98.9631	
		1.1382		0.9127		0.7260		0.5735
3	96.7150		97.3903		97.9429		98.3896	
		1.1838		0.9583		0.7696		0.6136
4	95.5312		96.4320		97.1733		97.7760	
		1.2311		1.0062		0.8157		0.6566
5	94.3001		95.4258		96.3576		97.1194	
		1.2803		1.0565		0.8647		0.7026
6	93.0198		94.3693		95.4929		96.4168	
		1.3316		1.1093		0.9166		0.7517
7	91.6882		93.2600		94.5763		95.6651	
		1.3848		1.1648		0.9716		0.8044
8	90.3034		92.0952		93.6047		94.8607	
		1.4402		1.2230		1.0299		0.8606
9	88.8632		90.8722		92.5748		94.0001	
		1.4978		1.2842		1.0916		0.9210
10	87.3654		89.5880		91.4832		93.0791	
		1.5577		1.3484		1.1572		0.9858
11	85.8077		88.2396		90.3260		92.0938	
		1.6201		1.4158		1.2266		1.0544
12	84.1876		86.8238		89.0994		91.0394	
		1.6848		1.4866		1.3002		1.1281
13	82.5028		85.3372		87.7992		89.9113	
		1.7523		1.5610		1.3782		1.2071
14	80.7505		83.7762		86.4210		88.7042	
		1.8223		1.6390		1.4309		1.2917
15	78.9282		82.1372		84.9601		87.4125	
		1.8952		1.7210		1.5485		1.3820
16	77.0880		80.4162		83.4116		86.0304	
		1.9710		1.8070		1.6415		1.4788
17	75.0620		78.6092		81.7701		84.5517	
		2.0499		1.8974		1.7399		1.5823
18	73.0121		76.7118		80.0302		82.9694	
		2.1319		1.9923		1.8443		1.6930
19	70.8802		74.7195		78.1859		81.2764	
		2.2171		2.0919		1.9550		1.8116
20	68.6631		72.6276		76.2309		79.4648	
		2.3059		2.1965		2.0724		1.9884
21	66.3572		70.4311		74.1585		77.5264	
		2.3980		2.3063		2.1966		2.0741
22	63.9592		68.1248		71.9619		75.4523	
		2.4940		2.4216		2.3284		2.2192
23	61.4652		65.7032		69.6335		73.2331	
		2.5937		2.5427		2.4682		2.3746
24	58.8715		63.1605		67.1653		70.8585	
		2.6975		2.6698		2.6162		2.5408
25	56.1740		60.4907		64.5491		68.3177	
		2.8054		2.8033		2.7732		2.7187
26	53.3686		57.6874		61.7759		65.5990	
		2.9176		2.9434		2.9396		2.9090
27	50.4510		54.7440		58.8363		62.6900	
		3.0343		3.0906		3.1160		3.1126
28	47.4167		51.6534		55.7203		59.5774	
		3.1557		3.2451		3.3029		3.3305
29	44.2610		48.4083		52.4174		56.2469	
		3.2819		3.4074		3.5011		3.5636
30	40.9791		45.0009		48.9163		52.6833	
		3.4132		3.5778		3.7112		3.8181
31	37.5659		41.4231		45.2051		48.8702	
		3.5498		3.7567		3.9389		4.0800
32	34.0161		37.6664		41.2712		44.7902	
		3.6916		3.9445		4.1699		4.3656

40-YEAR LIFE.—(*Continued.*)

Age in years.	Interest Rate. 4% Value.	Dep.	Interest Rate. 5% Value.	Dep.	Interest Rate. 6% Value.	Dep.	Interest Rate. 7% Value.	Dep.
33	30.3245		33.7219		37.1013		40.4246	
		3.8393		4.1417		4.4200		4.6712
34	26.4852		29.5802		32.6813		35.7534	
		3.9930		4.3488		4.6853		4.9982
35	22.4922		25.2314		27.9960		30.7552	
		4.1526		4.5662		4.9664		5.3480
36	18.3396		20.6652		23.0296		25.4072	
		4.3189		4.7946		5.2644		5.7225
37	14.0207		15.8706		17.7652		19.6847	
		4.4915		5.0343		5.5802		6.1229
38	9.5292		10.8363		12.1850		13.5618	
		4.6712		5.2860		5.9151		6.5516
39	4.8580		5.5503		6.2699		7.0102	
		4.8580		5.5503		6.2699		7.0102
40	0.0000		0.0000		0.0000		0.0000	
		100.0000		100.0000		100.0000		100.0000

45-YEAR LIFE.

Age in years.	Value 4%	Dep.	Value 5%	Dep.	Value 6%	Dep.	Value 7%	Dep.
0	100.0000		100.0000		100.0000		100.0000	
		0.8262		0.6262		0.4700		0.3500
1	99.1738		99.3738		99.5300		99.5600	
		0.8593		0.6575		0.4988		0.3744
2	98.3145		98.7163		99.0317		99.2756	
		0.8937		0.6903		0.5283		0.4007
3	97.4208		98.0260		98.5034		98.8749	
		0.9294		0.7249		0.5597		0.4287
4	96.4914		97.3011		97.9437		98.4462	
		0.9666		0.7611		0.5934		0.4587
5	95.5248		96.5400		97.3503		97.9875	
		1.0053		0.7992		0.6290		0.4908
6	94.5195		95.7408		96.7213		97.4967	
		1.0455		0.8392		0.6668		0.5252
7	93.4740		94.9016		96.0545		96.9715	
		1.0872		0.8810		0.7068		0.5620
8	92.3868		94.0206		95.3477		96.4095	
		1.1308		0.9251		0.7492		0.6013
9	91.2560		93.0955		94.5985		95.8082	
		1.1760		0.9714		0.7941		0.6484
10	90.0800		92.1241		93.8044		95.1648	
		1.2230		1.0200		0.8418		0.6884
11	88.8570		91.1041		92.9626		94.4764	
		1.2720		1.0710		0.8923		0.7366
12	87.5850		90.0311		92.0703		93.7398	
		1.3229		1.1245		0.9459		0.7882
13	86.2621		88.9086		91.1244		92.9516	
		1.3757		1.1807		1.0025		0.8433
14	84.8864		87.7279		90.1219		92.1083	
		1.4308		1.2398		1.0628		0.9024
15	83.4556		86.4881		89.0591		91.2059	
		1.4880		1.3018		1.1265		0.9655
16	81.9676		85.1863		87.9326		90.2404	
		1.5476		1.3668		1.1941		1.0331
17	80.4200		83.8195		86.7385		89.2073	
		1.6094		1.4352		1.2657		1.1055
18	78.8106		82.3843		85.4728		88.1018	
		1.6738		1.5070		1.3417		1.1828
19	77.1368		80.8773		84.1311		86.9190	
		1.7408		1.5823		1.4222		1.2657
20	75.3960		79.2950		82.7089		85.6533	
		1.8104		1.6614		1.5075		1.3542
21	73.5856		77.6336		81.2014		84.2991	
		1.8828		1.7445		1.5979		1.4490

45-YEAR LIFE.—(*Continued.*)

Age, in years.	Interest Rate. 4%		Interest Rate. 5%		Interest Rate. 6%		Interest Rate. 7%	
	Value.	Dep.	Value.	Dep.	Value.	Dep.	Value.	Dep.
22	71.7028		75.8891		79.6085		82.8501	
		1.9581		1.8317		1.6939		1.5504
23	69.7447		74.0574		77.9096		81.2997	
		2.0365		1.9233		1.7954		1.6590
24	67.7082		72.1341		76.1142		79.6407	
		2.1180		2.0195		1.9033		1.7751
25	65.5902		70.1146		74.2109		77.8656	
		2.2026		2.1205		2.0174		1.8994
26	63.3876		67.9941		72.1935		75.9662	
		2.2907		2.2264		2.1383		2.0323
27	61.0969		65.7677		70.0552		73.9339	
		2.3824		2.3378		2.2668		2.1746
28	58.7145		63.4299		67.7884		71.7593	
		2.4777		2.4548		2.4028		2.3268
29	56.2368		60.9751		65.3856		69.4325	
		2.5768		2.5773		2.5469		2.4897
30	53.6600		58.3978		62.8387		66.9428	
		2.6798		2.7062		2.6997		2.6640
31	50.9802		55.6916		60.1390		64.2788	
		2.7870		2.8417		2.8617		2.8504
32	48.1932		52.8499		57.2773		61.4284	
		2.8986		2.9837		3.0334		3.0499
33	45.2946		49.8662		54.2439		58.3785	
		3.0144		3.1328		3.2155		3.2635
34	42.2802		46.7334		51.0284		55.1150	
		3.1350		3.2896		3.4083		3.4920
35	39.1452		43.4438		47.6201		51.6230	
		3.2605		3.4539		3.6129		3.7363
36	35.8847		39.9899		44.0072		47.8867	
		3.3909		3.6267		3.8296		3.9979
37	32.4938		36.3632		40.1776		43.8888	
		3.5264		3.8081		4.0594		4.2777
38	28.9674		32.5551		36.1182		39.6111	
		3.6676		3.9983		4.3029		4.5772
39	25.2998		28.5568		31.8153		35.0339	
		3.8142		4.1984		4.5612		4.8976
40	21.4856		24.3584		27.2541		30.1363	
		3.9669		4.4083		4.8348		5.2404
41	17.5187		19.9501		22.4193		24.8959	
		4.1255		4.6286		5.1249		5.6073
42	13.3932		15.3215		17.2944		19.2886	
		4.2905		4.8600		5.4323		5.9997
43	9.1027		10.4615		11.8621		13.2889	
		4.4621		5.1032		5.7584		6.4197
44	4.6406		5.3583		6.1037		6.8692	
		4.6406		5.3583		6.1037		6.8692
45	0.0000		0.0000		0.0000		0.0000	
		100.0000		100.0000		100.0000		100.0000

50-YEAR LIFE.

0	100.0000		100.0000		100.0000		100.0000	
		0.6550		0.4777		0.3444		0.2460
1	99.3450		99.5223		99.6556		99.7540	
		0.6812		0.5015		0.3651		0.2632
2	98.6638		99.0208		99.2905		99.4908	
		0.7085		0.5267		0.3870		0.2816
3	97.9553		98.4941		98.9035		99.2092	
		0.7368		0.5529		0.4102		0.3014
4	97.2185		97.9412		98.4933		98.9078	
		0.7663		0.5806		0.4349		0.3224
5	96.4522		97.3606		98.0584		98.5854	
		0.7969		0.6097		0.4609		0.3450

50-YEAR LIFE.—(*Continued.*)

Age, in years.	Interest Rate. 4%		Interest Rate. 5%		Interest Rate. 6%		Interest Rate. 7%	
	Value.	Dep.	Value.	Dep.	Value.	Dep.	Value.	Dep.
6	95.6553		96.7509		97.5975		98.2404	
		0.8288		0.6401		0.4886		0.3692
7	94.8265		96.1108		97.1089		97.8712	
		0.8620		0.6722		0.5179		0.3950
8	93.9645		95.4386		96.5910		97.4762	
		0.8964		0.7057		0.5489		0.4226
9	93.0681		94.7329		96.0421		97.0536	
		0.9323		0.7410		0.5819		0.4522
10	92.1358		93.9919		95.4602		96.6014	
		0.9696		0.7781		0.6169		0.4839
11	91.1662		93.2138		94.8433		96.1175	
		1.0084		0.8170		0.6538		0.5178
12	90.1578		92.3968		94.1895		95.5997	
		1.0487		0.8578		0.6931		0.5540
13	89.1091		91.5390		93.4964		95.0457	
		1.0906		0.9008		0.7346		0.5928
14	88.0185		90.6382		92.7618		94.4529	
		1.1343		0.9457		0.7787		0.6343
15	86.8842		89.6925		91.9831		93.8186	
		1.1797		0.9931		0.8255		0.6786
16	85.7045		88.6994		91.1576		93.1400	
		1.2268		1.0427		0.8749		0.7262
17	84.4777		87.6567		90.2827		92.4138	
		1.2759		1.0948		0.9275		0.7771
18	83.2018		86.5619		89.3552		91.6367	
		1.3270		1.1496		0.9831		0.8314
19	81.8748		85.4123		88.3721		90.8053	
		1.3800		1.2071		1.0421		0.8896
20	80.4948		84.2052		87.3300		89.9157	
		1.4353		1.2674		1.1046		0.9519
21	79.0595		82.9378		86.2254		88.9638	
		1.4926		1.3307		1.1710		1.0185
22	77.5669		81.6017		85.0544		87.9453	
		1.5523		1.3974		1.2411		1.0898
23	76.0146		80.2097		83.8133		86.8555	
		1.6144		1.4672		1.3156		1.1661
24	74.4002		78.7425		82.4977		85.6894	
		1.6791		1.5405		1.3946		1.2477
25	72.7211		77.2020		81.1031		84.4417	
		1.7461		1.6176		1.4782		1.3351
26	70.9750		75.5844		79.6249		83.1066	
		1.8161		1.6984		1.5670		1.4285
27	69.1589		73.8860		78.0579		81.6781	
		1.8887		1.7834		1.6610		1.5285
28	67.2702		72.1026		76.3969		80.1496	
		1.9642		1.8726		1.7606		1.6355
29	65.3060		70.2300		74.6363		78.5141	
		2.0427		1.9661		1.8662		1.7500
30	63.2633		68.2639		72.7701		76.7641	
		2.1245		2.0645		1.9783		1.8725
31	61.1388		66.1994		70.7918		74.8916	
		2.2095		2.1677		2.0969		2.0086
32	58.9293		64.0317		68.6949		72.8880	
		2.2979		2.2761		2.2227		2.1438
33	56.6314		61.7556		66.4722		70.7442	
		2.3897		2.3899		2.3561		2.2989
34	54.2417		59.3657		64.1161		68.4503	
		2.4854		2.5095		2.4975		2.4545
35	51.7563		56.8562		61.6186		65.9958	
		2.5847		2.6347		2.6473		2.6263
36	49.1716		54.2215		58.9713		63.3695	
		2.6882		2.7666		2.8061		2.8101
37	46.4834		51.4549		56.1652		60.5594	
		2.7957		2.9056		2.9745		3.0068
38	43.6877		48.5499		53.1907		57.5526	
		2.9075		3.0501		3.1530		3.2173

50-YEAR LIFE.—(*Continued.*)

Age, in years.	Interest Rate. 4%		Interest Rate. 5%		Interest Rate. 6%		Interest Rate. 7%	
	Value.	Dep.	Value.	Dep.	Value.	Dep.	Value.	Dep.
39	40.7802		45.4998		50.0377		54.8353	
		3.0238		3.2027		3.3422		3.4425
40	37.7564		42.2971		46.6955		50.8928	
		3.1448		3.3629		3.5427		3.6835
41	34.6116		38.9342		43.1528		47.2093	
		3.2706		3.5309		3.7553		3.9414
42	31.3410		35.4033		39.3975		43.2679	
		3.4013		3.7075		3.9805		4.2172
43	27.9397		31.6958		35.4170		39.0507	
		3.5375		3.8929		4.2194		4.5124
44	24.4022		27.8029		31.1976		34.5383	
		3.6789		4.0875		4.4726		4.8284
45	20.7233		23.7154		26.7250		29.7099	
		3.8261		4.2919		4.7410		5.1662
43	16.8972		19.4235		21.9840		24.5437	
		3.9791		4.5065		5.0253		5.5280
47	12.9181		14.9170		16.9587		19.0157	
		4.1383		4.7319		5.3270		5.9149
48	8.7798		10.1851		11.6317		13.1008	
		4.3038		4.9683		5.6465		6.3289
49	4.4760		5.2168		5.9852		6.7719	
		4.4760		5.2168		5.9852		6.7719
50	0.0000		0.0000		0.0000		0.0000	
		100.0000		100.0000		100.0000		100.0000

Sinking Fund and Present Worth Formulas. — If V is the fund to be accumulated after n years by investing the annuity x at the annually compounded interest rate r (expressed as a decimal); and if W is the present worth of an annuity y — or the sum which, if placed at compound interest r will provide a given annuity y for n years before it is used up — then:

$$x = V \frac{r}{(1+r)^n - 1},$$

$$V = \frac{x[(1+r)^n - 1]}{r},$$

$$W = \frac{y[1 - (1+r)^{-n}]}{r}.$$

Where D_l = loss of value after l years and n = years length of assumed life:

$$D_l = \frac{(1+r)^l - 1}{(1+r)^n - 1}.$$

For Semi-annually Compounded Interest. — The accompanying table shows a sinking fund table by Peter Mogensen, first printed in Engineering News, Oct. 21, 1897, and based on semi-annual compounding of interest. The formula for computation was $x = \frac{V(s^2 - 1)}{s^{2n} - 1}$ where the new quantity s is \$1 plus a half year's interest added.

ANNUAL PAYMENTS TO A SINKING FUND NECESSARY TO ACCUMULATE ONE DOLLAR AT THE END OF A GIVEN NUMBER OF YEARS

Int. Per Ann.	1%	2%	3%	4%	5%	6%	7%	8%	9%	10%
r	1.005	1.010	1.015	1.020	1.025	1.030	1.035	1.040	1.045	1.050
n										
2	0.4975	0.4951	0.4923	0.4903	0.4877	0.4853	0.4829	0.4803	0.4781	0.4756
3	0.3298	0.3262	0.3235	0.3199	0.3170	0.3138	0.3106	0.3076	0.3044	0.3014
4	0.2463	0.2425	0.2389	0.2353	0.2318	0.2283	0.2248	0.2214	0.2180	0.2147
5	0.1953	0.1916	0.1881	0.1845	0.1807	0.1771	0.1734	0.1699	0.1664	0.1630
6	0.1625	0.1585	0.1545	0.1506	0.1468	0.1431	0.1394	0.1358	0.1322	0.1288
7	0.1387	0.1345	0.1304	0.1265	0.1226	0.1188	0.1151	0.1115	0.1080	0.1046
8	0.1206	0.1165	0.1124	0.1084	0.1045	0.1007	0.0970	0.0935	0.0900	0.0867
9	0.1061	0.1025	0.0983	0.0943	0.0904	0.0867	0.0831	0.0795	0.0761	0.0729
10	0.0953	0.0913	0.0871	0.0832	0.0793	0.0755	0.0719	0.0685	0.0652	0.0620
12	0.0788	0.0745	0.0704	0.0664	0.0626	0.0590	0.0555	0.0522	0.0491	0.0461
15	0.0620	0.0577	0.0537	0.0498	0.0462	0.0427	0.0394	0.0363	0.0335	0.0308
20	0.0453	0.0411	0.0371	0.0334	0.0300	0.0269	0.0241	0.0215	0.0191	0.0170
25	0.0353	0.0311	0.0273	0.0239	0.0208	0.0179	0.0155	0.0133	0.0114	0.0098
30	0.0287	0.0246	0.0209	0.0177	0.0149	0.0124	0.0104	0.0086	0.0071	0.0058
35	0.0239	0.0199	0.0165	0.0135	0.0109	0.0087	0.0070	0.0056	0.0044	0.0035
40	0.0204	0.0165	0.0132	0.0104	0.0082	0.0062	0.0048	0.0037	0.0028	0.0021
45	0.0177	0.0139	0.0107	0.0082	0.0062	0.0046	0.0034	0.0025	0.0018	0.0013
50	0.0154	0.0118	0.0088	0.0064	0.0047	0.0032	0.0024	0.0016	0.0011	0.0008
60	0.0122	0.0087	0.0060	0.0041	0.0028	0.0018	0.0012	0.0007	0.0005	0.0003
70	0.0099	0.0065	0.0043	0.0028	0.0017	0.0009	0.0006	0.0003	0.0002	0.0001
80	0.0082	0.0051	0.0031	0.0018	0.0010	0.0005	0.0003	0.0001	0.0001	0.0000
100	0.0059	0.0032	0.0016	0.0008	0.0004	0.0002	0.0001	0.0000	0.0000	0.0000

APPENDIX C

TYPICAL LIFE EXPECTATION TABLES FOR PUBLIC-UTILITY PROPERTY

TYPICAL LIFE-EXPECTATION FIGURES FOR PUBLIC-UTILITY PROPERTY

	Years	Authority *	Control †
Railways			
Bridges, steel........................	20-50	*	Obs.
wood......................	10	*	Det.
Buildings, office, masonry............	70	*	Obs.
dwellings, etc., wood-frame.	30	*	Obs. or Det.
stations, masonry..........	40	*	Obs.
wood..............	20	*	Obs.
shops, first class............	75	Wis. R. R. Comm.	Obs.
second class..........	50	Wis. R. R. Comm.	Det.
sheds, wood-frame..........	20	*	Det.
Cars, freight, wood...................	10-20	*	Det.
steel.....................	15-30	*	Det.
passenger, wood................	20-25	*	Obs.
steel.................	25-30	*	Det.
dining, parlor and sleeping, wood	15-20	*	Obs.
steel	20-25	*	Obs.
Locomotives, freight..................	15-20	*	Det. (1,000,000 m.)
passenger................	15-20	*	Det. (1,000,000 m.)
switching..............	20	*	Det.
Signals..............................	30	*	Obs.
Track, rail, main-line tangent.........	2-8	*	Det. and Obs. ‡
main-line curve........	1-5	*	Det. and Obs. ‡
sidings and yards........	10-20	*	Det. ‡
ties, ordinary light wood.......	5-10	*	Det.
ordinary hard wood......	10-15	*	Det.
treated and protected.....	30	*	Det.
Electric Railways			
Bridges (see Railways)			
Cars................................	30	B. J. Arnold	Det.
Car bodies, open-type...............	25	Chicago Trac. Val. Comm.	Det.
closed-type...............	20	" " " "	Det.
trucks..........................	30	" " " "	Det.
motors.........................	5	Wis. R. R. Comm.; H. Floy	Det.
misc. elec. equipment............	10-15	*	Det.

* Where no authority is cited the data are those of the author — average or approximate figures secured by examination or enquiry.

† Probable action limiting service life; deterioration (due to wear and tear and weathering) and obsoletion. Where both are cited, both actions have been observed, the first named predominating in a majority of cases.

‡ Main-line rail is removed after 5 to 10% reduction of weight, and is used as relayer rail on less important service like sidings and branches. Here it is good for many years of service. The wear on level main-line tangent rail is in the order of 1.3% per year per 100,000,000 tons passage over it. This wear probably increases by an extra 0.1% per 1% grade and by 0.3% extra per 1 degree curvature.

TYPICAL LIFE-EXPECTATION FIGURES FOR PUBLIC-UTILITY PROPERTY. — *Continued*

	Years	Authority *	Control †
Electric Railways			
Feeder conduit....................	30–50	Wis. R. R. Comm.	Obs.
Feeders, insulated aerial..............	10–15	" " "	Det.
Overhead construction, trolley wire, No. 0, 1 min. headway.............	2	Wis. R. R. Comm.	
Overhead construction, trolley wire, No. 00, 1 min. headway............	2½	" " "	Det. Reduced 25% in size
Overhead construction, trolley wire, No. 000, 1 min. headway...........	3	Wis. R. R. Comm.	
Overhead construction, single-catenary support..........................	15–20	*	Det.
Overhead construction, double-catenary support........................	20–25	*	Det.
Overhead construction, cross spans and brackets...........................	15–20	Wis. R. R. Comm.	Det.
Poles, cedar in earth...................	14	Wis. R. R. Comm.	Det.
wood in concrete...............	20	" " "	Det.
iron or steel.....................	40	" " "	Det.
Power station equipment (see Electricity-supply Works)			
Track, tangent.......................	18	Wis. R. R. Comm.	Det.
curves.....................	5	*	Det.
special work..................	5	*	Det.
Trestles (see Railways)			
Water-works			
Buildings, masonry..................	40–50	L. Metcalf	Obs.
wood-frame...............	20–50	"	Det.
Boilers, fire-tube.....................	12–16	"	Det.
water-tube....................	20–30	Wis. R. R. Comm.	Det.
Filter beds...........................	30–50	" " "	Obs.
Hydrants............................	40–50	L. Metcalf	Det.
Mains, large cast-iron (6 in. and over) .	20–40	"	Obs.
small cast-iron (4 in. and under)	50–75	"	Obs.
steel...........................	15–50	"	Det.
wood..........................	30–50	Wis. R. R. Comm.	Det.
Meters.............................	20–30	L. Metcalf	Det.
Pumps and engines...................	20–30	"	Det.
duplex.............	20–25	Wis. R. R. Comm.	Det.
triplex.............	20–30	" " "	Det.
crank and flywheel	30–40	" " "	Obs. and Det.
centrifugal	20–30	" " "	Det.
Reservoirs...........................	50–100	{ L. Metcalf Wis. R. R. Comm. }	Obs.
Standpipes..........................	30–50	L. Metcalf	Det.
Service pipes, lead...................	50–100	Wis. R. R. Comm.	Det. and Obs.
galvanized iron or steel..	30–50	" " "	Det.
Suctions and intakes.................	30–50	" " "	Det. and Obs.
Valves..............................	40–50	L. Metcalf	Det.
Wells, driven or drilled...............	50–75	Wis. R. R. Comm.	Det.
open and lined.................	75–100	" " "	Obs.
Gas Works			
Blowers............................	15	Wis. R. R. Comm.	Det.
Ammonia concentrators..............	15	" " "	Det.

TYPICAL LIFE-EXPECTATION FIGURES FOR PUBLIC-UTILITY
PROPERTY. — *Continued*

	Years	Authority *	Control †
Gas Works			
Ammonia storage tanks...............	15	Wis. R. R. Comm.	Det.
Coal-gas benches......................	25	" " "	Det.
Exhausters............................	25	" " "	Det.
Gas holders...........................	50	" " "	Obs. and Det.
Governors.............................	50	" " "	Det. and Obs.
Mains, small cast-iron (4 in. and under)	50	" " "	Obs.
Mains, large cast-iron (6 in. and over)	75	Wis. R. R. Comm.	Obs.
small steel or iron (3 in. and under)	20	" " "	Det.
large steel or iron (above 3 in.) .	30	" " "	Det.
Meter cases (station).................	50	" " "	Obs.
drums "	20	" " "	Det.
Meters and governors (consumer's)....	25	" " "	Det.
Purifiers.............................	50	" " "	Obs.
Scrubbers and condensers.............	30	" " "	Det.
Service pipes.........................	20	" " "	Det.
Tar and ammonia wells...............	50	" " "	Obs.
extractor.........................	40	" " "	Obs.
Water-gas machines..................	30	" " "	Det.
Electricity-supply Works			
Anchors and guys....................	10–20	Wis. R. R. Comm.	Det.
Arc lamps and hangings...............	10–15	Wis. R. R. Comm. / St. Louis P. S. Comm.	Det. and Obs.
Belting..............................	20–25	Wis. R. R. Comm.	Det.
Boilers, fire-tube.....................	10–15	" " "	Det.
water-tube...................	20–30	" " "	Det.
Buildings, masonry..................	75	" " "	Obs.
wood-frame or second class	50	" " "	Det. and Obs.
Chimneys and stacks, masonry.......	30	*	Obs.
steel...........	10	*	Det.
Condensers...........................	20–30	Wis. R. R. Comm. / Chicago Trac. Val. Comm.	Det.
Conduits and manholes...............	30–50	Wis. R. R. Comm.	Obs.
Conveyers, coal or ash................	10	" " "	Det.
ash or combined coal and ash.....................	5	*	Det.
Cross arms...........................	10–15	Wis. R. R. Comm.	Det.
Engines, gas..........................	10–15	" " "	Det. and Obs.
steam, high-speed...........	15–20	" " "	Det.
steam, slow-speed...........	25–30	" " "	Det. and Obs.
Feed-water heaters...................	20–30	" " "	Det.
Fuse boxes...........................	10–12	" " "	Det.
Fuel-oil equipment...................	25	Chicago Trac. Val. Comm.	Det.
Generators, motors and converters			
high-speed................	15	*	Det.
slow-speed................	20	*	Obs.
new types.................	20	Wis. R. R. Comm.	Det.
old types.................	15	" " "	Obs.
turbine driven...........	20	" " "	Det.
Lightning arresters	15–20	Wis. R. R. Comm.	Det.
Piping and covering..................	20–30	" " "	Obs. and Det.
Poles, cedar in concrete..............	12–18	" " "	Det.

TYPICAL LIFE-EXPECTATION FIGURES FOR PUBLIC-UTILITY
PROPERTY. — *Concluded*

	Years	Authority *	Control †
Electricity-supply Works			
Poles, cedar in earth..................	10–18	Wis. R. R. Comm.	Det.
iron or steel in concrete.........	15–30	*	Obs. and Det.
iron or steel in earth............	10–15	Wis. R. R. Comm.	Det.
reinforced-concrete..............	50	*	Obs.
Pumps, boiler feed......................	15–20	Wis. R. R. Comm.	Det.
small centrifugal..............	20–30	" " "	Det.
Service boxes.........................	10–12	" " "	Det.
Shafting..............................	20–40	" " "	Obs.
Station wiring, etc.....................	30	" " "	Obs. and Det.
Stokers...............................	20	Chicago Trac. Val. Comm.	Det.
Storage batteries......................	15	Wis. R. R. Comm.	Det.
Switchboard instruments and wiring..	25–30	" " "	Obs. and Det.
Switchboards, old types..............	20–30	" " "	Obs.
new types..............	15–20	" " "	Obs.
Turbines, hydraulic, old types........	25–40	" " "	Obs.
new types........	30–50	" " "	Obs.
steam, large units	20	" " "	Det. and Obs.
auxiliary units	10–20	*	Det. and Obs.
Transformers, consumers..............	10–15	Wis. R. R. Comm.	Det.
station and substation..	20	" " "	Obs. and Det.
Watt-hour meters (consumer's)........	10–15	" " "	Det.
Wire, insulated copper line............	10–15	" " "	Det.
lead covered aerial cable.........	10–15	" " "	Det. and Obs.
underground cable	20–25	" " "	Obs.
Telephone Utilities			
Buildings.............................	40	Chicago Tel. Comm.	Obs.
Cables, lead-covered aerial.	12	Wis. R. R. Comm.	Det. and Obs.
underground.....	20	" " "	Obs. and Det.
Central exchange equipment..........	10	" " "	Obs. and Det.
Conduit..............................	50	Chicago Tel. Comm.	Obs.
Cross arms...........................	8–12	Wis. R. R. Comm.	Det.
Furniture and tools...................	7	" " "	Det.
Poles, wood in earth..................	12–15	" " "	Det.
Power plant..........................	8	" " "	Det. and Obs.
Private-branch exchange equipment...	8	Chicago Tel. Comm.	Det. and Obs.
Substations (subscribers').............	10	Wis. R. R. Comm.	Det. and Obs.
Wire, copper, line.....................	40	Chicago Tel. Comm.	Obs.
copper, interior.................	30	" " "	Obs.
galv. iron, line.................	8–15	Wis. R. R. Comm.	Det. and Obs.

APPENDIX D

TYPICAL CITATION ABBREVIATIONS OF LAW REPORTS, ETC., MET WITH IN UTILITY DECISIONS

Following these paragraphs is a list of a very few of the abbreviated titles of the most important law reports, etc., apt to be cited in commission and court public-utility cases. The law reports are collections of authoritative expositions by courts, arranged by the court reporters generally and commonly bearing their names. Each case reported contains, among other things, the opinion of the court, showing the questions presented and the principles applied, and the judgment which is a summary of the result arrived at. Not all cases in the many courts are published — though all are filed. In citations the volume number precedes the abbreviation and the page number follows it.

The number of possible titles, including the many state-court reports, is legion and a list may be found in most law dictionaries. Some of the state reports will be found cited simply by the state name, thus; "90 Ala. 300," "30 Ariz. 300," "40 Cal. 400," etc. The court system may require something like the following; "100 N. Y. App. Div. 100," "20 Del. Ch. 200," "30 Ills. App. 300," etc. But the great accumulation of abbreviated titles, for both federal and state reports, exhibits the names of the compilers with such added designation as is needed, for instance; "10 Ben. 100" (Benedict's U. S. District Court Reports), "23 How. 230" (Howard's U. S. Supreme Court Reports), "3 Hughes (U. S.) 300" (Hughes' U. S. Circuit Court Reports), "3 Hughes (Ky.) 300" (Hughes' Kentucky Reports) "12 Ired. 120" (Iredell's North Carolina Law Reports), "8 Ired. Eq. 80" (Iredell's North Carolina Equity Reports), etc.

The several state public-utility commission citations are abbreviated in various unstandardized ways, but, whatever the form the meaning is usually apparent, for example; "3 Wis. R. R. Comm. 200" or "3 Wis. R. C. R. 300," "2 Ill. P. U. Comm. 200," or "2 Ill. P. U. C. R. 200," "1 Mass. P. S. Comm. 100," etc.

Am. Rep.,	American Reports.
Am. State Rep.,	American State Reports (Bancroft and Whitney).
Atl. Rep.,	Atlantic Reporter.
C. C. A., ·	U. S. Circuit Court of Appeals Reports.
Cyc.,	Encyclopedia of Law and Procedure.
Fed.,	Federal Reports.
Fed. Rep.,	Federal Reporter.
I. C. C. or I. C. C. R.,	Interstate Commerce Commission Reports.
N. E. Rep.,	Northeastern Reporter.

N. W. Rep.,   Northwestern Reporter.

P. U. R.,   Public Utilities Reports, Annotated.

(The only compilation exclusively of court and commission public-utility decisions, and the official publication of the Association of Railroad Commissioners; published by the Lawyers Cooperative Publishing Co., Rochester, N. Y.)

Pac. Rep.,   Pacific Reporter.

S. E. Rep.,   Southeastern Reporter.

So. or South Rep.,   Southern Reporter.

Sup. Ct., or Sup. Ct. Rep.,   Supreme Court Reports.

U. S.,   United States Supreme Court Reports.

U. S. App.,   United States Circuit Court of Appeals Reports.

INDEX

373

CPSIA information can be obtained
at www.ICGtesting.com
Printed in the USA
BVOW06s0823200517
484373BV00020B/84/P